Woman Defamed and Woman Defended

Woman Defamed and Woman Defended

AN ANTHOLOGY OF MEDIEVAL TEXTS

Edited by
ALCUIN BLAMIRES
with
KAREN PRATT and C. W. MARX

CLARENDON PRESS · OXFORD

*This book has been printed digitally and produced in a standard specification
in order to ensure its continuing availability*

OXFORD
UNIVERSITY PRESS

Great Clarendon Street, Oxford OX2 6DP

Oxford University Press is a department of the University of Oxford.
It furthers the University's objective of excellence in research, scholarship,
and education by publishing worldwide in

Oxford New York

Auckland Bangkok Buenos Aires Cape Town Chennai
Dar es Salaam Delhi Hong Kong Istanbul Karachi Kolkata
Kuala Lumpur Madrid Melbourne Mexico City Mumbai Nairobi
São Paulo Shanghai Singapore Taipei Tokyo Toronto
with an associated company in Berlin

Published in the United States
by Oxford University Press Inc., New York

ISBN 0-19-871039-9 (Pbk.)

Cover illustration: Woman and Dominican Friar Jousting. Detail from an Arthurian
manuscript (northern French, late 13th century). Yale University, Yale MS.229, fo. 100.
Reproduced by courtesy of the Beinecke Rare Book and Manuscript Library

for Barbara

Preface

The burgeoning of women's studies in recent times has yielded a rich harvest of volumes presenting medieval woman in her own voice and in the voice of others. Yet, whether because of an impulse to blaze new trails or because the territory has seemed noxious, the familiar literature of antifeminism in the Middle Ages has been somewhat overlooked by anthologists. Although it *seems* familiar, anyone who has tried to study the field will have discovered that certain authors frequently named in this connection—Marbod of Rennes, for instance, or Jacques de Vitry—are locked away in the pages of remote Latin texts, if they have been printed at all. Not only are the texts sometimes difficult of access: they are daunting in their chronological sweep. Chaucer imagines his Wife of Bath enduring her husband's daily recitals from a lavish but cleverly comprehensive anthology in which Ovid rubs shoulders with Tertullian (one of the dourest of the Church Fathers), while letters against marriage by passionate Heloise are jostled by the Book of Proverbs. The contents even include an elusive physician known as 'Trotula', perhaps in acknowledgement of the 'scientific' corroboration of woman's shortcomings which prevailed in those times.

Chaucer challenges us to confront the whole phenomenon of antifeminism, crammed between the boards of one manuscript volume. The present anthology seeks in its turn to introduce the major antifeminist texts from the twelfth century to the beginning of the fifteenth. First it reaches back to identify what they borrow from traditional misogyny in the Roman satirists and in the Bible, not forgetting the infrastructure supplied by ancient physiology. Then it presents some readings from the Fathers, Jerome especially, since one of the cornerstones of the tradition is the 'Book of Theophrastus' which lies embedded in his belligerent defence of virginity. But both here and in later sections, the less celebrated will be found alongside the more: St Ambrose's rather disparaging commentary on Mary Magdalene as well as St Augustine's on the Fall; and the systematic rehearsal of a wife's secondary status in Gratian's book on ecclesiastical law, as well as the classic manifestations of misogyny in the *Romance of the Rose* or the Goliardic satire *Against Marrying*.

Originally a short section was envisaged at the end, with extracts from Christine de Pizan to demonstrate how antifeminist allegations were eventually answered. Research disclosed the existence of a more substantial counter-tradition than expected—that is, more than expected in terms of specific argument, as distinct from the mode of encomium available to Jerome and others. Christine serves still as a suitable terminus; indeed, a second volume would be required to cope with her successors in the debate. But she is here preceded by voices raised interestingly against (for instance) the burden of sexual guilt hung insistently upon women by their antagonists. There is a heretic, too, who tries to oppose the doctrine which excludes women from the priesthood, and whose arguments are translated from the relevant manuscript especially for this volume.

Although the materials as a whole are somewhat various in the degree to which they consciously take sides in the medieval sport of woman-baiting, it is hoped that readers will welcome an element of variegation in this book. The chief objective is nevertheless to show how deeply etched were the conventions and the rhetoric of misogyny, and how people started to engage with them. Experience suggests that anthologies, like railway systems, have exasperating lacunae just where one was hoping for a through route. If that is inevitably sometimes the case in the following pages, one might reflect that the modern reader has not hitherto generally been offered much opportunity to travel around this particular network at all.

Note: Medieval quotation from the Bible was from the Catholic 'Vulgate' Latin text (which, incidentally, included a few books now frequently regarded as apocryphal). The Douai–Rheims translation of the Vulgate into English is adopted widely for new materials in this volume, but this policy has not been imposed on reprinted materials.

Vulgate Bible designations differ from those of the King James version, as follows:

King James	Vulgate
1 Samuel	1 Kings
2 Samuel	2 Kings
1 Kings	3 Kings
2 Kings	4 Kings

A. B.

Lampeter, Wales
1991

Acknowledgements

Among the many colleagues who have given kind assistance during the preparation of this book, I should like to thank in particular: George Rigg, for devoted transatlantic attention to numerous questions about medieval Latin texts; David D'Avray, for volunteering meticulous transcriptions of sermons by Jacques de Vitry; and Oliver Pickering, for a dialogue in which he gave more than he gained. My greatest debt must be to my two assistant editors, whose contribution extends well beyond the specific translations with which their names are associated. Thanks are extended also to Glyn Burgess, Del Kolve, Priscilla Barnum, Sophie Oosterwijk, and Douglas Wurtele for productive suggestions; to Kathy Miles, indefatigable in her pursuit of obscure articles; to Andrew Lockett, for his agreeable combination of courtesy and purposefulness in steering the book through the Press; and finally to St David's University College for a term's study leave at an opportune time.

Publishers and authors who have allowed extracts to be reprinted are acknowledged at the appropriate point in the volume.

Contents

xii CONTENTS

List of Plates
between pages 144 and 145

1. *Pasiphaë and the 'Bull'*. Reproduced by permission of Erlangen Universitätsbibliothek.
2. *Aeneas' Departure: Dido Commits Suicide by Falling on a Sword*. Reproduced by permission of the British Library.
3. *David and Bathsheba*. Reproduced by permission of the British Library.
4. *Expulsion from Paradise: Adam Pulls Eve's Hair and Kicks Her*. Marburg Bildarchiv Foto.
5. *Aristotle Ridden by Phyllis*. Reproduced by permission of the Augustinermuseum, Freiburg im Breisgau. Photo by Bildverlag, Freiburg im Breisgau.
6. *Jerome Tempted by Dancing Girls*. Reproduced by permission of the Metropolitan Museum of Art, New York.
7. *Sensuality*. Marburg Bildarchiv Foto.
8. *Samson and Delilah*. Reproduced by permission of the Pierpont Morgan Library, New York.
9. *The Virgin, Archangel Gabriel, and Tree of Virtues*. Reproduced by permission of the British Library.
10. *Judith Beheading Holofernes*. Reproduced by permission of the Librarian, St David's University College, Lampeter.
11. *The Women at Christ's Tomb*. Reproduced by permission of the British Library.
12. *Catherine of Alexandria Bound to a Column*. Reproduced by permission of the Metropolitan Museum of Art, New York.

Abbreviations

Ag. Jov.	*Against Jovinian* (*Adversus Iovinianum*: Jerome)
Ag. Marr.	*Against Marrying* (*De coniuge non ducenda*, tr. A. G. Rigg)
Brut	Trial of Walter Brut
CCSL	Corpus Christianorum, Series Latina
City	*City of Ladies* (Christine de Pizan)
CNRS	Centre National de la Recherche Scientifique
Corb	*Il Corbaccio* (Boccaccio)
CSEL	Corpus Scriptorum Ecclesiasticorum Latinorum
EETS	Early English Text Society
FOC	Fathers of the Church
Juv.	Juvenal
Leesce	*Le Livre de Leesce* (Jehan Le Fèvre)
Letter	*The Letter of Cupid* (Christine de Pizan)
Math.	*Les Lamentations de Matheolus* (Jehan Le Fèvre)
Miroir	*Le Miroir de Mariage* (Deschamps)
PG	*Patrologia Graeca*, ed. J.-P. Migne
PL	*Patrologia Latina*, ed. J.-P. Migne
RR	*Romance of the Rose* (Guillaume de Lorris and Jean de Meun)
Rule	*Rule for Anchoresses* (*Ancrene Riwle*)
Tert.	Tertullian
SATF	Société des Anciens Textes Français
S. Passion	*The Southern Passion*, ed. Beatrice Brown
S. Th.	*Summa theologiae* (Aquinas)
WoB	*The Wife of Bath's Prologue*

Introduction

A preliminary insight into the phenomenon of medieval antifeminism can be gained from a book called 'The Love of Books' (*Philobiblon*) written by Richard de Bury, who was an avid reader as well as a powerful figure in Church and State in early fourteenth-century England. He imagines books uttering a protest against clerics, who, instead of being their allies, now neglect them and allow them to be thrown out of their homes:

> Our place is usurped by pet dogs, or by hunting hawks, or by that two-legged animal with whom clerics were long since forbidden to live together, and whom we have always taught our pupils to shun even more than a snake or a cockatrice. For that reason she has always been jealous of any devotion to us: she cannot be placated. Eventually, when she spies us languishing undefended (except by some dead spider's web) in a corner, she begins to scowl, abusing us and scorning us in malignant language. She points out that we are the only items in the household that are unnecessary; she complains that we serve no domestic purpose whatever; and she advises that we should quickly be exchanged for expensive hats, fine silk fabrics and deep-dyed scarlets, frocks and fancy furs, wool and linen. And with good reason, if she could see what lies within our hearts, if she had attended our private deliberations, if she had read the book of Theophrastus or Valerius, or if she had only listened with comprehending ears to the twenty-fifth chapter of Ecclesiasticus.[1]

This passage introduces us to three of the four areas of discussion to be explored below. First—all in a spirit of fun, of course—it indicts women on traditional counts. She is 'animal' (*bestia*), 'snake', or other venomous creature; she is inveterately jealous of rivals; she nags in abrasive language (*virulentis sermonibus*); she presumes to offer her 'counsel', but her counsel is one long shopping list of consumables, notably for her wardrobe, which she would substitute for un-utilitarian writings; and the Word is beyond the scope of her limited understanding in any case. Second, Richard picks unerringly on a trio of texts central to misogyny: Jerome's 'Theophrastus', Walter Map's 'Valerius', and the gloomiest of the wisdom books of the medieval Bible. (Of this trio, the first two have been observed to

---

[1] My translation, from Richard de Bury 1960, 42–4. *Philobiblon* dates from 1344–5.

circulate together with the Book of Proverbs in medieval manu-scripts.[2]) And finally, there is a knowing diagnosis not only of a key factor, i.e. clerical celibacy, underlying the propagation of such books in the period, but also of the continuing male monopoly of literacy which licensed a 'private' circulation of antifeminist 'deliberations' among Europe's coterie of intellectuals.[3]

Let us enlarge these points in reverse order, beginning with the wellsprings of medieval misogyny. The subject is too vast to en-compass here other than in a provisional way, being characterized (for instance) by a frustrating infinity of regression.[4] By one route it leads back into ancient Judaic law; by another route it leads back to the dawn of Greek culture, where notions were already current in Hesiod's poetry (c.750 BC) of woman as the deceitful plague of man, responsible for bringing evil into the world.[5] Ovid, in whose footsteps medieval culture often trod, is really a latecomer in these matters. Although this volume opens with him, study of the scholarship on his works quickly discloses that he is merely an overnight stop in the long haul of satire on women; but a very important one because many of his predecessors became temporarily lost to view in the Middle Ages. He must have *seemed* to be a founding father of such satire.

Another starting point might be found in Greek physiology, for there we can locate part of the substructure for the gender divisions in Richard de Bury, whereby women are of an animal, material, household, pragmatic realm while men (intelligent men, anyway) are of a realm of higher deliberation which shuns the 'animal'. The substructure lurks in Aristotle's formulations of the male principle as 'soul' or 'form' and the female principle as 'body' or 'matter'. Since form is what 'shapes', it followed that man appropriated another divine faculty too, the faculty of 'movement': his was the 'active', formative role, woman's the 'passive', receptive role (supplying, in procreation, just inert substance for the superior male semen to 'move' into shape like a carpenter). And all this was summed up in the ultimate derogation of woman, as 'deformed' or 'defective' male, one who could not reach the male standard of perfection because her menstruation signalled that her body was physiologically inferior.[6]

[2] Pratt 1962, 13.
[3] Richard's own associates included Bradwardine, Fitzralph, Burley, and Holkot.
[4] On the history of misogyny, see: Wulff 1914, Moore 1943, Hays 1966, Rogers 1966, Hodgart 1969, Bullough 1973, Ruether 1972, Lucas 1983, Allen 1985.
[5] Allen 1985, 14–15.
[6] See Ch. 1 (iii) below.

Christine de Pizan saw that this sort of thinking (which we might suppose to be on some level an attempt to rationalize male distaste for what was considered the ritual 'uncleanness' of menstruation) had to be quashed if there was to be any progress in building the confidence of women. (Two hundred and fifty years later the doctrine was still turning up in Milton, whose Adam asks why God who 'peopled highest Heaven / With Spirits masculine' should have wanted to create also 'this *fair defect* / Of Nature'.[7])

It is an exaggeration, but not a crazy one, to assert that 'in the misogynistic thinking of the Middle Ages, there can, in fact, be no distinction between the theological and the gynaecological'.[8] In the theological sphere, after all, woman was again associated with 'matter' as with various other inferior categories. Even Augustine, who took to heart the message of Galatians 3: 26–8 that all people become 'the children of God by faith' because therein race, status, and gender disappear ('there is neither male nor female'), thought woman more than man represented an orientation of the mind towards the material rather than the spiritual.[9] In a cruder form of such thinking, woman *becomes* bodily sensation, disrupting the serenity of the male mind. Thus Ambrose, for example, proposes an allegory in the Fall, whereby the serpent is 'a type of the pleasures of the body', woman 'stands for our senses', and the man 'for our minds'. The paradigm of the Fall, then, is that 'pleasure stirs the senses, which, in turn, have their effect on the mind'.[10]

The danger of that effect naturally obsessed the early Church. In confronting it, those who committed themselves zealously to the new faith were much taken up with the problem of *distraction* represented by the ties of marriage and family. St Paul had commented on this distraction as something that could reduce the prayer capacity of a person of either sex: the Fathers of the Church followed suit, in that they used this argument in discouraging female virgins from marrying, or widows from remarrying, as much as they used it to champion male celibacy.[11] But, being male, they gave a special force and prominence to the supposition that the male would only reach the summit of spiritual and mental development by abjuring this distraction of family and woman. 'What happiness to be the bond-

[7] *Paradise Lost* x. 889–91.
[8] Bloch 1987, 20.
[9] Børresen 1981, 25–30.
[10] *Paradise* xv. 73 (Ambrose 1961, 351). Woman had been equated with bodily senses in Philo, but Augustine disagreed in *De Trinitate* xii. 13.
[11] e.g. Jerome, *Against Helvidius* xxii, in Fremantle 1893, 344–5.

4 INTRODUCTION

servant, not of a wife but of Christ, to serve not the flesh but the spirit!'[12] Christ Himself was thought to have endorsed such a way of life when He seemed to commend 'eunuchs, who have made themselves eunuchs for the kingdom of heaven'.[13]

Such a vision of the untrammelled Christian, the philosopher–ascetic, had tremendous appeal during the Middle Ages. Abelard was very struck by it, and through him, so was Heloise. But there was an unfortunate side-effect in the reduction of woman not just to the status of a 'distraction', but to a being who constantly risked sinning almost by her very *existence*, if that existence caused a man to have lustful thoughts. A woman who cultivates her looks 'draws a sword to kill her neighbour', declares Guibert of Tournai in the thirteenth century; she 'bears a flame to burn a home; carries poison for anyone who wishes to take; she uncovers a pit so that an animal may fall into it'.[14] A girl only has to show a bare neck, or sway a bit as she walks through town, proclaims another preacher, Bromyard, and in a single day she may be guilty of inflaming with lust maybe twenty men who see her, 'damning the souls whom God has created'.[15] The guilt is hers, not theirs. Moralists found it only too easy to omit the crucial rider which was added to a similar admonition a thousand years earlier: 'the beauty of a woman is the greatest snare—or rather, not the beauty of woman, but unchastened gazing!'[16]

As the Church struggled gradually to establish a fully celibate priesthood, bidding its clerics to 'shun the two-legged she-beast', it is not surprising that there was a hardening of the inclination among those same clerics to see woman not merely as a sexual snare employed by the devil, but even as a voluntary one. It is interesting to note that one of the reasons usually given for the male monopoly on preaching was that a woman preacher, however virtuous, would incite immoral thoughts in her auditors.[17] Speaking in public, she would compound her threat to men's souls. (It does not seem to have occurred to anyone to ask whether male preachers would unintentionally damn the souls of women responding erotically to their

[12] Jerome, *Ag. Jov.* I. 11.
[13] Matt. 19:12; discussed in Jerome, *Ag. Jov.* I. 12.
[14] D'Avray and Tausche 1980, 102. The 'drawn sword' is also in Ch. 2 Tert. 5, and the 'pit' in Ch. 3, *Rule 4*.
[15] Owst 1933, 395.
[16] Chrysostom, quoted in Bloch 1987, 15. In Ch. 4, Marbod 1 commences with the 'snare' commonplace.
[17] Humbert of Romans, quoted in Owst 1926, 5; and see Ch. 8, Brut A3.

spell.) Patterson is therefore right to speculate, when contemplating the speeches of the Wife of Bath and her forebears, that 'for the male audience [of the time] feminine speaking is never wholly divested of the titillating ambivalences of eroticism'.[18]

Given this climate of opinion, no wonder moralists were so preoccupied with restraining women from 'seeing and being seen' (Ovidian phraseology, much repeated in misogyny). It is an absorbing question whether one can resolve the paradox of the simultaneous vogue for courtly worship of women *and* acerbic denigration of them, so conspicuous during the twelfth century and after it, precisely by finding the origin of both in the seductiveness of the prolonged gaze.[19]

Associated, perhaps, with the clerical suspicion of the female body's power to provoke sexual arousal was a deep-seated male apprehension about, or inferiority complex about, the female capacity for extended sexual activity. Not only did women excite men to sinful thoughts; women were actually held to be more lustful creatures by nature.[20] From here it was a short step to the equation, woman equals lust. Whether other kinds of male fear—for instance, of castration, or of dependency on the mother—have anything to do with misogyny seems to me harder to prove, though there are signs that theories of this kind are enjoying a renaissance in critical studies.[21] A confident case might be made, on the other hand, that misogyny was (and is?) in part a reflex of men's anxiety that women are quicker-witted than they, and can 'run rings round them'. This seems to have been readily acknowledged in the same medieval culture which insisted that woman's reason and intelligence were paltry—which was, incidentally, a second excuse sometimes offered for her exclusion from preaching.[22] Notwithstanding lack of reason, she was admitted to have mental agility, adroitness, and verbal cleverness; and she was good for on-the-spot decisions, because 'Women ben wise in short avysement' according to Pandarus in Chaucer's *Troilus and Criseyde*.[23] That is certainly taken for granted in the racy short stories of the time. Pretending to tut-tut over female guile and cunning, the raconteurs are actually mesmerized by it: 'feminine wit often constitutes a prominent motif in the *fabliaux*', it

---

[18] Patterson 1983, 662.
[19] Bloch 1987, 15.
[20] See Ch. 1, Isidore 2.
[21] e.g. Straus 1988.
[22] Owst 1926, 5: see further Ch. 8 Brut, A3–A8.
[23] IV. 936; corroborated by Criseyde at IV. 1261–3.

has been said, to the extent that 'heroines possess super-human prescience, their spouses sub-normal stupidity'.[24] One can envisage a plausible psychological mechanism whereby male envy and fear of this female faculty of *short avysement* engendered determination to assert superiority and close ranks in other departments of the intellect. Although an analysis which projects hostility from fear is rather modern-sounding, it is anticipated to some extent as early as the fourteenth century, for Jehan Le Fèvre canvasses the idea that women have been kept out of the legal profession precisely because men fear their wits (*engin*) and knowledge, allied with their great subtlety.[25]

So much for contributory factors. Our survey supplements, but also confirms, what de Bury intimates: the centrality of clerical celibacy, and a male determination to defend an inherited domain of intellectual pursuits aggressively against female encroachment. What of the corpus of texts, of which he identifies just three?

In pre-modern times the art of discussion was an art founded on what we would nowadays call 'precedent'. Among the Church Fathers of the first six centuries AD precedent was constituted above all by scriptural quotations, discreetly reinforced by quotations from Roman literature. Among the writers of antifeminist texts from the eleventh century onwards, precedent meant quotation from scripture; quotation from the Fathers; and quotation from a range of classical literature, or at least from repositories of sayings culled from that literature—above all Ovid's and Juvenal's. The textual foundations of the bulk of this anthology up to Chapter 7 are, therefore:

1. a relatively small number of gloomy remarks about women in Proverbs, Ecclesiastes, and Ecclesiasticus (the latter now excluded from non-Catholic bibles as apocryphal); the second of the twin creation narratives in Genesis, together with the account of the Fall and Eve's punishment; certain stories of celebrated biblical heroes who gave way to sexual sin; and the Epistles of St Paul:
2. apophthegms from Ovid, Juvenal, Virgil, and others such as Valerius Maximus (compiler of a collection of anecdotes, first century AD):
3. as time went on, statements extracted from the Fathers:
4. eventually, extracts from the first wave of antifeminist texts, i.e.

---

[24] Spencer 1978, 211.
[25] *Leesce* 1156–61; echoed in Christine de Pizan, *City* I. 8. 8: and see Fiero *et al.* 1989, 75.

Walter Map's *Letter of Valerius*, Jerome's *Against Jovinian* (which was, as it were, re-released in the twelfth century), and Andreas Capellanus's *On Love*:

5. numerous anonymous Latin or vernacular proverbs.

Two things are likely to raise the eyebrow of the newcomer to this corpus. One is that the sayings and anecdotes are so coolly manipulated, and rarely interpreted with critical rigour or in the light of original context. The other is that antifeminist discourse proves to be such a 'small world'. Old friends (or enemies) keep turning up over and over again, facilitating the compilation of an anthology such as the present one because the tradition is sufficiently homogeneous, while also generating an intricate web of absorbing relationships among the texts. But the two points are worth pausing over.

Exploitative use of quotations was not something confined to debate about women; but it was nevertheless disconcertingly endemic in that quarter. For one thing, quotations from (say) the Book of Proverbs about 'wicked' or 'strange' women were lifted quite without acknowledgement that an adjacent passage might be a commendation of the 'good' woman.[26] Even more disconcerting is the silent deletion of some explanatory element from a quotation. Ambrose and some other Fathers convinced themselves that a verse in Ephesians 4:13 indicated that the more perfect a woman was in faith, the more she attained 'maleness'. The relevant verse is within a capacious paragraph declaring that Christ gave the world apostles, evangelists, pastors, etc., to further His work in various ways 'Until we all meet into the unity of faith, and of the knowledge of the Son of God, unto a perfect man, unto the measure of the age of the fulness of Christ'—a pronouncement discomforting indeed for women, If one stops there. But the next verse proceeds, 'That henceforth we be no more children tossed to and fro . . .', implying surely that 'manhood', while still challenging in its marginalization of 'womanhood', is here essentially opposed to 'childhood'.[27]

This would seem a little less objectionable (even though the dignity of one-half of the human race is at stake), if it were not that precisely this accusation—that they snatch bits of scripture without 'turning the page' to confirm the sense—can be found levelled at women in medieval literature. In Langland's *Piers Plowman*, Lady

[26] See Rogers 1966, 6–7. In the present volume, considerations of length have inhibited the selection of positive biblical statements about women.

[27] Biblical remarks about women's dress were likewise taken out of context, as observed in Ch. 8, *Dives 20*.

Mede is one who so blunders; earlier, Chrétien de Troyes had allowed Fénice to remember correctly only part of St Paul's *dictum* on 'marrying if one cannot remain continent'.[28]

But the impression of tacit deletion in antifeminism extends beyond simple quotation to encompass whole narratives, that of David and Bathsheba being a prime example, and one which can be amply followed through in this volume.[29] The Bible gives no evidence that Bathsheba bathed naked in her house *because* David might be gazing from an adjacent house. Yet the example is trotted out rather frequently as though it self-evidently showed culpable seduction by a woman. Even Walter Map, unless I am misjudging his tone, tries to sustain that interpretation, perhaps against his better judgement, when he says: 'Bathsheba was silent, and spoke no wrong; yet she became a spur which caused the fall of her perfect husband, the arrow of death for her innocent spouse.'[30] To jolt the complacency of anyone prematurely convinced of her innocence, however, let it be said that a biblical commentator writing in 1983 perpetuates old suspicions: 'Nothing is said ... about Bathsheba's responsibility. It appears from I Kings 1 [i.e. Vulgate III Kings 1] that she lacked neither ambition nor resourcefulness, so perhaps it is not altogether a coincidence that she happened to be bathing just when and where David could see her.'[31]

A whole arsenal of miscellaneous proverbs, drawn from here and there, reinforced misogyny. The female sex *en bloc* was a target of proverbial utterance, where the male sex was not. 'Dogs keep on pissing, and women keep on weeping' is one example. 'One cockerel suffices fifteen hens, but fifteen men don't suffice one woman' is another.[32] It is the biblical imprecations upon women which haunt the ear more, though, because they are more incessantly repeated. No apology is offered for their repetition in this volume, without which the operative conventions would not be adequately represented. They, along with recurrent trios or quartets of lecherous, or wrathful, or deceitful women assembled evenhandedly from scripture and classical poetry, together with the key allegations laid out in Theophrastus, are above all responsible for the impression that the texts adopting them are excessively formulaic: 'in this vast echo-

---

[28] *Piers Plowman* 'B' IV. 331–53; and *Cligés* 5324.
[29] See 'David' in the Index.
[30] Ch. 4, Map 10.
[31] Conroy 1983, 115–16.
[32] My translations of a French proverb quoted in Roy 1974, 325; and a Latin one quoted in Leotta's edn. of Marbod 1984, 100.

chamber of anti-feminist commonplace, the voices blur into each other, endlessly repeating the same message'.[33]

And yet, there is a danger of hearing less variety in the echo-chamber than is truly the case. Much depends on one's starting point, the particular texts one is hoping to elucidate with reference to the broad tradition. Two sophisticated modern analysts have concurred in giving primacy to the allegation of female nagging, which we noticed in Richard de Bury's vignette. (We are now broaching the third point; conventional medieval indictments of women.) For one of these analysts, a major premise of medieval antifeminism is that woman is 'a bundle of verbal abuses'. For the other also, woman's supposedly wagging tongue, 'feminine copiousness' or 'verbal licentiousness' are similarly a crucial factor.[34] Their emphasis (which perforce I am simplifying) is appropriate so long as we stay within the orbit of the *Lamentations of Matheolus*, the *Wife of Bath's Prologue* and *Tale*, and perhaps the *Romance of the Rose*, the texts which they chiefly address. (One might add that Chrysostom gave a sharp impetus to that emphasis centuries before, when he indicted Eve for 'ruining all' the minute she opened her mouth in paradise.[35]) It works somewhat less happily if we focus instead on Andreas Capellanus, who, though not unperturbed by woman's 'slanderous tongue', seems primarily overcome with amazement at female greed; and it works hardly at all in relation to Walter Map, for whom 'verbal abuse' would have been too vulgar a dimension to admit to the cultivated exhibition which he seeks to mount in his gallery of anti-matrimonial vignettes.

Misogyny was not unvariegated, then. But how far is it possible to identify any presiding structural principles in its expression? One verdict has been that misogynistic treatises are extremely loosely structured, 'with the charges and invectives juxtaposed in an order defying logic'.[36] On the whole this is not an unjust criticism. Its force is particularly apparent in the stretched-out canvas of the *Lamentations of Matheolus*, which betrays a lack of the kind of continuity that even the most sprawling medieval romance could muster through that genre's underlying rhythms of suspense and resolution. The *Lamentations* proceed by fits and starts. Every so often, just as his

---

[33] Mann 1991, 50. John of Salisbury said of anti-matrimonial literature: 'the whole chorus of correct thinkers chant the same tune': John of Salisbury 1938, 355.

[34] Bloch 1987, 4–5; and Patterson 1983, 660–1.

[35] See Ch. 2, Chrysostom 3.

[36] Cassell 1975, p. xx.

poem begins to founder, the author generates a new structuring
format, and sets off again refreshed. Examples of such formats are
'The Five Sophisms of Women' (i. 843–1166); 'The Five Senses
of Husbands which are Oppressed in Marriage' (i. 1167–322);
'Churches as Rendezvous and as Salons' (ii. 947–1068); 'Critique of
Reasons for Marrying' (ii. 2807–3824). What this alerts us to is the
paucity of received designs in literary antifeminism capable of
sustaining a poem of several thousand lines. The author has to draft
in models—the seven sins, the five senses—from other sectors of
medieval writing in order to lament marriage and women on the
cavernous scale he has chosen. Subsequent authors who took a hint
from the general strategy, but confined themselves to just one
transplanted model (for instance, the *Fifteen Joys of Marriage*, parodying a devotional work on the Fifteen Joys of Our Lady),[37] frequently
found more satisfying ways of developing the old material.

Four models were most closely associated with antifeminism. The
simplest, deriving probably from Ovid (though by no means invented
by him), was the catalogue of illustrative examples: the name
Pasiphaë would head a procession of women notorious for lust; or, in
panegyric, the heroine of the Book of Judith (say) would lead a
parade of noble women renowned for courageous and 'virile' deeds.
Walter Map scored a greater success than one might have predicted
with the catalogue formula; but he was an early runner and his
classical repertoire was fancied to such an extent that his short prose
piece attracted enormous scholarly commentaries for educational
purposes. More often deployed in short incidental bursts than as a
controlling structure, the catalogue device never lost its hold in the
period covered by this anthology.

A second model appears in Juvenal, although 'model' is perhaps
too strong a word. Juvenal's *Satire VI* is not noted for its structural
finesse. Purportedly addressed to one Postumus on the brink of
marriage, it first offers him some magnificently mordant recommen-
dations on more convenient ways to commit suicide. Staying with
the 'beware marriage' theme for only a short while, Juvenal seems to
slip increasingly into a random 'modern' version of the Ovidian
catalogue, in a series of sharply observed satirical caricatures of types
of Roman women. The caricatures are arresting, but there seems no
reason why they should stop, or why they stop where they do.

Far and away the most influential model was furnished by

'Theophrastus on Marriage', incorporated in Jerome's treatise *Against Jovinian*. The Fathers themselves were so accustomed to practising the ancient formulae of anti-matrimonial polemic that 'to describe the difficulties of marriage', in Jerome's view, was 'to revel in rhetorical commonplaces'.[38] But these commonplaces elsewhere in Jerome seek to dissuade women, whereas the Theophrastan essay aims to dissuade men. Ideal conditions exist for marriage, he begins, but very rarely. A wise man shuns marriage because he cannot concentrate on books as well as a wife. Wives require all sorts of luxuries. They grumble all night, full of jealousy and suspicion (a sample is given, mimicking such a wife's idiom). A poor wife is difficult to provide for; a rich one hard to put up with. You have to take her as you find her, for you cannot inspect her before acquisition, as you can other household goods. She requires constant attentions. Your every decision will offend her. It is impossible to secure her fidelity, since a pretty woman attracts swarms of lovers and an ugly one seeks them. If you want someone to look after the home or provide company in sickness, a servant or friend is a better choice. The wise man is never alone in the mind, anyway. As for the pretext of children, they will bring nothing but disappointment.

The spell which this piece cast over subsequent writers must have derived, I think, from its terseness as much as from its aura of authoritative antiquity. It was a splendid little store of off-the-peg items, ready for embellishment and rearrangement in new contexts. The goods were neatly labelled and clearly displayed—but not in any compelling order (why deal with reasons for marrying at the *end?*). No overall shape was provided here, therefore, but rather a sequence of individually compelling formulae. Of these, the most treasured were the sample utterances of the wife, and the *reductio ad absurdum* proving that rich or poor, pretty or not, wives mean trouble. This rhetoric of elimination proved exasperatingly popular, though Chaucer made sure the Wife of Bath gave it the kind of retort it deserved: 'So the devil takes the lot, by your account!'[39] Her own monologue, of course, attests to the huge potential eventually to be found in the mode of first-person complaint of which a snippet is tucked into Theophrastus's essay, and which was transmitted also by Juvenal. This could be identified as a fourth model, variously emulated in this anthology, but conspicuously so in parts of *The Widow*, in *Matheolus* 18–21, and *Corbaccio* 3.

[38] *Ag. Jov.* I. 13.   [39] See Ch. 7, *WoB 17*.

I2   INTRODUCTION

The selection of antifeminist readings in this anthology is really
only the tip of an iceberg. A roll-call of authors or texts potentially
available for inclusion could include Hildebert of Tours, Hugh of
Fouilloy, Peter of Blois, John of Salisbury, Pope Innocent III, medieval
comedies (e.g. *Pamphilus*), numerous short poems (e.g. those in the
Fiero volume), and productions in different vernaculars by (for
instance) Juan Ruiz, Cecco d'Ascoli, and Deschamps. There was
indeed, as Christine de Pizan observed, such a torrent of this writing
that literary culture seemed univocal in its denunciation of woman-
kind.[40] The questions which arise naturally in the face of this are, Do
we need to take very much of it seriously? and What kind of reaction
did it prompt?

There can be little doubt that the intelligentsia did regard the
rhetorical formulae of misogyny as a game, or at least that they
considered misogyny a suitable arena in which to show off their
literary paces. Noting that 'writers have much to say everywhere
against the frivolity of the sex', John of Salisbury concedes that
'possibly at times much of this is invention'—and then seems to
retract the concession by continuing, 'yet nothing prevents telling
the truth with a laugh', the truth being 'how easily women are
infatuated, how they cherish hatred', and so on.[41] Le Fèvre perhaps
comes near to giving the 'game' away at the very moment when he
is justifying his satire, since he admits that he is driven on 'to push
my argument to its logical, if extreme conclusion', and declares
besides that his position is reinforced by all sorts of 'commonplaces
and similes' which are the fruits of long study.[42] His posture, then, is
one of conscious extravagance and calculated embellishment. Besides, he proved that he could play the game on either side when he
un-wrote his *Lamentations* soon after he had written them, by
refuting their allegations one by one in his *Livre de Leesce*. In that
respect, he inherited the mantle of Marbod of Rennes, who paired off
attack and defence consecutively (literally on the same page) so as to
demonstrate facility in either mode. What both authors were also
doing was to exercise their own, and their readers', dialectical skills.
The issue itself (are women for good or for ill?) was not necessarily
one meant to excite passionate team support either way, any more
than other topics proposed for literary disputation, such as the
relative merits of summer and winter, or the relative merits of a

[40] See Ch. 9, *City* I–2.   [41] See John of Salisbury 1938, 360.
[42] See Ch. 6, *Math.* 26–7.

cleric/non-cleric as a lover. However, the further we take this
interpretation, the greater the risk of underestimation. If misogyny
dwindles to a puff of post-prandial smoke, then the indignation of
several writers in Chapters 8 and 9 of this book must become the
embarrassing indignation of the solemn *naif*, who mistakes game for
earnest. Although we need not deny that there was an element of
debate for debate's sake, there was surely too much at stake in this
particular debate (apportioning of responsibility for the Fall, for one
thing, and woman's continuing exclusion from public office for
another) for us to dismiss it all as fundamentally unserious.

Having mentioned that Le Fèvre and Marbod both defended what
they attacked, we should take stock of how much there was for them
to draw upon, in terms of pro-female polemic. In the period of the
Fathers there had already developed several varieties of (male-
authored) female panegyric. They fell into categories relating to the
three tiers of perfection thought to be attainable by women, with
faithful wifehood at the bottom, and chaste widowhood and virginity
higher up the scale. Catalogues of Old Testament heroines in each
sector were already making an appearance in Ambrose and Jerome,
though the greatest admiration was inevitably reserved for virgins.
The chief alternatives for eulogy were, so to speak, Iron Virgins and
Demure Virgins. In the former division, the greatest impact was
subsequently to be exerted by the *Lives* of female martyrs, such as
that of St Catherine of Alexandria rendered in Chapter 9 below, still
functioning for Christine de Pizan as it had down the centuries, as a
demonstration that woman has it in her to be no less resolute than
man. Iron virgins were characteristically praised in earlier times for
'transcending their sex',[43] and to that extent there was always a
catch in their usefulness as defence witnesses. Demure virgins
functioned rather more as role models, exemplifying the norms of
womanhood, from which the termagants and harlots of antifeminist
rhetoric deviated. Naturally, the Virgin Mary was the presiding
model and, where debate on women was concerned, she constituted
a trump card, able to trounce opposition almost by the mention of
her name alone (as in *The Thrush and the Nightingale*; see Chapter 8).

Yet, without devaluing her enormous significance in medieval
culture, we may observe that the Virgin Mary was not a very
convincing trump card on behalf of her sex, precisely because the
virgin birth made her unique (as Marbod noted[44]), and because

[43] Discussed in Clark 1979.   [44] See Ch. 8, Marbod 6.

description of her underlined the faults implicitly considered normative in women the more admiringly it distanced her from them. (Thus,
Ambrose writes that she was *untouched* by guile, *frugal* of speech,
without envy of her fellows. Also, 'there was nothing forward in her
words, nothing unseemly in her acts, there was not a frivolous
movement, not an unrestrained step, nor was her voice petulant.'[45])
She does not so much demonstrate that low estimates of woman's
behaviour are unjust, as triumph over shortcomings which the
reader is implicitly being asked to register, one by one, as prevalent in
the sex.

   At best, Ambrose could be said to have fallen into the trap—as it
would now seem to many—of trying to defend woman by bare denial
of the prosecution's charges. Reflex response of that kind was not
infrequent in the Middle Ages. Occasional exceptions come to light.
In a poem *To Muriel* by Serlo of Bayeux (born c.1050), written to
support its addressee in her resolve to remain a virgin, the old
arguments to dissuade a woman from marriage are powerfully
energized from a woman's point of view in a description of the abuse
and pain suffered by wives. (Unfortunately, the text has not survived
in a very good state, so it has not been included in this anthology.[46])
But Serlo's poem does not take aim at antifeminism *per se*, and it
remains undeniable that explicit defence of women was often
conducted on the basis laid down by the attack: doubtless an entirely
natural phenomenon, but one which has been criticized because it is
a reductive fallacy to 'argue that women are by nature good' and
hence to 'accept the conceptual foundation for the opposite view:
that they are by nature bad'.[47]

   As this anthology shows, defenders nevertheless persisted in their
attempts to match antifeminist dogma blow for blow. Countering the
obsession with Eve's secondariness to Adam in creation, they dwelt
on both the superiority of the rib-bone from which she was formed,
and the symbolism of parity derivable from her origin in Adam's side,
not his feet. They were closing in on the real issues more powerfully
when they saw ways in which their opponents' arguments could be
turned against them. Thus, the hypothesis that males were 'active'
and females 'passive' (part of the hierarchy which demoted
females[48]) could be used to prove that men must be more guilty in

   [45] *On Virgins* II. 7: Ambrose 1896, 374–5.
   [46] Text in Wright 1872, 233–40; comment in Raby 1957, II. 45–6.
   [47] Delany 1990, 159.
   [48] See Ch. 3, Aquinas *I*, quoting Augustine.

sexual matters than women. Scrutiny of responsibility becomes, in fact, a leading element in the later texts, affecting all areas of the debate and yielding interesting appraisals of the culpability of key 'witnesses' such as Bathsheba and, crucially, Eve herself.

Much of this took place within the confines of assumptions which no modern feminist would countenance. For instance, woman's 'weakness' was less often challenged than welcomed as a reason for greeting her moral accomplishments with special applause. Some will wince at Marbod's idea of the contributions to society for which woman is to be commended, since most of his criteria are identifiably androcentric.[49] Nevertheless, it was from such beginnings that reaction against antifeminism took root. The 'weapons' with which to combat misogyny 'had dropped from male hands', Mann says, and goes on to claim that Christine de Pizan adopts them without managing to 'shift the ground on which the battle is fought'.[50] The former is fair except in so far as it underestimates how much Christine promotes her experience of contemporary women's lives as evidence. The latter, I would have thought, scants the fresh power of Christine's offensive, particularly against the suppression and dispar-agement of woman's intellect, and against the authority of the 'authorities' massed against her sex. The present anthology will begin to fulfil its editors' dreams if it helps equip readers to judge such matters themselves.

[49] Cf. Fiero et al. 1989, 75, on Le Bien des Fames which 'enumerates the ways in which man benefits from the existence of woman'.
[50] Mann 1991, 3.

|Fig. 1. *Woman and Dominican Friar, Jousting*. Detail from an Arthurian manuscript (northern French, late 13th century). Yale University, Yale MS. 229, fo. 100ᵛ. Reproduced by courtesy of the Beinecke Rare Book and Manuscript Library.

I

The Roots of Antifeminist Tradition

(1) ANCIENT SATIRE

OVID* (43 BC–AD 18)

Ovid's poetry became quite widely known in the Middle Ages, particularly from the twelfth century onwards. Christine de Pizan was to target him as a bastion of misogyny,[1] and although her verdict might be open to question it is undeniable that, among the Ovidian epigrams which people loved to remember, not a few were antifeminist. 'A girl's word is lighter than leaves in autumn'; 'A wife's dowry is wrangling'; 'Her chastity consists in not having been asked'; 'Provided he's rich, they'll warm to an absolute oaf'[2]—such sayings might be absorbed at school and become the stock-in-trade of any (usually male) literate person. Of course, they simplify the attitude to women in his poetry, which is elusive because of the kaleidoscope of dramatic poses he explores, from the medley of erotic lyricism and suavity in the short poems of the *Amores*, through the mock-lectures on love psychology in the *Art of Love*, to the voice of woman betrayed in the *Heroides*. Generalizations are perilous. It would be especially misleading to highlight passages in which Ovidian women are associated with deceit and two-timing, because duplicity is equally urged upon men.[3] In fact, an intention to treat the sexes evenhandedly is explicitly paraded. 'I'm giving arms to both sides', asserts the narrator in *Cures for Love* (*Remedia Amoris*, 49–50), and the same holds true for *The Art of Love*.

Since Ovid's archness makes one suspect ironies at every turn, the extent of antifeminist *insinuation* in his poetry remains hard to gauge. The present selection confines itself to overtly misogynistic readings which caught the eye of later writers. Prominent among these is a cheerful discourse imputing wild (*furiosa*) sexual urges to women, by contrast with men's more law-abiding libido (see 1 below). It is illustrated with reference to lurid sex-motivated crimes of women in received legend (the catalogue itself being an ancient rhetorical device much favoured in subsequent antifeminist tradition). However, except in a rhetorical passage (3) alleging woman's infinite wrath upon discovery of a rival, Ovid does not elsewhere sustain the notion

---

* Tr. Peter Green, *Ovid: The Erotic Poems* (Harmondsworth: Penguin, 1982), 98–9, 127, 174–6, 186–7, 202, 214, 232–4, 249. © Peter Green, 1982. Reprinted by permission of Penguin Books Ltd.

[1] *City of Ladies* I. 9. 2, and see Ch. 9 below, Letter 4–5.

[2] Respectively, *Amores* II. 16. 45; *Art of Love* II. 155; *Amores* I. 8. 43; *Art of Love* II. 276.

[3] *Art of Love* III. 673 ff. (women) and I. 611 ff. (men).

of lawless extravagance in female desire. He is more bent on elaborating society's games of manipulative flirtation, with conspicuous attention given (see 5) to women's supposed designs on suitors' wallets. Doubtless it is always important to listen for an element of tongue-in-cheek exaggeration. Ovid does not usually cultivate high moral ground and outrage: these are more characteristic of Juvenal, and of those who imitated him.

1   Libido: *The Art of Love*, I. 269–343

The first thing to get in your head is that every single
   Girl can be caught—and that you'll catch her if
You set your toils right. Birds will sooner fall dumb in springtime,
   Cicadas in summer, or a hunting-dog
Turn his back on a hare, than a lover's bland inducements
   Can fail with a woman.[4] Even one you suppose
Reluctant will want it. Like men, girls love stolen passion,
   But are better at camouflaging their desires:[5]
If masculine custom precluded courtship of women
   You'd find each besotted girl
Taking the lead herself. A heifer amid lush pastures
   Lows to a bull, a mare
Whinnies at stallions; but our male libido's milder,[6]
   Less rabid: man's sex has bounds
Imposed by convention. Incest is out. Think of wretched Byblis—
   Burned up by her brother, expiating her crime
With a suicide's noose.[7] Myrrha loved her father (but hardly
   As a daughter should), and now she's straitjacketed
Behind tree-bark, oozing those fragrant tears we use for
   Perfume, named after her: myrrh.[8]

     . . . Pasiphaë
Proudly rejoiced in her role as bull's mistress . . .
   Plucked leaves and lush grass

---

[4] This rhetorical figure of *adunaton*, 'impossibility', was often imitated.
[5] A 'common doctrine' according to Hollis's edn. of Ovid 1977, 90, citing Euripides.
[6] This claim, and some of the ensuing illustrative examples, are also found in Ovid's contemporary, Propertius (III. 19).
[7] Byblis was involved in an incestuous relationship with her brother Caunus. When he fled she hanged herself (or, was transformed into a stream or fountain).
[8] Aphrodite destined Myrrha (or Smyrna) to an incestuous relationship with her unwitting father Cinyras: when he recognized her and pursued her, the gods turned her into a myrrh-tree.

For this bull, went off with the herds, unrestrained by concern for
   Her husband.
   . . . Yet the herd-leader, taken in by a wooden cow, contrived to
   Fill her: their offspring betrayed
Its paternity.[9] Had Aerope restrained her love for Thyestes
   (And to forgo even one man
Is a serious matter), Phoebus would never have turned backwards
   In mid-flight, have driven his steeds
And chariot Dawnwards.[10] From Nisus his daughter stole that
   purple
   Lock—and now fights down
The mad dogs that swarm from her groin.[11] Agamemnon lived
   through battles
   On land, and great storms by sea,
To become his wife's victim.[12] Who's not wept for flame-racked
   Creüsa, for the children whose bloody death
Stained Medea's hands?[13] . . .
   Each one of these crimes was prompted
   By woman's lust—lust that far
Outstrips ours in keenness and frenzy. Why doubt that you can
   conquer
   Any girl in sight?

2   Equivocal Resistance: *The Art of Love*, I. 663–78

What sensible man will not intersperse his coaxing
   With kisses? Even if she doesn't kiss back,
Still force on regardless! She may struggle, cry 'Naughty!',
   Yet she wants to be overcome . . .[14]

[9] Pasiphaë the wife of Minos became mistress of a bull, being impregnated inside a
wooden cow designed by Daedalus—who subsequently built a labyrinth to imprison
her man-bull offspring, the Minotaur.
[10] Aerope committed adultery with Thyestes, brother of her husband Atreus, who
took revenge by killing Thyestes' children and serving them to him at dinner.
According to some, the sun (Phoebus) went backwards in revulsion from this deed.
[11] Scylla fell in love with Minos when he was besieging her father Nisus. To help
Minos she plucked out a red lock of hair said to sustain Nisus' life, but Minos later
drowned her. Here confused with a monster also named Scylla.
[12] Agamemnon escaped the hostility of the winds and the sea, and of assailants on
land, only to become victim to his wife Clytemnestra and her lover Aegisthus.
[13] Medea helped Jason to win the Golden Fleece, and eloped with him; but
subsequently Creon of Corinth persuaded him to divorce Medea in favour of his
daughter Creüsa. Medea retaliated by sending her a poisoned robe which burnt her
up, then murdered her own two children by Jason.
[14] A theory repeated in *Art of Love* I. 485–6: it provoked Christine de Pizan, in *City*
II. 44.1.

It's all right to use force—force of *that* sort goes down well with
    The girls: what in fact they love to yield
They'd often rather have stolen. Rough seduction
    Delights them, the audacity of near-rape
Is a compliment—so the girl who *could* have been forced, yet
        somehow
    Got away unscathed, may feign delight, but in fact
Feels sadly let down.

3   Jealous Wrath: *The Art of Love*, II. 373–86

    More savage than the tawny
Boar in his rage, as he tosses the maddened dogs
On lightning tusks, or a lioness suckling her unweaned
    Cubs, or the tiny adder crushed
By some careless foot, is a woman's wrath, when some rival
    Is caught in the bed *she* shares. Her feelings show
On her face. Decorum's flung to the wind, a maenadic
    Frenzy grips her, she rushes headlong off
After fire and steel. Deserted, barbarian Medea
    Avenged her marital wrongs
On Jason by killing their children—like Procne the swallow,
    Another ruthless mother, breast stained red
With blood.[15] Such acts destroy the most strongly bonded
    Passions . . .

4   How Girls Outsmart Guardians: *The Art of Love*, III. 618–52

    With as many watchers around you as Argus had eyes
You'll outsmart them all. Can a guard stop you writing letters
    When you're shut in the bathroom? Will he find
All the places where your girl-accomplice can hide them—tablets
    Snugly tucked in her bra,
A package of papers strapped to one calf, a seductive message
    Slipped between sandal and foot?
        . . . Think of Danaë's father, and all the trouble
    He took to protect his daughter—yet she contrived

---

[15] On Medea, see n. 13. Procne was wife of Tereus, who raped her sister Philomela, cutting off her tongue to prevent disclosure: but Philomela wove a communication to Procne. In revenge the sisters served up the flesh of Tereus' son to him as food. When he pursued them, the gods transformed all three into birds.

To make him a grandfather.[16] The city's full of theatres,
    Girls love the races—what
Can a guardian do? Say she worships Egyptian Isis,
    And goes where no watchful male
May follow, clashing her sistrum? What about the Good Goddess,
    Banning men from her temple (except her own
Chosen adherents)?[17] The public baths provide plenty of private
    Fun for girls—while their guardians sit outside
In charge of their clothes. How cope with the sharp girlfriend
    Who's 'ill' on demand (but never too ill to vacate
Her bed for the length of a visit)? How counter those duplicate
    And duplicitous passkeys? How block the door—and all
Those other ways in? A guardian's wits can be fuddled. . . .
But what's the point of such unimportant digressions, when any
    Guard can be bought with a trifling bribe?

5   Cashing in on Sex: from *Amores*, i. 8

Here Ovid achieves a virtuoso performance using the conventional framework of an old woman's advice on how a girl should exploit admirers.[18] An
old bawd named Dipsas (*dipsa* is Greek for 'thirst') is in the process of training
a novice in the Arts of Manipulation. In the development of antifeminist
tradition, the old, ugly, cunning instructress—the *lena* (bawd) or *vetula* (little
old woman)—is often the butt of virulent mockery, and perhaps projects a
certain male fear. The narrator of this poem first gives an extravagant sketch
of Dipsas' knowledge of secret potions, her magical control of weather, and
her awesome incantations; he then reports the words of the overheard
tutorial.

'Dearie, you made a great hit with that rich young gentleman
    Yesterday. He'd got eyes for nobody else—
And why should he have? There's no girl more beautiful. Such a
    pity
    Your turn-out doesn't match your face.

   [16] Acrisius tried to keep his daughter virgin by shutting her up in a tower; but Zeus
impregnated her in the form of a shower of gold.
   [17] Roman satirists refer to the temple of the goddess Isis as a place for picking up
partners. Worship of the Good Goddess (*Bona dea*) was exclusive to women, who
according to Juvenal perverted her rites into orgies (*Satire* VI, 314 ff.). Later writers
often alleged that women pursued sexual intrigue under cover of religious observance.
   [18] Plautus' *Mostellaria* has a scene with a young prostitute instructed by her aged
maid while a lover eavesdrops; and cf. Juv. *Satire* VI, 231–41. The satire on gold-
digging is repeated in *Art of Love* i. 405–36.

I'd like to see you become as wealthy as you're good-looking—
Once get you in the money, I shan't ever starve. . . .

While you're spreading your net, go easy. Don't show too
    rapacious
Or your bird may fly off. Once you've caught him, anything
    goes.[19]
Some show of love does no harm: let him fancy himself your
    darling,
But take good care you collect a *quid pro quo*.
Don't say Yes every night. Pretend that you have a headache,
Or make Isis your excuse, then you can plead
Religious abstention. Enough's enough, though—he may get
    accustomed
To going without, over-frequent rebuffs may cool
His passion off. Take gifts, but be deaf to entreaties—
Let the lucky man hear his rival cursing outside.
You've hurt him? *He* started it. Throw a quick tantrum. This kind
    of
Counter-attack will very soon choke him off. . . .
Another trick you must learn is control of the tear-ducts,[20]
How to weep buckets at will—
And when you're deceiving someone, don't let perjury scare you:
Venus ensures that her fellow-gods
Turn a deaf ear to such gambits. You must get yourself a
    houseboy
And a well-trained maid, who can hint
What gifts will be welcome. Don't let them demand exorbitant
Tips for themselves. Little presents soon add up.
Your sister and mother, your nurse, these can all help fleece a
    lover—
Many hands make quick loot.
When you've run through all other excuses for getting presents
Say it's your birthday, show him the cake.
Don't let him get cocksure, without any rivals:
Love minus competition never wears well.
Leave the bed suspiciously rumpled, make sure he sees it,
Flaunt a few sexy bruises on your neck—

[19] The Bible also likens woman to a snare for birds (e.g. Prov. 7: 23, in Scripture 17,
below).
[20] Cf. Juv. 6, below.

Above all, show him his rival's presents (if none are forthcoming,
    Order some yourself, from a good shop).
When you've dug enough gold, then protest he's being far too
    generous
    And ask him for a *loan*—which you'll never repay.
Beguile with sweet words, and blandish while you despoil him:
    A taste of honey will mask the nastiest dose.
These tactics are guaranteed by a lifetime's experience,
    So don't ignore them. Follow my advice,
And you'll never regret it. Ah, many's the time you'll bless me
    While I'm alive, and pray that my old bones
Lie easy after I'm gone—'
        At this point my shadow
    Betrayed me.[21] I was dying to get my hands
On those sparse white locks, to tear at the old hag's raddled
    Cheeks and drink-bleary eyes.
May the gods strip the roof from her head, end her days in
    poverty,
    Send her horrible winters and an eternal thirst!

6   The Cause of Warfare: from *Amores*, II. 12

In an extended parody of militarism, the speaker announces the successful
outcome of his active service—his conquest of Corinna. This prompts a
rhetorical meditation on precedents for conflict over women.

No novelty, either, about the cause of warfare. Europe
    And Asia would never have been
Embroiled without Helen's abduction.[22] It was a woman
    Brought Centaurs and Lapiths to blows
Over the wine at that wedding.[23] A woman, Lavinia, got the
    Trojans fighting again, for the second time,
When they set foot on Latin soil.[24] While our City was still new-
    founded
    Those Sabine girls screaming rape

[21] The 'shadow' of Ovid, erotic instructor, is present in more than the literal sense.
[22] Helen was wife of Menelaus of Sparta. Her 'abduction' by Paris provoked the
famous siege of Troy by Menelaus and his brother Agamemnon.
[23] They came to blows at the wedding of Pirithous and Hippodameia.
[24] When Aeneas landed in Italy Lavinia's father gave her to him, arousing the
hostility of prince Turnus, to whom she had been betrothed.

Provoked most bloody reprisals.[25] I've seen two bulls battling
Over a snow-white heifer—she egged them on.

7   Defence of Women, or Mock-defence? *The Art of Love*, III. 9–43

Don't pin the evil reputation
Of one or two on them all, judge each girl by
Her own proper merits. It's true that Helen and Clytemnestra
Must face sisterly charges from both
The sons of Atreus[26]; it's true that what Eriphyle plotted
Sent Amphiaraus and his horses down,
Still living, to Styx[27]; yet Penelope stayed constant
For ten years, while her husband was at the wars,
And ten more of his wanderings.[28] Look at Protesilaus
And Laodameia—who cut short her span on earth
To follow the man she loved.[29] Alcestis redeemed Admetus'
Life by pledging her own, was borne to the grave
In his stead.[30] Evadne cried, 'Ah take me, Capaneus!
We'll mingle our ashes', and sprang
On to the pyre.[31] Virtue herself, by name and fashion,
Is a lady . . .
You seldom see the ladies
Using bows and flaming arrows on their men—
Men are often deceivers, girls hardly ever: enquiries
Will prove the feminine cheat
A rare bird indeed. Medea, already a mother, was dumped by
Perfidious Jason for another bride,
And as far as Theseus knew, deserted Ariadne
Had long been food for gulls
On that lonely beach.[32] How did Nine Ways get its title?
How did the very woods come to shed their leaves

[25] At the founding of Rome, Romulus' men lacked partners. Inviting the nearby Sabines, they seized the Sabine women, who later effected a reconciliation between the two sides.
[26] Atreus' sons Menelaus and Agamemnon lost their wives Helen and Clytemnestra to other men: cf. nn. 12 and 22.
[27] Eriphyle was bribed with a necklace to persuade her husband Amphiaraus to join a war against Thebes even though he knew it would be his death.
[28] She was wooed by many men during Odysseus' absence.
[29] Laodameia committed suicide after pining for her dead husband Protesilaus.
[30] Apollo persuaded the Fates to spare Admetus' life if he could find a substitute: his wife Alcestis volunteered—and was later rescued from Hades by Hercules.
[31] Capaneus died in the battle for Thebes.
[32] On Medea see n. 13. Ariadne fell in love with Theseus, helping him escape from the labyrinth after killing the Minotaur (see n. 9): but he deserted her on the island of Naxos.

And weep for Phyllis?[33] Remember that guest with the reputation
For *piety? He* left poor Dido a sword—
And a motive for suicide.[34] What ruined all these ladies?
Erotic ineptitude, lack of technique. It takes
Technique to make love last. . . .

JUVENAL (EARLY SECOND CENTURY AD)

Like Ovid, Juvenal was a master of the quotable epigram, for example 'Who's
to guard the guards themselves?'—his comment on the futility of chaperon-
ing women.[35] His misogynistic *dicta* were eagerly collected and might be
recycled anywhere (e.g. by Abelard, discussing abbesses; or sandwiched
between scriptural citations in a thirteenth-century sermon on marriage[36]).
But tonally, Juvenal differs fundamentally from Ovid, cultivating not so
much the conspiratorial grin as moral outrage at the sordid animalism and
chill cynicism he ascribes to women. Ovid asserts woman's keen libido only
half-seriously and in a context where sexual interest is taken as the healthy
norm. Juvenal more searingly indicts female lust in a context where
recognition of normative sexual drives is offered only as the tawdry excuse of
a wife brazening out her adultery (see 6 below). There is nothing in Ovid to
match Juvenal's revolting glimpse of a man, going to meet dignitaries early
one morning, getting his shoes wet in the puddles of stale urine left by his
wife and her tipsy friends around civic statues during the night.[37] However,
medieval misogyny was rather selective in what it extracted from Juvenal: so
the midnight urinations of this angry sketch (rather too open to retort,
anyway, in terms of male drunkenness and street vomit) did not catch on.
The full impact of Juvenal's sixth satire is best seen in Boccaccio's *Il Corbaccio*
(Chapter 6 below).

FROM *SATIRE VI**

1 Suicide Beats Marriage: 28 32

Surely you used to be sane. Postumus, are you taking a wife?
Tell me what Fury, what snakes, have driven you on to this
madness?
Can you be under her thumb, while ropes are so cheap and so
many,

[33] Phyllis was abandoned by her fiancé Demophöon at Nine Ways, whose name
Ovid derives from her walking nine times to the sea before taking her life.
[34] Virgil called Aeneas *pius*. When he cut short an affair with Dido and left
Carthage, she transfixed herself on his sword.
[35] *Satire* VI, 347–8.
[36] See Ch. 3, Heloise and Abelard 8; and Ch. 5, Jacques de Vitry 1.
[37] *Satire* VI, 313.
* Tr. Rolfe Humphries (Bloomington: Indiana University Press, 1958), pp. 64–5,
67–71, 73–4, 81–5. © 1958, Indiana University Press. Reprinted by permission of
the publisher

When there are windows wide open and high enough to jump
   down from,
While the Aemilian bridge is practically in your back yard?

2   Scarcity of the Chaste Bride: 45-54

   You go seeking
A virtuous old-fashioned wife? It's time to summon the doctors.
How choosy you are![38] If a decent and modest woman
Falls to your lot, flop prone on your face at the Tarpeian altar,
Bow and adore, and slay a golden heifer to Juno.
Not many women are worthy to touch the fillets of Ceres . . .[39]
Will she be satisfied with one man, this Hiberina?[40]
Sooner, I think, with one eye.

3   The Insatiable Empress: 115-32

Look at those peers of the gods, and hear what Claudius suffered.
Soon as his august wife[41] was sure that her husband was sleeping,
The imperial whore preferred, to a bed in the palace,
Some low mattress; put on the hood she wore in the nighttime,
Sneaked through the streets alone, or with only a single com-
   panion,
Hid her black hair in a blonde-coloured wig, and entered a
   brothel.
Reek of old sheets, still warm—her cell was reserved for her,
   empty,
Held in the name of Lycisca. There she took off her dress,
Showed her golden tits, and the parts where Britannicus came
   from,
Took the customers on, with gestures more than inviting,
Asked and received her price and had a wonderful evening.
Then, when the pimp let the girls go home, she sadly departed
Last of them all to leave, still hot, with a woman's erection,
Tired by her men, but unsatisfied still,[42] her cheeks all discoloured,
Rank with the smell of the lamps, filthy, completely disgusting,

---

[38] Substituted for Humphries, 'What a real sweetheart you are!' in light of Courtney
1980, 268, n. on l. 47.
[39] Juno, as goddess of marriage, and Ceres, as an especially chaste goddess.
[40] The name 'Hiberina' is restored instead of Humphries, 'this piece of perfection.'
[41] Messalina, wife of Emperor Claudius and mother of Britannicus.
[42] This phrase, *lassata necdum satiata*, was often recalled, even in the context of
scientific discussion of woman's 'excess moistness'; Jacquart and Thomasset 1988, 81,
213.

Perfumed with aroma of whore-house, and home, at last, to her
pillow.

4   The Unendurably Perfect Wife: 161–6

'Isn't there one from all of these crowds who seems to you
worthy?'
Let her be well-behaved, good-looking, wealthy, and fertile,
Let her have ancestors' busts and portraits all over her hallways,
Let her be more intact than all the pre-ravished Sabines,[43]
Let her be a rare bird, the rarest on earth, a black swan—
Who could endure a wife endowed with every perfection?

5   Capricious Domineering Wives: 206–30

If you are simply devoted to one alone, bend your neck,
Bow to the yoke; no lover finds mercy in any woman.
Passionate she may be, but she loves to plunder and torment.
The better you are, as husband and man, the less the advantage
You will get from a wife. You will never give anyone presents
If she says, No! If she stands in your way, there is nothing, but
nothing,
You can purchase or sell. She will regulate even your friendships,
Slam the door in the face of a lifelong boon companion. . . .
'Crucify that slave!' 'But what has he done to deserve it?
Who is witness against him? Who has informed on him? Lis-
ten[44]—
No delay's ever too long in the death of a human being.'
'A slave is a human being? You fool! All right, he's done nothing.
This is my wish, my command; my desire is good enough reason.'
So she is lord of her spouse. But soon she abandons this kingdom,
Occupies house after house, and her bridal veil gets pretty ragged.
Then she comes flying back to the bed she scorned and aban-
doned,
Leaving behind her the doors in festal array, and the garlands
New on the walls, and the branches still green over the lintel.
So her conquests grow: eight husbands in five Octobers—
O illustrious feat, worth being carved on her tombstone![45]

---

[43] See n. 25.
[44] Or, 'Let him speak.' In 479 ff. Juv. harps on the theme of women's cruel abuse of
attendants and slaves, recalled by Chaucer in the Prologue of the Monk's Tale.
[45] Tombstones commended wives married only once. Juvenal's record-breaking
eight husbands seem to be remembered in Jerome, and thence Chaucer: see Ch. 7,
WoB 2.

6   Bedroom Tactics and Brazenness: 268–85

The bed holds more than a bride; you lie with bicker and quarrel
Always, all night long, and sleep is the last thing you get there.
There she can really throw her weight around, like a tigress
Robbed of her young; or else, to atone for her own bad conscience,
She fakes the outraged sigh, and hates the boys whom her
        husband
Has, or she says he has, or sheds tears over a mistress
Purely fictitious, of course. Her tears come down like raindrops,
With plenty more where they came from, ready to flow at her
        bidding.[46]
Abject slug that you are, you think this proves that she loves you.
Aren't you pleased with yourself, as your lips go seeking those
        lashes
Wet with her pitiful tears? But what if you happened to open
The drawers of her desk, and found those notes, those fervent
        epistles,
Saved by your green-eyed wife, the hypocritical cheater?
You may catch her in bed with a slave or a knight. What
        happens?
All she can do in that case is invoke the art of Quintilian,
'Master of Rhetoric, help! Come to my aid, I implore you.'
'Sorry,' Quintilian replies, 'I'm stuck; get yourself out of this
        one.'[47]
This does not bother her much; her explanation is ready.
'Long ago,' she says, 'it was understood between us
Perfectly well, you could do what you pleased, and no double
        standard
Kept me from having my fun. So howl as much as you want to,
I am human, too.' Can you beat their nerve when you catch
        them?
That's when their very guilt supplies them anger and spirit.

7   Over-articulate Learning: 434–56

Even worse is the one who has scarcely sat down at the table
When she starts in on books, with praise for Virgil and pardon
For the way Dido died; she makes comparisons, placing

[46] Cf. Ovid 5 above.
[47] Woman's method of persuasion is beyond the ken of Quintilian, the authority on
rhetoric.

Virgil one side of the scales, and counterweights him with
    Homer.[48]
Critics surrender, professors are lost; the whole crowd is silent.
No one can get in a word edgewise, not even a lawyer,
No, nor an auctioneer, nor even another woman,
Such is the force of her words, the syllables pouring in torrents
Making a din like that when pots and kettles are rattled
In an eclipse of the moon. No need of trumpets or cymbals,[49]
All by herself she can make all of the noise that is needed. . . .
Postumus, my good friend, don't let the wife of your bosom
Ever acquire the style of an orator, whirling the sentence,
Heaving the enthymeme, or the undistributed middle.[50]
Don't let her know too much about historical matters,
Let there be some things in books she does not understand. How I
    hate them,
Women who always go back to the pages of Palaemon's gram-
    mar,
Keeping all of the rules, and are pedants enough to be quoting
Verses I never heard.

8   Plastered Faces: 457–73

There's nothing a woman won't do, nothing she thinks is
    disgraceful
With the green gems at her neck, or pearls distending her
    earlobes.
Nothing is worse to endure than your Mrs Richbitch, whose
    visage
Is padded and plastered with dough, in the most ridiculous
    manner.
Furthermore, she reeks of unguents, so God help her husband
With his wretched face stunk up with these, smeared by her
    lipstick.
To her lovers she comes with her skin washed clean. But at home
Why does she need to look pretty? Nard is assumed for the lover,
For the lover she buys all the Arabian perfumes.

---

[48] Dido is already a bone of contention—championed by a woman (as later by
Christine de Pizan: *Letter*, 445–60).
[49] Antifeminists mocked woman's utterance as clatter (later, as the noise of a
clock). Loud noise was thought to frighten off demons attending eclipses.
[50] She is imagined brandishing rhetorical devices like weapons.

It takes her some time to strip down to her face, removing the
   layers
One by one, till at last she is recognizable, almost,
Then she uses a lotion, she-asses' milk; she'd need herds
Of these creatures to keep her supplied on her northernmost
   journeys.
But when she's given herself the treatment in full, from the
   ground base
Through the last layer of mud pack, from the first wash to a
   poultice,
What lies under this—a human face, or an ulcer?

9   Credulity, Superstition: 517–31

The superstitious lady is consulting a visiting eunuch 'seer'.

In a solemn voice, he warns her, Beware of September,[51]
Beware of the hurricanes, unless she has made an oblation,
First, of a hundred eggs, or given him some old garments
The colour of vine leaves in autumn, by way of preventive magic
Whereby what danger there is, however appalling or sudden,
Passes into the clothes, a full year's expiation.
   On a winter day she'll go down to the Tiber,
Break the morning ice, plunge three times into the current,
Wash her fearful head where the waves crest high, and then,
   trembling,
Naked, with bleeding knees, crawl out on the field of Mars.
If white Io commands, she will go to the borders of Egypt,
Fetch from the sun-warmed Nile water, and sprinkle the temple
Sacred to Isis, that stands near the polling booths of the city.
She has no doubt that she's called by the actual voice of the
   goddess—
What a fine soul and mind for the gods to talk with by nighttime!

   [51] The seer makes easy prophecies, with an eye to gaining her colourful cast-off
clothes.

(ii) SCRIPTURE*

A full scriptural background for this anthology would occupy a whole volume, for ideally one would need the complete stories of Samson, Judith, Esther, etc., as well as extensive readings in Proverbs, Ecclesiastes, and Ecclesiasticus, the three books in which the most damaging assertions are made about women. Of these, the most extraordinary is probably Ecclesiasticus 42: 14 (included in *10* below), which Christine de Pizan struggled to neutralize.[52] Some conspicuous possibilities, such as St Paul's comments on marriage and virginity in 1 Corinthians 7, are omitted because they are quite fully reported in the anthology's readings from Jerome and others. The selection makes no claim to be representative of 'woman in the Bible'; it merely supplies, for quick reference, a number of excerpts particularly influential in literature attacking and defending women.

Creation of Adam and Eve: Genesis 1: 25–7 and 2: 15–3: 7

1   (1: 25) And God made the beasts of the earth according to their kinds, and cattle, and every thing that creepeth on the earth after its kind. And God saw that it was good. (26) And He said: Let us make man to our image and likeness: and let him have dominion over the fishes of the sea, and the fowls of the air, and the beasts, and the whole earth, and every creeping creature that moveth upon earth. (27) And God created man to His own image; to the image of God He created him: male and female He created them. . . .

2   (2: 15) And the Lord God took man, and put him into the paradise of pleasure, to dress it, and to keep it. (16) And He commanded him, saying: Of every tree of paradise thou shalt eat: (17) But of the tree of knowledge of good and evil, thou shalt not eat. For in what day soever thou shalt eat of it, thou shalt die the death. (18) And the Lord God said. It is not good for man to be alone: let us make him a help like unto himself. . . . (21) Then the Lord God cast a deep sleep upon Adam: and when he was fast asleep, He took one of his ribs, and filled up flesh for it. (22) And the Lord God built the rib which He took from Adam into a woman: and brought her to Adam. (23) And Adam said: This now is bone of my bones, and flesh of my flesh; she shall be called woman, because she was taken out of man.

---

* From The Holy Bible, tr. from the Latin Vulgate, part first published at Douai in 1609 and part at Rheims in 1582 (Belfast, 1852 edn.).
[52] See Ch. 9, *Quarrel 4.*

3   (3: 1) Now the serpent was more subtle than any of the beasts of the earth which the Lord God had made. And he said to the woman: Why hath God commanded you, that you should not eat of every tree of paradise? (2) And the woman answered him, saying: Of the fruit of the trees that are in paradise we do eat: (3) But of the fruit of the tree which is in the midst of paradise, God hath commanded us that we should not eat; and that we should not touch it, lest perhaps we die.[53] (4) And the serpent said to the woman: No, you shall not die the death. (5) For God doth know that in what day soever you shall eat thereof, your eyes shall be opened: and you shall be as Gods, knowing good and evil. (6) And the woman saw that the tree was good to eat, and fair to the eyes, and delightful to behold: and she took of the fruit thereof, and did eat, and gave to her husband who did eat. (7) And the eyes of them both were opened. . . .

David and Bathsheba: 2 Kings 11: 1–27

4 (1) And it came to pass at the return of the year, at the time when kings go forth to war, that David sent Joab and his servants with him, and all Israel, and they spoiled the children of Ammon, and besieged Rabba: but David remained in Jerusalem. (2) In the mean time it happened that David arose from his bed after noon, and walked upon the roof of the king's house: and he saw from the roof of his house a woman washing herself, over-against him: and the woman was very beautiful. (3) And the king sent, and enquired who the woman was. And it was told him, that she was Bethsabee the daughter of Eliam, the wife of Urias the Hethite. (4) And David sent messengers, and took her, and she came in to him, and he slept with her: and presently she was purified from her uncleanness:[54] (5) And she returned to her house having conceived. And she sent and told David, and said: I have conceived.

5 (6) And David sent to Joab, saying: Send me Urias the Hethite. And Joab sent Urias to David. (7) And Urias came to David. And David asked how Joab did, and the people, and how the war was carried on. (8) And David said to Urias: Go into thy house, and wash thy feet. And Urias went out from the king's house, and there went out after him a mess of meat from the king. (9) But Urias slept before the gate of the king's house, with the other servants of his lord, and

[53] In *Paradise* xii, Ambrose attributes blame to Eve for adding a new clause to the original prohibition: Ambrose 1961, 334–7.

[54] i.e., she had just finished menstruating; so the bath could have marked the end of ritual impurity.

went not down to his own house. (10) And it was told David by some
that said: Urias went not to his house. And David said to Urias: Didst
thou not come from thy journey? why didst thou not go down to thy
house? (11) And Urias said to David: The ark of God and Israel and
Juda dwell in tents, and my lord Joab and the servants of my lord
abide upon the face of the earth: and shall I go into my house, to eat
and to drink, and to sleep with my wife?[55] By thy welfare and by the
welfare of thy soul I will not do this thing. (12) Then David said to
Urias: Tarry here today, and to-morrow I will send thee away. Urias
tarried in Jerusalem that day and the next. (13) And David called
him to eat and to drink before him, and he made him drunk: and he
went out in the evening, and slept on his couch with the servants of
his lord, and went not down into his house. (14) And when the
morning was come, David wrote a letter to Joab: and sent it by the
hand of Urias, (15) Writing in the letter: Set ye Urias in the front of
the battle, where the fight is strongest: and leave ye him, that he may
be wounded and die. (16) Wherefore as Joab was besieging the city,
he put Urias in the place where he knew the bravest men were. (17)
And the men coming out of the city, fought against Joab, and there
fell some of the people of the servants of David, and Urias the Hethite
was killed also.... (26) And the wife of Urias heard that Urias her
husband was dead, and she mourned for him. (27) And the
mourning being over, David sent and brought her into his house,
and she became his wife, and she bore him a son: and this thing
which David had done, was displeasing to the Lord.

The Temptress: Proverbs 7: 4–27

6 (4) Say to wisdom: Thou art my sister: and call prudence thy
friend, (5) That she may keep thee from the woman that is not thine,
and from the stranger who sweeteneth her words. (6) For I looked
out of the window of my house through the lattice, (7) And I see little
ones, I behold a foolish young man, (8) Who passeth through the
street by the corner, and goeth nigh the way of her house, (9) In the
dark, when it grows late, in the darkness and obscurity of the night,
(10) And behold a woman meeteth him in harlot's attire, prepared to
deceive souls: talkative and wandering, (11) Not bearing to be quiet,
not able to abide still at home, (12) Now abroad, now in the streets,
now lying in wait near the corners.

---

[55] Presumably referring to the ancient religious custom of observing continence
during military campaigns.

7 (13) And catching the young man, she kisseth him, and with an impudent face, flattereth, saying: (14) I vowed victims for prosperity, this day I have paid my vows. (15) Therefore I am come out to meet thee, desirous to see thee, and I have found thee. (16) I have woven my bed with cords, I have covered it with painted tapestry, brought from Egypt. (17) I have perfumed my bed with myrrh, aloes, and cinnamon. (18) Come let us be inebriated with the breasts, and let us enjoy the desired embraces, till the day appear. (19) For my husband is not at home, he is gone a very long journey . . . (21) She entangled him with many words, and drew him away with the flattery of her lips. (22) Immediately he followeth her as an ox led to be a victim, and as a lamb playing the wanton, and not knowing that he is drawn like a fool to bonds. (23) Till the arrow pierce his liver: as if a bird should make haste to the snare, and knoweth not that his life is in danger. (24) Now therefore, my son, hear me, and attend to the words of my mouth. (25) Let not thy mind be drawn away in her ways: neither be thou deceived with her paths. (26) For she hath cast down many wounded, and the strongest have been slain by her. (27) Her house is the way to hell, reaching even to the inner chambers of death.

None in a Thousand: Ecclesiastes 7: 26–30

8 (26) I have surveyed all things with my mind, to know, and consider, and seek out wisdom and reason: and to know the wickedness of the fool, and the error of the imprudent; (27) And I have found a woman more bitter than death, who is the hunter's snare, and her heart is a net, and her hands are bands. He that pleaseth God shall escape from her: but he that is a sinner, shall be caught by her. (28) Lo this have I found, said Ecclesiastes, weighing one thing after another, that I might find out the account, (29) Which yet my soul seeketh, and I have not found it. One man among a thousand I have found, a woman among them all I have not found.[56] (30) Only this I have found, that God made man right, and he hath entangled himself with an infinity of questions.

The Wicked Woman: Ecclesiasticus 25: 22–31

9 (22) There is no head worse than the head of a serpent: (23) And there is no anger above the anger of a woman. It will be more agreeable to abide with a lion and a dragon, than to dwell with a

---

[56] Obsessively quoted in the Middle Ages: critically considered in Ch. 8, Albertano 3.

wicked woman. (24) The wickedness of a woman changeth her face: and she darkeneth her countenance as a bear: and showeth it like sack-cloth. In the midst of her neighbours, (25) Her husband groaned, and hearing he sighed a little. (26) All malice is short to the malice of a woman, let the lot of sinners fall upon her. (27) As the climbing of a sandy way is to the feet of the aged, so is a wife full of tongue to a quiet man. (28) Look not upon a woman's beauty, and desire not a woman for beauty. (29) A woman's anger, and impudence, and confusion is great. (30) A woman, if she have superiority, is contrary to her husband. (31) A wicked woman abateth the courage, and maketh a heavy countenance, and a wounded heart.

The Risk of Women: Ecclesiasticus 42: 11–14

10 (11) Keep a sure watch over a shameless daughter: lest at any time she make thee become a laughing-stock to thy enemies, and a by-word in the city, and a reproach among the people, and she make thee ashamed before all the multitude. (12) Behold not everybody's beauty: and tarry not among women. (13) For from garments cometh a moth, and from a woman the iniquity of a man. (14) For better is the iniquity of a man, than a woman doing a good turn,[57] and a woman bringing shame and reproach.

Women, the Passion and Resurrection: John 20: 1–18.

Each gospel gives a slightly different account. In St Matthew, (i) several women followers (including Mary Magdalene and Mary the mother of James) watch the death of Christ at a distance. (ii) The two Maries then attend the sepulchre. (iii) Having apparently left it for the Sabbath, they return next morning, to find an open tomb and an angel who bids them tell the disciples of the Resurrection. As they run to do so Christ meets them; they worship at His feet; He says that they should tell the disciples to go to Galilee to see Him. In the other gospels (i) and (ii) remain relatively constant, but there are marked variations in (iii). St Mark has the women reassured by the angel, but Christ appearing to Mary Magdalene alone, with the rider that when she went to tell the grieving disciples, they did not believe she had seen Him alive. St Luke has several women together reporting the Resurrection news to the disciples; the latters' incredulity; and Peter running to the sepulchre and wondering at what he sees (Matt. 27: 55–28: 10; Mark 15: 40–16: 11; Luke 23: 49–24: 12). St John differs more extensively. Instead of (i) he situates the Virgin as well as the two Maries close to the cross (19: 26).

[57] The Douai–Rheims translation carries an explanation: 'That is, there is, commonly speaking, less danger to be apprehended to the soul from the churlishness or injuries we receive from men, than from the flattering favours and familiarity of women.'

He omits (ii). And his (iii) turns the spotlight on to Mary Magdalene in her lone vigil at the tomb and in her personal encounter with Christ.

11   (20: 1) And on the first day of the week, Mary Magdalene cometh early, when it was yet dark unto the sepulchre: and she saw the stone taken away from the sepulchre. (2) She ran therefore, and cometh to Simon Peter, and to the other disciple whom Jesus loved, and saith to them: They have taken away the Lord out of the sepulchre, and we know not where they have laid Him. (3) Peter therefore went out, and that other disciple, and they came to the sepulchre. (4) And they both ran together, and that other disciple did outrun Peter, and came first to the sepulchre. (5) And when he stooped down, he saw the linen cloths lying: but yet he went not in. (6) Then cometh Simon Peter, following him, and went into the sepulchre, and saw the linen cloths lying. (7) And the napkin that had been about His head, not lying with the linen cloths, but apart, wrapt up into one place. (8) Then that other disciple also went in, who came first to the sepulchre: and he saw, and believed. (9) For as yet they knew not the scripture that He must rise again from the dead. (10) The disciples therefore departed again to their home.

12   (11) But Mary stood at the sepulchre without, weeping. Now as she was weeping, she stooped down, and looked into the sepulchre: (12) And she saw two angels in white, sitting, one at the head, and one at the feet, where the body of Jesus had been laid. (13) They say to her: Woman, why weepest thou? She saith to them: Because they have taken away my Lord: and I know not where they have laid Him. (14) When she had thus said, she turned herself back, and saw Jesus standing; and she knew not that it was Jesus. (15) Jesus saith to her: Woman; why weepest thou? whom seekest thou? She thinking that it was the gardener, saith to Him: Sir, if thou hast taken Him hence, tell me where thou hast laid Him: and I will take Him away. (16) Jesus saith to her: Mary: She turning, saith to Him: Rabboni (which is to say, Master). (17) Jesus saith to her: Do not touch me, for I am not yet ascended to my Father: but go to my brethren, and say to them: I ascend to my Father and to your Father, to my God and your God. (18) Mary Magdalene cometh and telleth the disciples: I have seen the Lord, and these things He said to me. [John does not indicate their response.]

On Widows: First Epistle of St Paul to Timothy, 5: 9–15

13   (9) Let a widow be chosen[58] of no less than threescore years of age, who hath been the wife of one husband, (10) Having testimony for her good works, if she have brought up children, if she have received to harbour,[59] if she have washed the saints' feet, if she have ministered to them that suffer tribulation, if she have diligently followed every good work. (11) But the younger widows avoid.[60] For when they have grown wanton in Christ, they will marry: (12) Having damnation, because they have made void their first faith. (13) And withal being idle they learn to go about from house to house: and are not only idle, but tattlers also, and busy-bodies, speaking things which they ought not. (14) I will therefore that the younger should marry, bear children, be mistresses of families, give no occasion to the adversary to speak evil. (15) For some are already turned aside after Satan.

Women Not to Teach: First Epistle of St Paul to Timothy, 2: 8–15

14   (8) I will therefore that men pray in every place, lifting up pure hands without anger and contention. (9) In like manner women also in decent apparel: adorning themselves with modesty and sobriety, not with plaited hair, or gold, or pearls, or costly attire, (10) But as it becometh women professing godliness with good works. (11) Let the woman learn in silence, with all subjection. (12) But I suffer not a woman to teach, nor to use authority over the man: but to be in silence. (13) For Adam was first formed; then Eve, (14) And Adam was not seduced; but the woman being seduced was in the transgression. (15) Yet she shall be saved through childbearing: if she continue in faith and love and sanctification with sobriety.

---

[58] Either 'chosen as deaconesses' (so Abelard, 'Origin of Nuns': see Scott Moncrieff 1974, 148); or, 'entitled to receive material support from the Church' (so Jerome, *Ag. Jov.* 1. 14); or, 'selected to give spiritual or charitable assistance in the Church'.
[59] 'Practised hospitality'.
[60] 'Refuse to place on the list'.

(III) PHYSIOLOGY AND ETYMOLOGY

Where women were concerned, menstruation was the preoccupation of medieval medicine and physiology. If, in the realms of religion, menstruation rendered her unclean and untouchable,[61] in the realms of physiology it signified her inability to match the fully developed human, i.e. the male, because unlike him she displayed evidence of an inefficient bodily system that had to keep on clearing itself of residual 'bilge-water'.[62] The beliefs derived from scientific observation about this ran from the mildly to the grotesquely sinister: any woman might be 'venomous' during menstruation, but in a woman menstruating irregularly or in an older woman whose menstrual system was deteriorating, baneful fluids seeking an outlet could be transmitted through the eyes and could poison small infants, according to a popularizing work of the thirteenth century spuriously attributed to Albert the Great, *On the Secrets of Women* (*De secretis mulierum*).[63] Since women were for the most part excluded from the medieval universities, they lacked opportunities to refute *ex cathedra* these wilder excesses of medical lore. The authenticity of treatises by one woman, known as Trotula, who practised at Salerno in the eleventh/twelfth century, is hard to establish—but in any case she seems not to have raised any serious challenge.[64] Possibly no one before Christine de Pizan treated in writing the 'lies' of the *De secretis* material with the disdain they deserved.[65]

Some traditional beliefs about male physiology implied that woman's power over a man's life through sexual attraction was biologically adverse. Andreas Capellanus remembers 'once reading in a medical treatise that sexual activity makes men senile earlier'.[66] Since male semen was taken to be a sort of highly refined (or 'concocted') residue of blood, it was supposed in medical opinion as handed down from Aristotle and Galen that frequent sexual activity would literally drain away the vitality of a man's blood, shrinking his brain perhaps, or debilitating his eyes.[67] This is an example of a tenet that remained fairly constant amidst the shifting physiological lore of the Middle Ages. So, generally, did the idea that the production of male sperm is facilitated by man's body heat, by contrast with woman, who is

---

[61] See Levit 15: 20 ff. It was imagined in the Middle Ages that a man having sex with a menstruating woman risked catching leprosy: Jacquart and Thomasset 1988, 186.

[62] Jacquart and Thomasset 1988, 27, translating a twelfth-century anatomical treatise.

[63] Jacquart and Thomasset 1988, 75–6; and see Lemay 1978, 392, on the diffusion of this text. On other baneful effects, see Isidore 3 below.

[64] Benton 1985.

[65] See Ch. 9, *City* 4.

[66] *On Love* III. 61.

[67] Aristotle, *Generation of Animals* 725^b, 726^b; Rousselle 1988, 12–20; Jacquart and Thomasset 1988, 55–6.

definitively colder so that she cannot refine her fluids to the same extent: hence their accumulation as menses which require purging.

ARISTOTLE (384–322 BC)

FROM *GENERATION OF ANIMALS* * *(DE GENERATIONE ANIMALIUM)*

Aristotelian physiology had considerable impact from the late twelfth century onwards, when his rediscovered writings began to be studied in the University of Paris.[68] He reduced the role of woman in procreation to that of 'prime matter' awaiting the 'forming' or 'moving' agency of the man's semen. He defined female sex in terms of its 'inability' to emulate male functions. Physicians and commentators sometimes disputed his most damaging deductions about woman—e.g. that she is a 'deformed male' or 'male whose purpose has been thwarted' and that she contributes no active 'seed' of her own in the act of procreation. But Aristotle's considerable authority certainly did substantiate an unflattering equation between woman and 'matter', which found an echo in commonplace etymology. The following is a selection of the points arising from Aristotle's discussion of semen and menstrual discharge, and from his enquiry whether women contribute anything to generation other than a place for it to occur.

1 (726[b]) Semen is pretty certainly a residue from that nourishment which is in the form of blood and which, as being the final form of nourishment, is distributed to the various parts of the body. This, of course, is the reason why semen has great potency—the loss of it from the system is just as exhausting as the loss of pure healthy blood . . .

2 Now (i) the weaker creature too must of necessity produce a residue, greater in amount and less thoroughly concocted;[69] and (ii) this, if such is its character, must of necessity be a volume of bloodlike fluid.[70] (iii) That which by nature has a smaller share of heat is weaker; and (iv) the female answers to this description. . . .

3 (727[a]) Now it is impossible that any creature should produce two seminal secretions at once, and as the secretion in females which answers to semen in males is the menstrual fluid, it obviously follows

* Tr. A. L. Peck, *Aristotle: Generation of Animals* (London: Heinemann; and Cambridge, Mass.: Harvard University Press, 1963), pp. 91–3, 97, 101–3, 109, 173–5, 185, 459–61. © The President and Fellows of Harvard College, 1963. Reprinted by permission of the publishers and the Loeb Classical Library.

[68] Allen 1985, Ch. V.

[69] The process whereby nourishment is converted, especially into blood.

[70] Because not reaching the further stage of 'concoction', into semen.

that the female does not contribute any semen to generation; for if there were semen, there would be no menstrual fluid; but as menstrual fluid is in fact formed, therefore there is no semen. . . .

4 (727ᵇ) By now it is plain that the contribution which the female makes to generation is the *matter* used therein, that this is to be found in the substance constituting the menstrual fluid, and finally that the menstrual fluid is a residue. (728a) . . . A woman is as it were an infertile male; the female, in fact, is female on account of inability of a sort, viz., it lacks the power to concoct semen out of the final state of nourishment . . . because of the coldness of its nature. . . .

5 (729ᵃ) The male provides the 'form' and the 'principle of the movement', the female provides the body, in other words, the material. Compare the coagulation of milk. Here, the milk is the body, and the fig-juice or the rennet contains the principle which causes it to set. . . .

6 (737ᵃ) When the semen has entered the uterus it 'sets' the residue produced by the female and imparts to it the same movement with which it is itself endowed. The female's contribution, of course, is a residue too, . . . and contains all the parts of the body *potentially*, though none in *actuality*; and 'all' includes those parts which distinguish the two sexes. Just as it sometimes happens that deformed offspring are produced by deformed parents, and sometimes not, so the offspring produced by a female are sometimes female, sometimes not, but male. The reason is that the female is as it were a deformed male; and the menstrual discharge is semen, though in an impure condition; i.e. it lacks one constituent, and one only, the principle of Soul.

7 (738ᵇ) An animal is a living body, a body with Soul in it. The female always provides the material, the male provides that which fashions the material into shape; this, in our view, is the specific characteristic of each of the sexes: that is what it means to be male or female. Hence, necessity requires that the female should provide the physical part, i.e. a quantity of material, but not that the male should do so, since necessity does not require that the tools should reside in the product that is being made, nor that the agent which uses them should do so. Thus the physical part, the body, comes from the female, and the Soul from the male, since the Soul is the essence of a particular body.

8 (775ª) Once birth has taken place everything reaches its perfection sooner in females than in males—e.g. puberty, maturity, old age—because females are weaker and colder in their nature; and we should look upon the female state as being as it were a deformity, though one which occurs in the ordinary course of nature. While it is within the mother, then, it develops slowly on account of its coldness, since development is a sort of concoction, concoction is effected by heat, and if a thing is hotter its concoction is easy; when, however, it is free from the mother, on account of its weakness it quickly approaches its maturity and old age, since inferior things all reach their end more quickly.

GALEN (131–201)

Galen served as court physician to Emperor Marcus Aurelius and wrote extensively about medicine and anatomy in his native Greek. During the Middle Ages his authority—transmitted especially through Arab writings on the subject—became legendary. Although he differed from Aristotle in some respects, for example in reinstating the presence of female 'seed' in coitus (largely because he knew of the ovaries where his predecessor did not), he explicitly backed the philosopher's hierarchical theory of the sexes, and indeed grounded his medical thinking on the affirmation of a gradation of temperature between them. That difference, he believed, gave rise to a complementarity of generative organs whereby woman's are the inverse of man's.

FROM *ON THE USEFULNESS OF THE PARTS OF THE BODY**
(*DE USU PARTIUM*: LATE SECOND CENTURY AD)

1 (II. 299) Now just as mankind is the most perfect of all animals, so within mankind the man is more perfect than the woman, and the reason for his perfection is his excess of heat, for heat is Nature's primary instrument. Hence in those animals that have less of it, her workmanship is necessarily more imperfect, and so it is no wonder that the female is less perfect than the male by as much as she is colder than he. In fact, just as the mole has imperfect eyes, though certainly not so imperfect as they are in those animals that do not have any trace of them at all, so too the woman is less perfect than the man in respect to the generative parts. For the parts were formed within her when she was still a foetus, but could not because of the defect in the heat emerge and project on the outside, and this,

* Tr. Margaret Tallmadge May, *Galen: On the Usefulness of the Parts of the Body* (Ithaca, NY: Cornell University Press, ii. 630–2). © 1968 by Cornell University. Reprinted by permission of the publisher.

though making the animal itself that was being formed less perfect than one that is complete in all respects, provided no small advantage for the race; for there needs must be a female. Indeed, you ought not to think that our Creator would purposely make half the whole race imperfect and, as it were, mutilated, unless there was to be some great advantage in such a mutilation.

2   (II. 300) Let me tell what this is. The foetus needs abundant material both when it is first constituted and for the entire period of growth that follows. . . . Accordingly, it was better for the female to be made enough colder so that she cannot disperse all the nutriment which she concocts and elaborates. . . . This is the reason why the female was made cold, and the immediate consequence of this is the imperfection of the parts, which cannot emerge on the outside on account of the defect in the heat, another very great advantage for the continuance of the race. For, remaining within, that which would have become the scrotum if it had emerged on the outside was made into the substance of the uteri, an instrument fitted to receive and retain the semen and to nourish and perfect the foetus.

3   (II. 301) Forthwith, of course, the female must have smaller, less perfect testes,[71] and the semen generated in them must be scantier, colder, and wetter (for these things too follow of necessity from the deficient heat). Certainly such semen would be incapable of generating an animal. . . .[72] The testes of the male are as much larger as he is the warmer animal. The semen generated in them, having received the peak of concoction, becomes the efficient principle of the animal. Thus, from one principle devised by the Creator in his wisdom, that principle in accordance with which the female has been made less perfect than the male, have stemmed all these things useful for the generation of the animal: that the parts of the female cannot escape to the outside; that she accumulates an excess of useful nutriment and has imperfect semen and a hollow instrument to receive the perfect semen; that since everything in the male is the opposite [of what it is in the female], the male member has been elongated to be most suitable for coitus and the excretion of semen; and that his semen itself has been made thick, abundant, and warm.

---

[71] Galen calls the ovaries the female testes.
[72] i.e., on its own: but Galen allows female 'semen' a contributory role in conception.

ISIDORE OF SEVILLE (c. 570–636)

Raised in Spain during the rule of the Visigoths, Isidore was educated in a monastery, took vows himself, and became Archbishop of Seville. His great encyclopaedia of knowledge (known as *Etymologiae* owing to its emphasis on the derivations of key words under each subject heading) achieved phenomenal popularity throughout Europe and continued to be cited for many centuries.

FROM *ETYMOLOGIES** (*ETYMOLOGIAE*)

Man and Woman

1 (XI. ii. 17) Man [*vir*] is so named, because there is greater force [*vis*] in him than in women [*feminis*]—hence also the word 'strength' [*virtus*]—or, he is so named because he controls woman [*feminam*] forcefully [*vi*]. (18) Woman [*mulier*] gets her name from 'softness' [*mollitie*], or as it were 'softer', *mollier*, with a letter taken away or changed.[73] (19) For the two sexes are differentiated in the strength [*fortitudine*] and weakness [*imbecillitate*] of their bodies. Thus there is the greatest strength [*virtus*] in man [*viri*], and less in woman [*mulieris*] so that she might be forbearing to man; otherwise, if women were to repel them, sexual desire might compel men to desire something else or rush off to another sex . . .

2 (XI. ii. 23) What is now called a 'female' [*femina*], antiquity called *vira* [i.e. female of *vir*, 'man'] . . . (24) The word 'female' [*femina*] derives from the area of the thighs [*femorum*] where her gender is distinguished from a man's. But some think she is called 'female' [*femina*] through the Greek etymology for 'burning force' [i.e. Greek *fos*] because of the intensity of her desire.[74] For females [*feminas*] are more lustful than males, among women [*mulieribus*] as much as among animals. Hence the word 'effeminate' [*femineus*] was applied to an excess of love [*amor*] in antiquity.[75]

---

* New translation by Alcuin Blamires from W. M. Lindsay (ed.), *Isidori Hispalensis Episcopi: Etymologiarum sive originum libri xx*, 2 vols. (Oxford: Oxford University Press, 1911).

[73] Gratian maintained that 'man' [*vir*] was from 'strength of mind' [*virtus animi*], and that 'woman' [*mulier*] arose from 'softness of mind' [*mollities mentis*]; Friedberg 1955, i. col. 1145.

[74] A derivation seized on in Ch. 6, *Math*. 25, whereas defenders of women (e.g. *Leesce* 1241–3) preferred the link with *mollities*.

[75] A notion still widespread in the Middle Ages: hence Andreas Capellanus urges his protégé 'to restrain your physical pleasure [*voluptatem*] like a man [*viriliter*]': *On Love* III. 50. See also Ch. 8, Gower 1 and 3.

Father, Mother, Procreation

3   (IX. v. 3) A father [*pater*] is the one from whom the beginning of a family line derives its origin. Hence he is termed the head of the family [*paterfamilias*]. The father is so named because he procreates a son by carrying through an accomplishment [*patratione*]; for this 'accomplishment' [*patratio*] is the consummation of the business of Venus. (4) Those who 'engender' [*genitores*] are named from 'bringing forth' [*gignendo*], while 'parents' are those who 'bear' [*parientes*]. (5) The same is true of 'creators' [*creatores*]—the semen of the male, whence the bodies of animals and humans are conceived, is 'growth' [*crementum*], hence parents are called 'creators'. (6) A 'mother' [*mater*] is so called because from her something is made: for 'mother' [*mater*] is as it were 'matter' [*materia*], while the father is the cause.[76]

The Menses

4   (XI. i. 140) The *menstrua* are the superfluous blood of women. They are called *menstrua* after the cycle of the moon, in accordance with which this flow usually comes—the moon being named *mene* in Greek. They are also called 'womanish things' [*muliebria*], since woman is the only menstruating animal. (141) From contact with this blood, fruits fail to germinate, grape-must goes sour, plants die, trees lose their fruit, metal is corroded with rust, and bronze objects go black. Any dogs which consume it contract rabies. The glue of bitumen, which resists both metal and water, dissolves spontaneously when polluted with that blood.[77]

Eve

Isidore's reflections on 'Eve', in a chapter about the prophetic character of certain names, note both positive and bleak possibilities in etymological tradition: but these possibilities do not yet include the wordplay whereby the Latin *Eva* could be seen to be reversed in the *Ave* of Gabriel's *Ave Maria* ('Hail, Mary') so as to suggest that whatever woman undid in the Fall was remedied by another woman, a 'Second Eve', in the Nativity.[78]

5   (VII. vi. 5) *Eva* can be interpreted as 'life' [*vita*];[79] or as 'disaster'

---

[76] Cf. Aristotle 5 and 7, above.

[77] This superstitious catalogue originated in Pliny and appeared widely, e.g., in Vincent of Beauvais, *Speculum naturale* XXXI. 24, and in Innocent III *De miseria condicionis humane*, I. 4 (Innocent III 1978, 100–1). It was imagined that conception during menstruation would produce deformed or leprous offspring.

[78] See Fyler 1988; and Ch. 2, Jerome 25.

[79] Cf. Gen. 3: 20.

[*calamitas*], or 'woe' [*vae*]. As life, because she was the origin of being born; disaster and woe, because by her transgression she became the cause of dying, and from her falling 'disaster' took its name. (6) But some say that Eve is called 'life' and 'disaster' because woman is often the cause of man's welfare, and often the cause of his disaster and death (which is woe [*vae*]).[80]

[80] See Innocent III, *De miseria*, i. 6 for an ingenious elaboration—that all infants are born bawling 'Ah' or 'Ee', indicating the pain of human life and of childbirth, after Eve's sin (Innocent 1978, 102–3).

(iv) 'MATTER' AND 'FORM' IN LATER
WRITINGS

St ANSELM (1033–1109)

FROM *MONOLOGIUM**

A Benedictine monk, prior of Bec in Normandy and later Archbishop of Canterbury, Anselm accomplished writings that were distinctive and influential. Among them, he composed a lyrical prayer to Paul in which Jesus is imagined as a mother, labouring to bring forth and nurture new life through death.[81] In the context of a philosophical analysis in the *Monologium*, he was again prepared to challenge preconceptions about sacred gender, asking whether the Divine Nature of God and Jesus might be female. However, it is significant that here he retreated under the impetus of the Aristotelian view—known to him, perhaps, through the work of Galen or Porphyry—that the father takes precedence as 'principal cause' in generation.

1   (Ch. 42) I should now like to infer, if I can, that the Supreme Spirit is most truly father and the Word most truly son. Yet, I think I ought not to bypass the question of which set of terms is more suitable for them—'father and son' or 'mother and daughter'—for there is no sexual distinction in the Supreme Spirit and the Word. For if the Supreme Spirit is appropriately father and its offspring appropriately son because each is spirit, then by parity of reasoning why is it not appropriate for one to be mother and the other to be daughter on the grounds that each is truth and wisdom?[82] Is it [preferable to call them father and son] because among those natures which have a difference of sex it is characteristic of the better sex to be father and son and of the inferior sex to be mother and daughter? Now, although such is naturally the case for many beings, for others the reverse holds true. For example, in some species of birds the female sex is always larger and stronger, the male sex smaller and weaker.

   * Ed. and tr. Jasper Hopkins and Herbert Richardson, *Anselm of Canterbury*, 4 vols. (London: SCM Press; Toronto: Edwin Mellen Press, 1974), i. 55–6. © SCM Press Ltd and Edwin Mellen Press, 1974. Reprinted by permission of the publishers.
   [81] Allen 1985, 265–6.
   [82] Latin *spiritus* ('spirit') is a masculine noun, whereas *veritas* ('truth') and *sapientia* ('wisdom') are grammatically feminine, the latter being especially well known as a female personification.

2 But surely, the Supreme Spirit is more suitably called father than mother because the first and principal cause of offspring is always the father. For, if the paternal cause always in some way precedes the maternal cause, then it is exceedingly inappropriate for the name 'mother' to be applied to that parent whom no other cause either joins or precedes for the begetting of offspring.[83]

St THOMAS AQUINAS (1225–74)

FROM THE *SUMMA THEOLOGIAE**

The Aristotelian equation between woman and 'matter' appealed to St Thomas[84] because it explained why Christ, though born of woman, was not a recipient of Original Sin. That was transmitted always by the active, formative seed of the male—but Christ had no human father.[85] In the *Summa*, however, the Aristotelian position is most concisely recapitulated in answering the question, Should one love one's mother more than one's father?

1 (II. ii. 26. 10: Reply) It is the father who ought to be loved more than the mother. For one's father and mother are loved as principles in our natural origin. But the father, as the active partner, is a principle in a higher way than the mother, who supplies the passive or material element. And so, speaking *per se*, the father should be loved the more.

2 Hence: (1) In human generation, the mother provides the matter of the body which, however, is still unformed, and receives its form only by means of the power which is contained in the father's seed.

[83] Cf. the father as 'cause' in Isidore 3 above.
* Tr. R. J. Batten OP, *St Thomas Aquinas, Summa Theologiae*, xxxiv (London: Blackfriars, in conjunction with Eyre & Spottiswoode; and New York: McGraw-Hill, 1975), 149. © Blackfriars 1975. Reprinted by permission of Cambridge University Press.
[84] See further the Aquinas section in Ch. 3.
[85] Børresen 1981, 219–22; Aquinas, *S. Th.* III, Q. 32 art. 4, 'whether the Virgin played any active part in the conception of Christ's body'.

GUIDO DELLE COLONNE

FROM *THE HISTORY OF THE DESTRUCTION OF TROY**
(*HISTORIA DESTRUCTIONIS TROIAE*: 1287)

Physiological considerations were doubtless subsumed under the general notion of woman's 'weakness' in most antifeminist literature. However, in the important version of the Troy story by Guido, an erudite and sourly misogynistic Italian writer, the celebrated episode of Medea's love affair with Jason when he comes to Colchis in quest of the Golden Fleece is narrated with a sarcasm which builds explicitly on the terminology of 'matter' and 'form'.

1   (From Book II) Just before it was time to eat, the king, desirous of showing the Greeks all the courtesy of his noble nature, sent for his daughter [Medea] to come and graciously be present at the feast with the newly arrived guests, whom the king himself was receiving with great pleasure.... Medea, however, having heard the command of her father, although she was an extremely beautiful maiden, tried, as is the custom of women, to add beauty to beauty, that is, through beautiful ornaments. For this reason, she came to the tables of the dinner guests decked out with precious ornaments and royal attire, elegant in her entire bearing, not with a familiarity to put one off. Her father ordered her to sit next to Jason. Oh, unfortunate and infatuated generosity, what do you owe to politeness in the hazard of your reputation and the loss of your honour for courtesy? Is it wise to trust to feminine constancy or the female sex, which has never been able, through all the ages, to remain constant? Her mind always remains in motion and is especially changeable in girlhood, before the woman, being of marriageable age, is joined to her husband. For we know the heart of woman always seeks a husband, just as matter always seeks form.[86] Oh, would that matter, passing once into form, could be said to be content with the form it has received. But just as it is known that matter proceeds from form to form, so the dissolute desire of women proceeds from man to man, so that it may be believed without limit, since it is of an unfathomable depth, unless by

---

* Tr. Mary Elizabeth Meek, *Historia Destructionis Troiae* (Bloomington: Indiana University Press, 1974), 13–16. © Indiana University Press, 1974. Reprinted by permission of the publisher.

86   Both St Bonaventure ('the imperfect nature of woman seeks man as matter seeks its form'; quoted in Allen 1985, 428) and the twelfth-century Jewish physician Maimonides (quoted in Allen 1987, 100) think of woman as matter hungry for form. In *Legend of Good Women*, 1582–8, Chaucer coolly switches Guido's analogy to make Jason, not Medea, represent appetitive 'matter'.

chance the taint of shame by a praiseworthy abstinence should restrict it within the limits of modesty. Why, therefore, O King Aeëtes, were you so bold as to place a tender young woman side by side in intimacy with the foreign hero? If with trembling heart you had considered the frailty of the sex, you would not later have lamented that the only heir of your kingdom was carried away to a foreign realm in a disgraceful flight by sea, at such a great cost that you were deprived both at once and at the same time of your daughter and of an unheard of amount of treasure. What did the protection of Mars avail you against the tricks and snares of a woman? . . .

2   Medea, therefore, was between her father and Jason, and although she was covered with blushes, still she could not control the glances of her eyes; in fact, when she could, she turned their glance with sweet looks toward Jason, so that, by gazing with eager imagination at his face and at the features of his face, his blond hair, and his body and the limbs of his body, she suddenly burned with desire for him, and conceived in her heart a blind passion for him.

2

The Church Fathers

TERTULLIAN, QUINTUS SEPTIMIUS FLORENS
(c.160–c.225)

FROM *THE APPEARANCE OF WOMEN** (*DE CULTU FEMINARUM*)

Tertullian was a pagan of Carthage converted to Christianity before AD 197, but details of his career—even whether he became a priest or remained a layperson—are scanty. His elaborately rhetorical and passionately ascetic writings were avidly absorbed by Jerome two hundred years later. Through Jerome, some of Tertullian's thinking was to enter the mainstream of Christian polemic, and of medieval misogyny too. Of course Tertullian himself was following in the footsteps of earlier ascetics, but it has justly been suggested that he made 'the first consequential statement' in the Christian Latin world 'of the belief that abstinence from sex was the most effective technique with which to achieve clarity of soul'.[1] He wrote of women as creatures of dangerous sexual allure, whose urgent duty it was to suppress their attractiveness in order to minimize the spiritual damage it wrought in men. His most strident assertions are made in *On the Appearance of Women, De cultu feminarum*, a composite text consisting of an unfinished first book, plus a second book more comprehensively (but slightly less harshly) treating the same material. Even making allowance for rhetorical exaggeration, Tertullian exemplifies the unlovely virulence of ascetic antifeminism, so it may be worth mentioning that he can be quite funny too: wondering whether, if he gets to clamber from the ground at the day of the resurrection of the body, he will find angels ferrying aloft women in full make-up and their finest hats (see *10*).

This treatise seems to have been written for women recently converted.[2] It communicates the social tensions surrounding a faith struggling to dissociate itself from pagan *mores*—no easy task in the case of wealthy convertees with an inbred assumption about cutting a figure in society. Among the sources used by Tertullian to counter this is the Book of Enoch, which held that ornament was introduced to the world by fallen angels. This Jewish text does not appear to have been very influential in the Latin West after Tertullian, so it is not otherwise represented in this anthology.

---

* New translation by C. W. Marx from *Tertulliani Opera*, pt. 1, ed. A. Kroymann, CCSL, i (Turnhout: Brepols, 1954). © C. W. Marx 1992
[1] Brown 1988, 78. See esp. *De exhortatione castitatis*, ch. X.
[2] Tert. 1959, 111.

1 (I. 1) If there were faith on earth equal to the reward for faith which is hoped for in heaven, none of you, my most beloved sisters, from when you became aware of the living God and came to understand your nature as women, would have wanted a very glamorous or ostentatious style of dress. Rather, you would go about in mourning clothes and even neglect your appearance, giving the impression of a mourning and repentant Eve so that, by adopting all the clothing of the penitent, you might atone more fully for what derives from Eve, namely the disgrace of the first sin and the hatred which followed because of the fall of the human race. 'In sorrows and care you will give birth, woman, and be dependent on your husband; and he is lord over you.'[3] Do you not know that you are Eve?

2 The judgement of God upon this sex lives on in this age; therefore, necessarily the guilt should live on also. You are the gateway of the devil; you are the one who unseals the curse of that tree, and you are the first one to turn your back on the divine law; you are the one who persuaded him whom the devil was not capable of corrupting; you easily destroyed the image of God, Adam. Because of what you deserve, that is, death, even the Son of God had to die. And do you still think of adorning yourself above and beyond your tunics of animal skin?

3 (II. 1) Most women either through simple ignorance or bold deception behave as if chastity consisted only in the chastity of the flesh and disgust at sexual intercourse, as if nothing external mattered such as the arrangement of clothes and ornaments. They persist in their former eagerness for beauty and glamour, and they display the same outside appearance as the women of the pagan peoples in whom there is no perception of true chastity.

4 (II. 2) You should know that in order to achieve perfect, that is, Christian, chastity you must not only *not* seek to be the object of desire, but also despise the very idea of being one. First, because the desire to please through appearance does not come from a sound conscience, since we know that appearance naturally excites sexual desire. Why therefore do you arouse this evil towards yourself? Why do you excite what you declare to be foreign to you? Second, because we ought not to open the way to temptations. These sometimes, by their urgency, perpetrate sin—and may God drive this away from His

[3] Gen. 3: 16.

own—and indeed they stir up the spirit by offering opportunities to sin.

5   Why are we a danger to another? Why do we cause desire in another? If the Lord in elaborating the law does not make a distinction in penalty between the fact of sexual intercourse and desire,[4] I do not know whether He may leave unpunished a person who has brought someone else to damnation. For that man is lost as soon as he desires your beauty, and he has committed already in his mind what he desired and you have become his sword, so that, although the sin may not be yours, you may not be free from hatred. The same thing happens when a robbery is committed on someone's land: the crime is not blamed on the owner, but while the farm has a bad reputation, he also acquires a bad name. Are we to put on make-up so that others are destroyed? What about 'Love your neighbour as yourself; do not take care only for your own things, but for those of another'?[5] . . . Since we and others are concerned about the desire for beauty which is so dangerous, you should now realize not only that you must reject the preparation of false and contrived beauty, but also that you must remove the splendour of *natural* beauty by concealing and neglecting it as dangerous to the sight of the eyes. For, although we should not find fault with beauty as something good bestowed on the body by nature, as an additional gift of divine creation, and as good clothing for the soul, we must however be wary of it, because of the injury and violence which it brings to those who pursue it.

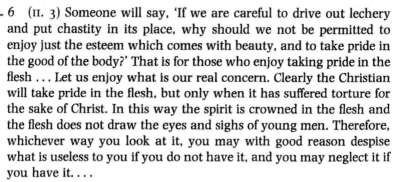

6   (II. 3) Someone will say, 'If we are careful to drive out lechery and put chastity in its place, why should we not be permitted to enjoy just the esteem which comes with beauty, and to take pride in the good of the body?' That is for those who enjoy taking pride in the flesh . . . Let us enjoy what is our real concern. Clearly the Christian will take pride in the flesh, but only when it has suffered torture for the sake of Christ. In this way the spirit is crowned in the flesh and the flesh does not draw the eyes and sighs of young men. Therefore, whichever way you look at it, you may with good reason despise what is useless to you if you do not have it, and you may neglect it if you have it. . . .

7   (II. 5) I make these suggestions not in order to recommend that

---

[4] Matt. 5: 28.
[5] Matt. 19: 19, and 1 Cor. 10: 24.

TERTULLIAN   53

your appearance be uncultivated and entirely unkempt;[6] and we are
not aiming to persuade you that there is any good in squalor and
filth, but rather, there is a way of caring for the body which is both
natural and proper. We must not go beyond what simple and
necessary neatness requires, that is, beyond what pleases God. For
they offend Him who rub their skin with creams, stain their cheeks
with rouge, and make their eyes seem larger with eye-liner. Surely
what God created displeases them; indeed, in themselves they
censure and criticize the creator of all things. For they are finding
fault when they try to improve and add to His creation, taking the
embellishment from a rival artist.[7] This rival is the devil. For who
would instruct how to change the body except the one who
transformed the spirit of man through wickedness? Without doubt,
he was responsible for devices of the kind we have been discussing, so
that by using these you may show by your own hands that in a way
you do violence to God. Whatever is born is the work of God.
Therefore, what is contrived later is the business of the devil. How
wicked it is, to add to divine work the inventions of Satan! . . . How
far removed are these things from your instruction and your
promises; how unworthy of the name 'Christian' it is for those who
are compelled to adopt simplicity in all things, to have a face which is
not natural. You lie with your appearance though you are not
permitted to lie with the tongue;[8] you desire what is not yours
though you are commanded not to take the possessions of another;
you commit adultery in outward appearance though you should be
intent on chastity. Believe me, blessed sisters: how may you keep the
commandments of God if you do not keep in yourselves the features
which He has created?

8 (II. 6) I see certain women dye their hair blonde by using saffron.
They are ashamed of their own nation—that they are not by birth
Germans[9] or Gauls. . . . Indeed, the strength of these dyes damages
the hair; frequent use of even any natural liquid ruins the head, just

---

[6] Plainness, not slovenliness, is the objective: but cf. Jerome, Letter 107.11,
commending the virgin who 'by a deliberate squalor makes haste to spoil her natural
good looks': Fremantle 1893, 194.
[7] Imitated by others such as Ambrose, who warns of the provocation to a great
artist if a hack presumes to work over his painting: *Hexaemeron* VI. 18, in Ambrose
1961, 259–60. Jerome, Letter 54.7, wonders how confidently a woman can 'raise
features to heaven which her Creator must fail to recognize': Fremantle 1893, 104.
[8] The designation of make-up as a 'lie' has an ancient history: see e.g. *Oeconomicus*
by Xenophon (c.430–357), quoted in Allen 1985, 56.
[9] German wigs are attested in Ovid, *Amores* I. 14; and cf. Ch. 1 above, Juv. 3.

as the heat of the sun, although it is beneficial for enlivening and
drying the hair, may harm it. What beauty can come from harm?
What beauty can come from using impure substances? Shall a
Christian woman pour saffron on her head as upon an altar? . . . But
the Lord says, 'Which of you can make a white hair black or create a
white one from a black?'[10] In this way they contradict the Lord; they
say, 'Look, we can make blonde hair from white or from black, which
is more attractive.' . . .

9 (II. 7) What does such elaborate labour in arranging your hair
contribute to your salvation? Why can you not leave your hair
alone? One minute you tie it up, the next you let it hang free; one
minute you pile it up, the next you take it down again. Some women
long to force it into curls; others let it fall, flying wild, which is not a
good example of simplicity. Further, you attach I don't know what
kind of monstrosities of sewn and woven wigs, sometimes in the form
of a cap, like the covering for the head, and protection for the crown,
sometimes in the form of a veil for the back of the neck. Should we be
surprised if this does not contradict the commandments of the Lord,
one of which declares that no one can of his own accord add to his
stature?[11] You, however, do add to your weight, by building up head-
dresses, or rather shield-bosses, on your necks. . . . God commands
that women be veiled,[12] and I think He does this so that the heads of
some of them may not be seen!

10 I hope that I, most wretched man that I am, on the day of
Christian joy may raise up my head at least as high as your heels! I
will see then whether you, with your faces whitened by make-up,
and your rouge, and your hair dyed blonde and the display on your
heads, will arise, and whether the angels will carry up women
painted in this way to meet Christ in the clouds. If these things are
fitting for the present time and are godly, then they will also come
together with your body at the resurrection and take their own
places. But nothing can arise except flesh and spirit, pure and simple.
What does not arise in flesh and spirit, is damned because it is not of
God. At this time have nothing to do with things that are damned; let
God see you today just as He will see you on the day of the
resurrection.

11 (II. 8) Of course now as a man jealous of that sex (you may say),
I am trying to deter women from the things which are their own. Are

[10] Matt. 5: 36.   [11] Matt. 6: 27.   [12] I Cor. 11: 5.

there not certain things forbidden to *us*, out of consideration for the dignity we must maintain in our respect for God? Since indeed by a fault of nature there is in men, because of women, and in women because of men, a desire to please, the male sex acknowledges its own devices to enhance its appearance: cutting the beard very closely, plucking it here and there, trimming the edges, arranging the hair and dyeing it and removing the first grey hair, rubbing the hair which covers the whole body with a dye normally used by women, smoothing the rest of the body with rough powder, then looking into the mirror at every opportunity, gazing anxiously into it.

12 Nevertheless, when we have come to know God and when we have set aside this desire to please, because we are free from sensuality, we reject all those things as superfluous and as detrimental to chastity. For where God is, there is chastity, and where there is chastity, there is dignity its helper and companion. How shall we practise chastity if we do not practise dignity which is the way to achieve it? How shall we practise dignity in achieving chastity unless we display seriousness in appearance, in dress, and in the bearing of the whole man?

13 (II. 9) For this reason you must take care to cut away and cast off the more excessive sumptuousness of your clothing and the rest of the trappings of your make-up. For what good does it do to display a virtuous face both unadorned in its simplicity and worthy to receive divine teaching, if the rest of the body uses frilly display and absurd luxuries? It is easy to see how these fineries are closely connected with the pursuit of lechery and how they impede the principles of chastity. . . .

14 (II. 10) Doubtless God showed men how to dye wool with the juice of herbs and the slime of shells? It had escaped Him, when He commanded all things to be created, to specify purple and scarlet sheep![13] No doubt it was God too who invented the manufacture of these same clothes which are light and thin, and heavy only in their price; no doubt it was God who produced such masterpieces of gold for the careful fitting and setting of gems; no doubt it was God who caused ears to be pierced, and for this reason, that from these bodily wounds there might hang some kind of cut stones which, as is well

[13] Abbreviating a point elaborated in I. 8, that what God did not choose to create cannot be good.

known, the Parthians insert in their shoes in place of studs. This is a practice which causes distress to His own creation and torments innocent children suffering pain for the first time.

15 As a matter of fact, pagan literature tells us that this same gold whose glory preoccupies you was used by a certain people for chains. Therefore these things are not good because of their intrinsic value but because they are rare. When these crafts had been introduced by the fallen angels who discovered these same materials,[14] elaborate workmanship along with the rarity of the materials caused them to be thought precious and thereby incited the desire of women to possess them for their value. If these same angels who uncovered these materials and their attractions, I mean of gold and bright gems, and passed on their crafts and taught among other things the use of eye make-up and the dyeing of wool, are damned by God, as Enoch tells us, how will we please God if we take pleasure in things developed by those who on this account have incited the anger and censure of God? . . . Would we not behave much more profitably and carefully if we were to understand that all things were provided at the beginning and placed in the world and now may be used to test the character of His servants, so that in being free to use them, they might overcome trials of their own chastity? . . .

16 (II. 11) What reason do you have for appearing in public so elaborately dressed, since you have nothing to do with those occasions when it is necessary? You do not go from one temple to another, nor wish to go to public shows, nor to celebrate the feast days of the pagans. For all these splendid clothes are displayed in public at these gatherings and because of the desire to see and be seen,[15] either for the business of lechery or to bolster vanity. But you have no reason to go out in public except on urgent business. You may go out to visit a sick brother or to attend mass, or to hear the word of God. Any one of these is a serious or holy matter, for which there is no need for extraordinary, elaborate and loose appearance. . . .

To the objection that a lowering of one's standards of dress on becoming Christian might appear a 'blasphemy' against the faith, Tertullian retorts that it would be a greater 'blasphemy' for converts to resemble prostitutes.

---

[14] Tertullian draws on 1 Enoch 8: 1, an apocryphal account of angels who slept with human women and passed to them the secret of ornaments and cosmetics; see Prusak 1974, 90 ff.
[15] Recalling Ovid *Art of Love* 1.99; see also Ch. 7, *WoB* 39.

17 (II. 12) Even the scriptures suggest that the enticements of beauty are usually associated with and linked to prostitution. That powerful city which ruled over seven mountains and many waters deserved to be called a 'whore' by the Lord, because she was dressed like a whore.[16] Indeed, she sits in purple and scarlet, and gold and precious stones. How cursed are those things without which the cursed prostitute could not work. It was because Thamar had painted and made herself up that Juda suspected that she was soliciting trade, and so, because she hid herself under a veil and by the nature of her dress suggested that she was a prostitute, he concluded that she was, addressed her as such, and made an agreement with her.[17] ...

18 (II. 13) Some women perhaps may say, 'I do not need the approval of men, for I do not ask for the witness of men; it is God who sees my heart.' We all know that; nevertheless, let us remember what the Lord said through the Apostle: 'Let your virtue appear before men.'[18] Why would He have said this except to ensure that evil should have no access to you at all or that you might be an example and witness to the wicked? It is not enough for Christian chastity to be so but it must seem so. Your chastity should be so great that it may shine from your soul to your clothes and emanate from the conscience to your outer appearance, so that the special characteristics of chastity, which unite to maintain the faith forever, may be visible for all to see.[19] You must get rid of trivial things which can undermine the strength of faith because they are themselves without purpose and transitory. ...

19 For the lives of Christians are characterized less by gold than by iron, for the robes are being prepared for the martyrs, and the angels who will bear them up are being made ready. Go forth adorned with the ointments and ornaments of the prophets and the apostles, taking your radiance from simplicity, your rosy complexion from your chastity; paint your eyes with modesty and your mouth with silence; hang on your ears the word of God and fasten round your necks the collar of Christ.[20] Bow your heads to your husbands and

---

[16] Apoc. 17: 1 ff.
[17] Gen. 38: 11–16.
[18] Phil. 4: 5.
[19] Christine de Pizan argues in *City* II. 62.1 that one's conscience should not be judged by one's dress.
[20] A *tour de force* on 'Christian make-up' taking its cue from 1 Tim. 2: 9–10, in Ch. 1, Scripture 14, and mingling other biblical reminiscences.

that will be ornament for you. Keep your hands busy with spinning[21] and stay at home, and you will be more pleasing than if you were adorned with gold. Dress yourselves in the silk of modesty, with the linen of holiness, and with the purple of chastity. Dressed up in this way, you will have God as your lover.

St JOHN CHRYSOSTOM (c.347–407)

John Chrysostom had studied law and experienced hermit life before he was ordained and began a campaign of reformation in his native city of Antioch. He was an influential expositor of scripture, remembered in the Middle Ages for his advocacy of chastity and for his censure of women. There is pathos in the bleak end of his career when he was unseated from his eventual office as Patriarch of Alexandria and exiled, partly because his moral rigour had antagonized Empress Eudoxia: there is irony too, because Chrysostom's was one of the strongest voices to be raised among the Fathers in denial of authority to women, or of any right to teach.

Woman Not to Teach

FROM *HOMILY IX ON ST PAUL'S EPISTLE TO TIMOTHY**

1   The blessed Paul requires great modesty and great decorum of women, and not only as regards their dress and appearance: he proceeds even to regulate their speech. And what does he say? 'Let the woman learn in silence'; that is, let her not speak at all in the church; a rule he has also given in his Epistle to the Corinthians, where he says, 'It is a shame for women to speak in the church';[22] and the reason is that the law has made them subject to men. Furthermore, 'if they will learn any thing, let them ask their husbands at home'. At that time, under such instruction, women did indeed keep silence; but now there tends to be a lot of noise among them, much racket and talking, and nowhere so much as in this place. They may all be seen here talking more than in the market, or at the baths. They are all busily conversing on unfruitful matters, as if they came here for relaxation. So there is general confusion and

---

[21] Cf. Ch. 8, Marbod 4; Ch. 9, *City* 7; and *Book of Margery Kempe* (Meech and Allen, 1940), 129.

* From *The Homilies of S. John Chrysostom on the Epistles of St Paul to Timothy, Titus and Philemon*, Library of Fathers of the Catholic Church (Oxford: John Henry Parker, 1843), Homily IX, 69–72, revised by Alcuin Blamires. Greek text in *PG* 62.544. This sermon is on 1 Tim. 2: 11–15; see Ch. 1, Scripture 14.

[22] 1 Cor. 14: 35, a text quoted also by Jerome to deny a Pelagian opinion that 'every woman ought to have a knowledge of the Law': see *Against the Pelagians* 1. 25, in Fremantle 1893, 461.

they do not seem to understand that unless they are quiet they cannot learn anything useful. For when our preaching has to compete with the chatter and no one attends to what is said, what good can it do them? The extent of the silence required of women is that they are not to speak even of spiritual matters, let alone worldly ones, in the church. This is good order and decorum; this will make her fairer than any dress.[23] 'Clothed' like this, she will be able to offer her prayers most pleasingly.

2 'But I suffer not a woman to teach.' ... Having said that he wished them not to speak in the church, in order to eliminate every reason for conversation, he says, let them not teach, but have the status of learners. In this way they will show submission by their silence. For their sex is somewhat talkative by nature; on that account he restrains them on all sides. 'For Adam', he says, 'was first formed, then Eve. And Adam was not deceived, but the woman being deceived transgressed.'

3 It may be asked, What has this to do with today's women?—It shows that the male sex enjoyed the higher honour. Man was formed first; and elsewhere Paul shows man's superiority: 'Neither was the man created for the woman, but the woman for the man.'[24] Why does he say this? He wishes for the man to have the pre-eminence in every way; let man take precedence, he means, both for the reason already given [man's prior creation] and because of what happened afterwards. The woman taught the man once and made him guilty of disobedience, and ruined everything.[25] Therefore, because she made bad use of her power over the man, or rather her equality with him, God made her subject to her husband. 'Your desire shall be for your husband [and he shall rule over you].'[26]

St AMBROSE (c.339–97)

Ambrose was of aristocratic Roman background, studied rhetoric and law, and became a provincial governor. After popular pressure persuaded him to accept the bishopric of Milan, he emerged as one of the most impressive church leaders in the West. Despite the pressures of office, he found time for extensive writing. His reputation for misogyny in the Middle Ages[27] rested

[23] Cf. Tert. 19 above.
[24] I Cor. 11: 9.
[25] In any case, the Fathers suspected women of having shallow intellects, vulnerable to heresy; see 2 Tim. 3: 6–7 and Jerome, Letter 75: Fremantle 1893, 156.
[26] Gen. 3: 16.
[27] e.g. in Ch. 9, Christine, *Quarrel* 4.

partly on the anti-matrimonial propaganda of treatises such as *On Widows* and *On Virgins*. Since that propaganda overlaps with materials selected in the present volume from Tertullian and Jerome, the treatises are represented here only by an encomium on the biblical widow, Deborah, which typifies the Fathers' enthusiasm for female efforts to overcome innate 'weakness'. Ambrose's devaluation of women is more palpable in some extracts from his scriptural commentary, where he shows an almost perverse willingness to discover criticism of women just where others were to find them vindicated.

A Widow Transcends her Sex

FROM *ON WIDOWS** (*DE VIDUIS*: *C.*378)

Ambrose presents the story of Deborah from the fourth book of Judges to prove that gender limitations need not prevent a woman matching the courage or *virtus* of a man.

I   (VIII) She showed not only that widows have no need of the help of a man, but that they can be reinforcements for men. Without being at all restrained by the weakness of her sex, she undertook to perform the duties of a man—and did even more than she had undertaken. And at last, when the Jews were being ruled under the leadership of the judges, because these could not govern them with manly justice or defend them with manly strength, so that wars broke out on all sides, they chose Deborah, to be ruled by her judgement. And so one widow both ruled many thousands of men in peace and defended them from the enemy. There were many judges in Israel, but no woman before was a judge; just as, after Joshua, there were many judges but none of them was a prophet. And I think that her career as judge has been narrated, and her deeds described, so that women should not be restrained from valorous actions by the weakness of their sex. A widow, she governed the people; a widow, she led armies; a widow, she chose generals; a widow, she made military decisions and had charge of triumphs.[28] Evidently it is not nature which is answerable for the fault or subject to weakness. It is not sex, but valour which gives strength.

---

* Tr. H. de Romestin, *The Principal Works of St Ambrose*, Select Library of Nicene and Post-Nicene Fathers, x (Oxford: Parker & Co; New York: Christian Literature Co., 1896), 398–9. Rev. Alcuin Blamires. Latin text in *PL* 16.247–75 (248).

[28] But Deborah's status as widow at this point is questionable, as Jerome observes in Letter 54.17: Fremantle 1893, 108.

Creation of Adam and Eve

FROM PARADISE* (DE PARADISO: C.375)

2 (IV) 'And God took the man whom He had created and placed
him in Paradise to till it and keep it.'[29] ... Note the fact that man was
made outside Paradise, whereas woman was made inside it. This gives
us to understand that every individual acquires grace through
virtue, not through location or through family stock. Indeed, although created outside Paradise, that is in an inferior place, man is
found to be superior, whereas woman was created in a better place,
that is in Paradise, yet is found to be inferior.[30] The woman was first
to be deceived and it was she who deceived the man. Hence the
apostle Peter told that holy women were subject to the stronger
vessel, obeying their husbands as their masters.[31] And Paul says:
'Adam was not deceived, but the woman was deceived and was in
sin.'[32]

Critique of Mary Magdalene

FROM THE COMMENTARY ON LUKE* (EXPOSITIO
EVANGELII SECUNDUM LUCAM: 388–9)

In the events of the Passion[33] Ambrose strains for confirmation of his own
low estimate of women. Thus, although he can hardly avoid commending
their attentiveness and devotion (Commentary x. 144) he manages to
dampen this by detecting in their coming and going from Christ's sepulchre
a sign that their sex typically 'wavers' (hardly fair, given that the men have
fled altogether). In the extract given, his discussion of woman's role in
carrying news of the Resurrection to the disciples betrays his anxiety lest this
should seem to qualify women for an evangelizing role. Moreover, he
reduces Mary Magdalene's privilege of being the first to see the risen Christ
(which other writers were to find remarkable) to a lesson in her deficient
faith.[34]

_____

* New translation by Alcuin Blamires, from Ambrose, Opera, ed. C. Schenkl, CSEL
32.1 (Vienna, 1896), 280.
[29] Gen. 2: 15.
[30] The 'privilege' of Eve in her place of creation, rather than the sour lesson derived
by Ambrose, was later a traditional point in woman's favour, found in Jacques de
Vitry and e.g. Ch. 9, Letter 10, City 4.
[31] 1 Pet. 3: 1.
[32] 1 Tim. 2: 14.
* New translation by Alcuin Blamires from Expositio in Evangelium Secundum
Lucam, ed. M. Adriaen, CCSL xiv, pt. IV (Turnhout: Brepols, 1957).
[33] See Ch. 1, Scripture 11–12. Ambrose does not restrict himself to Luke's account.
[34] See Ch. 8, Abelard 2; S. Passion 1.

3   (x. 155) Deservedly, surely, [Mary Magdalene] is forbidden to touch the Lord, since we touch Christ not with bodily contact but with faith. 'For I have not yet ascended to my Father,'[35] He says; that is, 'I have not yet ascended for you, who seek the living among the dead.' Therefore she is sent to those who are stronger (by whose example let her learn to believe), in order that *they* may preach the Resurrection.

4   (156) Just as woman was the author of man's sin in the beginning, and he the follower in error, so now she who had previously tasted death had first sight of the Resurrection, and in turn was first in the remedy for sin. So as not to endure the opprobrium of man's perpetual blame, she transmitted grace too, and compensated for the misery of the original fall by her disclosure of the Resurrection. Through woman's mouth death had proceeded: through woman's mouth life was restored. (157) But since she is too inferior in steadfastness for preaching, and her sex is weaker in carrying things through, the evangelical role is assigned to men. . . .

Ambrose now compares Mary unfavourably with Stephen, who experienced a vision of Christ.

5   (160) Neither over the earth nor on the earth nor in a physical way should we look for You if we want to find You, for 'Henceforth we do not know Christ in a physical way.'[36] Accordingly, Stephen did not look for You on the earth when he saw You standing at the right hand of God,[37] whereas Mary, who sought on earth, could not touch. Stephen touched, who looked in heaven: in the very midst of the Jews he saw You when You were absent, whereas Mary in the midst of angels did not see You though You were present. The evangelist himself teaches us why she could not touch: it was because, when she saw You, she did not know who You were. . . .[38]

6   (161) Then we have this: 'Jesus said to her, "Woman".' She is 'woman' to the extent that she does not believe, because a woman who believes hastens 'unto perfect manhood, unto the measure of the age of the fulness of Christ',[39] lacking then her temporal name, her bodily sex, the wantonness of youth, the garrulity of old age.

[35] John 20: 17.
[36] 2 Cor. 5: 16.
[37] Acts 7: 55.
[38] John 20: 14.
[39] Eph. 4: 13; discussed in the Introduction.

Hence Jesus says: 'Woman, what are you weeping about?'—as if He were saying, 'God does not require tears alone, but faith. The tears would be good, if you recognized Christ.' . . .

7 (165) So, what is the point of 'Do not touch me'?—'Do not apply your hand to great things beyond you, but go to my brothers' (that is, to those who are more perfect: 'For whosoever shall do the will of my Father, that is in heaven, he is my brother, and sister, and mother'[40]), because the Resurrection cannot easily be grasped except by the more perfect. The prerogative is reserved for those who are more the foundation of this faith; but 'women I do not permit to teach' in church, 'let them ask their husbands at home'.[41] Thus she is sent to those who are Christ's family, and she accepts the instructions given.

St JEROME (c. 342–420)

The Inferiority of Marriage; and the Distraction of Women

FROM *AGAINST JOVINIAN** (*ADVERSUS JOVINIANUM*: c. 393)

Jerome was a figure of great authority in the Middle Ages, revered for having produced the Vulgate or 'standard' translation of the Bible from Hebrew into Latin. In his lifetime, however, he was a controversial figure, a champion of radical asceticism at Rome who inevitably provoked resentment with his sarcastic polemic. In particular, he alarmed fellow-Christians by his vigorous extension of arguments in Ambrose and other Fathers, propounding the superiority of virginity over marriage. The backbone of this position was already laid out in Chapters 22–3 of a treatise *Against Helvidius* (AD 383).

Although Jerome had to leave Rome for the East under a cloud of censure in 385, his friend Pammachius contacted him some eight years later on behalf of ascetic sympathizers in the capital when they were disturbed by the teachings of a monk named Jovinian. The four points which incensed Jerome in the 'nauseating trash' of this 'Epicurus of Christianity'[42] were: (i) that baptized Christians can attain equal spiritual merit whether married, single, or widowed; (ii) that sincere, baptized Christians cannot be overcome by the devil; (iii) that a life of fasting is not more deserving than the grateful acceptance of food and drink; and (iv) that the baptized faithful will receive undifferentiated reward in heaven. Jovinian's appears to have been a serious position based on 'a high estimate of baptismal regeneration', but it resulted

---

[40] Matt. 12: 50.
[41] 1 Tim. 2: 12, and 1 Cor. 14: 35.
* Tr. W. H. Fremantle, *The Principal Works of St Jerome*, Select Library of Nicene and Post-Nicene Fathers, vi (Oxford: James Parker & Co.; and New York: Christian Literature Co., 1893), 346–416; rev. by C. W. Marx. Latin text in *PL* 23.221–352.
[42] *Ag. Jov.* i. 4, i. 1

in his excommunication.[43] Meanwhile Jerome was scandalized by the notion of putting sexual abstinence spiritually on a par with marriage, and relished an opportunity to pulverize all his opponent's propositions, especially the first, in his *Against Jovinian*. The treatise went too far and was counter-productive, prompting Augustine to write pointedly on *The Good of Marriage*, while Pammachius even tried to stop copies circulating.

As it turned out, Jerome had the last laugh. Thanks to the eye-catching witticisms his treatise incorporated from classical sources, and above all thanks to the inclusion of a memorably vehement antifeminist passage arguing that the wise man must not marry, which he attributed to Theophrastus, his piece was endlessly quarried by subsequent writers.[44] Theophrastus (c.372–288) was an important pagan philosopher who took on the mantle of Aristotle. The *Book on Marriage* (*Liber de nuptiis*) from which Jerome says he is quoting is otherwise unknown, so the attribution remains uncertain, as does Jerome's immediate source for the passage—which could have been a lost work by Seneca or Tertullian. Anyway it seemed valuable evidence that celibacy was not a modern Christian invention, and the Theophrastan excerpt later exerted a phenomenal influence on the evolution of misogyny once it was put into circulation by writers such as Abelard (in *Theologia Christiana* II. 94–106, c.1124), and John of Salisbury (*Policraticus* VIII. 11, c.1159).

In the first six chapters of *Against Jovinian* Jerome identifies the relative status of marriage and virginity as a key issue, and, while carefully denying that he discredits marriage, ranks it third after virginity and widowhood in its spiritual 'yield'. Finding that his opponent resorts to 1 Corinthians 7 among other scriptural evidence, he grounds his counter-attack on interpretation of the same text.

1   (1. 7) . . . Let us turn to the main point of the evidence: 'It is good', St Paul says, 'for a man not to touch a woman.'[45] If it is good not to touch a woman, it is bad to touch one: for there is no opposite to goodness but badness. If however it is bad and the evil is pardoned, it is for this reason that the allowance is made, namely to prevent a worse evil. But surely, a thing which is only allowed because there may be something worse has only a slight degree of goodness. He would never have added 'let each man have his own wife', unless he had previously used the words 'to avoid fornication'. Do away with fornication, and he will not say 'let each man have his own wife'. Just as though one were to lay it down: 'It is good to feed on wheaten bread, and to eat the finest wheat flour' and yet, to prevent a person pressed by hunger from devouring cow-dung, I may allow him to eat barley. Does it follow that the wheat will not have its peculiar purity, if barley is preferred to excrement? That is naturally good which does

not admit of comparison with what is bad, and is not eclipsed because something else is preferred.⁴⁶

2   At the same time, we must take note of the Apostle's good sense. He did not say, 'it is good not to have a wife', but, 'it is good not to touch a woman': as though there were danger even in the touch; as though he who touched her would not escape from her who 'hunts for the precious life,' who causes the young man's judgement to fly away.⁴⁷ 'Who can hold fire firmly to his chest and not be burnt or can walk upon burning coals and not be scorched?'⁴⁸ Just as he who touches fire is instantly burned, so by mere touch the peculiar nature of man and woman is perceived, and the difference of sex is understood. Heathen fables relate how Mithras and Ericthonius were begotten of the soil, in stone or earth, by raging lust.⁴⁹ Hence it was that our Joseph, because the Egyptian woman wished to touch him, fled from her hands, and, as if he had been bitten by a mad dog and feared the spreading poison, threw away the cloak which she had touched.⁵⁰

3   'Do not refuse each other except by consent for a period of time so that you may devote yourselves to prayer.'⁵¹ I ask you, what kind of good thing is that which impedes prayer? Which does not allow the body of Christ to be received? So long as I do the husband's part, I fail in continency. The same Apostle in another place commands us to pray always. If we are to pray always, it follows that we must never be in the bondage of wedlock, for as often as I render my wife her due, I cannot pray.⁵²

Jerome goes on to underline Paul's representation of marriage as an optional concession.

---

⁴⁶ Jerome draws on Tertullian (e.g. *De exhortatione castitatis* 3–4) and on Ambrose (*On Widows* 13), with lurid addition of cow-dung.
⁴⁷ Prov. 6: 26.
⁴⁸ Prov. 6: 27–8.
⁴⁹ Mithras was a Persian sun-god adopted by Romans, Erichthonius a mythical king of Athens supposedly conceived when Hephaestus' semen fell on the earth as he struggled to rape Athena.
⁵⁰ Joseph repulsed the advances of Potiphar's wife, pulling himself from her grasp so that she tore his clothes; later she alleged attempted rape (Gen. 39: 7 ff.).
⁵¹ i.e. refuse the reciprocal 'debt' of sexual gratification (1 Cor. 7: 4, and cf. Ch. 3, Gratian 2; and Ch. 7, *WoB* 9).
⁵² Jerome expected that husbands would 'swell with rage' at this view of marriage and sex as an impediment to prayer (Letter 48: 15: Fremantle 1893, 75), but he was committed to it.

4 (I. 9) Then come the words, 'But I say to the unmarried and to
widows, it is good for them if they so continue even as I. But if they
do not contain themselves, let them marry: for it is better to marry
than to be burnt.'[53] Having conceded to married persons the
enjoyment of wedlock and pointed out his own wishes or what he
might allow, he passes on to the unmarried and to widows, sets
before them his own practice for imitation, and calls them happy if
they so continue. 'But if they do not contain themselves, let them
marry', just as he said before, 'to avoid fornication', and 'Lest Satan
tempt you, because of your incontinency'. And he gives a reason for
saying 'If they do not contain themselves, let them marry', namely,
'It is better to marry than to be burnt.' The reason why it is better to
marry is that it is worse to burn. Destroy burning lust and he will not
say it is better to marry. The word *better* always implies a comparison
with something worse, not a thing absolutely good and incapable of
comparison. It is as though he said, 'it is better to have one eye than
neither, it is better to stand on one foot and to support the rest of the
body with a stick, than to crawl with broken legs'.

Jerome elaborates his interpretation with reference to 1 Corinthians 7: 10–
24, then qualifies Paul's admission that virginity lacks the prescriptive
backing of Christ.

5 (I. 12) Christ loves virgins more than others, because they
willingly give what was not commanded them. And it indicates
greater grace to offer what you are not bound to give, than to render
what is exacted of you. The Apostles, contemplating the burden of a
wife, exclaimed, 'If such is the condition of a man with a wife, it is not
advantageous to marry.'[54] Our Lord thought well of their view. 'You
rightly think', He said, 'that it may not be advantageous for a man
who is striving for the kingdom of heaven to take a wife: but it is a
hard matter, and all men do not receive the saying, but only they to
whom it has been given. Some are eunuchs by nature, others by the
violence of men. Those eunuchs please me who are such not of
necessity, but of free choice. Willingly do I take them into my bosom
who have made themselves eunuchs for the kingdom of heaven's
sake, and in order to worship me have renounced the condition of
their birth.'

[53] 1 Cor. 7: 8–9, translating the passive verb (*uri*) in the Vulgate.
[54] Matt. 19: 10 ff.

Jovinian's Old Testament exemplars of marriage are critically scrutinized. Then his observation that some of the Apostles had wives is answered in the claim that they seem to have left them to follow Christ. As for women being 'saved through childbearing' (1 Timothy 2: 10), this means that she can make up for the loss of her own virginity if she produces children who then remain virgins. Jerome now returns to an Old Testament witness; Solomon, author of Proverbs.

6 (1. 28) Let us show what this Solomon with his many wives and concubines thought of marriage. For no one can know better than he, who suffered through them, what a wife or woman is. Well, then, he says in the Proverbs: 'The foolish and bold woman comes to want bread.'[55] What bread? Surely, that bread which comes down from heaven: and he immediately adds: 'The earth-born perish in her house, rush into the depths of hell.'[56] Who are the earth-born that perish in her house? They of course who follow the first Adam, who is of the earth, and not the second, who is from heaven. And again in another place: 'Like a worm in wood, so a wicked woman destroys her husband.'[57] But if you assert that this was spoken of bad wives, I shall briefly answer: Why should I be obliged to run the risk of the wife I marry proving good or bad? 'It is better', he says, 'to dwell in a desert land, than with a contentious and irritable woman.'[58] How seldom we find a wife without these faults, he knows who is married. Hence that nobly sublime orator, Varius Geminus, says well 'The man who does not quarrel is a bachelor.'[59]

7 'It is better to dwell in the corner of the housetop, than with a contentious woman in a shared house.'[60] If a house common to husband and wife makes a wife proud and breeds contempt for the husband, how much more if the wife is the richer of the two, and the husband only a lodger in her house! She begins to be not a wife, but mistress of the house; and if she offends her husband, they must part. 'A continual dripping of water on a wintry day'[61] turns a man out of doors, and so will a contentious woman drive a man from his own house. She floods his house with her constant nagging and daily chatter, and ousts him from his own home, that is the Church. Hence the same Solomon earlier commands: 'My son, may you not drift

---

[55] Prov. 9: 13 (minus the reference to bread).
[56] Prov. 9: 18.
[57] Prov. 25: 20 (but Jerome has switched the gender).
[58] Prov. 21: 19.
[59] Epigrammatist often quoted by Seneca.
[60] Prov. 21: 9, 25: 24.
[61] Prov. 27: 15.

away [from the Church].'[62] And the Apostle, writing to the Hebrews, says: 'Therefore we ought to give the more earnest heed to the things spoken, lest perhaps we drift away.'[63]

8 Who may resist explaining what is expressed allegorically? 'The leech had three daughters, dearly loved, but they could not be satisfied, and a fourth is not satisfied to say "it is enough"; hell, the love of a woman, the earth which is not satisfied with water, and fire do not say "it is enough".'[64] The leech is the devil; the daughters of the devil are dearly loved, and they cannot be satisfied with the blood of their slain—hell, and woman's love, and the parched earth and the glowing fire. It is not the whore, or the adulteress, who is spoken of; but woman's love in general is accused of ever being insatiable— put it out, it bursts into flame; give it plenty, it is again in need; it deprives a man's mind of its vigour, and engrosses all thought except for the passion which it feeds. What we read in the parable which follows is to the same effect: 'For three things the earth trembles; indeed, there are four things which it cannot bear: if a servant becomes king; if a fool is filled with bread; if a hateful woman has a good husband; and if a female servant supplants her mistress.'[65] See how a wife is classed with the greatest evils. But if you reply that it is a *hateful* wife, I will give you the same answer as before—the mere possibility of such danger is in itself no light matter. For he who marries a wife is uncertain whether he is marrying a hateful woman or one worthy of his love. If she be hateful, she is intolerable. If worthy of love, her love is compared to the grave, to the parched earth, and to fire.

After citing Ecclesiastes, Jerome expounds the Song of Songs as a hymn to virginity; surveys the prophets of the virgin birth; protests that baptism cannot level virgins with prostitutes; argues that priestly office is not properly compatible with marriage and its sexual functions; asserts that continence is not an unnatural curb on the sex drive and is unlikely to halt generation; and collects scriptural texts elevating the spiritual over the fleshly. Then, in refutation of Jovinian's allegation that virginity is a Christian novelty, he catalogues examples testifying to pre-Christian respect for virginity, then for monogamy.

9 (I. 43) I will proceed to married women who were reluctant to survive the decease or violent death of their husbands for fear they might be forced into a second marriage, and who entertained a

---

[62] Prov. 3: 21.   [63] Heb. 2: 1.   [64] Prov. 30: 15–16.   [65] Prov. 30: 21–3.

marvellous affection for the only husbands they had. This may teach us that second marriage was repudiated among the heathen. Dido, the sister of Pygmalion, having collected a vast amount of gold and silver, sailed to Africa, and there built Carthage. And when her hand was sought in marriage by Iarbas, king of Libya, she deferred the marriage for a while until she might complete the city. Not long after, having raised a funeral pyre to the memory of her former husband Sichaeus, she preferred to 'burn rather than to marry'.[66]

10 (1. 44) What need to tell of the wife of Niceratus, who unable to bear any wrong to her husband, inflicted death upon herself rather than subject herself to the lust of the thirty tyrants whom Lysander had set over conquered Athens?[67] Artemisia also, wife of Mausolus, is related to have been distinguished for chastity. Though she was queen of Caria, and is extolled by great poets and historians, no higher praise is bestowed upon her than that when her husband was dead she loved him as much as when he was alive, and built a tomb so great that even to the present day all costly sepulchres are called after his name, *mausoleums*.[68]

Next Jerome turns to Roman examples, Lucretia and others.

11 (1. 46) ... Marcia, Cato's younger daughter, when asked after the loss of her husband why she did not marry again, replied that she could not find a man who wanted her more than her money. Her words teach us that men in choosing their wives look for wealth rather than chastity, and that many in marrying use not their eyes but their fingers. That *must* be an excellent thing which is won by avarice! When the same lady was mourning the loss of her husband, and the matrons asked what day would see the end of her grief, she replied, 'The same that sees the end of my life.' I think that the one who continued to desire her husband after his death had no thought of marrying again. Porcia, whom Brutus took as wife, was a virgin; ... Porcia could not live without Brutus, for women attach themselves closely to particular men, and to keep to one is a strong link in the chain of affection. When a relative urged Annia to marry again

---

[66] Jerome borrows from Tert., *De exhortatione castitatis*, 13, this pre-Virgilian narrative of Dido, as well as the witty inversion of 1 Cor. 7: 9.

[67] Niceratus was son of an Athenian leader who had died before the Spartan, Lysander, supported the rule of the Thirty Tyrants after defeating Athens, 404 BC.

[68] The celebrated tomb of King Mausolus (d. 353 BC), built by Pythius, not by his widow (who was also his sister) Artemisia.

(she was mature and a goodly person), she answered: 'I shall certainly not do so. For if I find a good man I have no wish to be in fear of losing him: if a bad one, why must I put up with a bad husband after having had a good one?'

Theophrastus on Marriage

Jerome admits that his catalogue of chaste women has been protracted, but, introducing the 'Theophrastus' excerpt, protests:

12 (I. 47) What am I to do when the women of our time press me with apostolic authority, and before the first husband is buried, repeat over and over again from memory the precepts which allow a second marriage? May those who despise the faithfulness of Christian purity at least learn chastity from the heathen. The Book of Theophrastus on marriage is said to be worth its weight in gold.[69] In it the author asks whether the wise man marries. And after laying down the conditions—that the wife must be fair, of good character, and honest parentage, the husband in good health and of ample means—and after saying that under these circumstances a wise man sometimes enters the state of matrimony, he immediately proceeds thus: 'But all these conditions are seldom satisfied in marriage. A wise man therefore must not take a wife. For in the first place his study of philosophy will be hindered, and it is impossible for anyone to attend to his books and his wife at the same time. Married women want many things, costly dresses, gold, jewels, expensive items, maidservants, all kinds of furniture, litters and gilded coaches. Then come prattling complaints all the night:[70] that one lady goes out better dressed than she; that another is looked up to by all. "I am a poor despised nobody at women's gatherings." "Why did you ogle that creature next door?" "Why were you talking to the maid?" "What did you bring from the market?" We are not allowed to have a single friend or companion; her husband's friendship going elsewhere would entail his hate for her, she suspects. There may be in some neighbouring city the wisest of teachers; but if we have a wife we can neither leave her behind, nor take the burden with us.

13 'To support a poor wife is hard: to put up with a rich one is torture. Notice too that in the case of a wife you cannot pick and

---

[69] Or, 'the brilliant book', or, *The Golden Book*: the status of the adjective *aureolus* is unclear.

[70] Cf. Ch. I, Juv. 6.

choose: you must take her as you find her. If she has a bad temper or is a fool, if she has a blemish or is proud, or has bad breath, whatever her fault may be—all this we learn after marriage. Horses, asses, cattle, dogs, even slaves of the smallest worth, clothes, kettles, wooden seats, cups, and earthenware pitchers, are first tried and then bought: a wife is the only thing that is not shown before she is married, for fear she may not give satisfaction.

14 'Our gaze must always be directed to her face, and we must always praise her beauty: if you look at another woman, she thinks that she is out of favour. She must be called "My lady", her birthday must be kept, we must swear by her health and wish that she may survive us; respect must be paid to the nurse, to the gossip, to the father's slave, to the foster-child, to the handsome hanger-on, to the effeminate steward who manages her affairs, and to the eunuch who ministers to the safe indulgence of her lust; names which are only a cloak for adultery.[71] Whatever people she sets her heart on, you must love too whether you like it or not.[72]

15 'If you give her the management of the whole house, you are reduced to being her servant. If you reserve some control for yourself, she will not think you are loyal to her; but she will turn to strife and hatred, and unless you quickly take care, she will have the poison ready. If you admit to the house old women, and soothsayers, and prophets, and vendors of jewels and silk clothing, you "imperil her chastity"; if you shut the door on them, she is injured and fancies you suspect her. But what is the good of even a careful guardian, when an unchaste wife cannot be watched, and a chaste one ought not to be?[73] For compulsion is an unreliable keeper of chastity, and a woman only deserves to be called "chaste" who is free to sin if she chooses. If a woman is beautiful, she is soon desired; if she is ugly, she is soon stirred to lust. It is difficult to guard what many long for; it is annoying to have what no one thinks worth possessing. But the misery of having an ugly wife is less than that of watching over a beautiful one. Nothing is safe, for which a whole population sighs and longs. One man entices with his figure, another with his mind, another with his wit, another with his presents. Somehow, or sometime, a fortress is captured which is attacked on all sides.

[71] Cf. Juv. *Satire* VI, 014–029, for suspicions about attendant 'eunuchs'.
[72] Cf. Ovid, *Art of Love* II. 198–202.
[73] On the futility of 'guarding' cf. Ch. 1, Ovid 4.

16 'Men marry so as to get someone to run the household, to comfort them when they are low, and to banish loneliness; but a faithful servant makes a far better manager, more obedient to the master, more observant of his ways, than a wife who thinks she proves herself mistress if she acts in opposition to her husband, that is, if she does what pleases her, not what she is told. But friends, and servants who are under the obligation of favours received, are better able to wait upon us in sickness than a wife, who makes us liable for her tears (and will shed a flood in anticipation of being the heir); and whose ostentatious anxiety drives her sick husband to the distraction of despair. But if she herself is poorly, we must fall sick with her and never leave her bedside. Or, if she be a good and agreeable wife (how rare a bird she is![74]), we have to share her groans in childbirth, and suffer torture when she is in danger.

17 'The truly wise man can never be alone. He has with him the good men of all time, and turns his mind freely wherever he chooses. What is inaccessible to him in person he can embrace in thought. And, if men are scarce, he converses with God. He is never less alone than when alone.

18 'Then again, to marry for the sake of having children, so that our name may not perish, or that we may have support in old age, and leave our property without dispute, is the height of stupidity.[75] For what is it to us when we are leaving the world if another bears our name, when even a son does not necessarily take his father's title, and there are countless others who are called by the same name? Or what support in old age is he whom you bring up, and who may die before you, or turn out to be a lout? Or at all events, when he reaches mature age, you may seem to him to die too slowly. Friends and relatives whom you can judiciously love are better and safer heirs than those whom you must make your heirs whether you like it or not. Indeed, the surest way of having a good heir is to ruin your fortune in a good cause while you live, not to leave the fruit of your labour to be used you know not how.'

19 (1. 48) When Theophrastus speaks like this, are there any of us Christians, whose inclination is for heaven and who daily say 'I long to be dissolved, and to be with Christ',[76] whom he does not

---

[74] Cf. Ch. 1, Juv. 4.
[75] Continuing from *16* the conventional ancient catalogue of 'reasons for marrying'.
[76] Phil. 1: 23.

embarrass? Shall a co-heir of Christ really long for human heirs? And shall he desire children and delight himself in a long line of descendants, who will perhaps fall into the clutches of Antichrist, when we read that Moses and Samuel preferred others to their own sons, and did not count as their children those whom they saw displeasing God?

20 When Cicero after divorcing Terentia was requested by Hirtius to marry his sister, he put the matter altogether aside, and said that he could not possibly devote himself to a wife and to philosophy.[77] . . . Socrates had two wives, Xanthippe and Myron, granddaughter of Aristides. They frequently quarrelled, and he used to mock them for disagreeing over a man so ugly as himself, with snub nose, bald forehead, rough-haired, and bandy-legged. At last they planned an attack upon him, and having punished him severely and put him to flight, plagued him for a long time. On one occasion when he opposed Xanthippe, who was heaping abuse upon him from above; she doused him with dirty water, but he only wiped his head and said, 'I knew thunder like that was bound to be followed by a shower.'

From this flows a succession of criticisms of wives in Roman culture, of which the following are examples.

21 We read of a certain Roman noble who, when his friends found fault with him for having divorced a beautiful, chaste, and rich wife, stretched out his foot and said to them, 'And the shoe before you looks new and elegant, yet no one but myself knows where it pinches.' Herodotus tells us that a woman takes off her modesty with her clothes;[78] and our own comic poet [Terence] thinks the man fortunate who has never been married.[79] Do I need to refer to Pasiphaë, Clytemnestra, and Eriphyle, the first of whom—the wife of a king and ruining herself in pleasure—is said to have lusted for a bull, the second to have killed her husband for the sake of an adulterer, the third to have betrayed Amphiaraus, and to have preferred a gold necklace to the well-being of her husband?[80] In all

[77] Despite Cicero's witty reply to his neighbour, he did remarry.
[78] This is the answer given in Herodotus, *Histories* I. 8, when a king suggests to his subject that he should judge the incomparable beauty of the queen by seeing her naked.
[79] Terence, *Hecyra* II. 1.4.
[80] Ancient epitomes of womanly vice: see Ch. I, Ovid I (Pasiphaë and Clytemnestra) and 7 (Eriphyle).

the bombast of tragedy and the overthrow of houses, cities, and kingdoms, it is the wives and mistresses who stir up trouble. Parents take up arms against their children; unspeakable banquets are served; and on account of the rape of one foolish woman Europe and Asia are involved in a ten years' war.[81]

22   (I. 49) Aristotle and Plutarch and our Seneca have written treatises on marriage, from which we have already given some extracts and now add a few more. The love of beauty buries reason and is close neighbour of madness; a foul blot little in keeping with a sound mind.[82] It confuses counsel, breaks high and generous spirits, drags men away from great thoughts to mean ones; it makes men peevish, angry, foolhardy, cruelly overbearing, servile flatterers, good for nothing, at last not even for love itself. For, although in the intensity of passion it burns like a raging fire, it wastes much time through suspicions, tears, and complaints: it begets hatred of oneself, and at last hates itself.

Woman and Sexual Temptation; and the Era of Female Virginity

FROM *LETTER 22, TO EUSTOCHIUM** (384)

Jerome is writing a letter of advice to his friend Paula's daughter, Eusto-chium, who has committed herself to a life of virginity. Reflections on the need for unremitting vigilance against desire prompt a disclosure of the way his own contemplations in the desert have been threatened by fantasies of nubile girls.

23   (VII) When I was living in the desert, that vast solitude which is parched by the burning sun and affords a savage home for hermits, how often I fantasized that I was among the pleasures of Rome! I used to sit alone because I was filled with bitterness. Sackcloth disfigured my unshapely limbs and through long neglect my skin had become as black as an Ethiopian's. Tears and groans were my daily routine; and whenever drowsiness overcame my struggles against it, I bruised my bare bones, which hardly held together, against the ground.... Now, although in my fear of hell I had consigned myself to this prison, where I had no companions but scorpions and wild beasts, I often found myself surrounded by

[81] Alluding to the abduction of Helen by Paris, source of the Trojan War.

[82] In *Ag. Jov.* II. 8–9 Jerome returns to the 'insanity' of sexual desire and the philosopher's need to avoid it through seclusion.

* Tr. W. H. Fremantle, *Principal Writings of Jerome*, 22–41 (24–5, 26, 30), revised by Alcuin Blamires. Latin text in Jerome 1933.

dancing girls! My face was pale from fasting, my body was ice-cold; yet my mind was burning with desire, and the fires of lust kept boiling up within me when my flesh (before its tenant) was as good as dead. — QUOTE —

Citing Job's characterization of the devil—'His strength is in his loins, and his power in his navel'[83]—Jerome demonstrates the devil's power through 'the loins' in what was to be a classic sequence of scriptural examples.

24   (XII) Do you wish for proof of my assertions? Samson was braver than a lion and tougher than rock. Alone and unprotected he pursued a thousand armed men; and yet, in Delilah's embrace, his resolution melted away.[84] David was a man after God's own heart,[85] and his lips had often sung of the holy one, the future Christ, yet as he walked upon the roof of his house he was fascinated by Bathsheba's naked beauty, and added murder to adultery.[86] Notice here how, even in his own house, a man cannot use his eyes without danger. Then, repenting, he says to the Lord: 'Against thee, thee only, have I sinned and done this evil in thy sight.'[87] Being a king he feared no one else. So, too, with Solomon. Through him Wisdom spoke, discoursing on plants 'from the cedar tree that is in Lebanon even to the hyssop that springeth out of the wall'.[88] Yet he went back from God because he was a lover of women.[89] And, as if to show that near relationship is no safeguard, Amnon burned with illicit passion for his sister Thamar.[90]

Jerome argues that, whereas under the Old Law celibacy was confined to 'sons of prophets', the transition from Eve to Mary has inaugurated a glorious new era of female virginity.

[83] Job 40: 11.
[84] Judg. 15–16. Among other exploits, Samson slew a thousand Philistines with an ass's jaw-bone and escaped an ambush in the city of Gaza by hoisting the city gates from their mountings. But when he fell in love with Delilah, the Philistines bribed her to wheedle out of him the key to his strength—his uncut hair. It was shaved while he was asleep 'in her bosom', so Samson was finally imprisoned and blinded, only to wreak destruction upon his enemies when his hair grew again, by convulsing the pillars of the building where he was brought to entertain them.
[85] I Kgs. 13: 14.
[86] 2 Kgs. 11: 2–27. See Ch. 1, Scripture 4.
[87] Psalm 51: 4.
[88] 3 Kgs 4: 33.
[89] 3 Kgs. 11: 1–10 gives an account of Solomon's love of foreign women, who turned him towards the worship of 'strange Gods', angering the God of Israel.
[90] 2 Kgs. 13.

25   (XXI) The virtue of continence used to be found only in men, and
Eve went on sustaining the labour-pains of childbirth. But now that
a virgin has conceived in the womb and borne for us a child of which
the prophet says that 'Government shall be upon his shoulder, and
his name shall be called the mighty God, and everlasting Father',[91]
the chain of the curse is broken. Death came through Eve, but life has
come through Mary. And thus the gift of virginity has been bestowed
most richly upon women, seeing that it has had its beginning from a
woman. As soon as the Son of God set foot upon earth, He formed a
new household for Himself there, so that, just as He was adored by
angels in heaven, angels might also serve Him on earth.

Objection to the Sexual Double Standard

FROM *LETTER 77, TO OCEANUS** (399)

In this eulogy of his protégé Fabiola, Jerome had to confront the harshness of
the doctrine that a woman must not remarry if separated from her first
husband, whether on grounds of adultery, sodomy, or worse.[92] While
upholding the doctrine (transgressed by Fabiola, who later enacted public
penance in order to be received back into the Church), Jerome protests
against society for condoning in husbands what it censures in wives.

26   (III) Because at the very outset there is a rock in the path and
she is overwhelmed by a storm of censure for having abandoned her
first husband and taken a second, I will not praise her for her
conversion till I have first cleared her of this charge. So terrible were
the vices imputed to her former husband that not even a prostitute or
a common slave could have put up with them. If I were to recount
them, I should spoil the heroism of a wife who chose to bear the
blame of a separation rather than to blacken the character and
expose the stains of the man who was one body with her. I will only
urge this one plea which is sufficient to exonerate a chaste matron
and a Christian woman. The Lord has given a commandment that a
wife must not be put away 'except it be for fornication, and that, if
put away, she must remain unmarried'.[93] Now a commandment
which is given to men logically applies to women also. For it cannot
be that, while an adulterous wife is to be put away, an unfaithful

---

[91] Isa. 9: 6.
* Tr. W. H. Fremantle, *Principal Works of Jerome*, 157–63 (158). Latin text in
Jerome 1933.
[92] Further discussed in Letter 55.3.
[93] Matt. 19: 9; 1 Cor. 7: 11.

husband is to be retained. The Apostle says: 'he who is joined to a harlot is one body with her'.[94] Therefore she who is joined to a filthy fornicator is one body with him, too. It is true, the laws of Caesar are different from the laws of Christ: Papinianus[95] commands one thing, our own St Paul another. Earthly laws give a free rein to the promiscuity of men, merely condemning seduction and adultery; lust is allowed to range unrestrained among brothels and slave girls, as if the guilt were constituted by the rank of the person assailed and not by the purpose of the assailant. But with us Christians what is unlawful for women is equally unlawful for men, and as both serve the same God, both are bound by the same obligations.[96]

St AUGUSTINE (354–430)

The influence of St Augustine's teaching in western Christendom was enormous for well over a thousand years. He was by no means a fanatical ascetic, since he wrote constructively on marriage and strongly defended the inherent good of the physical human body against the Manichaeans. Nevertheless, he was appalled by the uncontrollability, or 'insubordination', of sexual arousal, something visited upon humanity with a kind of poetic justice immediately after the Fall, he thought.[97] Before his own conversion Augustine had a common-law wife for years, though she had to be sent away when his mother planned (futilely, it turned out) a marriage for him. After his conversion he claimed that the recollection of sexual desire now horrified him, and that he had ruled out marriage because a man's mind is 'cast out of its citadel' by 'female blandishments and intimate contact'.[98] Possibly his ideas on sexuality were coloured by his own life as one 'who never married and whose experience of sexual pleasure was illicit and guilt-provoking'.[99]

Augustine's specific doctrines on women were relatively more neutral and sophisticated than those of some of the Fathers, even though he envisaged for her a secondary ranking in the simple hierarchy, the 'natural order observed among men, that women should serve men, and children their parents, because it is just that the weaker mind should serve the stronger'.[100] Among other aspects, he was concerned with fine-tuning the debate as to whether woman was or wasn't 'in God's image'—both at once, in his

[94] I Cor. 6: 16.
[95] A reputable Roman jurist.
[96] Resistance to the 'double standard' can also be found in Chrysostom, *Homily 5 on I Thessalonians* and *Homily 19 on I Corinthians* (Clark 1983, 73–6); in Augustine's *On Adulterous Marriages* (Huegelmeyer 1955, 108–9) and in his sermon *De decem cordis,* recapitulated in *Dives and Pauper* (see Ch. 8). Further discussion in Ch. 4, Andreas 1; Ch. 8, S. Passion 2; and Ch. 9, City 14.
[97] Pagels 1990, 110–12, 140–1; and Brown 1988, 406–8, 416–19.
[98] *Soliloquies* i. 10.17, in Augustine 1953, 33–4.
[99] Pagels 1990, 141. Such views are challenged in Truax 1990.
[100] See Ch. 3 below, Gratian 3.

opinion, thanks to a subtle conception of her as, under her physical aspect, symbolizing (without quite *constituting*) an inferior, sense-oriented dimension of humankind.[101] His attitude to Eve was not shrill, but insidiously condescending nevertheless in the underlying opinion that Adam cannot seriously have shared her credulity in the face of the serpent's claims. On the other hand, he staunchly affirmed the bodily resurrection of woman *as* woman. Moreover, he strongly endorsed the objections of predecessors such as Chrysostom and Jerome to the 'double standard' whereby husbands claimed a sexual licence which they would not dream of allowing to their wives.[102] The catch was that he based his objection on the 'superior' male's obligation to set a good example to the 'weaker' sex. Nevertheless, his strictures against male hypocrisy made him a useful ally in the defence of women throughout the Middle Ages, as is demonstrated by the full report of his argument in *Dives and Pauper* (Chapter 8).

Hierarchy of Man and Woman in Creation

FROM *CONFESSIONS** (*CONFESSIONES*: AD 398)

Near the end of the book comes a hymn of thanks for the created world.

I (XIII. 32) And finally we see man, made in your image and likeness, ruling over all the irrational animals for the very reason that he was made in your image and resembles you, that is, because he has the power of reason and understanding. And just as in man's soul there are two forces, one which is dominant because it deliberates and one which obeys because it is subject to such guidance, in the same way, in the physical sense, woman has been made for man. In her mind and in her rational intelligence she has a nature the equal of man's, but in sex she is physically subject to him in the same way as our natural impulses need to be subjected to the reasoning power of the mind, in order that the actions to which they lead may be inspired by the principles of good conduct.

---

[101] See Børresen 1981, 21–30; and Augustine, *De Trinitate* XII.
[102] See Jerome 26 and n. above.
* Tr. R. S. Pine-Coffin, *Saint Augustine: Confessions* (Harmondsworth: Penguin, 1961), 344, © R. S. Pine-Coffin, 1961. Reprinted by permission of Penguin Books Ltd. Latin text in *PL* 32.659–868.

Eve as 'Helper'; Her Role in the Fall

FROM *THE LITERAL MEANING OF GENESIS** (*DE GENESI AD LITTERAM*: 401–16)

2   (IX. 5) Now, if the woman was not made for the man to be his helper in begetting children, in what was she to help him? She was not to till the earth with him, for there was not yet any toil to make help necessary. If there were any such need, a male helper would be better, and the same could be said of the comfort of another's presence if Adam were perhaps weary of solitude. How much more agreeably could two male friends, rather than a man and woman, enjoy companionship and conversation in a life shared together. And if they had to make an arrangement in their common life for one to command and the other to obey in order to make sure that opposing wills would not disrupt the peace of the household, there would have been proper rank to assure this, since one would be created first and the other second, and this would be further reinforced if the second were made from the first, as was the case with the woman. Surely no one will say that God was able to make from the rib of the man only a woman and not also a man if He had wished to do so. Consequently, I do not see in what sense the woman was made as a helper for the man if not for the sake of bearing children.

In subsequent discussion of the Fall, Augustine suggests that Eve's explicit consciousness of the prohibition made her transgression the more inexcusable. He also argues that she would not have been swayed by the serpent's temptation had there not already been some streak of presumption in her. Her punishment prompts Augustine to ponder the nature of her 'servitude'.

3   (XI. 37) We must give consideration to the statement, 'And you shall be subject to your husband, and he shall rule over you',[103] to see how it can be understood in the proper sense. For we must believe that even before her sin woman had been made to be ruled by her husband and to be submissive and subject to him. But we can with reason understand that the servitude meant in these words is that in which there is a condition similar to that of slavery rather than a bond of love (so that the servitude by which men later began to be

* Tr. John Hammond Taylor, SJ, *St Augustine: The Literal Meaning of Genesis*, 2 vols., Ancient Christian Writers, no. 42 (New York and Ramsey, NJ: Newman Press, 1982), ii, 75, 170–1, 175–6. © 1982 by Revd. Johannes Quasten, Revd. Walter J. Burghardt, SJ, and Thomas C. Lawler. Latin text in *PL* 34.245–486.
    [103] Gen. 3: 16.

slaves to other men obviously has its origin in punishment for sin). St Paul says, 'Through love serve one another.'[104] But by no means would he say, 'Have dominion over one another.' Hence married persons through love can serve one another, but St Paul does not permit a woman to rule over a man.[105] The sentence pronounced by God gave this power rather to man; and it is not by her nature but rather by her sin that woman deserved to have her husband for a master.[106] But if this order is not maintained, nature will be corrupted still more, and sin will be increased.

Augustine offers a final reflection on the Fall.

4 (XI. 42) ... If Adam was a spiritual man, in mind though not in body, how could he have believed what was said through the serpent, namely, that God forbade them to eat of the fruit of that one tree because He knew that if they did they would be gods in their knowledge of good and evil? As if the Creator would grudge so great a good to His creatures! It is surely strange if a man endowed with a spiritual mind could have believed this. Was it because the man would not have been able to believe this that the woman was employed on the supposition that she had limited understanding, and also perhaps that she was living according to the spirit of the flesh and not according to the spirit of the mind?

5 Is this the reason that St Paul does not attribute the image of God to her? For he says, 'A man indeed ought not to cover his head, since he is the image and glory of God, but woman is the glory of man.'[107] This is not to say that the mind of woman is unable to receive that same image, for in that grace St Paul says we are neither male nor female.[108] But perhaps the woman had not yet received the gift of the knowledge of God, but under the direction and tutelage of her husband she was to acquire it gradually. It is not without reason that St Paul said, 'For Adam was formed first, then Eve; and Adam was not seduced but the woman was seduced and fell into sin.'[109] In other words, it was through her that man sinned. For Paul calls him a sinner also when he says, 'in the likeness of the sin of Adam, who is a type of the One to come'.[110] But he says that Adam was not seduced.

[104] Gal. 5: 13.   [105] I Tim. 2: 12.
[106] The sense appears to be that woman's subjection symbolizes the beginning of human domination generally *and* that the Fall rendered more extreme the submission wherein she already—but in a 'bond of love'—served man: cf. Ch. 3, Aquinas 2.
[107] I Cor. 11: 7.   [108] Gal. 3: 28.
[109] I Tim. 2: 13–14.   [110] Rom. 5: 14.

In fact, Adam under interrogation did not say, 'The woman whom Thou gavest to be my companion seduced me and I ate'; but, 'She gave me fruit of the tree and I ate.' On the other hand, the woman said, 'The Serpent seduced me.'

6 Can we imagine that Solomon, a man of incredible wisdom, believed that there was any advantage in the worship of idols? But he was unable to resist the love of women drawing him into this evil....[111] So it was in the case of Adam. After the woman had been seduced and had eaten of the forbidden fruit and had given Adam some to eat with her, he did not wish to make her unhappy, fearing she would waste away without his support, alienated from his affections, and that this dissension would be her death. He was not overcome by the concupiscence of the flesh ... but by the sort of attachment and affection by which it often happens that we offend God while we try to keep the friendship of men.... I do not think that the wiles of the serpent by which the woman was seduced could have been in any way the means of his seduction.

Women at the Resurrection of the Body

FROM *CITY OF GOD** (*DE CIVITATE DEI:* 412–27)

7 (XXII. 17) Because of these sayings, 'Until we reach the perfection of manhood, the stature of the full maturity of Christ',[112] and 'Being shaped into the likeness of God's Son',[113] some people suppose that women will not keep their sex at the resurrection; but, they say, they will all rise again as men, since God made man out of clay, and woman out of man. For my part, I feel that theirs is the more sensible opinion who have no doubt that there will be both sexes in the resurrection. For in that life there will be no sexual lust, which is the cause of shame. For the first human beings, before their sin, 'were naked, the man and the woman, and they were not ashamed'.[114]

8 Thus, while all defects will be removed from those bodies, their essential nature will be preserved. Now a woman's sex is not a defect: it is natural. And in the resurrection it will be free of the necessity of

[111] 3 Kgs. 11: 1–11.
* Tr. Henry Bettenson, *St Augustine: City of God* (Harmondsworth: Pelican, 1972), 1057–8. © Henry Bettenson 1972. Reprinted by permission of Penguin Books Ltd. Latin text in CCSL 47–8 or PL 41.13–804.
[112] Eph. 4: 13; cf. the use of this in Ambrose 6 above.
[113] Rom. 8: 29.
[114] Gen. 2: 21.

intercourse and childbirth. However, the female organs will not subserve their former use; they will be part of a new beauty, which will not excite the lust of the beholder—there will be no lust in that life—but will arouse the praises of God for His wisdom and compassion, in that He not only created out of nothing but freed from corruption that which He had created.

9   He who established the two sexes will restore them both. And indeed, Jesus was questioned by the Sadducees, who denied the resurrection; and they asked to which of seven brothers a wife would belong, to whom they had all been married . . . ; and Jesus replied . . . 'in the resurrected life men and women do not marry; they are like the angels of God in heaven'.[115] That is, 'they are like them in immortality and felicity, not in body. . . .' Thus Christ denies the existence of marriage in the resurrected life; He does not deny the existence of women in heaven.

[115] Matt. 22: 29 ff.

3

The Legacy of the Church Fathers

Although they were succeeded by many notable theologians, the Church Fathers remained monumentally important, and of course their 'legacy' is ubiquitous among medieval authors, including many who are assigned to later chapters in this volume. The rationale of the present chapter is to review a diversity of essentially non-satirical contexts, within which there reappeared emphases from the Fathers which were hostile to women.

GRATIAN
(TWELFTH CENTURY)

FROM THE *DECRETUM**

One way for us to measure the continuing influence of the Fathers is to see how deeply embedded they are—together with their views on women—in the *Decretum*, one of the central reference books of the Middle Ages which was compiled by Master Gratian of Bologna from a wide variety of sources about 1140. It is among the most important collections of canon (i.e. ecclesiastical) law. Of its three parts, the second, from which the extract below is taken, consists of thirty-six *causae* or 'causes', divided into 'questions' and 'chapters'. *Causa* 33 raises questions concerning marriage and separation, and Question 5 takes up the issue of *continentia*, i.e. sexual self-denial. The obligations of both husband and wife are reviewed: *continentia* in marriage is only possible if both parties are in agreement; a wife cannot be forced to make a vow of chastity; the husband can refuse to comply with vows of chastity which a wife made without his consent, but cannot cancel vows which the wife made with his consent. A husband is entitled to the rewards of *continentia* even if, because of his wife's *incontinentia* (unwillingness to refrain), he is obliged to have sex with her. The underlying issue is the notion of sexual intercourse as a reciprocal 'debt' which, in line with St Paul's teaching, neither partner may formally withhold lest the other should turn elsewhere. But when it is a question of *abstinentia*, i.e. of other kinds of self-denial, such as fasting, reciprocity disappears and numerous statements by the Fathers are forthcoming to assert the husband's authority.[1] In reading these statements, we should remember that in the Middle Ages the observations of the Fathers 'were considered as genuine legal evidence and as such had the same standing as decisions of councils and papal dispensations'.[2]

* New translation by C. W. Marx, from *Corpus Juris Canonici*, i, ed. Aemilius Friedberg (Graz, 1955), col. 1253–6. © C. W. Marx 1992.
[1] See further Raming 1976, 31–2.
[2] Raming 1976, 33.

1   (xi) Vows of abstinence which a woman makes with her husband's consent; she is not compelled to abide by those vows if he forbids her. From Augustine, 'Questions on Numbers'. 'It is evident that the law has wanted woman to be under the authority of man so that none of the vows which she makes for the sake of abstinence may be enacted by her unless her husband has authorized it by giving his permission. But when the law wishes to consider if a man is at fault in the case of his first permitting and afterwards prohibiting promises, it does not judge that a woman may do what she had vowed because she was first permitted to do this by the man. Rather, the law says that the fault rests with the man because he denied what he had previously granted; its purpose is not, however, to grant permission to the woman to fulfil her vows. But the man may be condemned because he first granted and afterwards forbade it.'[3]

2   Gratian: From what has been described previously, it is apparent that neither a woman without the agreement of a man, nor a man without the consent of a woman is able to enact before God vows of continence. If, however, it shall be promised by one with the consent of the other, and if afterwards he who allowed it shall wish to set aside the vow of continence, nevertheless it is not possible, because in fulfilling the sexual obligation of marriage the woman holds power equally with a man. Thus if either one of them shall release the other from the marriage right, he or she is not then able to recall the other to the former servitude. But, since in other respects the man is the head of the woman and the woman is the body of the man, a woman is able to make vows of *abstinence,* with the man's permission; but if he prohibits her, she may not fulfil her promises, and this, as we have said, is because of the conditions of servitude by which she ought to be subject to the man in all things. On this see Augustine in his book of questions about Genesis:

3   (xii) Women ought to be subject to their husbands. 'It is the order of nature among human beings that women obey man and sons obey their parents, because it is justice in these matters that the lesser obey the greater.'[4]

---

[3] This is an abbreviated account of legislation in Num. 30: 3–16. From Augustine, *Quaestionum in Heptateuchum libri septem,* iv, *Quaestiones in Numeros,* in PL 34.717–48 (745–6).

[4] *Quaestionum in Heptateuchum libri septem,* i, *Quaestiones in Genesis,* in PL 34.547–98 (590). What Augustine calls the natural order simply amounts to the actual hierarchy operative at the time—thought of as a universal: Raming 1976, 35.

4 (XIII) *Man is the head of woman. From Augustine's 'Questions on the Old and New Testaments'.* 'The image of God is in man so that there may be one created from which the rest may originate, having the power of God, as it were his deputy, because he has the image of the one God, and so woman is not made in the image of God. So indeed it is said, "And God made man; He made him in the image of God." Also the Apostle said, "A man ought not to cover his head because it is the image and glory of God; but a woman covers her head because she is not the glory and image of God."'[5]

5 (XIV) *From the same source.* 'Here it is clear enough that women are subject to men and the law wishes wives to be almost servants, and it has been ordained that a man may give testimony against his wife by which she may be executed by stoning if his testimony may be shown to be true. On the other hand, he himself may not be executed by stoning if his testimony may be shown to be false, but he is merely chastized and denounced and ordered to remain forever with her whom he had wanted to imprison. However, in other instances, the law orders that person to be killed who might have harmed anyone through false testimony—if it can be proved; it is ordered that he be punished with the same punishment by which the accused would have been punished if the testimony were true.'[6]

6 (XV) *On the same topic: Jerome on the Epistle to Titus.* 'Since man is the head of woman, as Christ is the head of man,[7] any wife who does not submit to her husband, that is, to her head, is guilty of the same crime as is a man who does not submit to his head [Christ]. When she who is a Christian desires to rule over a man, the word of God is blasphemed, just as when the first commandment of God is condemned and brought to nothing or when the gospel of Christ is disgraced. This is against the law of nature and belief. Even pagan women serve their men according to the common law of nature.'[8]

7 (XVI) *It is necessary that woman follow the will of man in all things. From Augustine, 'Questions on Numbers'.* 'The law, therefore, has not wanted anyone to promise something to God against His will, so that

---

[5] Not authentic Augustine, but pseudo-Augustine, now known as Ambrosiaster. Here, and in 10 below, Ambrosiaster distorts 1 Cor. 11: 6 ff. by addition. *Quaestiones veteris et novi testamenti: Quaestiones ex utroque mixtim,* in PL 35.2301–92 (2320).
[6] This regulation is in Deut. 22: 13–21. Augustine, *Quaest. in Hept,* v, *Quaestiones in Deuteronium,* in PL 34.747–76 (762).
[7] 1 Cor. 11: 3.
[8] Jerome, *Commentarium in Epistolam ad Titum,* ii. 3, PL 26.582.

in the very promises to abstain from things which are lawful and granted, the authority of a woman may not have force but only that of a man.' ...[9]

8 (XVII) A woman has no power but in all things may be subject to the power of a man. From Ambrose, in his book of Questions on the Old Testament. 'It is agreed that a woman is subject to the power of a man, and has no authority; nor is she able to instruct nor to be a witness nor to make a promise nor to make a legal judgement.'[10]

9 (XVIII) From Ambrose on the Hexameron, in the tract on the fourth day. 'Adam was deceived by Eve, not Eve by Adam. It is just that the one whom the woman brought to sin may take control over her, lest woman fall again through self-indulgence.'[11]

10 (XIX) From Ambrose on the First Epistle to the Corinthians. 'A woman ought to cover her head since it is not the image of God. But she ought to wear this sign in order that she may be shown to be subordinate and because error was started through woman. In church she may not have her head uncovered but veiled on account of reverence for the bishop, and she is not allowed to speak because the bishop assumes the role of Christ. Therefore, just as it will be before the judge Christ, so may it be before the bishop because he is the deputy of the Lord: because of original sin she ought to be seen to be subordinate.'[12]

11 (XX) From Ambrose's book on Paradise. 'Nor is it without significance that woman was created not from earth itself, from which Adam was fashioned, but from the rib of Adam, so that we might know that there is one bodily nature in man and woman, one source of the human race. So in the beginning man and woman were not created from two sources, nor were two men created, nor were two women, but man was made first and then woman from him. God, wishing to establish humankind in one nature, began this from one original creature and preserved it from the possibility of many and different natures.'[13]

[9] *Quaest. in Numeros* (see n. 3), PL 34.745.
[10] Not Ambrose but Ambrosiaster, *Quaestiones ex veteri testamento,* in PL 35.2215–52 (2247). Woman's exclusion from legal office reflects Roman law.
[11] *Hexaemeron libri sex,* in PL 14.133–288 (277).
[12] *Commentarium in Epistolam B. Pauli ad Corinthios Primam,* in PL 17.193–290 (253–4). The author is Ambrosiaster; see Raming 1976, 34.
[13] *De Paradiso,* in PL 14.291–332 (315).

12 Gratian: Therefore it is completely obvious that the husband is so much the head of the wife that she is not allowed to offer to God any vows of *abstinence,* or to enter the religious life, without the permission of a man. Although such vows may be affirmed with the permission of her husband, she is not allowed to fulfil the promise by her own agency when the man wishes to revoke his permission. Where vows of *continence* are concerned, they can be offered by one with the permission of the other, but after the permission is granted, the promises cannot be given up for any reason.

HELOISE (1101–1164) AND ABELARD (1079–1142)

The authenticity of the correspondence attributed to Heloise and Abelard has long been disputed, among other things because the letters only seem to have come to light in the latter part of the thirteenth century.[14] For present purposes the letters are assumed authentic, though they would still warrant inclusion in this anthology if proved to be clever forgeries.

Abelard was one of the intellectual giants of the twelfth century in philosophy and theology. His passionate liaison with Heloise, a girl of conspicuous intellectual attainment who became his student, went sensationally wrong when it provoked her guardian Fulbert into castrating Abelard soon after the couple (much against the will of Heloise) had married. Both then retreated into the monastic life, Abelard eventually assisting with advice for her community. The couple's interaction is absorbing and subtle, as are the views on women which each expresses or implies. Heloise in effect gives a magnificent personal answer to misogyny's slurs about fickle and domineering women in the profundity and altruism of the love expressed for Abelard in her first letter: a love which she had not wanted to spoil with the 'chains' and self-interest she associated with marriage. Yet at the same time she absorbed not only the period's rhetoric about the 'weakness' of her sex (instanced in Abelard's own statement, 'men are naturally, both in mind and in body, stronger than women'[15]) but also the received disparagement of women as an impediment to the flowering male intellect. Despite various hints of pride in her sex,[16] Heloise was prepared to apply in real life the misogynistic rejection of marriage derived from Jerome's writing. Thus, she 'inadvertently becomes the first woman to argue for the devaluation of woman in western thought'.[17] However, there is a complication: her arguments are mainly *reported,* by Abelard to a third party in a letter called *The Story of his Misfortunes (Historia Calamitatum).* Heloise did later give them

[14] The controversy is summarized in Brooke 1989, 93–102; and Luscombe 1980.
[15] Letter 6: Scott Moncrieff 1974, 137.
[16] Radice 1974, 165–6.
[17] Allen 1985, 293. But her verdict on herself was not shared by those who commented on the couple's affair: Mann 1991, 53; and Dronke 1976.

general endorsement, though she pointedly added as a major motive her distrust of the mercenary streak in marriage;[18] but there is no knowing the extent to which Abelard 'polished' her views in reproducing them.

Heloise on Marriage

FROM *THE STORY OF HIS MISFORTUNES*[*]

1 What honour could she win, she protested, from a marriage which would dishonour me and humiliate us both?[19] The world would justly exact punishment from her if she removed such a light from its midst. Think of the curses, the loss to the Church and grief of philosophers which would greet such a marriage! Nature had created me for all mankind—it would be a sorry scandal if I should bind myself to a single woman and submit to such base servitude. She absolutely rejected this marriage; it would be nothing but a disgrace and a burden to me. Along with the loss to my reputation, she put before me the difficulties of marriage, which the apostle Paul exhorts us to avoid when he says: 'Has your marriage been dissolved? Do not seek a wife . . . those who marry will have pain and grief in this bodily life, and my aim is to spare you.' And again: 'I want you to be free from anxious care.'[20]

2 But if I would accept neither the advice of the Apostle nor the exhortations of the Fathers on the heavy yoke of marriage, at least, she argued, I could listen to the philosophers. . . . For example, St Jerome in the first book of his *Against Jovinian* recalls how Theophrastus sets out in considerable detail the unbearable annoyances of marriage and its endless anxieties, in order to prove by the clearest possible arguments that a man should not take a wife. . . .[21]

3 'Consider', she said, 'the true conditions for a dignified way of life. What harmony can there be between pupils and nursemaids, desks and cradles, books or tablets and distaffs, pen or stylus and spindles? Who can concentrate on thoughts of Scripture or philosophy and be able to endure babies crying, nurses soothing them with lullabies,

[18] Radice 1974, 113–14.
[*] Tr. Betty Radice, *The Letters of Abelard and Heloise* (Harmondsworth: Penguin, 1974), 70–4, 130–1, 101–2. © Betty Radice 1974. Reprinted by permission of Penguin Books Ltd. Latin text in Muckle 1950/1953/1955.
[19] Although ecclesiastics of the time not infrequently had mistresses and children (and Heloise had already borne Abelard's son), marriage would be a 'humiliation' as a bar to promotion, eclipsing his career.
[20] 1 Cor. 7: 27, 28, 32.
[21] See Ch. 2, Jerome 12 ff.

and all the noisy coming and going of men and women about the house? Will he put up with the constant muddle and squalor which small children bring into the home? ... Consequently, the great philosophers of the past have despised the world, not renouncing it so much as escaping from it, and have denied themselves every pleasure so as to find peace in the arms of philosophy alone.[22] The greatest of them, Seneca, gives this advice to Lucilius: "Philosophy is not a subject for idle moments. We must neglect everything else and concentrate on this, for no time is long enough for it. Put it aside for a moment, and you might as well give it up, for once interrupted it will not remain. We must resist all other occupations, not merely dispose of them but reject them."[23]

4 '... But if pagans and laymen could live in this way, though bound by no profession of faith, is there not a greater obligation on you, as clerk and canon, not to put base pleasures before your sacred duties, and to guard against being sucked down headlong into this Charybdis, there to lose all sense of shame and be plunged forever into a whirlpool of impurity?[24] If you take no thought for the privilege of a clerk, you can at least uphold the dignity of a philosopher, and let a love of propriety curb your shamelessness if the reverence due to God means nothing to you. Remember Socrates' marriage ...'

The story of Xanthippe is rehearsed (see Chapter 2, Jerome 20); after which is briefly mentioned Heloise's argument 'that the name of mistress instead of wife would be dearer to her'. Heloise's internalization of the ascetic male suspicion of woman becomes further apparent in Letter 3, where a sense of guilt about his injury—though 'we were both to blame'—prompts an anguished outburst setting herself in the lineage of Eve.

Heloise as Eve

FROM LETTER 3: HELOISE TO ABELARD

5 What misery for me—born as I was to be the cause of such a crime! Is it the general lot of women to bring total ruin on great men? Hence the warning about women in Proverbs: 'But now, my son, listen to me, attend to what I say: do not let your heart entice you into her ways, do not stray down her paths; she has wounded and

---

[22] A theme developed in *Ag. Jov.* ii. 9, and imitated by Abelard in *Theologia christiana*.

[23] Seneca, *Epistulae ad Lucilium*, 72.3.

[24] Cf. Ch. 4, Marbod 5.

laid low so many, and the strongest have all been her victims. Her house is the way to hell, and leads down to the halls of death.'[25] And in Ecclesiastes: 'I put all to the test . . . I find woman more bitter than death; she is a snare, her heart a net, her arms are chains. He who is pleasing to God eludes her, but the sinner is her captive.'[26]

6 It was the first woman in the beginning who lured man from Paradise, and she who had been created by the Lord as his helpmate became the instrument of his total downfall. And that mighty man of God, the Nazarite whose conception was announced by an angel, Delilah alone overcame; betrayed to his enemies and robbed of his sight, he was driven by his suffering to destroy himself along with his enemies.[27] Only the woman he had slept with could reduce to folly Solomon, wisest of all men; she drove him to such a pitch of madness that, although he was the man whom the Lord had chosen to build the temple in preference to his father David, who was a righteous man, she plunged him into idolatry until the end of his life, so that he abandoned the worship of God which he had preached and taught in word and writing.[28] Job, holiest of men, fought his last and hardest battle against his wife, who urged him to curse God.[29] The cunning arch-tempter well knew from repeated experience that men are most easily brought to ruin through their wives, and so he directed his usual malice against us too, and attacked you by means of marriage when he could not destroy you through fornication. Denied the power to do evil through evil, he effected evil through good.

7 At least I can thank God for this: the tempter did not prevail on me to do wrong of my own consent, like the women I have mentioned, though in the outcome he made me the instrument of his malice. . .

Although this *cherchez la femme* attitude was also offered at one point as a kind of excuse by Abelard to Heloise's uncle,[30] it is notable that Abelard generally accepted personal responsibility for the sexual initiative in their affair. But his view of woman was ambivalent. His high estimate of women's importance in Christian history can be seen below in Chapter 8. Yet as a commentator on Genesis, if anything, he disparaged Eve more sharply than

[25] Prov. 7: 24–7; in Ch. 1, Scripture 6.
[26] Eccles. 7: 27; in Ch. 1, Scripture 8.
[27] Samson, Solomon, and David are a conventional trio: see Ch. 2, Jerome 24.
[28] 3 Kgs. 8: 17–20; and 3 Kgs. 11: 1–8: but Heloise distinctively transforms plural ('strange women') into singular.
[29] Job 2: 9–10. Job's wife appears rarely in misogynistic writing.
[30] Radice 1974, 70.

others.[31] Moreover, his acceptance of the prevailing generalization that the sex was 'weaker' led to a condescending attitude to convents lacking masculine guidance—a touchy subject in the period but especially so for him, since his continuing association with Heloise in her community made tongues wag.

Abelard on the 'Weaker Sex'

FROM *THE STORY OF HIS MISFORTUNES*

8 The weaker sex needs the help of the stronger, so much so that the Apostle lays down that the man must always be over the woman, as her head, and as a sign of this he orders her always to have her head covered.[32] And so I am much surprised that the custom should have been long established in convents of putting abbesses in charge of women just as abbots are set over men, and of binding women by profession according to the same rule, for there is so much in the Rule which cannot be carried out by women, whether in authority or subordinate. In several places too, the natural order is overthrown to the extent that we see abbesses and nuns ruling the clergy who have authority over the people,[33] with opportunities of leading them on to evil desires in proportion to their dominance, holding them as they do beneath a heavy yoke. The satirist has this in mind when he says that 'Nothing is more intolerable than a rich woman.'[34]

ST THOMAS AQUINAS (1225–1274)

In his *Summa*, the Dominican philosopher-theologian St Thomas conducted a systematic review of Christian doctrine. He was extensively influenced by Augustine: for example, he settled the question 'whether Eve's sin was graver than Adam's' against Eve by quoting Augustine's arguments that Adam did not share the presumption which made her believe the serpent, and that Adam's sin was lessened because committed for the sake of companionship.[35] Wherever possible, however, he wanted to reconcile the teachings of Augustine and other Fathers with Aristotelian philosophy, which had quite recently become available in the Latin West. In the case of doctrine on women, his best efforts could not mask a disparity between Aristotle's concept of her as 'defective male' and the Church's belief that, as a

[31] McLaughlin 1975, 305–6.
[32] I Cor. 11: 5: cf. Gratian 4 and 10.
[33] Controversy had been stirred by the situation at Fontevrault, where the abbess was exercising authority over male clergy assigned to her nuns' service.
[34] See Ch. 1, Juv. 8. Abelard felt strongly that abbesses should not come from powerful families or conduct themselves in lordly fashion, but saw the male supervision as consultative (Radice 1974, 209–14).
[35] *S. Th.* IIa IIae. Q. 163 art. 4; cf. Ch. 2, Augustine 4 and 6.

creation of God, woman—even if weaker—must be undefective (see 1–3 below).

FROM THE *SUMMA THEOLOGIAE** (1266–1272)
1a. 92, article 1

1   Should woman have been made in that original creation of things? THE FIRST POINT: 1. It seems that woman ought not to have been produced in the original production of things. For the Philosopher says that the female is a male *manqué*.[36] But nothing *manqué* or defective should have been produced in the first establishment of things; so woman ought not to have been produced then.

2. Again, subjection and inferiority are a result of sin; for it was after sin that woman was told, 'Thou shalt be under the power of the man';[37] and Gregory says that where we have done no wrong, we are all equal.[38] Yet woman is by nature of lower capacity and quality than man; for the active cause is always more honourable than the passive, as Augustine says.[39] So woman ought not to have been produced in the original production of things before sin....

2   ON THE OTHER HAND, there is Genesis: 'It is not good for man to be alone; let us make him a help that is like himself.'[40]

REPLY: It was absolutely necessary to make woman, for the reason Scripture mentions, as a help for man; not indeed to help him in any other work, as some have maintained, because where most work is concerned man can get help more conveniently from another man than from a woman; but to help him in the work of procreation.[41] ...

Hence: 1. Only as regards nature in the individual is the female something defective and *manqué*. For the active power in the seed of the male tends to produce something like itself, perfect in masculinity; but the procreation of a female is the result either of the debility of the active power, of some unsuitability of the material, or of some change effected by external influences, like the south wind, for example, which is damp, as we are told by Aristotle.[42]

---

* Tr. Edmund Hill OP, *St Thomas Aquinas, Summa Theologiae*, xiii (London: Blackfriars, in conjunction with Eyre & Spottiswoode, and New York: McGraw-Hill Book Co., 1963), 35–9. © Blackfriars 1963. Reprinted by permission of Cambridge University Press.
[36] See Ch. 1, Aristotle 6.
[37] Gen. 3: 16.
[38] *Moralia in Job* XXI. 15; PL 76.203.
[39] *De Genesi ad litteram* XII. 16; PL 34.467.
[40] Gen. 2: 18.
[41] See Ch. 2, Augustine 2.
[42] Aristotle, *Generation of Animals* 766ᵇ.

But with reference to nature in the species as a whole, the female is not something *manqué*, but is according to the tendency of nature, and is directed to the work of procreation. Now the tendency of the nature of a species as a whole derives from God, who is the general author of nature. And therefore when He established a nature, He brought into being not only the male but the female too.

2. Subjection is of two kinds; one is that of slavery, in which the ruler manages the subject for his own advantage, and this sort of subjection came in after sin. But the other kind of subjection is domestic or civil, in which the ruler manages his subjects for *their* advantage and benefit. And this sort of subjection would have obtained even before sin.[43] For the human group would have lacked the benefit of order had some of its members not been governed by others who were wiser. Such is the subjection in which woman is by nature subordinate to man, because the power of rational discernment is by nature stronger in man.

In the second Article some objections to Eve's creation from man are raised, and answered as follows.

3 REPLY: It was right for woman to be formed from man in the original establishment of things, for reasons that do not apply to the other animals. In the first place, this was desirable in order to maintain a certain style and dignity for the first man, by making him, in virtue of his likeness to God, the original[44] of his whole kind, just as God is the original of the whole universe. So Paul says that God 'made the whole of mankind from one'.[45]

In the second place, this was good in order to make the man love the woman more and stick to her more inseparably, knowing that she had been brought forth from himself. . . .

Thirdly, as Aristotle says, 'with man male and female are not only joined together for purposes of procreation, as with the other animals, but to establish a home life, in which man and woman work together at some things, and in which the man is head of the woman'.[46] So the woman was rightly formed from the man, as her origin and chief. . . .

---

[43] See Ch. 2, Augustine 3.
[44] 'Original' and 'origin' in these paragraphs translate *principium*, a key term also in St Thomas's discussion of the primacy of father over mother: see Aquinas extract in Ch. 1.
[45] Acts 17: 26.
[46] *Ethics* VIII, 12; 1162ª.

94   THE LEGACY OF THE CHURCH FATHERS

GOTTFRIED VON STRASSBURG

FROM *TRISTAN** (C.1210?)

Gottfried's adaptation of the Tristan and Isolde story projects the lovers with
a strange blend of partisan lyricism and knowing cynicism. Their return at
one point to endure the torment of suspicion and surveillance at the court of
Isolde's husband Mark generates an ambivalent exoneration of the heroine
and womankind. It is ambivalent because Gottfried roots his enthusiasm for
woman in an assumption (reminiscent of the Fathers) that woman at her
summit approximates to man, by transcending the self-destructiveness
inherited from the 'daughters of Eve'.

1   (17971) And since women are heirs to it, and nature promotes it
in them, all honour and praise to the woman who nevertheless
succeeds in abstaining! For when a woman grows in virtue despite
her inherited instincts and gladly keeps her honour, reputation, and
person intact, she is only a woman in name, but in spirit she is a
man![47] One should judge well of all her doings, and honour and
esteem them. When a woman lays aside her woman's nature and
assumes the heart of a man, it is as if the fir dripped with honey, the
hemlock yielded balm, or what rooted as a nettle bore roses above
ground! What can ever be so perfect in a woman as when, in alliance
with honour at her side, she does battle with her body for the rights
of both body and honour? She must so direct the combat that she
does justice to them both and so attends to each that the other is not
neglected. She is no worthy woman who forsakes her honour for her
body, or her body for her honour, when circumstance so favours her
that she may vindicate them both. Let her deny neither the one nor
the other, let her sustain the two, through joy and through sorrow,
however she sets about it. Heaven knows, a woman has to rise in
merit at the cost of great effort.[48] Let her commend her ways to
seemly moderation,[49] let her restrain her instincts and adorn herself
and her conduct with it!

---

* Tr. A. T. Hatto, *Gottfried von Strassburg: Tristan* (Harmondsworth: Penguin,
1960), 277–8. © A. T. Hatto 1960. Reprinted by permission of Penguin Books Ltd.
   [47] Cf. Ch. 2, Ambrose 6; other parallel statements are quoted in Raming 1976, 162;
and Bullough 1973, 499.
   [48] The doctrine of woman's 'handicap', reiterated in Ch. 8, Marbod 6, and Ch. 8,
Abelard 5.
   [49] From what follows it seems that the 'moderation' in question is largely the
avoidance of casual sexual gratification.

*RULE FOR ANCHORESSES (ANCRENE RIWLE)**

This medieval English prose treatise of the thirteenth century (or earlier) addresses young women who have voluntarily secluded themselves in individual cells or 'anchorages' in order to devote themselves to the religious life. In many respects the advice is humane and sympathetic, but it is conspicuously conditioned by the Fathers' obsession with female beauty as a threat which it is women's own responsibility to neutralize. After laying out a programme of daily prayer in Part I, its author turns to the question of controlling bodily senses in Part II, beginning with the risk of the wandering eye. Anchoresses should not be so foolhardy as to allow themselves to 'peep out' of their cells, for this is to repeat the perilous glance of a Dinah or an Eve. (Dinah had already been a negative model in Jerome: but she was more recently so in the commentaries by St Bernard and Hugh of St Victor which the *Rule*-author seems to have consulted.[50])

Perils of Seeing, and Being Seen

FROM PART II, 'THE CUSTODY OF THE SENSES'

I 'Dina, the daughter of Jacob, went out to see the strange women.'[51] There is a story told in Genesis of a maiden called Dina, the daughter of Jacob, who went out to look at the strange women. It does not say that she looked at men. What happened, do you think, as a result of that looking? She lost her maidenhood and became a harlot. Later, also as a result of it, the promises of great patriarchs were broken, and a great city burned to the ground, and the king and his son and the men of the city were killed and the women led away; her father and her brothers, noble princes though they were, were outlawed. This is what came of her looking. All these things the Holy Ghost caused to be written down in order to warn women against their foolish eyes. And observe that Dina's evil was not the result of her seeing Sichem the son of Hamor, with whom she sinned, but the result of her allowing him to look at her; for what he did to her was, at the beginning, much against her will.

2 Bethsabee also, by unclothing herself before David's eyes, caused him to sin with her, even though he was so holy a king and a prophet of God.[52] And after all this, a weak man comes forward, thinks

---

* Tr. M. B. Salu, *The Ancrene Riwle* (London: Burns & Oates, 1955), 23–5, 120–2. © Burns & Oates. Reprinted by permission of the publisher.
[50] Robertson 1989, 115–25, discusses afresh the *Rule*'s modifications of these sources; and see Jerome, Letter 107.6.
[51] Gen. 34: 1 ff.
[52] 2 Kgs. 11: 2 ff.; see Ch. 1, Scripture 4–5.

himself formidable in his wide hood and closed cloak, and wishes to see some young anchoresses, and must needs look, as if he were made of stone, to see how the beauty of a woman whose face is not burned by the sun pleases him, saying that she may look without fear at holy men, such as he himself is, indeed, in his wide sleeves! But oh, overweening man, do you not hear what happened to David, the darling of God, of whom God Himself said, 'I have found a man according to my own heart'?[53] This man, whom God Himself in these precious words called His chosen king and prophet, this man, through looking at a woman while she was bathing, let out his heart and betrayed himself so far that he committed three most grave and deadly sins: adultery with Bethsabee, the lady on whom he had looked; treachery; and murder of his true soldier, Urias her lord. And you, a sinful man, have the hardihood to cast your foolish eyes upon a young woman.

3   Ah, my dear sisters, if anyone insists on seeing you, believe no good of it and trust him the less for it. I do not want anyone to see you without the special leave of your director, for all those three sins which I have just spoken of, and all the evil that came about through Dina, of which I spoke above, all happened, not because the women looked lustfully upon the men, but because they unclothed themselves before the eyes of men, thus being the occasion of sin in them.[54]

4   For this reason it was commanded in God's name in the Old Law that a pit should always be covered; and if an animal fell into an uncovered pit, the man who had uncovered the pit had to pay the penalty. These are very terrible words for the woman who shows herself to men's sight. It is she who is represented by the man who uncovers the pit. The pit is her fair face, and her white neck, and her light eye, and her hand if she holds it out before his eyes; and further, her speech is a pit, if it is not controlled, and all other things whatsoever that belong to her, through which sinful love may be aroused. All this our Lord calls a pit. He commands that this pit should always be covered with a lid, lest any animal should fall into it and perish in sin. 'Animal' here means the animal man who gives no thought to God and who does not use his reason as a man ought to do, but goes on to fall into the pit of which I am speaking, if he

---

[53] Acts 13: 27.

[54] Having just attributed responsibility to the males (cf. Ch. 8, *Dives* 16), the author now reverts towards the kind of judgement made in Ch. 2, Tert. 4–6.

finds it uncovered. But the judgement on the woman who uncovers the pit is very stern, for she must pay for the animal that has fallen into it. She is guilty before our Lord of the animal's death and must answer for his soul on the Day of Judgement, and make restitution for the loss of the animal when she has no coin but herself. This is a hard penalty; but it is God's judgement and His command that it must be paid without fail, because she uncovered the pit in which the animal perished. You uncover this pit, you who do anything by which a man is bodily tempted by you, even though you may be unaware of it. Have great fear of this judgement; and if the man is tempted in such a way that he commits mortal sin through you in any way, even though it is not with you, but with desire for you, or if he tries to yield with another person to the temptation awakened in him through your doing, be quite sure of the judgement: you must pay for the animal because you laid open the pit, and unless you are absolved, you must, as they say, suffer the rod, that is, feel pain for his sin. The dog goes gladly in wherever he finds an entrance.

Reason Grown Weak

FROM PART IV, 'TEMPTATIONS'

5 We read in the Book of Kings[55] that Isboseth lay sleeping and had appointed a woman to be doorkeeper, who was winnowing wheat. Rechab and Baana, the sons of Remmon, came and found the woman, having stopped her winnowing, fallen asleep, and they went in and slew the wretched Isboseth who had guarded himself so badly. It is very necessary to understand the meaning of this. The Hebrew 'Isboseth' means in English 'a man confused', and is not he indeed confused and out of his mind who lies down to sleep in the midst of his enemies? The doorkeeper is Reason, whose duty it is to winnow the wheat, to separate the straw and chaff from the clean grain, that is, through unceasing discrimination, distinguish good from evil, put the wheat into the granary, and always blow away the devil's chaff, which is fit for nothing but to increase the smoke of hell. But the dazed Isboseth, see with what confusion he acted! He appointed a woman to be doorkeeper. A poor sort of guardian! But alas for all those who do the like! 'Woman' is Reason grown weak when it should be manful, stalwart and bold in true faith. The keeper of the door lies down to sleep as soon as one begins to consent to sin and to

---

55 2 Kgs. 4: 5–6.

allow desire to enter and enjoyment to develop. When the sons of Remmon, the children of hell, find a doorkeeper thus negligent and lacking in vigilance, they go in and slay Isboseth, that is, the dazed spirit which is off its guard, sleepy and unwatchful. . . . St Gregory says: 'Isboseth would not have died his sudden death had he not appointed a woman, that is, a lax custodian, to guard the entrance to his soul.'[56] All this misfortune came about because of the sleeping of the doorkeeper, who was not waking and on guard; not like a man, but like a woman, easily overthrown.

[56] *Moralia*, bk. i; in *PL* 75.549.

4

The Satirical Tradition in Medieval Latin

To be 'lettered', in the Middle Ages, generally presupposed an education for a career in the Church. The language of the Church was Latin. Not surprisingly, amongst a readership of 'clerks' or *clerici* (those in, or intending, a career in the priesthood, which in theory was celibate), there was a continuous recycling of received misogyny. Some of this was probably done in a facetious spirit, seeking to upstage tradition. But one might also view it as a form of individual or group therapy in support of celibacy.

Among influential writers who dabbled in misogynistic material, John of Salisbury (*Policraticus, c.* 1159) would most warrant inclusion here—were it not that his main contribution is to repeat Theophrastus verbatim. The selection offered ranges through several other texts, each well known in its period, including formal invective in poetry and prose, pseudo-rustic mock-vision, and anecdotal sermon, but beginning with a little exercise in corrosive definition whose first line was later immortalized by Chaucer, when he assigned it to Chauntecleer the cockerel in the *Nun's Priest's Tale*.[1]

THE LIFE OF SECUNDUS*
(LATE TWELFTH CENTURY)

What is Woman?

A Greek Life of 'Secundus', perhaps first composed as early as the second century AD, represents a 'philosopher' of this name as having sworn himself to silence out of horror at the circumstances of his mother's death. (She committed suicide after failing his own test of her chastity.) Even Emperor Hadrian's threats would not break his silence. Hadrian had to be content with terse written answers to his questions ('What is the Universe? God? Day? . . . the Earth? Man? Beauty? Woman? a Friend?', etc.). This biography, together with its 'verbally smart definitions',[2] circulated for centuries in the East before one Willelmus brought a Greek copy back from Constantinople to the abbey at St Denis in 1167, and translated it into Latin.[3] This Latin version in turn had a great vogue in the West. The 'woman' answer was easy to pluck out and add to one's manuscript notebook of quotations.

[1] *Canterbury Tales* VII. 3163–4.
* New translation by Alcuin Blamires from Ben E. Perry (ed.), *Secundus the Silent Philosopher*, Philological Monographs no. 22, ed. Walton Morris (Ithaca: American Philological Association, 1964), 96.
[2] Perry 1964, 1.
[3] Perry 1964, 23–4.

What is Woman?—Man's undoing;[4] an insatiable animal; perpetual trouble and non-stop combat; man's daily ruin; a storm in the home; an impediment to peace of mind; the wreck of a weak-willed man; instrument of adultery; expensive war; the very worst creature and heaviest burden; fatal snake; human property.[5]

MARBOD OF RENNES (c. 1035–1123)

THE FEMME FATALE* (DE MERETRICE), FROM THE BOOK WITH TEN CHAPTERS (LIBER DECEM CAPITULORUM), CHAPTER III

Marbod studied and then taught at the cathedral school of Angers, becoming Bishop of Rennes in Brittany in his sixties. He was a keen writer on a wide range of topics, often cultivating a difficult form, the leonine hexameter. The *Book with Ten Chapters* seems to have been written in old age; it looks back over a literary career that began in what now seems to him youthful levity. The second chapter surveys the stages of human life, drawing particular attention to the licentious behaviour sometimes associated with the schools. Then come the twin chapters—a diptych, as it were—attacking and praising woman. The eulogy is to be found in Chapter 8 below.

1   Countless are the traps which the scheming enemy[6] has set throughout the world's paths and plains: but among them the greatest—and the one scarcely anybody can evade—is woman. Woman the unhappy source, evil root, and corrupt offshoot, who brings to birth every sort of outrage throughout the world. For she instigates quarrels, conflicts, dire dissensions; she provokes fighting between old friends, divides affections, shatters families.[7] But these are trivia I speak of: she dislodges kings and princes from the throne, makes nations clash, convulses towns, destroys cities, multiplies slaughters, brews deadly poisons. She hurls conflagration as she rampages through farmsteads and fields. In sum, there lurks in the

[4] Latin *Hominis confusio*: Willelmus derived this notorious opening expression from a corruption in his Greek MS of a phrase meaning 'the object of man's desire'.

[5] Apparently mistranslating the Greek for 'service rendered in the procreation of men'. The expressions 'insatiable animal' and 'non-stop combat' are also more abusive than the Greek: Perry 1964, 36–7.

* New translation by Alcuin Blamires from Marbod of Rennes, *Liber decem capitulorum*, ed. Rosario Leotta (Rome: Herder, 1984); see also PL 171 cols. 1698–9. Ch. III is alternatively entitled 'The Whore' (*De meretrice*), or 'The Evil Woman' (*De muliere mala*, used by Leotta) in the MSS.

[6] The devil. For 'traps', cf. Eccles. 7: 27, in Ch. 1, Scripture 8. The metaphor often reappears, e.g. in *The Fifteen Joys of Marriage*: Pitts 1985.

[7] Cf. Ch. 1, Ovid 6, and Ch. 2, Jerome 21.

universe no manifestation of evil in which woman does not claim some part for herself.[8]

2 (15) Her sex is envious, capricious, irascible, avaricious, as well as intemperate with drink and voracious in the stomach. She relishes revenge and is always panting for the upper hand, without the slightest qualm about crime or deceit so long as she wins; she is intent on achieving whatever she wants by fair means or foul. To her nothing seems illicit if it is pleasurable. She belies her own appearance as she goes, concealing her squalid secrets, a shameless liar who is by no means innocent of the crime of intrigue. Here gaping at wealth, there burning with the flame of lust, she is a babbler, and unreliable, and—on top of so much evil—arrogant.

3 (25) Armed with these vices woman subverts the world; woman the sweet evil, compound of honeycomb and poison,[9] spreading honey on her sword to transfix the hearts of the wise. Who urged the first parent to taste what was forbidden? A woman. Who drove a father to corrupt his daughters? A woman. Who eliminated a man's strength when his hair was cut off? A woman. Who lopped off the sacred head of a righteous man with a sword? A woman, who piled crime on her mother's crime, and branded shocking incest with yet more shocking murder.[10]

4 (34) Who led astray David the holy and who led wise Solomon astray with sweet charm so that one turned adulterer and the other committed sacrilege—who but seductive woman?[11] I pass over many women catalogued on the sacred page: the horrifying Jezebel, Athalia who dared to commit heinous sin,[12] and more whom it is unnecessary to enumerate. I mention only in passing many who are traditionally spoken of in the work of poets and historians: Eriphyle, Clytemnestra, Belides, Procne, and that harlot bred by Leda who was fought over in the ten-year Trojan war of nations, and others too whose stories the tragic poets often rehearse for the people.[13]

[8] Cf. Juv. *Satire* VI, 242–3.
[9] Cf. Ch. 1, Ovid 5, 'taste of honey'.
[10] Respectively, Eve; Lot's two daughters (the eldest proposed that they make him drunk then lie with him to 'preserve his seed': Gen. 19: 31–8); Delilah; and Salome, who added murder to the crime of incest (between her mother Herodias and Herod Antipas) by demanding the head of John the Baptist (Matt. 14: 1–11).
[11] Cf. Ch. 2, Jerome 24.
[12] Athalia usurped the throne by murdering heirs to it (4 Kgs. 11: 1 ff.), and Jezebel pursued the prophets sadistically (esp. 3 Kgs. 21: 7 ff.); the two are recalled in *Math.* II. 2550–66).
[13] On Eriphyle, Clytemnestra, and Procne, see Ch. 1, Ovid 7 and 3; Helen of Troy

5   (45) As exemplar of this dire monster to be avoided, ancient wisdom contrived the terrifying Chimaera. Not undeservedly, it is said a threefold shape was given to it: the front part lion, the rear a serpent's tail, and the middle parts nothing but red hot flame.[14] This image mimics the nature of a harlot, in that she seizes spoil to carry off in her lion's mouth, while feigning to be something with an impressive, quasi-noble appearance. With this façade she consumes her captives in the flames of love in which nothing of substance or weight is seen; only frivolous, irrational, furious lust. The back parts are crammed with deadly poison because death and damnation terminate sensual pleasures.

6   (58) Turbulent Charybdis, who sucks in and draws to its death everything near her, bears female form.[15] The Siren is also like this: she entices fools by singing lovely melodies, draws them towards her once they are enticed, and when they are drawn in she plunges them into the annihilating abyss. But Ulysses evaded this fate. He closed his crew's ears to the notorious songs while physically restraining himself from being able to change course, by being lashed with ropes to the mast of the speeding ship. No less successfully did he elude evil Circe's sweet poisons. Those who drank them took on the shapes of wild beasts, transformed into the likeness of dogs and filthy swine. They signify degenerates and sensualists living the life of a herd of animals under the sway of lust.

7   (71) Oh race of men! Beware the honied poisons, the sweet songs and the pull of the dark depths. Do not let the charm of contrived appearances seduce you; be in dread of the destructive flames and the fierce serpent. If a beautiful woman courts you aiming to deceive you, and if you have such confidence in yourself that you stout-heartedly prepare to enter the fray, you will deceive yourself with ignorance, if you scorn the darts of the enemy. It is not the rule in this type of struggle that you can win by close combat. It is better to undertake retreat and attain safety with your feet. If you run, you will get away: if you approach, you will be caught.[16] But I warn you

(daughter of Leda) was 'disputed over' in a catastrophic war such as the poem has already blamed on women; see also Ch.2, Jerome 21.

[14] The Chimaera's middle was usually (as in Map 6 below) described as a she-goat's, but was fire in Ovid, *Met.* IX. 647. A similar moralization is in Bernardus Silvestris 1979, 69.

[15] Antiquity portrayed Scylla and Charybdis (rocks flanking the treacherous Strait of Messina) as mythological monsters preying on ships; cf. Ch. 6, *Corb.* 14.)

[16] Recalling some famous advice in Ovid's *Cures for Love* (79 ff. and 213 ff.)

not to look back at her, since anyone who toys with desire can be turned to stone by the very sight of the Gorgon.[17]

8 (84) Whoever seeks earth's calm seas in the ship of the Church in order to arrive at the desired harbour of the homeland—avoiding sweet-sounding songs and dangerous attractions—should block up and protect the hearing with lawful doctrine and stay fastened to the timber with rope of divine fear. The timber is the cross our salvation, like a ship's mast. Nor is it without sailyards, which are the arms of the cross.

WALTER MAP (1140–c.1209)

THE LETTER OF VALERIUS TO RUFFINUS, AGAINST MARRIAGE* (C.1180)

Walter Map was a member of Henry II's court and later Archdeacon of Oxford. He wrote this letter around 1180, and at first (because of his use of the pseudonym) it was credited not to him, but usually to the ancient Roman author of a book of 'Notable Deeds and Sayings', Valerius Maximus. Eventually Map reclaimed it by inserting it into his capacious work, Courtiers' Trifles (De nugis curialium).

1   I had a friend who lived the life of a philosopher; after many visits over a long time I once noticed that he had changed in his dress, his bearing and his expression: he sighed a lot, his face was pale and his dress vulgarly ostentatious; he said little and was sombre, but was arrogant in a strange way; he had lost his old wit and jollity. He said he was not well, and indeed he wasn't. I saw him wandering about alone, and in so far as respect for me allowed he refused to speak to me. I saw a man in the grip of Venus' paralysis: he seemed all suitor, not at all a philosopher. However, I hoped that he would recover after his lapse: I pardoned what I didn't know; I thought it was a joke, not something brutally serious: he planned not to be loved but to be wived—he wanted to be not Mars but Vulcan.[18] My mind failed me; because he was bent on death, I began to die with him. I spoke to him, but was repulsed. I sent people to talk to him, and when he wouldn't listen to them I said 'An evil beast hath devoured him.'[19] To

[17] Medusa.
* Tr. and © A. G. Rigg. Latin text in Walter Map, De Nugis Curialium, Courtiers' Trifles, ed. and tr. by M. R. James, rev. C. N. L. Brooke and R. A. B. Mynors (Oxford: Clarendon Press, 1983), 287–313.
[18] Vulcan was Venus' husband; Mars her lover.
[19] Gen. 37: 33.

fulfil all the good turns of friendship I sent him a letter in which I altered the names, and called myself (Walter) Valerius and him (John, a red-head [Lat. *rufus*]) Ruffinus, and called the letter 'the letter of Valerius to Ruffinus the philosopher, against marrying'.

2   I am forbidden to speak, and I cannot keep silent. I hate the cranes, the voice of the night-owl, the screech-owl and the other birds which gloomily predict with their wails the sadness of foul winter, and you mock the prophecies of disaster which will surely come true if you continue as you are. Therefore I am forbidden to speak, for I am a prophet not of pleasure but of truth.

3   I love the nightingale and the blackbird, for with their soft harmony they herald the joy of the gentle breeze, and above all the swallow,[20] which fills the season of longed-for joy with its fullness of delights, and I am not deceived. You love parasites and hangers-on with their sweet flatteries, and above all Circe who pours on you joys full of sweet-scented delight, to deceive you: I cannot keep silent, lest you are turned into a pig or an ass.[21]

4   The servant of Babel pours out for you honeyed poison, which 'moveth itself aright'[22] and delights and leads astray your spirit: therefore I am forbidden to speak. I know that 'at the last it biteth like a serpent' and will give a wound which will admit no antidote: therefore I cannot keep silent.

5   You have many to persuade you to pleasure—and to your peril; I am a stumbling speaker of bitter truth which makes you vomit: therefore I am forbidden to speak. The voice of the goose is criticized among swans which are taught only to please, but it taught the senators to save the city from fire, the treasure-houses from plunder, and themselves from the arrows of their foes.[23] Perhaps you too will realize with the senators, for you are no fool, that the swans sing death, and the goose screeches safety: therefore I cannot keep silent.

6   You are all afire with longing, and, seduced by the nobility of its fine head, do not realize that you are seeking the Chimaera;[24] you refuse to recognize that that three-formed monster is graced with the

---

[20] This word usually means 'nightingale', but clearly Map had a different bird in mind from the first.
[21] i.e., by Circe: cf. Marbod 6 above.
[22] Prov. 23: 31.
[23] Alluding to a legend of how geese saved Rome from an attack by the Gauls.
[24] Cf. Marbod 5 above.

face of a noble lion, is sullied by the belly of a stinking goat, and is armed with the tail of a poisonous serpent: therefore I am forbidden to speak.

7 Ulysses was enticed by the harmony of the Sirens, but, because he knew the voices of the Sirens and the drinks of Circe, he restrained himself with the chains of virtue, in order to avoid the whirlpool.[25] I trust in the Lord and hope that you will imitate Ulysses, not Empedocles, who was overcome by his philosophy (or rather, melancholy), and chose Etna as his tomb.[26] I hope you will take notice of the parable you hear, I cannot keep silent.

8 But your present flame, by which the worse choice pleases you, is stronger than the flame which draws you to me; therefore, lest the greater flame draws the lesser to it, and I myself perish, I am forbidden to speak. That I may speak with the spirit by which I am yours, let the two flames be weighed in any scale, equal or not, and let your decision, whatever it is, be at my risk: you must pardon me, for the impatience of the love I have for you will not let me keep silent.

9 After the first creation of man the first wife of the first Adam sated the first hunger by the first sin, against God's command. The sin was the child of Disobedience, which will never cease before the end of the world to drive women tirelessly to pass on to the future what they learned from their mother. My friend, a disobedient wife is dishonour to a man: beware.

10 The Truth which cannot be deceived said of the blessed David, 'I have found a man according to my heart.'[27] But by love of a woman he fell conspicuously from adultery to homicide, to fulfil the saying 'scandals never come singly'.[28] For every iniquity is rich in followers, and whatever house it enters, it hands over to be soiled by abuse. My friend, Bathsheba was silent, and spoke no wrong; yet she became the spur which caused the fall of her perfect husband, the arrow of death for her innocent spouse. Is she innocent who strives with both eloquence, like Samson's Delilah, and beauty, like Bathsheba, when

[25] Cf. Marbod 6 above.
[26] See Ovid, *Met.* XIV, and Horace, *Ars poetica* 465–6, stating that Empedocles coolly jumped into burning Etna.
[27] I Kgs. 13: 14. Map introduces the familiar trio of men 'brought low' by women—David, Samson, Solomon: cf. Ch. 2, Jerome 24.
[28] Matt. 18: 7

the latter's beauty triumphed alone, even without intending to?[29] If you are no closer than David to the heart of God, do not doubt that you too can fall.

11   Solomon, Sun of men, treasure of God's delights, singular home of wisdom, was clouded over by the ink of darkness and lost the light of his soul, the smell of his glory, and the glory of his house by the witchcraft of women: finally, he bowed down before Baal, and from a priest of the Lord was turned into a servant of the devil, so that he can be seen to have fallen from a higher precipice than Phoebus in the fall of Phaëton, when he became Admetus' shepherd instead of Jupiter's Apollo.[30] My friend, if you are not wiser than Solomon—and no man is—you are not too great to be bewitched by a woman. Open your eyes and see.

12   The very best woman (who is rarer than the phoenix)[31] cannot be loved without the bitterness of fear, anxiety, and frequent misfortune. Wicked women, however—who swarm so abundantly that no place is free from their wickedness—sting sharply when they are loved; they give their time to tormenting a man until his body is divided from his soul. My friend, it is a pagan saying 'Take care to whom you give'; the proper advice is 'Take care to whom you give yourself.'

13   Lucretia, Penelope, and the Sabine women carried the banners of chastity and (with few followers) brought back their prizes. My friend, there are no Lucretias, Penelopes or Sabine women now:[32] beware of them all.

14   Arrayed against the ranks of the Sabine women are Scylla, daughter of Nisus, and Myrrha, daughter of Cynaras, and behind them come many crowds of all the vices, assembled in an army to bring sighs, groans, and finally hell to their captives. My friend, so that you don't fall prey to these merciless predators, do not fall asleep in their path when they pass by.

[29] Cf. Ch. 1, Scripture 4; and, on the question of 'intention'. Ch. 3, *Rule 4*; and Ch. 8, *Dives 16*.

[30] Appears to confuse a punishment suffered by Apollo (Phoebus) with the story of his son Phaëton's misdirection of Phoebus' chariot.

[31] In Theophrastus (Ch. 2, Jerome 16), a good woman is a 'rare bird'; in Juv. (Ch. 1 Juv. 4) a 'black swan'. Map's modification, 'phoenix' (the legendary unique bird which immolated itself every 500 years, to be reborn from its ashes), is imitated in Ch. 6, *RR 8*, where 'white crows' are added.

[32] In Ovid, Penelope and the Sabine women were exemplars of chastity, Scylla and Myrrha of wild passion: Ch. 1, Ovid 7, and 6, and 1.

15 Jupiter was king of the earth, and was also called king of heaven, because of his singular strength of body and incomparable refinement of mind; yet he was compelled to run after Europa, bellowing like a bull.[33] My friend, you see that even one whose virtue raised him above heaven was lowered to the level of the beasts by a woman. A woman will drive you too to bellowing, if you are not stronger than Jupiter, whose strength was unmatched.

16 Phoebus first encircled the whole world with the rays of his wisdom, and so alone deserved the glory of the name 'Sun'. He was besotted with love for Leucothoe, bringing shame on himself and death on her; for a long time he suffered an eclipse, was changed, and frequently lost his brightness (which the whole world needed).[34] My friend, avoid Leucothoe, so that your inner light does not turn into darkness.

17 Mars earned the title 'god of warriors' because of the well known frequency of his triumphs, which he won by his quickness and vigour. When he least expected it, he and Venus were bound together by Vulcan: the chains were invisible, but they could still feel them. This event earned the applause of satirists and the mockery of the court of heaven.[35] My friend, at least think about the chains which you do not see but already partly feel: get free while the chains can still be broken, lest that lame and ugly blacksmith (unfit to share a god's table or a goddess's bed), as is his habit, ties you to his Venus and makes you like himself, ugly and lame (or, what I fear more, deformed); you would not be able to acquire a cloven hoof[36] to make you clean; tied to Venus, you would be an object of sorrow and mockery to those that see you, applauded by the blind.

18 Paris, that false judge of goddesses, rejected Pallas because she promised profit rather than pleasure. My friend, would you make a similar decision?[37]

19 I see that already your fastidious mind is skimming over what you read as quickly as possible, not paying attention to the morals but looking for fine figures of speech. You are waiting for the muddied stream to flow past, for the mud to separate, and for clear

[33] Ovid, *Met.* VI. 103 ff.
[34] Ovid, *Met.* IV. 190 ff.
[35] Ovid, *Met.* IV. 171 ff.
[36] Based on Deut. 14: 6.
[37] Paris 'decided' in favour of Venus when she offered him a beautiful wife, as against Minerva, who offered success in war, and Juno, who offered greatness.

waters to appear, but you are waiting in vain, for streams must match their sources, whether muddied or clear. My faulty expression reflects the inexperience of my heart; the lumpy unevenness of my words offends a well bred mind. Fully conscious of this lack of polish, I would gladly have turned aside from my dissuasion, but, because I cannot keep silent, I have spoken to the best of my ability. If I had as much elegance of style as I have enthusiasm for the topic, I would be sending you such elegant words, joined together in such a noble union, that both separately and together they would be seen to bring a blessing on their author. But since you are indebted to me for whatever my love (still bare and unproductive but not, I hope, infertile) can deserve, in the meantime patiently give me your ear until I unfold what I have wrapped up. Do not ask me for an orator's purple or white (which I sadly admit I do not know), but accept the good will of the writer and the truth of what is written.

20   On the day on which a cruel Atropos dared to cut his noble thread, Julius Caesar (for whose greatness the world was too narrow) humbly lent his ear, at the door of the Capitol, to Tongilius, who was lowly but divine, as he foretold the daggers. If Caesar had paid attention, those to whom he paid the penalty would have paid it to him. But when I foretell the daggers that await you, you give ear to me like the serpent to the poisoners; you pay attention like a boar to barking dogs; you are as content as a snake that hides from the midsummer sun. You look after your own interests like a spurned Medea; you have as much pity on yourself as the sea does on shipwrecked sailors. You only restrain your hands out of respect for the king's peace. My friend, the conqueror of the world humbled himself to his faithful adviser, though this side of perfect humility; he almost withdrew his foot, because he almost obeyed; he succumbed to the penalty because he did not obey completely; his great humility did him no good because it was not complete. What will such wild inhumanity, such inflexible stubbornness, such disdainful arrogance do for you, who of your own accord rush unarmed into the ambushes of robbers? Please humble yourself as Caesar (who had humbled the world) humbled himself, and listen to your friend. If you think that Caesar was mistaken in not listening to advice, listen and take note of what happened to others, so that their misfortunes can benefit you: a rebuke supported by examples does no harm. I do not know in what refuge you are protected or in what sanctuary you lie idle. Caesar found the merciless to be traitors, and did not turn back;

if you ever escaped such a school, did you find the pious to be without pity?

21 King Phoroneus, who gladly published laws for the people and first embellished Greek culture with them, on the day on which he went the way of all truth said to his brother Leontius, 'I would not lack the highest summit of good fortune, if only I had never had a wife.' Leontius said, 'How has a wife impeded you?' He replied, 'All married men know!' My friend, I wish you had experienced marriage but were not now married, so that you would know what an impediment it is to felicity!

22 The Emperor Valentius, eighty years old and still a virgin, when on the day of his death he heard the praises of his triumphs recounted—and he had had many—said that he was only proud of one victory. Asked 'Which?' he said, 'When I conquered my worst enemy, my own flesh.'[38] My friend, this emperor would have left the world without glory, if he had not boldly resisted that with which you have now made a pact.

23 After his divorce from Terentia, Cicero would not marry again; he said it was not possible to give one's attention both to a wife and to philosophy.[39] My friend, I wish your mind would give you this answer, or that your tongue would reply to me; at any rate, deign to imitate the master of eloquence by at least speaking, to give me some hope, even if it is vain.

24 Canius of Cadiz, a poet of a light and pleasant wit, was reproved by the sombre hen-pecked historian Livy of Phoenicia, because he enjoyed the loves of many women: 'You cannot share in our philosophy when you yourself are shared by so many: Tityus does not love Juno with a liver torn into so many pieces by vultures!'[40] Canius replied: 'Whenever I slip, I get up more cautiously; when I am pushed down a little, I come up for air more quickly. The alternations of my nights make my days happier: a perpetuity of darkness is like hell. The first lilies of the springtime sun spread with a more effusive joy if they enjoy winds both from the south-east and the south-west—more than those which are blown over by the single blast of

---

[38] From Cicero's *De Senectute*, 47.
[39] Cf. Ch. 2, Jerome 20.
[40] Tityus' punishment for attempted rape (though not of Juno) was to have vultures tear perpetually at his liver in Tartarus. (Map seems to have invented this conversation.)

the fiery south wind. Mars broke his chains and sits at the heavenly banquet, from which hen-pecked Vulcan is excluded, held back by his own rope. Many threads bind less firmly than one chain: from philosophy I obtain pleasure—you go to it for relief!' My friend, I approve the words of both, but the lives of neither, but it is true that many diseases, which continually interrupt health, do less harm than a single disease which continually afflicts one with incurable illnesses.

25 Weeping, Pacuvius said to his neighbour Arrius, 'Friend, I have in my garden an unlucky tree: my first wife hanged herself on it, then my second wife, and now the third.' Arrius replied, 'I'm surprised you find yourself able to weep in all these successes'; then he said, 'Good Lord, think how many sorrows that tree has saved you!' Thirdly, he said, 'Friend, let me have some shoots of that tree to plant for myself.' My friend, I also say to you, I'm afraid you may have to beg shoots of that tree when you won't be able to find any.[41]

26 Sulpicius, who had divorced a noble and chaste wife, knew where his own shoe pinched him.[42] My friend, be careful that you don't have a pinching shoe which you can't take off.

27 Cato of Utica said, 'If the world could exist without women, our company would not differ from that of the gods.'[43] My friend, Cato said nothing that he hadn't experienced and known; none of these men who attack the deceits of women do so without having themselves been deceived—they are fully experienced and aware. You should believe them, for they tell the truth: they know that love pleases and stabs the loved one; they know that the flower of Venus is a rose, for under its bright colour lie hidden many thorns.

28 Metellus would not marry the daughter of Marius, although she was rich in dowry, beautiful to look at, famous in birth, and of good reputation; he said, 'I prefer to be mine than hers'; Marius said, 'But she will be yours'; Metellus retorted, 'A man has to be a woman's, because it is a point of logic that the predicates are only what the subject allow.'[44] Thus, by a joke Metellus turned away a load from his back. My friend, even if it is fitting to take a wife, it is not

[41] Cf. Ch. 7, WoB 56; the anecdote goes back to Cicero, De orat. II. 69.
[42] Cf. Ch. 2, Jerome 21.
[43] From a pseudo-Augustinian sermon: Christine de Pizan counters it in City I. 9.3.
[44] Puns on predicate and subject (that which is literally 'placed underneath', but logically governs the predicate) abound in medieval Latin antifeminist writings.

expedient. May it be love (and not blind love) that is in question, not income; may you choose beauty, not clothes; her mind, not her gold; may your bride be a wife, not a dowry. If it can possibly happen in this way, you may be able to be a predicate in such a way that you do not derive anger from the subject!

29 Lais of Corinth, a renowned beauty, only deigned to accept the embraces of kings and princes, but she tried to share the bed of the philosopher Demosthenes, so that she would seem, by breaking his notorious chastity, to have made rocks move by her beauty (as Amphion did with his lyre), and having attracted him by her blandishments she toyed with him pleasantly. When Demosthenes was enticed to her bedroom, Lais asked him for a hundred talents for the privilege; he looked up to heaven and said 'I don't pay so much to repent!'[45] My friend, I wish you would lift your attention to heaven, and avoid that which can only be redeemed by repentance.   .

30 Livia killed her husband whom she hated greatly; Lucilia killed hers, whom she loved to excess.[46] The former intentionally mixed poison, the latter was deceived and poured out madness as a cup of love. My friend, these women strove with opposite intentions, but neither was cheated of the natural end of female treachery, that is, evil. Women walk by varying and diverse paths, but whatever the paths they wander, whatever the by-ways they take, there is one result, one finishing-post for all their routes, one head and point of agreement of all their ways—mischief. Take the example of these two women as evidence that woman, whether she loves or hates, is bold in everything—crafty, when she wants to do harm (which is always), and when she tries to help frequently gets in the way, and so turns out to do harm even unintentionally. You are placed in the furnace: if you are gold, you will come out finer.

31 Deianeira clothed Hercules in a shirt, and brought vengeance on the 'hammer of monsters' with the blood of a monster: what she had contrived to bring her happiness resulted in her tears. My friend, Deianeira knew and saw that Nessus had been pierced by Hercules' spear, but nevertheless she trusted Nessus in her attempt on Hercules, and almost of her own accord enfolded in death the man whom she ought to have wrapped in a shirt.[47] A woman of unsound

---

[45] A story transmitted by Aulus Gellius.

[46] Livia was an accomplice in the poisoning of her husband Drusus, Emperor Tiberius' son; Lucilia is not known.

[47] The centaur Nessus, dying after Hercules wounded him for trying to rape his wife

and rash spirit, her will constantly unbalanced, thinks that what she wants is most important, not what is expedient; as she desires above all to please, she is determined to put her pleasure ahead of everything. Hercules fulfilled twelve inhuman labours, but by the thirteenth, which surpassed all inhumanity, he was consumed. Thus the bravest of men lay dead, to be lamented just as he lamented himself—he who had held up on his shoulders the span of the world without a groan.

32 Finally, what woman, among so many thousand thousands, ever saddened the eager and consistent suitor by a permanent refusal?[48] Which one ever invariably cut off the words of a wooer? Her reply always savours of her favour, and however hard she may be she will always have hidden in her words some hint of encouragement for your plea. Any woman may say 'No', but none says 'No' for ever. Gold broke through the defences of Acrisius' tower and violated Danaë's chastity although it was protected with a complex rampart.[49] My friend, this is how a debaucher rained from heaven on a maiden who had triumphed over earth; this is how someone of superior rank overcomes a woman whom a lowly suitor cannot deceive. The fierce north wind uproots a tree that stands firm against the gentle western breeze.

33 Perictione, an elderly virgin with a firm reputation for chastity, was finally overcome by the phantom of Apollo; she conceived and gave birth to Plato.[50] My friend, look how vigilance preserved her intact, but an illusion in a dream deflowered her, so that we can see that every rose bush is deprived of its crimson glory by some whirlwind. But it turned out well (if anything can be well like this), since Plato followed his father in his wisdom, and thus inherited the mystery and majestic name of his father.

34 My friend, are you more surprised or indignant that in my examples I suggest pagans as models for you to imitate, idolaters to you who are a Christian, wolves to a lamb, evil men to you who are

Deianeira, told her that his blood could act as a love-potion; but the blood was poisoned from Hercules' arrow, and when later she sent him a robe smeared with it, the robe clung to his flesh and tortured him: see Ovid, *Met.* IX. 99 ff.

[48] Cf. Ch. 1, Ovid *1*.
[49] The Ovidian assertion that women are all ultimately seducible is capped with an Ovidian example of the difficulty of protecting virginity: on Danaë, see Ch. 1, Ovid *4*.
[50] The legend that Plato was fathered on Perictione by an apparition of Apollo is in *Ag. Jov.* 1. 42.

good? I want you to be like the exemplary bee that gathers honey from the nettle, and to suck honey from the rock and oil from the hardest stone. I know that the pagan tales are superstitious, but every creation of God provides some model for good behaviour: God Himself is named lion, worm, and ram. Those who lack the faith do many things wrongly, but some things which, though of no merit in themselves, could yield an abundant fruit among us. But if they, who lacked hope, faith, charity and a preacher, wore leather belts [i.e. like John the Baptist], but we are asses or pigs or wild animals out of some lack of humanity, by what merit of faith, charity, and hope will we be found worthy, when we see the prophets, Apostles, and especially our great Lord, who can only be seen by those with pure hearts? Or, if the pagans, out of enthusiasm for their arts, wore themselves out by many struggles, with no vision of the future blessedness but only to avoid ignorance, what will happen to us, if we neglect the divine page which is directed to the truth, which is illumination, a lamp for the feet and a lantern to light the paths? I wish you would take out the divine page, read it, and take it into your room, so that the King will take you into His. You pledged your troth to Holy Scripture with the flowers of the springtime of your life; in your summertime she waits for you to bring grapes: do not hurt her by taking another bride, lest at harvest-time your grapes are the wild kind. I want you to be the bridegroom of Pallas, not of Venus.[51] Pallas will adorn you with fine necklaces and clothe you in wedding clothes. The marriage will be celebrated with Apollo as your best man; the wedding songs will be taught to the cedars of Lebanon by Mercury.[52] I have devoutly nurtured the hope of this long desired celebration, but in fear. This has been the purpose of this whole recital; although slow, this whole address will hasten to this end: the firmness of my dissuasion, of which you feel the iron-sharpened barbs, has been directed to this purpose.

35 *Conclusion of the preceding epistle.* The hand of the surgeon is hard, but healing. These words are also hard, but healthy: I hope that they are as useful to you as they are well meant. You say that I am imposing a strict way of life on you. Granted: for the way that leads to life is strict, and there is no smooth path to complete joy; indeed, it is through rough places that we get to even moderate joys.

---

[51] i.e. of wisdom, not of love.
[52] Conflation of allusions to S. of S. 5: 15, and Martianus Capella's 5th c. poem, *Marriage of Philology and Mercury.*

Jason learned that to reach the Golden Fleece he would have to pass through a sea still unravished by oars or boats, past sulphur-breathing bulls, and a watchful poisonous serpent. Following a plan that was sound, if not easy, he went and returned, and brought back a desirable treasure.[53] So the bitter wormwood of truth is accepted by a humble and well-disposed mind, is made fertile by assiduous care, and is brought to fruition by useful perseverance. Thus, the seed is sown by the south wind, pourer of rains; it is strengthened by the north wind, that sweeps the streets; it is brought to fulness by the west wind, that creates the flowers. So hard beginnings are rewarded by a sweet conclusion, and a narrow path leads to wide palaces, a slender track to the land of the living. But, to give support to my argument from the testimony of ancient writers, read Theophrastus' *Aureolus* and Ovid's *Medea*,[54] and you will find that almost nothing is impossible to a woman.

36   My friend, may almighty God not let you be deceived by the tricks of almighty woman;[55] may He light your heart, lest your eyes be bewitched and you go where I fear. But lest I seem to have written an *Orestes*, farewell.

ANDREAS CAPELLANUS

FROM *ON LOVE** (*DE AMORE*: C. 1 1 8 5)

Not much is known for sure about Andreas 'the chaplain', though there is a reasonable hypothesis that he was associated with the French royal court and knew Countess Marie de Champagne in the 1180s. His *De amore* is more or less a mock-textbook on the refinements of courtship, full of questions and answers and model debates within an overall structure loosely derived from Ovid's *Art of Love*.

The 'Double Standard'

In emulation of Ovid, Andreas elaborates an art of courting in Book 1, and proceeds to the art of *retaining* love in his shorter second book. In 11. 6, he addresses hypothetical problems of infidelity, starting with what is to happen if a woman discovers that her partner also loves a second woman. Unless it is

---

[53] The 'sound plan' which enabled Jason to succeed was that of Medea, whom he subsequently dumped, to his cost (see Ch. 1, Ovid 1): this is very cryptic.
[54] On *Aureolus* see Ch. 2, Jerome 12 and n. Ovid wrote a lost tragedy entitled *Medea*.
[55] Characteristic wordplay: *det tibi Deus omnipotens omnipotentis femine fallacia non falli.*
* Tr. P. G. Walsh, *Andreas Capellanus on Love* (London: Duckworth, 1982), 243 and 305–21. © 1982 by P. G. Walsh. Reprinted by permission of Gerald Duckworth & Co. Ltd.

a case of casual sex with 'someone's maid', the opinion given is that the first woman should reject him, but that stratagems for retrieving his full allegiance are possible. It transpires that more stringent criteria apply if the boot is on the other foot.

1 (II. 6.15) But now let us investigate the primeval sin, and see what should be done if a woman breaks faith with her lover. The long-standing opinion of some authorities has sought to claim that the same conventions should be wholly preserved in the case of a deceiving woman as were stated in the case of the deceiving lover.[56] But though this opinion is an ancient one, its age should not be revered because it launches on us the greatest error.

2 (16) God forfend that I should ever proclaim a pardon for a woman who was not ashamed to satisfy two men's lusts. Such behaviour is tolerated in men because of the prevailing convention and that privilege of the sex by which the performance of all shameful acts in this world is naturally more freely permitted to men. But in the case of a woman, the modesty of her chaste sex accounts it so wicked that once a woman has lent herself to the pleasure of several men, she is considered a lewd harlot, reckoned by all as unworthy to associate with other bands of ladies.[57] (17) So if the woman should return to her earlier lover, it is considered quite shameful for him to enjoy her embraces further, for he can realize with the certainty of truth that love in no sense continues in her case. So why should he repose his affections in her?

Why Not to Love Women

Book III of Andreas's work is not so much an Ovidian *Remedia* or guide to the removal of love's torments for those who find themselves unloved (as promised in the work's preface) as it is an outright repudiation of love. It runs through a medley of religious, moral, and prudential arguments: sexual love offends God, damages friendships, prompts violence and perjury and other crimes, is a form of enslavement, entails loss of public esteem, brings one under the devil's sway, and debilitates the body. Latterly Andreas seems to indicate clearly that, even though he is adopting a standpoint whereby 'fornication with a woman' is perceived to disfigure male dignity, he will refrain from using 'analysis of the nature or condition of woman' as a disincentive. To do so would be to broach a 'distasteful and tedious' topic and could be interpreted as a condemnation of Nature (III. 52–3).[58] Two pages

[56] See Ch. 2, Jerome 26 and n.
[57] Andreas refuses a 'remedy' for anyone who loves such a woman (II. 19), and repeats in III. 28 that sexual freedoms are allowed to males because of their 'recklessness' (*audacia*), but reduce women to whores.
[58] A point insisted on by Christine de Pizan: see Ch. 9, *Letter 1*, and *City* I. 8.3. In *Ag.*

later Andreas stops refraining, and launches into the misogynistic indictments which round off the treatise and which are excruciatingly—and
presumably deliberately—exasperating in their addiction to totalizing formulae such as 'every woman is . . .' and 'no woman can . . .'. Although the
treatise as a whole is replete with rhetorical exaggeration, this absolutist
phraseology reaches a crescendo in the present section. Has Andreas taken a
decision to expose the 'distastefulness' of misogyny in a *reductio ad absurdum*
of its negativity? Is Book III a kind of hoax, and its antifeminist passage a
hoax-within-a-hoax? Is this cheerlessly strident misogyny projected as the
inevitable concomitant of an anti-love posture, or does it conceivably
represent what Andreas 'really' thinks about women, with whose psychology and sexuality he has flirted extensively in Books I and II? If a hoax, it has
gone wrong, for modern taste finds this last book lacking in *élan*.[59]

3 (III. 62) Another reason why I urge you not to love is because
wisdom is dislodged from its role in a wise man by his love.[60] It does
not matter how full of sound sense a man is. Once enticed to sexual
intercourse he cannot observe moderation, deploy his wisdom to
control tendencies to sexual indulgence, or curb his lethal activities.
(63) Indeed, the wise are said to grow more deranged with love and
to satiate more eagerly desires of the flesh than those with less
knowledge to guide them. None had fuller or greater wisdom than
Solomon, but he sinned with boundless sexual indulgence, and
through love of women did not fear to worship foreign gods. (64)
What prophet was there of greater or more celebrated wisdom than
David, yet he had countless concubines, lusted foully after Uriah's
wife, debauched her in adultery, and like a treacherous murderer
killed her husband? What lover of women, then, could control his
lust, if these men had the support of such great instruction in
wisdom, yet love of women caused their wisdom to forget its function
and to be unable to control their sexual indulgence?[61]

4 (65) There is yet another argument by which we disconcert
lovers. You could never find the reciprocated love you look for in a
woman. No woman ever loved her husband, nor can she ever bind
herself to a lover with a reciprocal bond of love. For it is the woman's
way to look for wealth in love,[62] and not to grant to her partner the
consolations he likes; and one should not be surprised at this for it is

Jov. I. 8 St Paul's message is paraphrased: 'I acquiesce in marriage, lest I should seem
to condemn nature.'

[59] Andreas Capellanus 1982, 15.
[60] Cf. Ch. 2, Jerome 22; and Introduction to Augustine.
[61] On Solomon and David, see Map 10–11 above, and Ch. 2, Jerome 24.
[62] Ovid, *Art of Love* II. 279 ff.; and cf. Ch. 1, Ovid 5.

in her nature. (66) All women by the general make-up of their sex are disfigured by the vice of parsimony and greed, and carefully concentrate with ears pricked on financial profit and gain. I have travelled numerous parts of the world, and though I sought carefully I could never find a man to claim acquaintance with any woman who did not pressingly demand gifts if they were not offered gratuitously, and who did not impose delay on a love already begun if there were no full tally of gifts to acknowledge, whether spontaneously offered or demanded. (67) Even if you have bestowed riches beyond counting on a woman, once she finds you slack about giving her the usual presents, or discovers that you are now penniless, she will regard you as an unknown stranger, and you will be a boring nuisance to her in all you do.

5 There is no woman to be found who is bound to you with such affection and firm constancy that she will remain loyal to her love if some man approaches her with the slightest offer of gifts. (68) There is such an abiding flame of avarice in woman that generous gifts utterly break down the barriers of her chastity. If you seek to approach with open hands, there is no woman who will let you leave without your obtaining what you seek. But if you make no generous promises of gifts, do not approach women with any request, for even with the distinction of a king to adorn you you will get absolutely nothing from them if you come empty-handed; you will be turned away blushing from their halls. All women are thieves through avarice; we know they have pockets. (69) There is no woman alive of such distinction of blood or blessed with such position and abundance of wealth that an offer of money does not breach her virtue, and she can be undermined by the extensive material wealth even of a corrupt and worthless man. The reason is that no woman ever considers herself rich, just as no drunkard ever thinks he has had enough to drink. Even if land and water were all transformed together into gold, a woman's avarice could scarcely be diminished by it.

6 (70) Again, every woman is by nature not only miserly but also an envious backbiter of other women, a grabber, a slave to her belly, fickle, devious in speech, disobedient, rebellious against prohibitions, married with the vice of pride, eager for vainglory, a liar, a drunkard, a tongue-wagger who cannot keep a secret. She indulges in sexual excess, is inclined to every evil, and loves no man from the heart.

7   (71) Woman is miserly because there is no imaginable wickedness in the world she does not boldly do at the prospect of a gift, and
she cannot for all her plenty bring herself to help a person in need.
You could more easily scrape a piece off an unbreakable lodestone
with your fingernail than by human wit obtain anything from her
hoarded savings of her own free will. Epicurus believes that the
greatest good lies in service to the belly, and a woman believes that
nothing wins applause in this world except riches and parsimony.
(72) No woman is accounted so naive and foolish that she cannot
guard her property with greedy niggardliness, and win possession of
that of others with the most polished skill. Why, a guileless woman
goes about selling one hen more circumspectly than the wisest
lawyer transferring the possession of a good-sized castle. Then no
woman is ever joined in such ardent love with a man that she does
not devote all her brains to draining away her partner's wealth. This
rule of thumb is never found misleading; there are no exceptions to
it.

8   (73) As a general rule, every woman is also known to be envious,
always eaten with jealousy at another's beauty and discontented
with her material lot. Even if she hears her own daughter's beauty
praised she can scarcely stop herself being gnawed by the fire of inner
envy. (74) She sees the considerable poverty and excessive indigence
of neighbouring women as abundant wealth and plentiful riches. So
I think the old proverb sought to designate the female sex alone and
without exception when it says
  'The crops are lusher in a neighbour's field,
  Their neighbour's cattle heavier udders yield.'[63]
It is almost inconceivable that one woman should praise the moral
character or beauty of another. If she does happen to praise her in
one thing, she will at once add a criticism of something else to cancel
out the praise she uttered.

9   (75) So reasonably enough it follows that a woman is a slanderer, because slander is the outcome of nothing but envy and hate.
Woman has never sought to dispense with these prescriptive rights,
but tries to keep them wholly undiminished. It would be hard to find
a woman whose tongue could ever be merciful or leave slander
unsaid. (76) Every woman believes that she is advancing her glory
and her own good name if she seeks to detract in this way from the

---

[63]   *Art of Love* I. 349–50; and proverbial (Walther 1963–9, 19378).

praises of other women; and this is a clear indication to all that there is little wisdom stirring within women, for everyone in the world is aware of the general and constant rule that slander only damages the good name and harms the reputation of the slanderer.[64] (77) But this does not make women stop their slander or assaults on the praises of good men, and so I think we should maintain stoutly that there is no woman with a whit of sound instruction. All that wise men hold is quite foreign to a woman; she gets her notions at random, dwells happily on her own praises, and behaves contrary to wisdom in other ways which would be tedious for me to mention individually.

10   (78) Every woman is also disfigured with the vice of greed, for she strains every sinew to steal all the possessions not only of other men but also of the husband to whom she is happily wed. Once she has grabbed them, she strives to keep them so that they will aid no one. Such is the greed that prevails over a woman that she does not believe she is opposing the decrees of divine or human law; she seeks to become rich at the expense of others. (79) In fact, a woman thinks that refusing gifts to all, and zealously keeping things gained by fair means or foul, is the greatest of virtues and a quality which all should praise. No woman is an exception to this rule, not even a queen.

11   (80) Further, a woman is habitually such a slave to her belly that there is nothing she would blush to approve if she were sure of excellent food. If she is plagued with hunger for food, no amount of it could suffice for her to anticipate repletion, or for her to invite a companion to table. Instead, she always looks for the most private places in which to eat in secret, and her habit is to take pleasure in eating outside meal-times. (81) Though in other ways the female sex is always avaricious, and addicted invariably to clinging fast to possessions, she exhausts all she has most greedily through gluttony for food. No woman has ever been seen who did not yield when tempted to the vice of gluttony. We can observe all this in Eve, the first woman; though fashioned by God's hand and not by man's work, this did not make her any more afraid of taking the forbidden fruit, and she deserved to be expelled from her home in Paradise because of her voracious belly. (82) So if the woman created sinless by God's hand could not restrain her belly's vices, how will the rest

---

[64] Repeated in Christine de Pizan, *Letter* 737–47; and presumably applicable to the present slander.

fare, each conceived in sin in her mother's womb and never living without sin? Thus you can take it as a general rule that you can get anything out of a woman easily if you take the trouble to give her fine meals fairly often.

12   (83) Woman is also found fickle as a general rule. There is no woman so firmly determined on anything that her reliability cannot be soon dispelled by slight persuasion from someone. For woman is like melting wax, always ready to assume fresh shape and to be moulded to the imprint of anyone's seal.[65] (84) No woman could make you so certain of her promise that her intention and purpose with regard to that promise are not found to be changed in next to no time. No woman's mind remains unchanged for an hour, so that Martianus reasonably says: 'No more delays, for woman's always fickle in her ways.'[66] (85) You must therefore not expect to enjoy fulfilment of any promise from a woman unless you have first safely obtained the thing promised. It is useless to regard a woman's pledge by the light of the civil laws; you must always hold your bag ready when confronting her promises. The old proverb appears to brook no exception in the case of women when it says 'Once you're ready, no delays; procrastination never pays.'[67] (86) We know that everything every woman says is spoken with inner deceit, for they always have thoughts different from the words they say. No man could so rejoice in a woman's intimacy or affection as to be able to know the secrets of her heart or the degree of sincerity with which she addresses him, for a woman trusts no man as friend, believing that all are utter deceivers. So she continues always in her deceitful purpose, and all she says is spoken with a false heart and ambivalent mind.

13   (87) This is why you should never feel certain of a woman's promise or oath, because there is no lasting loyalty in her. Ensure that you always keep your inner purpose hidden from her, and do not reveal to her your hidden thoughts, so that in this way you may cheat guile by guile and repel her deceit. (88) Samson's honest character all men know, but we read that because he could not conceal his inner thoughts from a woman he was beguiled by her

---

[65] Woman's 'softness' was asserted by etymology (see Ch. 1, Isidore 1), and she is associated positively with 'wax' in Marbod 5 (Ch. 8 below): but there could be the innuendo of woman imprinted by phallic seals: Jacquart and Thomasset 1988, 37.

[66] A recollection of celebrated words from Virgil's *Aeneid* 4.569 f., where Mercury urges Aeneas on to leave Dido because 'women are fickle'! Andreas surprisingly misattributes them to Martianus Capella.

[67] Walther 1963–9. 31438.

deceitful heart, and so defeated by the army of his enemies, captured by them, and deprived of both bodily strength and eyesight.[68] We hear of countless other women too who are said basely to have betrayed their husbands and lovers by false words because these men could not conceal their secrets from them.

14 (89) Every woman is further polluted by the vice of disobedience. There is no woman alive in the world so wise and circumspect that, if she is forbidden the improper use of something, she does not fight the prohibition with all the strength of her body, and set out to transgress it. This is why the well-known utterance of the sage has rightly been found to apply to women without any exception: 'Forbidden fruit we strive to gain, and prize denied fain would attain.'[69]

15 (90) We read too of a man of great wisdom who had a loathsome wife. He was unwilling to kill her with his own hand, because he did not want to commit a crime. But he knew that she took joy in seeking forbidden things, and so he got a most expensive vessel and put in it a fine, fragrant wine mixed with poison. Then he said to his wife: 'My dearest wife, be sure not to touch this goblet, nor venture to sip a single drop of this liquid, for it is poisonous and lethal for humans to drink.' (91) The woman spurned her husband's prohibition; before he had gone any distance she took liberties with the forbidden drink, and the poison finished her off altogether. Yet why tell this story when we know more illustrious examples? Did not Eve, the first woman who was moreover fashioned by God's hand, die and lose the glory of immortality by the sin of disobedience, by her guilt dragging all her posterity to mortal destruction?[70] So if you want a woman to do anything, you will get your way by bidding her do the opposite.[71]

16 (92) Pride also regularly mars the female sex. When a woman is roused by the goad of pride she cannot control her tongue or hands from evil deeds or abusive words, but in her anger recklessly does all manner of wickedness. Anyone seeking to restrain an angry woman wearies himself with wasted effort; even if he keeps her tied hand and foot, and applies all manner of torture to her, he could not make her desist from her evil intention, or diminish her arrogance of mind.

[68] Judges 16: 15; and see Ch. 2, Jerome 24.
[69] *Amores* III. 4: 17; Walther 1963–9, 29695.
[70] Cf. Map 9 above.
[71] Cf. Ch. 5, Jacques de Vitry 2–3.

(93) Moreover, the anger of any woman is aroused at the slightest, most unsubstantial remark, sometimes without provocation. Then her arrogance swells without limit. I can never recall anyone succeeding in finding a woman who could restrain her arrogance. No woman has been found an exception to these rules.

17   (94) Then again, every woman seems to look down on another woman, a trait clearly stemming from arrogance alone, for no man could despise another except through haughty pride. Women too, doddering hags as well as young girls, strain every nerve to praise their own beauty, and these words of the sage clearly prove that this habit too results from arrogance alone:

'There's gross disdain and pride in beauty's train.'[72]
(95) So it is quite evident that women cannot be in full possession of outstanding character, for as the saying is,

'When arrogance is there, it sullies manners fair.'[73]

18   Vainglory also seriously preoccupies women. One could not find a woman in the world who is not delighted by people's praise more than all else, and who does not believe that all words spoken about her are addressed to her praises. (96) This fault can be observed even in the first woman, Eve, when she took the forbidden food so as to be able to have knowledge of good and evil. Moreover, no woman can be found of such low stock as not to maintain that she has notable parents and is descended from a family of high-ranking men, and who does not use all sorts of boasting to exalt herself. This is the kind of thing that vainglory seeks as its own.

19   (97) All women are known to be also liars. There is not a living woman who does not make pretence of what is untrue, and invent lies with reckless ingenuity. A woman will lie on oath a thousand times for some slight advantage, and devise countless lies for the smallest gain; (98) and indeed women slave to bolster all their lies by guile, and are fond of inventing untrue charges against other ladies by elaborate falsehood. But no man could have such strong suspicions against a woman as to make her confess her guilt unless she were caught in the very act of sinning.

20   (99) Moreover all women are drunkards, fond of drinking wine. None of them is ashamed to drink the best Falernian[74] in daylight in

---

[72] Ovid, *Fasti* I. 419; Walther 1963–9, 8874.
[73] Walther 1963–9, 12465.
[74] Juv. portrays a woman vomiting on Falernian wine: *Satire* VI, 430.

company with a hundred fellow-matrons. She is never so refreshed by drinking wine so many times that she refuses another cup if it is brought. Wine that has deteriorated she regards as her greatest foe, and drinking water is for her a most harmful practice; but if she comes upon wine in good condition unmixed with water, she would rather endure a huge loss to her estate than fail to drink her fill of it. This is why no woman escapes the sin of drunkenness on numerous occasions.

21 (100) All women are also free with their tongues, for not one of them can restrain her tongue from reviling people, or from crying out all day long like a barking dog over the loss of a single egg, disturbing the whole neighbourhood for a trifle. A woman gossiping with other women would never willingly give another a chance to speak; she always tries to dominate the conversation with her own opinions, and to go on talking longest.[75] Her tongue or breath could never be exhausted by talking. (101) We see, too, numerous women on many occasions who are so keen to talk that when they are alone they break into speech, and speak out aloud to themselves. Then too a woman recklessly contradicts everyone, and could never agree with anyone's opinion, but always strives to put her own view first on every topic.

22 (102) Besides this, no woman can keep a secret. The more she is bidden to keep something in confidence, the more eagerly she strains to tell it to everybody. No woman to this day has been found to keep any secret undivulged, no matter how important or even likely to cause someone's death. (103) Any secret confided to a woman's trust seems to burn her up inside if she does not first expose the confidences so disastrously reposed in her. You could not prevent women acting like this by bidding them do the opposite, the rule of thumb which I stated earlier, because all women take the greatest pleasure in gossiping about something new. So be sure to keep your secret from every woman.[76]

23 (104) Every woman in the world is also lustful. A woman may be eminent in distinction of rank and a man most cheap and contemptible, but if she discovers that he is sexually virile she does not refuse to sleep with him. But no man however virile could satiate a woman's lust by any means.[77] (105) Again, no woman is joined to

[75] Cf. Ch. 1, Juv. 7.
[76] Cf. Ch. 6, *RR* 34–7, and *Math.* 18–21; and Ch. 7, *WoB* 38.
[77] Cf. Ch. 1, Juv. 3.

a lover with such chaste loyalty, or is so united to her husband, that she does not welcome another as lover, especially if a wealthy man emerges. Then you see her wantonness in company with the most flagrant greed. No woman in this world is so faithful or so committed to any betrothal that if a lusting lover appears and entices her with expertise and persistence to enjoy love, she is minded to reject his request or defend herself against his advances, at any rate once he has applied heavy pressure. (106) This is a rule which does not mislead in the case of any woman. Realize, then, the reputation appropriate for a woman who is most fortunately placed and has the distinction of an honourable male friend or excellent husband, yet looks for lustful intercourse with another. A woman behaves like this because she is plagued by oppressive lust.

24 (107) The female sex is likewise disposed to every evil. Every woman fearlessly commits every major sin in the world on a slender pretext, and her mind readily bends to every evil under slight pressure from anyone. Again, there is no woman alive in the world, even an empress or a queen, who does not devote all her life to portents and to different ways of divining the future, as pagans do; her gullible mind is obsessed by them, and she diligently practises the unnumbered wickednesses of astrology.[78] (108) In fact, there is no task that a woman does without awaiting at the outset the appropriate day and hour, and without inaugurating it with the baneful art. She does not even marry, or conduct the ritual for a death, or cart seed into a field, or permit entrance into a new home, or anything else to be started without first inaugurating it in the woman's way, and having it approved by the magical prognostications of women. (109) This is why Solomon in his great wisdom, knowing as he did all the wickednesses and crimes of woman, made a general pronouncement on her vices and depravity. His words are: 'There is no good woman.'[79] So, Walter, why do you seek so eagerly to love what is evil?

[78] On superstition, cf. Ch. 1, Juv. 9; Ch. 5, Gautier 3–4, 14; *Corb.*, in Cassell 1975, 29; and John of Salisbury, *Policraticus* II. 18.
[79] Eccles. 7: 29.

AGAINST MARRYING*
(DE CONIUGE NON DUCENDA: c. 1222–50)

This jaunty, irreverent poem is found in fifty-five manuscripts, so must have circulated quite widely, perhaps especially in a clerical and university ambience. The author plunders and domesticates numerous fragments from Ecclesiasticus and Proverbs. While making only intermittent use of the literary antifeminist tradition derived from Roman satire, the poem contributed to later products of that tradition, notably to the *Lamentations of Matheolus* (see next chapter) which builds upon its sketches of household hell. Although it is not a text seriously concerned with celibacy, its editor has suggested that satires of this kind were indirectly 'sparked by the current debate on clerical celibacy culminating in the decree of the Fourth Lateran Council of 1215 forbidding clergy to marry'.[80]

Against Marrying is structured around the idea of the miraculous appearance of a trinity of 'angels'—one message in three speakers, as the poet puts it—to deter the protagonist from entering marriage at his friends' prompting. (A working man, he is named 'Gawain' in many manuscripts; this probably arises as a jesting reference to that knight's escapades with women.[81]) The 'angels' Peter, Lawrence, and John, sketchily conceived in the text as epitomizing power, wisdom, and grace, can be identified with specific people doubtless reputed at the time to be propagandists against marriage: Peter of Corbeil (d. 1222), Lawrence of Durham (d. 1154), and John Chrysostom (see Chapter 2 above). Peter speaks first, stressing primarily the sweat and weariness with which a husband must labour to provide for an ever-increasing family. The rest of the poem, given below, comprises the speeches of Lawrence and John.

Lawrence

L1   Then Wisdom's part to Lawrence goes,
     For laurel green in winter grows
     As full in leaf as in July;
     He next attacks the marriage tie.

L2   'A woman's silly, never staid,
     By many longings stirred and swayed.
     If husband can't her needs supply,
     Adultery's the way she'll try.

L3   She sells herself to get a gown
     And cool her burning passions down.
     With greed for presents all aflame
     She spurns her wretched husband's claim.[82]

* Tr. A. G. Rigg, *Gawain on Marriage: The 'De Coniuge Non Ducenda'* (Toronto: Pontifical Institute of Mediaeval Studies, 1986), 81–99. © Pontifical Institute of Mediaeval Studies, Toronto, 1986. Reprinted by permission of the publisher.
   [80] Rigg 1986, 12.   [81] Rigg 1986, 6.   [82] Cf. Andreas 4 ff. above.

L4   The wicked wife seeks leave to ride
To pilgrims' abbeys far and wide;
The brothels offer more delights
Than visiting the holy sites.[83]

L5   The wayward wife, by modest dress,
Avoids all blame for wantonness.
Like ships that cross the ocean's face
Her lustful exploits leave no trace.

L6   So Rancour grips the married male
Who keeps a wife who's up for sale.
He names as heir another's brat
And feeds what someone else begat.[84]

L7   Thus bitter grief and shame begin—
The child that's been conceived in sin.
Its mother knows its bastard line,
The foolish husband says: "It's mine."

L8   His wealth its owner soon forsakes,
When once his wife a lover takes.
She spurns her husband, then bestows
His hard-earned wealth on gigolos.

L9   She revels in unchastity
But still pretends fidelity;
Her husband groaning ever strives
To feed a wife another swives.

L10   The wicked hope of faithless wives
Is shortening their husbands' lives.
They steal to keep their lovers true—
Let Gawain therefore wife eschew!'

John

J1   John next, in whom God's grace abounds,
Inspired, a longer case propounds.
With eagle eye that penetrates
On marriage he expatiates.[85]

[83] On religious trips as pretexts, cf. Ch. 1, Ovid 4; and *Math.* 11. 947 ff. and 2145–54
[84] Juv. *Satire* VI, 76–81, culminates in the birth of a 'noble' son who turns out to have features like 'the mug of some gladiator'.
[85] John represents both Grace (third person of the Trinity), John Chrysostom, and John the evangelist, whose symbol was the eagle.

J2   'A married man's a slave for sure,
His flesh and spirit pain endure—
Like ox from market homeward led
To work the plough until he's dead.

J3   Who takes a wife accepts a yoke:[86]
Not knowing pain, with pain he'll choke.
Who takes a wife, himself is caught
And to eternal serfdom brought.

J4   To help their mates were wives designed,
To keep the seed of humankind.
Apart from this a wife's a pain
But rules the roost in his domain.

J5   By nature woman's quick to chide,
Deceitful, jealous, full of pride;
But donkey-like, the patient spouse
Accepts his burden like a mouse.

J6   "Whose wife is good is blest" it's said,[87]
But "good-wife" tales are rarely read.
She'll either nag or fornicate—
His lordship she'll not tolerate.

J7   Of good wives there's a scarcity—
From thousands there's not one to see.[88]
A man's injustice does less harm
Than woman's well-intentioned charm.[89]

J8   A woman will receive all males:[90]
No prick against her lust prevails.
For who could fill his spouse's spout?
Alone she wears the district out.

J9   Her lustful loins are never stilled:
By just one man she's unfulfilled.[91]
She'll spread her legs to all the men
But, ever hungry, won't say "When".[92]

[86] Traditional wordplay on *coniugium* ('marriage') and *iugum* ('yoke'); the latter is in Ch. 1, Juv. 5.
[87] Ecclus. 26: 1, 'Happy is the husband of a good wife.'
[88] Eccles. 7: 29; in Ch. 1, Scripture 8.
[89] Ecclus. 42: 14; in Ch. 1, Scripture 10.
[90] Ecclus. 36: 23: 'A woman will receive every man.'
[91] Cf. Ch. 1, Juv. 2.
[92] Lit., with her 'insatiable vulva' she is never 'satisfied': from Prov. 30: 15–16, discussed in Ch. 2, Jerome 8.

J10   Her appetite no man fulfils,
For too much copulation kills.
No man, as often as she'd choose,
Could pay to her his carnal dues.[93]

J11   Thus married women love to stray
And wish their husbands' lives away.
Since none a woman's lust can sate[94]
I don't commend the married state.

J12   Her tongue's a sword: its cutting blow
Like lightning brings her husband low.
Her tongue dispels her husband's joy;
Like wind her words his home destroy.[95]

J13   Of trust there's little left to show
When horns of pride begin to grow.
Her wicked spiteful tongue rains down
A thunderstorm upon his crown.[96]

J13A   In anger she'll his trust betray,
To murder open up the way.
With "love-sick" men she'll copulate
To pass the pox on to her mate.[97]

J13B   If she's of noble family born
She treats her lowly spouse with scorn.
To make a stand if he should think,
She'll poison him with bitter drink.[98]

J14   The wife's demands are always met;
If not, she'll quarrel, rage, and fret.
The noise defeats the patient spouse;
He yields to her and quits the house.

J15   A drip, the smoke, a wife—these three
Compel a man his house to flee.[99]

[93] See Ch. 1, introduction to (iii). The 'dues' are the reciprocal sexual 'debt' of marriage; cf. Ch. 3, Gratian 2.

[94] Cf. Andreas 23 above.

[95] Cf. Ch. 6, Math. 1.

[96] Recalling the story of Xanthippe; cf. Ch. 2, Jerome 20.

[97] By lying with a 'leprous man' (leproso), the woman could pass the contagion to the husband while herself uninfected, it was thought: Jacquart and Thomasset 1988, 189 and 193.

[98] On the wife's scorn, cf. Andreas 18 above; and on the poison, cf. Ch. 2, Jerome 15, also Juv. Satire VI, 610 ff.

[99] The dripping/wrangling wife are in Prov. 19: 13, quoted in Ch. 1, Jerome 7. Smoke makes up a trio in De contemptu mundi: Innocent III 1978, 120–1.

The man speaks words of peace; the wife
Piles on the quarrels and the strife.

J16 In cunning none outwits a snake;
For mischief women prizes take.
It's safer in a lion's cage
Than up against a woman's rage.[100]

J17 Than death there's no worse penalty,
Yet wives are worse for cruelty.[101]
For death takes but an hour or so,
But marriage pains are long and slow.

J18 Who takes a wife, to death is bound;
His mind decays that once was sound.
He starts to ail when he is wed,
But soon recovers once she's dead.

J19 A husband's never free from pain;
He longs to die but must remain.
This woe exceeds the worst of woes,
The bush must burn without repose.[102]

J20 In brief, to sum up marriage well,
It's either purgatory or hell.
In hell there's neither rest nor peace—
A husband's pains have no release.

J21 Hell's Mouth portrays the married state.
The wife's the Fury at the gate;
By Beasts his greedy brood is meant,
His many pains, his discontent.[103]

J22 Now who could stand the long misuse,
The many labours and abuse?
From marriage comes both wear and tear.
If wise, then marriage you'll forbear!'

J23 The angels having said their bit,
Their hands upon the Holy Writ,
From fire they tried to pull me free.
I answered briefly: 'I agree.'

[100] Ecclus. 25: 23; in Ch. I, Scripture 9.
[101] Eccles. 7: 27; in Ch. I, Scripture 8.
[102] Like the burning bush in Exod. 3: 2.
[103] This exposition of Hell's Mouth with a Fury and accompanying beasts as an analogy for marriage probably burlesques medieval commentaries on Hades. Marriage is 'hell' in *Math. I* (Ch. 6 below), and 'purgatory' in *Math. III*.

5

Antifeminist Tales

From about the eleventh century, the short exemplary tale enjoyed a huge popularity in the West, as poets and preachers began to draw eagerly on collections of stories of intrigue and comic mischief transmitted from eastern cultures (most conspicuously via the Muslim 'frontier' of Arabic Spain). The result was the flowering of the racy *fabliau*, or story of trickery, in which a dominant type concerned wives' stratagems in defying or cuckolding their husbands. (Of course there were anecdotes of faithful wives, too, but rather fewer.) Female deceit and sexual appetite are usually taken for granted. We are warned by Muscatine that it would be rash to suppose that these lustful *fabliau* women are a product of 'red-eyed clerics sublimating, in their fierce antifeminism, a deep fear of castration and of female domination'.[1] It seems more appropriate to talk in terms of the raconteurs' underlying admiration for the ingenuity shown by the women in circumventing sexually unattractive, possessive husbands. Some of the more popular tales will be found deployed in *The Lamentations of Matheolus* in the next chapter. The present chapter selects from the massive field of *fabliau* just a few, including two incorporated into a sermon.

THE BOOK OF THE WILES OF WOMEN* (EL LIBRO DE LOS ENGAÑOS E LOS ASAYAMIENTOS DE LAS MUGERES: 1253)

A preface states that this work was translated from Arabic into Spanish at the behest of Prince Fadrique of Castile in 1253. *The Wiles of Women* represents a part of what is known as the 'Sindibad' or 'Seven Sages' tradition—so named because, in the fiction which frames this collection, Sindibad is the wise man who teaches a prince; and the Sages subsequently have to save the prince's life by telling stories to make the king distrust allegations of sexual misconduct brought against the youth by one of the royal wives. To combat, and warn of, womanly trickery therefore becomes (even if facetiously) the *raison d'être* of the text; for although the wife tells counter-stories against counsellors, she appears to be outmatched both in quality and in quantity.

---

[1] Muscatine 1986, 121–2; and see Johnson 1983, Spencer 1978.
* Tr. John E. Keller, *The Book of the Wiles of Women*, University of North Carolina Studies in the Romance Languages and Literatures, 27 (Chapel Hill: University of North Carolina Press, 1956), 25–6, 30–2, 39–41. © University of North Carolina Press. Reprinted by permission of the publisher. Spanish text in Keller 1959.

I The Story of the Master and the Manservant, of the Wife and the Husband, and how they all found themselves together

'Sire, people have told me about the wiles of women. They say that there was a wife who had as a lover one of the king's privy-counsellors who held the whole city in fief from the hand of the king. Now this woman's lover sent a manservant to her house to find out if her husband was at home. When the servant entered the house, she was taken with him, for he was handsome, and he with her. She invited him to lie with her and he did so. Now the paramour, seeing that his servant was slow in returning, went to his mistress's house and knocked.

"What will become of me?" cried the manservant.

"Go and hide in that alcove," she commanded.

The servant's master entered just then, and she did not want him to go to the alcove where the young man was hiding. Just then her husband knocked at the door.

"Draw your sword," the woman instructed her paramour. "Stand there at the door of that room and threaten me. Then, without saying a word, be on your way."

He did so, and she went and opened the door for her husband, who, when he saw the man with the drawn sword, said, "What is this?"

The paramour said not a word to him and departed. Then the husband turned to his wife and cried, "Ah, you sinner! What business did that man have here who just went out insulting and threatening you?"

"The young man in that alcove", she replied, "came fleeing in terror from him, and finding the door unlocked, he came in crying for help, with his master on his heels ready to murder him. He ran to me, and I stood in front of him and prevented the man from killing him. That is why the man left here insulting and threatening me. But as God is my witness, he didn't frighten me!"

"Where is the young man?" asked the husband.

"He is in that alcove."

The husband went to the door to see if the young man's master had gone away, and not seeing him about, he called the fellow and said, "Go on out, for your master has departed."

Quite satisfied, the husband turned to his wife and said to her, "You played the role of a fine woman and you have done well, and I am very grateful to you."

And, Sire, I told you this story only so that you would not execute your son on the word of a woman, for in women are contained deceits without number.'

2   The Tale of the Man, his Wife, the Old Woman, and the She-Dog[2]

'Sire, I have heard that a man and his wife took an oath of loyalty and fidelity. The husband swore to return by a certain date, but he didn't. The wife went out one day to the street, and while she was there, a man saw her and was smitten with her and he asked for her love. She told him that she couldn't and that she wouldn't for anything.

The man then approached an old woman who dwelt nearby and he told her all about how he had fared with that woman. He begged her to get the woman for him and promised that he would give her whatever she wanted. The old woman told him she was willing to do so and that she would obtain the woman for him.

Going to her own house, she took honey and dough and pepper and kneaded it all together and made bread of it. Then she started for the house of the wife, calling after her a little dog she had, and tossing pieces of the bread to it so that the wife didn't notice. As soon as the dog had eaten the bread, it commenced to follow the old woman, fawning upon her so as to get more of the bread, and shedding tears because of the pepper that was in it. When the wife saw the dog in such a state, she was astonished.

"Old woman," she asked, "have you ever seen any other dog weep like this one?"

"She does so with reason," answered the old woman, "because this dog was once a woman, and very beautiful, and she used to live near me. A man fell in love with her, and she was not interested in him. He put a curse upon her, that man who was in love with her, and she was changed instantly into a she-dog. Now, whenever she sees me, she remembers it and bursts into tears."

"Woe is me!" cried the wife. "What shall I do? Just the other day a man saw me in the street and asked to be my lover, and I refused. Now I am afraid he will change me into a dog if he curses me! Go to him quickly and plead with him, and I will give him whatever he wants!"

"I shall bring him to you," said the old woman.

---

[2] This tale became widely dispersed: e.g. in Jacques de Vitry (Crane 1890, 239); *Math.* ii. 1855 ff.; and in the 13th-c. English *Dame Sirith* (Bennett and Smithers 1966, 77 ff.). But none of these has the denouement involving the return of the husband.

She arose and went out to look for the man. The wife went to beautify herself and then hastened to the old woman's house to see if she had located the man.

"I can't find him," said the old woman.

"What shall I do, then?" asked the wife.

The old woman went out and found a man and said to him, "Come here, for I have a woman who will do anything for you, anything I ask her to."

Now this man was the woman's husband, but the old woman did not know it.

"What will you give to one who gets you a fine room, and a beautiful woman, and good food and drink, if you want it?" she asked.

"Heavens! I would like that!" he cried.

She led the way, and he came close behind her. When he saw that the house was his own, he suspected that she was taking him to his own wife and he imagined that his wife acted in this fashion whenever he went away.

"Come in," said the evil old woman. "Sit here."

When his wife beheld his face and saw that he was her husband, she knew nothing to do but to carry the attack to him.

"So, Mr Whoremonger!" she cried. "Is this the faith you and I swore to keep? Now I know that you frequent bad women and wicked procuresses."

"Woe unto you!" roared her husband. "What are you trying to put over on me?"

"They told me", answered his wife, "that you were coming home, and I made myself beautiful and told this old woman to go out and test you to see if you went with bad women. And I see that right away you desired a prostitute! Never more will we live together and you will never touch me again!"

"May God forgive me," cried the husband, "and so may you! I thought only that she was leading me to my own house and to you, and it grieved me terribly when she brought me here. I thought that you had been doing this with other men."

The instant he said this, she tore her face and gashed it with her nails, crying, "Now I see well enough what you thought of me!"

She raved at him, and when he saw how angry she was, he began to coax her and to plead with her to pardon him; but she refused to forgive him until he had promised her, as a gift, a village that he owned.

And Sire, I gave you this story only to point out to you the perfidy of women, which is boundless.'

3   The Tale of the Young Man who did not wish to marry until he had learned all the Evils of Women

'Sire, they have told me that a man didn't want to marry until he had learned and discovered the evils of women and their wiles. He travelled until he arrived at a village where they told him that wise men dwelt, very deeply versed in the wiles of women, and that it would cost him dearly to learn their arts.

The one there who was the wisest said to him, "Do you want me to tell you something? You will never know nor will you ever completely learn the deceits of women until you sit for three days upon an ash heap and eat nothing except a little barley, bread made of barley, that is, and a little salt."

He answered that it was agreeable to him. Then he seated himself upon the ash heap and transcribed many books about the arts of women. After he had done so, he said that he wanted to return to his own land. He lodged in the house of a good man, and the host asked him all about himself. He told the man from whence he had come, and of how he had sat upon the ash heap while he transcribed those books, and of how he had eaten the barley bread, and of how he had endured a great deal of hardship and wretchedness, writing about the arts of women.

When he had finished speaking, the good man took him by the hand and led him to his wife, saying, "I have a good man who comes weary from travel."

And he told her his business and begged her to take him in charge until he was stronger, since he was weak. Having told her this, the husband went about his business. Now the wife knew perfectly well what she would teach him.[1] She questioned him as to who he was and what was his business, and he told her everything. When she understood all this, she took him for a booby and a simpleton, for she was well aware that he would never finish what he had set out to do.

"I firmly believe", she told him, "that no woman in the world will ever deceive you, nor will one ever be the equal of those books you have composed." But in her heart she said: "Be as wise as you may, for I shall make you see this stupidity of yours under which you labour. I am just the woman who knows how to show you!"

---

[1] Alternatively, 'she did what her husband asked'.

Then she called him and said, "Friend, I am a young woman and beautiful and I am ripe, and my husband is a tired old man. It has been a long time since he lay with me. If you want to, lie with me, since you are a smart fellow and full of experience. But say nothing to anybody!"

When she had spoken, he believed that she was in earnest. He stood up and tried to take her in his arms, but she said, "Not so fast! Let's undress."

He stripped, and she began to scream and shriek. The neighbours came running, and before they entered she told the fellow, "Stretch out on the floor. If you don't, you are a dead man!"[4]

He did so, and she placed a large bite of bread in his mouth. When the neighbours came in, they asked what had happened.

"This man is our guest," she replied. "He almost choked on a piece of bread and his eyes have rolled back in his head!"

Then she showed him to them, and she poured water upon him to revive him. He gave no signs of revival during all this while she was pouring cold water upon him and washing his face with a napkin. Finally, the men left and went about their business.

"Friend," said the woman, "in your books are there any arts like this one?"

"By my faith, never did I see one nor did I ever find one like this in my books!" he answered.

"You endured hardship and bad days for nothing," she told him. "Never expect anything else from all that, for what you sought you could never have, neither you nor any man alive!"

When he realized this, he took all his books and cast them into the fire, admitting that he had wasted his time.

Now Sire, I have told you this story so that you will not kill your son on the word of a woman.'

GAUTIER LE LEU

'THE WIDOW'* ('LA VEUVE': THIRTEENTH CENTURY)

Nothing seems to be known of Gautier's life, but he typifies the well-read French *jongleur*, skilled in boisterous *fabliaux*. His satirical representation of a

---

[4] Possibly she is instructing him to 'act dead'.

* Tr. Robert Hellman and Richard O'Gorman, *Fabliaux: Ribald Tales from the Old French* (New York: Thomas Crowell Co., 1965; reprinted Newport, Conn.: Greenwood Press, 1976), 145–6. © Robert Hellman and Richard O'Gorman, 1965. Reprinted by permission of Harper & Row Inc. and Weidenfeld & Nicolson Ltd. Old French text in Livingston 1951.

widow participates in the tradition which links Ovid's Dipsas, the wanton neighbourhood busy-bodies envisaged by St Paul in 1 Timothy, 11–13, the Old Woman in the *Romance of the Rose*, and the Wife of Bath—though Gautier's widow is most closely paralleled in *The Lamentations of Matheolus* 15–17, Chapter 6 below.

1 My lords, I should like to instruct you. We all of us must go off to the wars, on that expedition from which no man returns. And do you know how they dispose of someone who has been convoked to that army? They carry him to the church on a litter, toes up and with great speed; and his wife follows after him. Those who are closest to the wife lay hands and arms on her to keep her from, at the very least, beating her palms together. For she cries out in a loud voice: 'Holy Mother Mary, fair lady! It is a wonder I can keep going, I am so full of grief and affliction! I have more pain than I can bear! How grieved I am that I live on! How hard and bitter is this life! May it not be God's will that I travel much farther on this road, but let me be laid with my husband, to whom I swore my faith!'

2 So she carries on, acting her part, in which there is scarcely a word of truth. At the entrance of the church she begins again her business of shrieking and wailing. The priest, who would like to get on with the collection, quickly orders the candles to be lit; and when he has asked God's pardon for the dead man, he says the mass in a great hurry. When the service is finished and the corpse has been laid on his back in the black earth among the worms, then the good wife wants to jump into the open grave. Whoever should see her then, trembling and blinking her eyes open and shut and beating her fists together, would say: 'That woman could very well lose her mind.' And so they pull her back, and two of them hold her from behind and bring her all the way home. There her neighbours make her drink cold water to cool off her grief.

3 At the door of her house she begins all over again: 'My husband, what has become of you? You have not come back to me. My God, why have you been taken from me? When I think how your wealth had increased, how your business prospered, how well everything was going for you! How well your workaday clothes fit you and how becoming was your Sunday suit, which we had made on New Year's Day! Oh, Magpie, you told me the truth! And you, Heron, how I cursed you for squawking so much this year! You, Dog, how often you howled! And you, Chicken, you sang me a warning![5] Oh, Devil,

[5] Rustic version of the superstition ascribed to women; cf. Ch. 1, Juv. 9.

how have you bewitched me so that I cannot conjure my love in God's name to return to me! If it were possible to raise a dead man, I would pay any tribute to do so.

4 'God, how I dreamed this year—although I have said nothing about it—base, shameful dreams! May God turn them to my advantage! Husband, the day before yesterday I dreamt that you were in the church, and both the doors were locked. And now you are locked in the earth! And then, immediately after that, I dreamt that you had a black cloak and a pair of great leaden boots, and dressed so you dived into the water and never came up again. You died only a short time after. Those dreams really came true. I dreamt that you were dressed in a coat with a great hood. In your hands you held a stone with which you beat down the wall of the house. Lord, what a hole you left me there! No one mourned for you, but I do so again and again! Then it seemed to me—but I am very loath to speak of it—that in my dream a dove, white and beautiful, descended into my breast and made the wall whole again. I do not know what this last dream means.'[6]

5 Then begin the buzzings, the counsels, the parliaments[7] of relatives and neighbours, of nieces and cousins: 'In all charity, my good lady, you must find a good man, someone who is neither a fool nor a rascal, to take over this property and maintain this house.' Upon which the wife may be seen to make a sad face and answer sharply: 'Ladies, I have no inclination that way. Henceforth may God curse those who make such proposals to me, for they do not please me at all.' Then she curses all her pretty clothes.

6 So let us leave the lady to tell over her sorrows and misfortunes, and speak of her husband, who in all his life had never contented her. He is led to the great judgement seat up above, where he will be given short shrift if he cannot account for all his actions here below, and he is held accountable for the smallest things. He cries out and calls on his household, for whom he has provided so well, and on his relatives and friends, on whom he has bestowed his wealth, to come and help him, for the love of God. But this is something that no man may hope for. Then with a sad face he calls on his wife, who was so dear to him; but that lady has other concerns. A sweet sensation

[6] Cf. Ch. 7, WoB 41, for manipulation of dreams; and for the dream of the dove, cf. Chaucer, Troilus and Criseyde II. 925–31; Boccaccio, Decameron IV. 6.
[7] Juvenal mocks women's trivial 'councils' in Satire VI, 497–503; and Boccaccio in Corb.: Cassell 1975, 48–9.

pricks her heart and lifts up her spirit, and arouses in the bearded
counsellor under her skirts an appetite for meat, neither peacock nor
crane, but that dangling sausage for which so many are eager.

7 The lady is no longer concerned with the dead; so she washes
herself and dresses up and dyes her frock yellow and tucks up her
furbelows and does over her jabots, her ruffles, and her lace cuffs. She
puts on her best things, and as a new-moulted falcon goes flapping
through the air, so does the lady go sporting and showing herself off
from street to street.[8] She greets people with great ingenuousness,
bowing right down to the ground. Repeatedly she closes her mouth
tight and purses her lips. She is neither lazy nor bitter nor sour nor
quarrelsome, but sweeter than cinnamon, quicker turning and more
agile than a tambourine or a weather vane. Her heart flies on wings.
She is not inclined to grow angry or to complain or to scold, but
rather seeks to appear both good and full of humility. And she often
pulls her wimple forward to hide her hollow cheeks, which look like
open eggshells.

8 And now that I have told you of her manner and in what style
she was dressed, let me say briefly what sort of life she leads, both on
Sundays and weekdays. On Monday she sets out on her way; and
whoever she meets, be she blond or brunette, she lets her understand
what is on her mind. So she comes and goes the entire day. She has
many things to remember and when she goes to bed at night, then
does she begin to make her rounds. Her heart opens wide, and she
sends it forth to the many places where people have hardly any use
for her. No night is so dark as to keep her heart from voyaging. Then
she says over and over again: 'It's my opinion that I would suit this
one well; he is a fine young man. But that one wouldn't be interested
in me at all if my friends should bring up the subject. And there is
nothing for me in that other one; he's not worth two eggs.' So she
goes on all night, for there is no one to keep her from it. And, when
morning comes, she says to herself: 'I was born lucky! For there is no
one who can order me about. I need fear nobody, neither friend nor
stranger, neither brown nor blond nor redheaded. My halter is
broken.' She has no one to answer to. There is no feast or wedding
but she makes part of the company, and she needs no invitation. She

---

[8] The stereotype roving widow: cf. Jerome, Letter 77: 'most widows, having shaken
off the yoke of servitude, grow careless and allow themselves more liberty than ever,
frequenting the baths, flitting through the streets, showing their harlot faces everywhere' (Fremantle 1893, 159); and see Ch. 1, Scripture 13.

has plenty to eat and to drink. She lacks only one thing: that rod to chase away the pain in her bottom. And this she searches for and runs after.

9   She cannot bear the sight of her children and pecks at them the way a hen pecks at her chicks when she is kneeling before the cock.[9] She puts them away from her, becomes a sort of bogeyman for them. Often she makes wax candles and she habitually offers great numbers of them so that God may rid her of her children or that the plague may take them. 'Because of them,' she says, 'I cannot find anyone who will have me. No one would get mixed up in this.' And she takes to beating them and knocking them about; she slaps them and scratches them and bites them and calls down the plague on them. Because she does not have the love of a man, the children must pay.

10   This she does and a great deal more. If she has scraped some money together, she carries it about with her and says that this very morning a man came to her door to pay it to her. Then she speaks of Robert or Martin, who still owe her money, seven times what she has just collected, and who will pay her soon, perhaps in two weeks. To hear her tell it, she is very rich.

11   If she meets a gossip, someone who likes to go about repeating what she hears, she sidles up to her and says: 'There is something bothering me. I'm a very good friend of yours—for you're not stupid or proud   I've always liked you, and for a long time I've been meaning to ask you to come for a walk with me. I know you won't mind if I chat with you a little, because I'm sure we must be related, or so my mother used to say. But my heart is full of grief for my husband whom I have lost. My friends have forbidden me to put off my mourning, because I couldn't gain anything by doing so. And certainly my husband was very good to me. He gave me a great many things, both shoes and dresses. He made me mistress of himself and of his property. He was a very decent sort, but he wasn't much good in bed. As soon as he got into bed, he would turn his behind on me; and he would sleep that way all night. That was all the pleasure I had.[10] It used to make me very unhappy.

12   'Of course, I can't deny that he was a very wealthy man before I

<hr/>
[9] On the loathing of her children, cf. Ch. 6, *Math.* 15.
[10] The provocation of the husband's back turned at night is in Juv. *Satire* VI, 475 ff. For such intimacies revealed to 'gossips', cf. Ch. 7, *WoB* 38.

married him. But he was already quite bald when he came my way, and I was just a little girl with a dirty little face. You were only a baby then, running about like a little chick after your mother, who was a good friend of my mother's—they were close relatives. I swear by our Saviour, I am so grieved at his death! But one thing about my husband, he was a good provider; he knew how to rake in the money and how to save it, may his soul rest in peace! I have plenty of kettles and pots and white quilts and good beds and chests and chairs; and bonnets and coats and furs, which he had made in great quantity. Also I have plenty of sheets, both linen and woollen, and two kinds of firewood, the large and the small. My house is not exactly bare; I certainly have lovely kitchen equipment; I still have two cauldrons, one made in the old style with the edges turned all around it—my husband set great value on it. But I don't care to brag about what God has given me.

13 'You know Dieudonné very well? And you know Herbert well and Baudouin, Gombert's son? Do you know anything about their situations? I'm being pushed to marry again. But it's amazing about people: you imagine there is wealth where there is scarcely enough to eat. Many people are deep in debt, but I am truly rich. You can see the bark of the tree, but you can't tell what lies underneath. A great deal of so-called wealth is mostly wind, but mine is there to see. I make lots of sheets every year. I'm an honest woman and well brought up. The best people hereabouts often come calling on me. Some of them are relatives of yours. But I don't want to drop names. Are you related to Gomer? But as for Gomer, well, I won't say any more about him.

14 'But let me tell you something, my dear friend. Last year I went to a fortune teller, and he made me lie down flat in the middle of a circle, and he looked me over, and he said I would yet have a young man. Do you know of any worthy men in your neighbourhood? The one who lives next door to you seems like a very intelligent fellow. He gave me such a look the other day! But I was on my guard and took good care not to look back. A man who lives at Tournai and who is related to me on my father's side spoke to me of a friend of his, a very rich, propertied gentleman, who lives close by him. But he's old, they tell me, and I've come to despise him of late. I swear by Saint Leonard I will never take an old man![11] Because when it comes to getting a

---

[11] A jesting reference to Leonard as patron saint of prisoners; cf. Ch. 6, RR 14.

little bed exercise, I've no mind to go without seed and take the chaff.
I have enough property to get a handsome young man.

15   'Dear friend, think of me if there is any honest, sensible fellow
among your acquaintance; he would be well matched with me. Now
be nice and smart, and if you can find something for me, so may God
pardon me, you will have a good reward. I don't like making
promises or getting involved, but of one thing you can be sure: if this
business turns out well, you will be a very well-dressed woman. Look
around in the Chausée and Neufbourg sections of Valenciennes or at
Anzin. Who is this son of Dame Wiborc and of Geoffrey? The day
before yesterday when they proposed Isabel to him, he gave them the
cold shoulder. But if you don't mind, perhaps you might speak to him
secretly.

16   'But I've been here such a long time! I would stay the night, but
I'm afraid of putting you out. Let's make an appointment for Sunday.
Clemence will come too, and we'll have some apples and nuts and
some of that wine from Laenois; and I'll tell you about that relative of
mine—he doesn't live far from here—who wants to make a nun of
me.' Then she gives her a tap with the back of her hand and turns
away and goes home. The other one goes her way and repeats what
she has heard everywhere.

17   Meanwhile, this is how the widow fares. Her hairy Goliath so
pricks and excites her and the fire burns so high in her that at last she
succeeds in getting a man. And when she has caught him in her
trap, he can really complain of being worn out. Though he may
know his way about those tender nether-parts, though he be lively
and quick and can well strike and plunge, he will still be despised in
the morning. No one can help him there; he will get rough
treatment.[12]

18   As soon as the lady gets out of bed, she kicks the cat off the
hearth. Then all sorts of ill feelings come out, scoldings, reproaches:
'What have I got under my roof?—a poor thing, a wretch, a softling.
Aie! God must hate me! That I, who disdained proper young men,
gallants and gentlemen, that I should take up with such a born
weakling! May all who deal in such deceits have bad luck! And after
putting me to such torments! All he wants to do is eat and sleep. All
night long he snores like a pig. That's his delight and his pastime. Am

---

[12] Gautier harps on the widow's insatiability; cf. Ch. 4, *Ag. Marr. J9* and note.

I not ill treated then? When I stretch out next to him all naked and he
turns away from me, it almost tears the heart out of me. My
husband, my lord, you never treated me that way. You called me
your sweet beloved, and so I called you too, because you turned
toward me and kissed me sweetly and said to begin with: "My
beautiful wife and lady, what a sweet breath you have!" Husband,
those were your very words. May your soul rest in heaven! And this
vagabond treats me like the dung in his barnyard. But I well know,
by Saint Loy, that his morals are no better than those of an
Albigensian heretic. He doesn't care about loving women.'

19   To which the man replies: 'Lady, you are mistaken. You have
such a wry face that I find it hard to touch you. And I cannot keep
my agreement with you. Goliath gapes too often. I can't satisfy him;
I'm likely to die before I do.'

20   'Lying coward!' says the lady. 'You ought to be a monk and
enter a monastery. You have served me badly. Oh, it is easy to see
that I was not in my right mind when I gave up John, with his
property, good tillable land, and Geoffrey and Gilbert and Baudouin
and Foucuin, and took the worst man from here to Beauvais. Oh,
husband, you are ill replaced! You deserve to be deeply mourned, for
never was there a better man than you.[13] Alas! that all your good
qualities should be gone with you: your wisdom and your knowledge, your good manners and your kindness! You were always kind
and submissive. Never did you curse me or beat me or give me an ill
word. Whereas this whelp threatens me. It's only right that I hate
him.'

21   The young man answers angrily: 'Lady, you have a greedy
mouth in you that too often demands to be fed. It has tired my poor
old war-horse out. I've just withdrawn him all shrunken and sore.
One cannot work so much without getting weary and limp. The
peasant may be a good worker, but not every day is a working day.
You can drive the mare so hard as not to leave a drop of blood or
saliva in her. You have so milked and drained me that I am half dead,
and half mad too. I'll tell you straight out: a man must have a tough
skin indeed to let the devil trick him into taking a widow with
children, for he will never have a moment's peace thereafter. Come
on then, my sour old girl, give me the thirty marks you promised me

[13] Cf. Ch. 6, *Math. 15*, on wives using dead husbands as a reproach to their
successors.

on Tuesday or I won't do any more of this back-humping work. But by Saint Richier, if I don't get them, you'll pay dearly.'[14]

22   When she hears her young man ask for money, the good woman is furious. She sends him to all the devils in hell. She would sooner he beat her or killed her than that she should hand over that sum; he'll not have a single mark of her money. She begins once more to curse him and to quarrel and say foul things. 'Ah, wastrel!' she cries. 'All my goods are wasted. You have so bled me and robbed me that I no longer have a stick of firewood nor a grain of wheat. My house has been swept clean. You're a heavy burden to bear. And we know your family well—the stinking wretches—and your sisters and your aunts, who are all dirty whores. . . .'

23   At these words, the young man leaps up, and without so much as a by-your-leave he grabs her by the haunches and gives her such a thrashing, more than she bargained for, that he soon pays her in full for her foul words. Then he leaps on her again and beats and pounds her with his fists until he is all in a sweat and worn out. When she has had enough, the widow runs and hides in her chamber, without hat or headdress. She has been so roughly handled in the fray that her hair is all dishevelled. She goes to bed and covers up, forbids anyone to come in, and lies there licking her wounds.

24   But in the end she calls out: 'Oh, you thief, how you have hurt me! Now may God grant me a quick death and bring me where I can be with my husband. May my soul follow his and may I abide with him. For there is nothing I want more, dear husband, than to be with you.' And she speaks in an affectedly weak voice as though she were really dying; for she knows how to make the most of her wounds.[15] Then after a while, she begins to speak up a little; she calls for hot broth, for cheese tarts, for little cakes. Also she takes a great many baths, morning and even, early and late, until she is all healed and cured. Then, the quarrel over, the two of them come back together again.

25   For one thing I have learned is that if a man knows how to swing his balls he can overcome all ills. Where such a man lives, there the cat is commended to God—no one beats it or lays a hand on it; there the cushions are plumped up and the benches pushed

[14] Cf. Ch. 6, *Math. 15*, on widows who marry spendthrifts.
[15] A possible antecedent for Ch. 7, *WoB 59–60*.

against the wall, so that the man may not hurt himself on them; there not a log remains on the hearth; there is he loved and served and given everything he wants—chicken and other fowl; there is he lord and master; there is he washed and combed and his hair parted. For I tell you once again, according to the proverb: she who would have her husband soothe her tail must pile endearments on his head.

26   You who despise women, think of those endearments in that hour when she is under you and you on top. He who would experience that joy must give up to his beloved a great part of his will, no matter how much it grieves him to do so.[16] A man who is not distressed from time to time is neither kind nor honest. For if my wife scolds and says nasty things to me, all I need do is leave and she stops. Anyone who tried to answer her would be reasoning with madness.[17] And it is better for me to go away than to hit her with a piece of wood. Lords, you who are submissive, deceitful, and blusterers, do not be dismayed in any way: submissive men have more joy than do those quarrelsome rascals who are always looking for a fight. And finally, Gautier le Leu says that he who will oppress his wife or quarrel with her only because she wants what all her neighbours want does not have a gentle heart. But I do not choose to go any deeper into this question. A woman only does what she must. The tale is done. Set up the drinks.

JACQUES DE VITRY (c. 1170–1240)

FROM SERMON 66* IN *SERMONS FOR ALL* (*SERMONES VULGARES*)

Jacques de Vitry was an ecclesiastic of great energy and wide experience. He is remembered as a committed crusader and as a supporter of the female religious movement associated with Mary of Oignies. He also popularized the use of exemplary tales (*exempla*) in his huge repertoire of sermons. One collection of these, the *Sermones vulgares*, is written with an eye to numerous professions and social groups, and is packed with *exempla* which were later extracted to form one of the period's anthologies of ready-to-use preachers' stories.[18] Jacques includes three sermons 'to married people' (*ad coniugatos*) of which the first is represented below.[19] The sermon as a whole offers an

[16] Conciliatory remarks which qualify the antifeminism of 'The Widow': Johnson 1983, 305–6.
[17] On irrationality, cf. Ch. 4, Andreas 9; and Ch. 6, *Math.* 1.
* New translation by Alcuin Blamires from a transcription of the Latin text in MS B.N. Lat. 17509 (fos. 135ʳ–137ᵛ), kindly supplied by David D'Avray.
[18] The *exempla* are translated in Crane 1890.
[19] Discussed in D'Avray and Tausche 1980.

1. *Pasiphaë and the 'Bull'* (here interpreted as a man with a bull's nature). Detail from a manuscript of Christine de Pizan, *Epître d'Othéa*, Ch. XLV, illuminated by Willem Vrelant (*c.*1460). Universitätsbibliothek, Erlangen, MS 26361, fo. 59ʳ.

2. *Aeneas' Departure: Dido Commits Suicide by Falling on a Sword. Histoire Universelle* (Neapolitan, 1352–62), British Library, MS Royal 20. D. 1, fo. 199ʳ.

3. *David and Bathsheba. Liber humane salvationis* (German, c.1395), British Library Add. MS 38119, fo. 1ᵛ.

4. *Expulsion from Paradise: Adam Pulls Eve's Hair and Kicks Her.* Relief sculpture (12th century), Notre-Dame-du-Port, Clermont-Ferrand.

5. *Aristotle Ridden by Phyllis.* Detail from a tapestry of 'women's wiles' (German, c.1320–30), Augustinermuseum, Freiburg im Bresgau.

6. *Jerome Tempted by Dancing Girls. Belles Heures* of Jean, Duke of Berry, illuminated by the Limbourg brothers (*c.*1406–9). Metropolitan Museum of Art, New York, Cloisters Collection (54.1.1, fo. 186ʳ).

7. *Sensuality* (*Voluptas*). Relief sculpture (*c.*1290), porch of the Cathedral of Freiburg im Bresgau.

8. *Samson and Delilah*. Old Testament Picture Book (Parisian, *c*.1250), Pierpont Morgan Library, New York, MS 638, fo. 15ʳ.

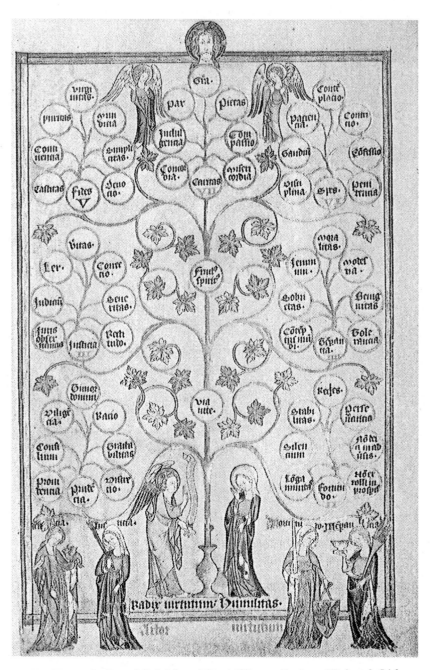

9. *The Virgin, Archangel Gabriel, and Tree of Virtues. Psalter of Robert de Lisle* (English, 14th century), British Library, MS Arundel 83. 11, fo. 129ʳ.

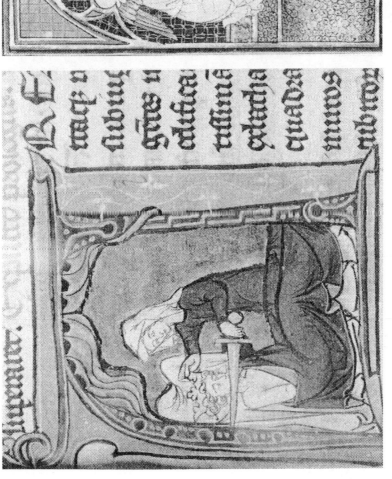

10. *Judith Beheading Holofernes.* Vulgate Bible (Normandy, 1279), St David's University College, Lampeter, MS 1, fo. 181ʳ.

11. *The Women at Christ's Tomb. Psalter of Robert de Lisle* (English, 14th century), British Library, MS Arundel 83. ΙΙ, detail of fo. 133ʳ.

12. *Catherine of Alexandria Bound to a Column. Belles Heures* of Jean, Duke of Berry, illuminated by the Limbourg brothers (*c.*1406–9). New York, Metropolitan Museum of Art, Cloisters Collection (54.1.1, fo. 17ʳ).

important reminder that misogynistic sentiment was constantly entwined with perspectives sympathetic to women. He begins by insisting on monogamy, and condemning promiscuous men. He goes on to touch on themes frequently found in commentary on marriage. Woman was created from the rib, not from foot or head, as a sign that she is man's 'companion',[20] and should be treated as such, not left half-starved at home while the husband boozes all day. If he beats her on his return, he must share her guilt should she abandon him for another man. God did not intend woman to be downtrodden, for He gave her special privileges.[21] After its denunciations of drunken husbands, however, the sermon switches forcibly into antifeminist mode.

1 Woman was not created from man's head, in case she should be inflated with arrogance towards man. 'I suffer not a woman to teach, nor to use authority over the man.'[22] Also, 'A woman, if she have superiority, is contrary to her husband.'[23] 'Let wives be subject to their husbands ... just as Sara obeyed Abraham, calling him "lord".'[24] For after woman sinned she was told: 'thou shalt be under thy husband's power',[25] that is, in being obedient to him; and a husband ought to take precedence over his wife, in ruling over her. But some wives are unwilling to be subject: they would rather take precedence, and they don't just despise their husbands, they lash out and beat them.... They always want to propose to put their will before their husbands' will. 'This is my will, and this is what I command: let will substitute for reason.' 'There was never a lawsuit which was not begun by a woman.' 'The marital bed is always a place of dispute and mutual bickering.' 'A wife's dowry is quarrelling.'[26] Then in Ecclesiasticus; 'It will be more agreeable to abide with a lion and a dragon than to dwell with a wicked woman.'[27]

2 I have heard of one bad woman who was so antagonistic towards her husband that she always opposed him, and did the contrary of his orders.[28] Whenever he invited people to a meal and asked her to receive the guests cheerfully, she did the opposite, and exasperated

[20] A commonplace: cf. Ch. 8, Dives 1.
[21] Her creation (i) inside paradise, and (ii) not from earth; and (iii) God's incarnation through human mother, not father. Adopted by Christine de Pizan, Ch. 9, Letter 10 and City 4.
[22] 1. Tim. 2: 12.
[23] Ecclus. 25: 30, in Ch. 1, Scripture 9; and cf. Ch. 8, Albertano 1 and 4.
[24] 1 Peter 3: 1, 6.
[25] Gen. 3: 16.
[26] A string of three quotations from Juv. Satire VI, 223, 242, 268 (see Ch. 1, Juv. 5–6); and a fourth from Ovid, Art of Love II. 155.
[27] Ecclus. 25: 23.
[28] Cf. Ch. 4, Andreas 15.

her husband very much. One day, when this man had invited some people to a meal, he had the table put up in his garden near a river. But she, sitting between it and the water, looked at the men who had been invited with a surly face, and kept herself some distance from the table. Her husband said, 'Be cheerful to our guests, and come nearer the table.' Hearing this, she immediately moved further away from the table, getting closer to the river bank behind her back. Her waiting husband now angrily said 'Come to the table!' But determined to do the opposite, she lunged so far away from the table that she fell into the river and, her breath stifled, disappeared.

3   With a show of grief he got into a boat and, steering *against* the current of the river, searched for his wife with a long pole in the water. When his neighbours asked why he was searching upstream, when he ought to be looking downstream, he replied: 'Don't you realize that my wife is always contrarious, and never goes the right way? I'm sure she would have gone against the current, not with it as others usually do.'

The middle of the sermon concentrates largely on a couple's equal obligations so far as sexual intercourse within marriage is concerned, but, Jacques continues:

4   It is clear that however much a married couple is equal as regards the carnal debt, in other things the husband is his wife's head,[29] to rule her, correct her (if she strays), and restrain her (so she does not fall headlong). For hers is a slippery and weak sex, not to be trusted too easily. Wanton woman is slippery like a snake and as mobile as an eel;[30] so she can hardly be guarded or kept within bounds. Some things are so bare that there is nothing by which to get hold of them. Just as whoever tries to grasp a sunbeam opens his hand to find it holds nothing, and just as a round glass container lacking handles to hold is not easily grasped by the hand and quickly slips away, so it is with woman: roving and lecherous once she has been stirred by the devil's hoe.[31] Put a frog on a silk cloth and it'll never rest until it jumps back into the mud; it cannot stay in a clean place.

5   She will bring tears to your eyes—but *their* eyes are schooled in

---

[29] Cf. Ch. 3, Gratian 2.
[30] Cf. 'eel in the Seine', Ch. 6, *RR 21*. 'Wanton' here translates *multivola* ('wanting many'), found in Catullus 68. 128.
[31] Reading *rastro* for MS *restro*, as suggested by D'Avray.

weeping.[32] Do not believe her, because 'the iniquity of a man is better than a well-meaning woman'.[33] When the time comes she will spread her wings, since if an opportunity discloses itself she'll fly off and quit. In this respect woman can be called a virtuoso artist, as they say; because she has one skill—that is, one way of deceiving—more than the devil.

6   I heard of one woman whose husband so kept watch on her that he would never allow her to go out without him. Being devious, she began to ponder how she could trick her guardian. Eventually she indicated to her lover (or rather, adulterer) that he should wait for her in a particular house. When she came in front of that house, she allowed herself to fall over into a lot of mud, pretending that her feet had slipped. Since all her clothing was filthy, she said to her husband: 'Wait here at the entrance, because I shall have to take my clothes off and clean them in this house.' But once she had gone in, she spent a long while with the adulterer, came out in cleaned clothes, and thus deceived her husband.

---

[32] Jacques adapts a passage on women's tears in Ovid, *Cures for Love* 687–90.
[33] Ecclus. 42: 14, in Ch. 1, Scripture 10.

6

Vernacular Adaptations in the
Later Middle Ages

Because the distinction between Latin and vernacular culture in the Middle
Ages was constantly blurred, it is rather artificial to compartmentalize them
in separate chapters. Nevertheless, Christine de Pizan makes the point that
one's first steps in learning Latin could lead towards misogynistic indoctrina-
tion because of the inclusion of exemplary material on David, Samson, etc.,
alongside Ovid, in the elementary Latin curriculum.[1] Since women were not
often educated in Latin, there was therefore a sense in which Latin remained
a linguistic enclave where antifeminism perpetuated itself and could be
indulged with particular impunity, safe from female retort. Richard de Bury
joked that women were justified in resenting books, full of antifeminist
'secrets' which, fortunately, they could not understand.[2] However, it was
often the Latin-trained 'clerks' who wrote in, or translated into, the
vernacular, too. So despite their wider dissemination, vernacular writings
from the thirteenth to the fifteenth centuries are not notable for being less
abrasively or less voluminously antifeminist, though courtly romance could
be considered a major sector of vernacular literature relatively positive about
women.

The three works represented in this chapter demonstrate between them
how a diversity of misogynistic conventions, including the most ancient,
could be refurbished, with typical late-medieval eclecticism. The Roman
satirists and Theophrastus are bedfellows in Jean de Meun; Boccaccio tries to
out-Juvenal Juvenal; and Le Fèvre faithfully renders what he finds in
Matheolus—a pot-pourri of the whole tradition.

JEAN DE MEUN (c. 1 240–c. 1 305)

FROM *THE ROMANCE OF THE ROSE** (*LE ROMAN DE LA
ROSE*: c. 1 2 7 5)

Jean de Meun was evidently widely read and is thought to have studied for a
time at the University of Paris. He translated a variety of philosophical and
other Latin works into French, though he is most celebrated for the
continuation he grafted on to Guillaume de Lorris's allegory about a lover's

---

[1] See Ch. 9, *Letter 3–4*.
[2] Discussed in the Introduction.
* Tr. Charles Dahlberg, *The Romance of the Rose by Guillaume de Lorris and Jean
de Meun* (Princeton: Princeton University Press, 1971), 156–78, 226–37, 276–81.
© Princeton University Press, 1971. Reprinted by permission of Princeton University
Press. Line references are to the edition by Langlois 1914–24).

quest for the 'rose'. Critics disagree substantially (as medieval readers of the text themselves disagreed) in their interpretation of the hugely influential hybrid poem thus produced, but most would admit that Jean cultivates a direction more overtly satirical and misogynistic, less emotionally sensitized, than that taken by Guillaume. Doubtless there is a groundswell of implicit misogyny in Guillaume, too: the unpleasant figures he portrays on the outside of the love-garden wall within which the rose is discovered—Hatred, Avarice, Old Age, and other 'undesirables'—are insistently female. Moreover, his whole narrative invites description in terms of phallocentric pursuit of a sex-object, though it can be countered that it is self-consciously so, and that Guillaume is exposing the 'courtly game' as one played by men for their own satisfaction.[3] Nevertheless, Jean de Meun is more explicitly indebted to misogynist tradition, as can frequently be observed in incidental disparagement. For instance, his stereotypical Old Woman/Procuress, La Vieille, reinforces two common medieval allegations against women simultaneously when she reproaches herself for showing 'a woman's poor judgement' because of her inability to end a relationship with a man who, though he abused her, was 'a hard rider in bed' (14489–512).

Readers have always had to remind themselves that the more notorious discourses, such as La Vieille's, ostensibly project the attitudes of Jean's *dramatis personae*. As his defenders in the early fifteenth-century 'Quarrel of the Rose' noted, it may be particularly necessary to remember this in the case of the misogynistic tirade launched by the Jealous Husband (Le Jaloux). Actually, the latter is not a member of the primary cast: he is *imagined* as a negative example of the bullying husband, criticizing a hypothetical wife, by the Friend when he is counselling the Lover on how to keep a sweetheart. According to Friend, this means retrieving a type of freedom within relationships that was characteristic of prehistoric times; it means eschewing the possessive and abusive behaviour displayed in marriage by a man like Le Jaloux. The antifeminist vitriol which the embittered husband pours forth is, therefore, intended to betray the destructiveness of a domineering male attitude. Jean has worked out a formula that courts his audience's (and maybe his own?) responsiveness to familiar misogynistic themes while simultaneously acknowledging their blatant invidiousness, mouthed by a man futilely bent on owning his wife. Friend declares that love and lordship cannot coexist.

The Jealous Husband

1 (8455) 'It is the same in marriages, where we see that the husband thinks himself wise and scolds his wife, beats her, and makes her live a life of strife. He tells her that she is stupid and foolish for staying out dancing and keeping company so often with handsome young men. They undergo so much suffering when the husband wants to have control over the body and possessions of his wife that good love cannot endure.

[3] Ferrante 1975, 111.

2 (8467) '"You are too giddy", he says, "and your behaviour is too silly. As soon as I go to my work, you go off dancing and live a life so riotous that it seems ribald, and you sing like a siren. And when I go off to Rome or Friesland with our merchandise, then immediately you become very coquettish⁴—for word of your conduct goes around everywhere, and I know through one who tells me of it—and when anyone speaks about the reason that you conduct yourself so demurely⁴ in all the places where you go, you reply, 'Alas! It is on account of my love for my husband.' . . . Everyone knows very well that you lie. For me, sorrowful wretch! For me! I formed evil gauntlets with my own hands and deceived myself cruelly when I accepted your faith, the day of our marriage. For me you lead this life of riot! For me you lead this life of luxury! Who do you think you go around fooling? I never have the possibility of seeing these quaint little games,⁴ when these libertines, who go around spying out whores, greedy for pleasure and hot with desire, gaze and look upon you from top to bottom when they accompany you through the streets. . . .

3 (8553) '"Didn't I take you to serve me?⁵ Do you think that you deserve my love in order to consort with these dirty rascals just because they have such gay hearts and find you so gay in turn? You are a wicked harlot, and I can have no confidence in you. The devils made me marry. Ah! If I had believed Theophrastus, I would never have married a wife. He considers no man wise who takes a wife in marriage, whether she is beautiful or ugly, poor or rich, for he says, and affirms it as true in his noble book, *Aureolus*⁶ (a good one to study in school), that married life is very disagreeable, full of toil and trouble, of quarrels and fights that result from the pride of foolish women, full, too, of their opposition and the reproaches that they make and utter with their mouths, full of the demands and the complaints that they find on many occasions. One has great trouble keeping them in line and restraining their silly desires. (8579) He who wants to take a poor wife must undertake to feed her, clothe her, and put shoes on her feet. And if he thinks that he can improve his situation by taking a very rich wife, he will find her so proud and

---

⁴ 'Coquettish', 'demurely', and 'quaint little games' are attempts to render the nuance of *cointe, cointe,* and *cointerie.*
⁵ Possibly recalling the words used by her in the marriage rite.
⁶ On the title *Aureolus* see Ch. 4, Map 35; and Ch. 2, Jerome *12.* What follows paraphrases the Theophrastus material in Jerome *12–18,* whether direct from Jerome or through an intermediary such as John of Salisbury.

haughty, so overweening and arrogant, that he will again have great torment to endure her. And if, in addition, she is beautiful, everybody will run after her, pursue her and do her honour; they will come to blows, will work, struggle, battle, and exert themselves to serve her; and they all will surround her, beg her, try to get her favour, covet her, and carry on until in the end they will have her, for a tower besieged on all sides can hardly escape being taken.

4 (8597) '"If, on the other hand, she is ugly, she wants to please everybody; and how could anyone guard something that everyone makes war against or who wants all those who see her? If he takes up war against the whole world, he cannot live on earth. No one would keep them from being captured, provided that they had been well-solicited. He who understood how to take a prize well would capture even Penelope, and there was no better woman in Greece.

5 (8608) '"In faith, he would do the same with Lucrece, even though she killed herself because King Tarquin's son took her by force. According to Titus Livius, no husband or father or relative could prevent her, in spite of all the trouble that they took, from killing herself in front of them. They urged her strongly to let go her sorrow; they gave her persuasive reasons; and her husband particularly comforted her with compassion and pardoned her with generous heart for the entire deed, and lectured her and studied to find lively arguments to prove to her that her body had not sinned when her heart did not wish the sin (for the body cannot be a sinner if the heart does not consent to it). But she, in her sorrow, held a knife hidden in her breast, so that no one might see it when she took it to strike herself; and she answered them without shame:[7] 'Fair lords, no matter who may pardon me for the filthy sin that weighs on me so heavily, no matter how I am pardoned, I do not pardon myself of the penance for that sin.' Then, full of great anguish, she struck and rent her heart and fell to the ground dead, in front of them. But first she begged them to work to avenge her death. She wanted to establish this example in order to assure women that any man who took them by force would have to die. As a result, the king and his son were sent into exile and died there. After that disturbance, the Romans never wanted to make anyone king.

[7] With the source material from Livy's *History* (1. 57–8) are mingled emphases (in part deriving from Augustine, *City of God* 1. 19) that mischievously discredit Lucretia, insisting on her refusal to compromise with her relatives' advice, and insinuating indecorousness here in the expression *sanz vergogne*.

6 (8651) '"And if one knows how to beseech women, there is no Lucrece, no Penelope in Greece, nor any worthy woman on earth. If a man knew how to take her, no woman ever defended herself.[8] The stories of the pagans tell us so, and no one ever found an exception. Many women even give themselves away when they lack suitors.

7 (8661) '"Again, those who marry have a very dangerous custom, one so ill-arranged that it occurs to me as a very great wonder. I don't know where this folly comes from, except from raging lunacy. I see that a man who buys a horse is never so foolish as to put up any money if he does not see the horse unclothed, no matter how well it may have been covered.[9] He looks the horse over everywhere and tries it out. But he takes a wife without trying her out, and she is never unclothed, not on account of gain or loss, solace or discomfort, but for no other reason than that she may not be displeasing before she is married. Then, when she sees things accomplished, she shows her malice for the first time; then appears every vice that she has; and then, when it will do him no good to repent, she makes the fool aware of her ways. I know quite certainly that no matter how prudently his wife acts, there is no man, unless he is a fool, who does not repent when he feels himself married.

8 (8687) '"By Saint Denis! Worthy women, as Valerius bears witness, are fewer than phoenixes. No man can love one but what she will pierce his heart with great fears and cares and other bitter misfortunes. Fewer than phoenixes? By my head, a more honest comparison would say fewer than white crows, however beautiful their bodies may be. Nevertheless, whatever I say, and in order that those who are alive may not say that I attack all women with too great impunity, a worthy woman, if one wants to recognize her, either in the world or in the cloister, and if he wants to put in some toil in seeking her, is a rare bird on earth, so easily recognized that it is like the black swan.[10] Even Juvenal confirms this idea when he reiterates it in a positive statement: 'If you find a chaste wife, go kneel down in the temple, bow down to worship Jupiter, and put forth your

----

[8] 'No Lucrece'; cf. Ch. 4, Map 13. On lack of resistance cf. Ch. 4, Map 32 and Andreas 23.
[9] The comparison with a horse (sexually symbolic: to be 'ridden' by the man?) is selected from Theophrastus' catalogue of things tried out before purchase: cf. Ch. 2, Jerome 13, and *Math*. II. 393 ff., III. 265 ff.
[10] To the phoenix found in Ch. 4, Map ('Valerius') 12, Jean adds the 'black swan' from Ch. 1, Juv. 4, and 'white crow' from Juv. *Satire* VII, 202.

effort to sacrifice a gilded cow to Juno, the honoured lady, for nothing more wonderful ever happened to any creature.'[11]

9   (8717) '"And if a man wants to love the wicked women—of whom, according to Valerius, who is not ashamed to tell the truth, there are swarms, here and overseas, greater than those of the bees that gather in their hives—if he wants to love them, what end does he expect to come to?[12] He brings harm to himself by clinging to such a branch; he who clings to it, I well recall, will lose both soul and body.

10   (8727) '"Valerius, who sorrowed because his companion Rufinus wanted to marry, made a stern speech to him: 'My friend', he said, 'may omnipotent God keep you from ever being put into the snare of an all-powerful woman who smashes all things through cunning.'[13]

11   (8735) '"Juvenal himself writes to Postumus on his marriage: 'Do you want to take a wife, Postumus? Can't you find ropes, cords, or halters for sale? Can't you jump out of one of the high windows that we can see? Or can't you let yourself fall from the bridge? What Fury leads you to this torment and pain?'[14]

12   (8745) '"King Phoroneus himself who, as we have learned, gave the Greek people their laws, spoke from his deathbed and said to his brother Leonce: 'Brother, I reveal to you that I would have died happy if I had never married a wife.' And Leonce straightway asked him the cause of that statement. 'All husbands', said Phoroneus, 'test it and find it by experiment; and when you have taken a wife, you will know it well in every detail.'[15]

13   (8759) '"Pierre Abelard, in turn, admits that Sister Heloise, abbess of the Paraclete and his former sweetheart, did not want to agree for anything that he take her as his wife. Instead, the young lady of good understanding, well educated, loving and well loved in return, brought up arguments to convince him not to marry; and she proved to him with texts and reasons that the conditions of marriage are very hard, no matter how wise the wife may be. For she had seen, studied, and known the books, and she knew the feminine ways, for she had them all in herself. . . ."'

[11] Cf. Ch. 1, Juv. 2.   [12] Ch. 4, Map 12.   [13] Ch. 4, Map 36.
[14] Ch. 1, Juv. 1.   [15] Cf. Ch. 4, Map 21.

(8777–824) The speaker mentions a couple of Heloise's arguments as well as her notorious claim that she would rather be Abelard's whore than an empress.

'"... I do not believe that any such woman ever existed afterward; and I think that her learning put her in such a position that she knew better how to overcome and subdue her nature, with its feminine ways. If Pierre had believed her, he would never have married her.[16]

14   (8833) '"Marriage is an evil bond, so help me Saint Julian, who harbours wandering pilgrims, and Saint Leonard, who unshackles prisoners who are truly repentant, when he sees them lamenting.[17] It would have been better for me to go hang, the day I had to take a wife, when I became acquainted with so quaint a woman. With such a coquette I am dead. For Saint Mary's son, what is that quaintness worth to me, that costly, expensive dress that makes you turn your nose up, that is so long and trails behind you, that irks and vexes me so much, that makes you act so overbearing that I become mad with rage? What profit does it give me? ..."'

(8851–89) Her elaborate dresses impede his attentions by day, and hang up uselessly at night.

15   (8889) '"And if any man, to confound me, wanted to oppose me by replying that the bounties of good things go well with many different kinds of people and that beautiful apparel creates beauty in ladies and girls, then, no matter who said so in fact, I would reply that he lied. For the beauties of fair things, violets or roses, silk cloths or *fleurs de lys*, as I find it written in a book, are in themselves and not in ladies.[18] All women should know that no woman will ever, as long as she lives, have anything except her natural beauty. And I say the same about goodness as I have told you about beauty. Thus, to begin my speech, I say that if one wanted to cover a dung-heap with silken cloths or little flowers, well-arranged and beautifully coloured, it would certainly still be a dung-heap, whose custom it is to stink just

---

[16] See Ch. 3, Heloise 1–4. The speaker's idea that she learned to 'subdue her feminine ways' by reading (men's?) books begs questions.

[17] Cf. Ch. 5, Gautier 14.

[18] Probably from Boethius, *Consolation of Philosophy*, II. pr. 5, arguing that the radiance of jewels belongs to the stones themselves, not to the wearers, and that whatever is underneath glittering ornaments remains 'in its filth'.

as it did before.[19] Someone might want to say, 'If the dung-heap is ugly within, it appears more lovely without; and in just the same way the ladies apparel themselves in order to appear more beautiful or to hide their ugliness.' If someone were to say thus, I do not know, by my faith, how to reply, except to say that such deception comes from the maddened vision of eyes that see them in all their fine apparel. As a result, their hearts are led astray because of the pleasing impression of their imaginations, and they do not know how to recognize a lie or the truth or how, for lack of clear vision, to explicate the sophism.[20] But if they had the eyes of a lynx, they would never, for any sable mantles, surcoats, or skirts, any head ornaments, kerchiefs, undergarments, or pelisses, for any jewels or objects of value, for any covert, smirking coquetries, if one considered them well, for any gleaming exteriors, which make them look artificial, and never for any chaplets of fresh flowers, would they seem to them to be beautiful. However well Nature had formed Alcibiades, whose body was always beautiful in colour and moulding, anyone who could see within him would want to consider him very ugly. So Boethius tells us. . . .'"[21]

(8957–9012) Le Jaloux ponders the incessant and one-sided conflict between Beauty and Chastity, the latter obliged to flee universal attack.

16   (9013) '"I swear by God, the celestial king, that a woman who wants to be beautiful, or who exerts herself to appear beautiful, examines herself and takes great trouble to deck herself out and look attractive, because she wants to wage war on Chastity, who certainly has many enemies. In cloisters and abbeys all the women are sworn against her. They will never be so walled in that they do not hate Chastity so strongly that they all aspire to shame her. They all do homage to Venus, with no consideration for worth or harm; they primp and paint in order to fool those who look at them, and they go searching along through the streets in order to see, to be seen,[22] and to arouse desire in people, so that they will want to lie with them.

---

[19] Moralists frequently compared the hypocrite, and the dressy woman, to a dungheap covered with snow: cf. *Corb.* 12 below, and *Math.* II. 3095–8.

[20] *Math.* 3 builds on this.

[21] *Consolation* III. pr. 8, in a discussion of the eye's inability to get beyond externals. Note the use of a *male* exemplar of beauty.

[22] Ovid, *Art of Love* I. 99 observes that women gather to watch, and be watched, at the amphitheatre: cf. Ch. 5, Gautier 7.

Therefore they wear their finery to carols and churches,[23] for not one of them would ever do so if she did not think that she would be seen and that she would thus more quickly give pleasure to those whom she could deceive. Certainly, if the truth be told, women give great shame to God. Misguided fools, they do not consider themselves rewarded with the beauty that God gives them. Each one has on her head a crown of flowers, of gold, or of silk. She preens herself and primps as she goes through the town showing herself off, and thus the unhappy wretch abases herself in a very wicked way when, to increase or perfect her beauty, she wants to draw on to her head an object lower and more base than she. Thus she goes around despising God because she considers Him inadequate, and in her foolish heart she thinks to herself that God did her a great outrage in that, when He proportioned the beauty in her, He acquitted himself very negligently. Therefore she searches for beauty in creations that God made with much worse appearance, things like metals or flowers or other strange things." '[24]

(9063–122) If men ornament themselves they offend God likewise. But Le Jaloux prefers simple clothes and resents buying elaborate dresses for his wife to show off to her boyfriends, who presumably find her more sexually obliging than he, and laugh at him meanwhile.

17 (9123) ' "It is through you, lady slut, and through your wild ways, that I am given over to shame, you riotous, filthy, vile, stinking bitch. May your body never see the end of this year when you give it over to such curs! Through you and your lechery I am placed in the confraternity of Saint Ernoul, the patron of cuckolds, from whom no man with a wife, to my knowledge, can be safe, no matter how much he may go about to guard her and spy on her, even though he may have a thousand eyes. All women get themselves attacked, and there is no guard worth anything. If it happens that they omit the deed, they never are without the wish, by which, if they can, they will jump to the deed, for they always carry their desire with them. But Juvenal gives one great comfort for this situation when he says, of the need that is called a woman's carnal need to be made happy, that it is the least of the sins by which the heart of a woman is stained, for their nature commands each of them to give her attention to doing

---

[23] The *carole* was a dance. On churches and courtship see Ch. 1, Ovid 4, and Ch. 4, *Ag. Marr.* L4.
[24] Paraphrasing Boethius, *Consolation*, II. pr. 5; cf. Ch. 2, Tert. 7, on tampering with God's image.

worse.[25] Do we not see how the mothers-in-law cook up poisons for
their sons-in-law, how they work charms and sorceries and so many
other diabolical things that, no matter how stout his powers of
thought, no man could count them?

18 (9155) '"All you women are, will be, and have been whores, in
fact or in desire, for, whoever could eliminate the deed, no man can
constrain desire. All women have the advantage of being mistresses
of their desires. For no amount of beating or upbraiding can one
change your hearts, but the man who could change them would
have lordship over your bodies."'

(9165–312) More outbursts against her presumed lovers, who under the
influence of this Deianeira, or Delilah, will fancy themselves as tough as
Hercules or Samson, ready to cripple him. Yet they probably treat her like a
whore and are really after her expensive accessories, which are useless to
him, but lead her into fornication.

19 (9313) '"But now tell me without making up any lies. Where,
for the sake of love, did you get that other rich new dress in which
you fixed yourself up here the other day when you went to the carols,
for I know very well that I am right to think that I never gave it to
you. You swore to me by Saint Denis, Saint Philibert, and Saint Peter
that it came to you through your mother, who sent you the cloth for
it because, as you gave me to understand, her love for me is so great
that she wants to spend her money in order to make me keep mine.
May she be grilled alive, that dirty old whore, that priest's concubine,
that mackerel, that pimping whore, and may you, for your merits,
fry along with her, if the case is not exactly as you say. I would
certainly ask her, but I would exert myself in vain; the whole thing
would not be worth a ball to me: like mother, like daughter. I know
that you have talked together, and it is obvious that you both have
hearts touched by the same wand. I know which foot you jump with,
and that dirty painted old whore agrees with your attitude; she used
to act in the same way. She has followed so many roads that she has
been bitten by many curs. But now, I know, her looks are so bad that
she can make nothing by herself, and so now she sells you. Three or
four times a week she comes in here and leads you out on the pretext
of new pilgrimages according to her old customs—for I know the
whole plan—and then she doesn't stop parading you, as one does
with a horse for sale, while she grabs and teaches you to grab."'[26]

[25] *Satire* VI, 133–5.
[26] Cf. Ch. 1, Ovid 5; and Juv. *Satire* VI 231–41.

(9357–402) Concluding the Jealous Husband's speech, the Friend imagines him assaulting his wife in a rage, provoking her smouldering resentment.

20   (9403) 'Afterward, if he sleeps in her company, he puts his life in very great peril. Indeed, sleeping and waking, he must fear most strongly that, in order to avenge herself, she may have him poisoned or hacked into pieces, or make him languish in a life of desperate ruses. Or he must fear that, if she cannot play any other way, she may take it into her head to flee. A woman values neither honour nor shame when anything rises up in her head;[27] this is the truth without doubt. A woman has no reason whatever.[28] Valerius even claims that, towards whatever she hates *and* whatever she loves, a woman is bold, cunning, and studious of bringing injury to others.'[29]

(9421–902) Friend reflects on the incompatibility between love and the authoritarianism which can beset it in marriage. Then he rounds off his miscellaneous advice to the Lover with various antifeminist insinuations, the first of which presupposes that male fickleness is apt in view of women's slipperiness.

21   (9903) 'For no woman will ever know so much or be so firm of heart, so loyal or serious, that one could ever be certain of holding her, no matter how much trouble one took, any more than if one held an eel by the tail in the Seine;[30] for he hasn't the power to prevent her saving herself, so that immediately she will have escaped, however strongly he might seize her. There is no animal so well trained that is always ready to flee; she has so many different changes that no man should have confidence in her.

22   (9917) 'I do not say these things on account of good women, who establish restraints through their virtues; but I have not yet found any, however many I may have tested. Not even Solomon could find them, no matter how well he knew how to test them, for he himself affirms that he never found a stable woman.[31] And if you take the trouble to seek one and find her, take her; you will have the pick of sweethearts, one who will be wholly yours. If she doesn't have the possibility of running about looking, so that she might provide for herself elsewhere, or if she does not find someone who will solicit her, such a woman will give herself up to Chastity.

---

[27] Echoing Ch. 1, Juv. 8.
[28] Probably recalling Prov. 9: 13: 'A foolish woman and clamorous, and full of allurements, and knowing nothing at all.'
[29] Cf. Ch. 4, Map 30.
[30] Cf. Ch. 5, Jacques de Vitry 4.
[31] Eccles. 7: 29; in Ch. 1, Scripture 8.

23 (9933) 'Now I want to say another brief word before I leave this subject. In short, a man who wants to keep the love of any girl, whatever she may be, ugly or beautiful, must observe this commandment of mine, and he should remember it always and consider it very precious: let him give any girl to understand that he cannot protect himself against her, so dumbfounded and amazed is he by her beauty and worth, for there is no woman, however good she may be, old, young, worldly or cloistered, no lady so religious, however chaste of body or soul, who does not take delight in hearing someone go about praising her beauty. No matter how ugly she may be called, one should swear that she is more beautiful than a fairy; one may do so securely, since she will easily believe him, for every woman, I know well, thinks of herself as one so beautiful, however ugly she may be proven, that she is indeed worthy to be loved.[32]

24 (9959) 'Thus should all handsome, worthy, and noble young men be diligent in keeping their sweethearts, without criticizing them for their follies. Women do not care for correction; instead, they have minds so constructed that it seems to them that they do not need to be taught their trade. And no man who doesn't want to displease them should dissuade them from anything that they want to do. Just as the cat knows by nature the science of catching, and cannot be diverted from it, because he is always born with such a faculty and was never put to school to learn it, just so a woman, however foolish she is, knows by her natural judgement that, whatever excess she commits, good or bad, wrong or right, or whatever you wish, she does nothing that she should not, and she hates whoever corrects her.'[33]

The Old Woman

In the allegory, the love-object's personified Responsiveness (her *Bel Acueill*) is imprisoned, and guarded somewhat ineffectually from the Lover's entreaties by La Vieille. The latter is the archetypal medieval literary Old Woman, survivor of a lifetime in the sex war and, like Ovid's Dipsas, a 'guide' to younger recruits who she hopes will learn under her tutelage to use men as she feels they have used her. Our realization that she has been goaded into retaliation by the cynicism and lies she has encountered in men makes her an ambivalent figure. If she is 'an illustration of the strongest antifeminist diatribes' who 'sketches all the ways women can deceive and fleece and

---

[32] Closely modelled on Ovid, *Art of Love* I. 611–14.
[33] Cf. Ovid, *Art of Love* II. 641 ff. ('don't criticize a woman's faults') and *Cures for Love*, 409–10 ('few women admit the truth').

tyrannize men',[34] men like the Friend are partly to blame. Or, to put it another way, in fashioning her Jean de Meun proves himself an observant disciple of Ovid, who told men to 'deceive [women] the deceivers' yet subsequently disclosed to women that men are the biggest cheats after all.[35] La Vieille especially wants her charge to beware of generosity and fidelity.

25   (13037) 'Never be generous; and keep your heart in several places, never in one. Don't give it, and don't lend it, but sell it very dearly and always to the highest bidder.[36] See that he who buys it can never get a bargain: no matter how much he may give, never let him have anything in return; it were better if he were to burn or hang or maim himself. In all cases keep to these points: have your hands closed to giving and open to taking. Certainly, giving is great folly, except giving a little for attracting men when one plans to make them one's prey or when one expects such a return for the gift that one could not have sold it for more. . . .

(13055-144) La Vieille will help in the quest to secure rich admirers, to each of whom a pledge should be sworn. The gods have given precedent for perjury in love, and stability is not to be expected from youth.

26   (13145) 'Know also another truth: he who is lord of the fair should collect his market-toll everywhere; and he who cannot at one mill—Hey! to another for his whole round! The mouse who has but one hole for retreat has a very poor refuge and makes a very dangerous provision for himself. It is just so with a woman: she is the mistress of all the markets, since everyone works to have her. She should take possessions everywhere. If, after she had reflected well, she wanted only one lover, she would have a very foolish idea. For, by Saint Lifard of Meun, whoever gives her love in a single place has a heart neither free nor unencumbered, but basely enslaved. Such a woman, who takes trouble to love one man alone, has indeed deserved to have a full measure of pain and woe. If she lacks comfort from him, she has no one to comfort her, and those who give their hearts in a single place are those who most lack comfort. In the end, when they are bored or irritated, all these men fly from their women.

27   (13173) 'No woman can come to a good end. Dido, the queen of Carthage, could not hold Aeneas, no matter how much she had done for him; she had received him poor, a wretched fugitive from the fair land of Troy, his birthplace, and had reclothed and fed him. Because

[34] Ferrante 1975, 116.
[35] *Art of Love* I. 645; III. 31, 456.
[36] On 'selling' see Ch. 1, Ovid 5; Ch. 4, *Ag. Marr. L3*; Ch. 7, *WoB 35.*

of her great love for him, she honoured his companions and, to serve and please him, had his ships rebuilt. To obtain his love she gave him her city, her body, her possessions; and he so reassured her in turn that he promised and swore to her that he was and would for ever be hers and would never leave her. She, however, had no joy of him, for the betrayer, without permission, fled by sea in his ships. As a result, the beautiful Dido lost her life. Before the second day, she killed herself in her chamber with the sword that he had given her in her own hand. Remembering her lover, and seeing that she had lost her love, she took the sword, quite naked, raised it point upward and placed it under her two breasts, then let herself fall on it. It was a great pity to see, whoever saw her do such a deed. He would have been a hard man who was not touched by pity when he thus saw the beautiful Dido on the point of the blade. Her sorrow over him who tricked her was so great that she fixed the blade within her body.

28 (13211) 'Phyllis was another.[37] She waited so long for Demophöon that she hanged herself because he overstayed the time when he was to return and thus broke both his oath and his faith.'

(13215–64) Paris deserted Oenone for Helen, and Jason left Medea despite all she had done for him.

(13265) 'Briefly, all men betray and deceive women;[38] all are sensualists, taking their pleasure anywhere. Therefore we should deceive them in return, not fix our hearts on one. Any woman who does so is a fool; she should have several friends and if possible act so as to delight them to the point where they are driven to distraction.'

(13273–516) Detailed advice on how a woman should cultivate her body and manners to the best advantage.

29 (13517) 'A woman should be careful not to stay shut up too much, for while she remains in the house she is less seen by everybody, her beauty is less well-known, less desired, and in demand less. She should go often to the principal church and go visiting, to weddings, on trips, at games, feasts, and round dances, for in such places the God and Goddess of Love keep their schools and sing mass to their disciples.[39]

30 (13529) 'But of course, if she is to be admired above others, she

---

[37] Dido and Phyllis are consecutive instances of betrayed women in Ch. 1, Ovid 7.
[38] La Vieille repeats that men are liars in 13781–94.
[39] Cf. Ovid *Art of Love*, III. 417 ff.; Ch. 5, Gautier 8.

has to be well-dressed. . . . If her dress drags or hangs down near the pavement, she should raise it on the sides or in front as if to have a little ventilation or as if she were in the habit of tucking up her gown in order to step more freely. Then she should be careful to let all the passersby see the fine shape of her exposed foot. And if she is the sort to wear a coat she should wear it so that it will not too much hinder the view of her lovely body which it covers. Now she will want to show off her body and the cloth in which she is dressed, which should be neither too heavy nor too light, with threads of silver and small pearls, and particularly to show off her purse, which should be right out for everyone to see;[40] therefore she should take the coat in both hands and widen and extend her arms, whether on clean streets or muddy ones. Remembering the wheel which the peacock makes with his tail, she should do the same with her coat, so that she displays openly both her body and the fur linings of her clothing, squirrel or whatever costly fur she has used, to anybody she might see staring at her.'

(13575—696) A woman's nets should be spread indiscriminately; prey should be carefully handled, and kept dangling as long as possible.

31   (13697) 'She is a fool who does not pluck her lover down to the last feather, for the better she can pluck the more she will have, and she will be more highly valued when she sells herself more dearly. Men scorn what they can get for nothing; they don't value it at a single husk. If they lose it, they care little, certainly not as much as does one who has bought it at a high price. Here then are the proper ways to pluck men: get your servants, the chambermaid, the nurse, your sister, even your mother, if she is not too particular, to help in the task and do all they can to get the lover to give them coats, jackets, gloves, or mittens; like kites, they will plunder whatever they can seize from him, so that he may in no way escape from their hands before he has spent his last penny. Let him give them money and jewels as though he were playing with buttons instead of money. The prey is captured much sooner when it is taken by several hands.[41]

32   (13725) 'On occasion let them say to him, "Sir, since we must tell you so, don't you see that my lady needs a dress? How can you allow her to go without? By Saint Gile! If she wanted to be with a

----

[40] Cf. Ch. 5, Gautier 10.
[41] On the joint campaign to fleece lovers, cf. Ch. 1, Ovid 5.

certain one in this town, she would be dressed like a queen and ride out in fine trappings. My lady, why do you wait so long before asking him for it? You are too shy towards him when he leaves you thus in your destitution." Then, however pleased she is, she should order them to keep quiet, she, who has perhaps relieved him of so much that she has harmed him seriously. And if she sees that he recognizes that he may be giving her more than he ought and that he may think himself seriously harmed by the large gifts on which he is in the habit of feeding her, and if she feels that she does not dare urge him to give anything, then she should ask him to lend to her, swearing that she is quite ready to pay him back on any day that he will name. But I certainly forbid that anything ever be given back.'[42]

The remainder of La Vieille's speech particularly emphasizes the instinctual imperative of human libido, which impels women towards sexual freedom in defiance of society's restraints. Since she makes clear that the imperative is powerful in men and women alike, what she says contributes to misogyny only (though importantly) to the extent that a libertarian view is being propounded *by* a woman. La Vieille also catalogues some Ovidian stratagems for evading a husband's watch: making him drunk, or drugged, or feigning a fever which necessitates a visit to the baths.

Genius Condemns the Disclosure of Secrets to Women

Later in Jean's continuation, the goddess Nature declares that she wishes to 'confess' her bitter sense of her own folly in having assisted humankind. Her 'priest', Genius, bidding her to calm her emotion, promises to keep secret anything she confesses. Then he launches into one of the poem's sharpest misogynistic outbursts, not very germane to Nature, and one which Christine de Pizan found particularly offensive.[43]

33 (16322) 'He who dares trouble you is a great fool. But it is also true, without fail, that a woman is easily inflamed with wrath. Virgil himself bears witness—and he knew a great deal about their difficulties—that no woman was ever so stable that she might not be varied and changeable.[44] And thus she remains a very irritable animal. Solomon says that there was never a head more cruel than the head of a serpent and nothing more wrathful than a woman, and that nothing, he says, has so much malice.[45] Briefly, there is so much vice in woman that no one can recount her perverse ways in rhyme

[42] Cf. Ch. 1, Ovid 5, 'ask him for a loan ...'.
[43] See Ch. 9, *Quarrel* 1.
[44] Referring to the adage in *Aeneid* iv. 569–70, 'woman is always changeable and fickle'.
[45] Ecclus. 25: 22–3, 26; in Ch. 1, Scripture 9.

or in verse. Titus Livius, who knew well what the habits and ways of women are, says that women are so easily deceived, so silly, and of such pliable natures that with their ways entreaties are not worth as much as blandishments.[46] Again, Scripture says elsewhere that the basis of all feminine vice is avarice.[47]

34   (16347) 'Whoever tells his secrets to his wife makes of her his mistress.[48] No man born of woman, unless he is drunk or demented, should reveal anything to a woman that should be kept hidden, if he doesn't want to hear it from someone else. No matter how loyal or good-natured she is, it would be better to flee the country than tell a woman something that should be kept silent. He should never do any secret deed if he sees a woman come, for even if there is bodily danger, you may be sure that she will tell it, no matter how long she may wait. Even if no one asks her anything about it, she will certainly tell it without any unusual coaxing; for nothing would she keep silent.[49] To her thinking she would be dead if the secret did not jump out of her mouth, even if she is in danger or reproached. . . . And do you know what the wretch who confides in her does to himself? He binds his hands and cuts his throat; for if, just one single time, he ever dares grouch at her or scold her or get angry, he puts his life in such danger—if he deserved death for his deed—that she will have him hanged by the neck, if the judges can catch him, or secretly murdered by friends. Such is the unfortunate harbour at which he has arrived.'

(16389–576): The uneasiness of the man hiding a secret will be obvious to his wife in bed. She will cajole, complain, resort to sexual tactics until he reveals it. (See *Matheolus 18–21* below for an imitation.) Then, she will wait until she can use it against him.

35   (16577) 'Fair lords, protect yourselves from women if you love your bodies and souls. At least, never go to work so badly that you reveal the secrets that you keep hidden inside your hearts. Fly, fly, fly, fly, fly, my children; I advise you and urge you without deception or guile to fly from such an animal. Note these verses of Virgil, but know them in your heart so that they cannot be drawn out

---

[46] Livy commented (*History*, 1. 9.16) that the abducted Sabine women were placated by the men's romantic talk of having been driven by love, 'the most moving of pleas to a woman's heart'.

[47] 1 Tim. 6: 10, here misapplied to women.

[48] Cf. Ch. 4, Andreas 13.

[49] On loquacity cf. Ch. 1, Juv. 7; Ch. 2, Chrysostom 1; Math 1, 8, 10–11; and Ch. 8, Albertano 1.

therefrom: O child who gather flowers and fresh clean strawberries, here lies the cold serpent in the grass.[50] Fly, child, for he poisons and envenoms every person that comes near. O child, seeking along the earth for flowers and new strawberries, the evil chilling serpent, who goes about here hiding himself, the malicious adder who covers up and conceals his venom, and hides it under the tender grass until he can pour it out to deceive and harm you; O child, give thought to avoiding him. Don't let yourself be seized if you want to escape death, for it is such a venomous animal in body, tail, and head, that if you approach it you will find yourself completely poisoned, for it treacherously corrodes and pierces whatever it reaches, without remedy. No treacle may cure the burning of that venom. No herb or root is worth anything against it. The only medicine is flight.

36 (16617) 'However, I do not say, and it was never my intent to say, that you should not hold women dear or that you should flee from them and not lie with them.[51] Instead I recommend that you value them highly and improve their lot with reason. See that they are well clothed and well shod, and labour always to serve and honour them in order to continue your kind so that death does not destroy it. But never trust them so much that you tell them anything to keep quiet about. Certainly allow them to go and come, to keep up the household and the house if they know how to take care of it; or if it happens by chance that they know how to buy or sell they can busy themselves with such activity; or if they know any trade let them do it if they need to; and let them know about the things that are open and that don't need to be hidden. But if you abandon yourself so much that you give them too much power, you will repent later, when you feel their malice. Even Scripture cries out to us that if the woman has lordship she opposes her husband when he wants to say or do anything.[52] . . . Think about holding your tongue, for nothing can come to any conclusion when they share secrets, so proud and haughty are they, with such corrosive, venomous, and harmful tongues. But when fools come to be held in their arms and hug and kiss them in the games that are so pleasing to them, then nothing can be hidden from them. There the secrets are revealed; there husbands reveal themselves and afterward they are sorry and

---

[50] Virgil warns the child against the snake in the grass in *Eclogues*, III. 92–3.

[51] Genius's *volte-face* (undermined by the adjectives 'corrosive, venomous' used just below) is noted by Christine: Ch. 9, *Quarrel 1*.

[52] Ecclus. 25: 30; in Ch. 1, Scripture 9.

chagrined. All of them reveal their thoughts except the wise men who have pondered well.

37   (16677) 'Malicious Delilah, through her poisonous flattery, cut off Samson's hair with her scissors as she held him softly close, sleeping in her lap. As a result, this man who was so valiant, worthy, strong, and fierce in battle, lost all his strength when she thus sheared off his locks. She revealed all his secrets, which the fool, not knowing how to hide anything, had told her.[53] But I don't want to tell you any more examples; one can very well suffice you for all of them. Even Solomon speaks of it . . . "In order to flee from danger and reproach, guard the gates of your mouth against her who sleeps in your bosom."[54] Whoever hold men dear should preach this sermon so that they may guard against women and never confide in them.'

GIOVANNI BOCCACCIO (1313–1375)

FROM *THE CORBACCIO** (*IL CORBACCIO: C.1355*)

Boccaccio found women a constantly interesting topic. He wrote a whole volume *On Famous Women* (*De mulieribus claris*), a kind of biographical dictionary of celebrated women in pagan culture. In his romances there is often a Don Juanism in his attitude, though—a combination of admiration and desire with rakish cynicism. *The Corbaccio* (meaning perhaps 'Evil Crow', alluding to a fable in which the bird attempts to hide its ugliness beneath peacock's feathers) is no romance, but a mordant experiment in unalloyed contempt, deeply indebted to Juvenal's *Satire* VI but drawing besides on a wide harvest of antifeminist texts. Boccaccio had stored them away in a personal anthology or *florilegium* known as the *Zibaldone laurenziano*, begun before 1350. *Il Corbaccio* adopts the structure of a medieval literary dream-vision, parodying that form's presentation of enlightenment by an authority figure. Its narrator, crushed by a fantasy of unfulfilled love for a widow, dreams of a desolate purgatorial landscape where an incongruously grave and Dantesque personage, the Spirit of her former husband, exposes this fantasy by savagely de-romanticizing women in general and the widow in particular.[55] It is a classic case of a fiction in which woman is the absent centre of discussion and target of verbal abuse thinly veneered with wit. It is also a classic development of the subcategory of antifeminism aimed at the figure of the old woman or widow.

[53] Cf. Ch. 4, Andreas 13
[54] Not 'Solomon', but Micheas 7: 5.
* Tr. Anthony K. Cassell, *The Corbaccio, Giovanni Boccaccio* (Urbana, Chicago, and London: University of Illinois Press, 1975). Reprinted by permission of the translator: © Anthony Cassell. Italian text: Nurmela 1968.
[55] The germ of this could be the 'Phoroneus' anecdote, that only husbands know why one should not marry; see *RR* 12; and Ch. 4, Map 21.

Boccaccio's strategy gives misogynistic conventions a double run, because the Spirit (i) argues that for the narrator to subject himself to the love of any woman is a debasement of his masculine and intellectual excellence because women *en bloc* are vile and inferior beings; and (ii) disabuses the narrator of his awe of the widow's personality by depicting the vileness of this woman in particular from a perspective of extreme, Swiftian proximity. The latter tactic perhaps represents (no less than the monologue of Le Jaloux by Jean de Meun) an attempt to update and give individual colour to the conventional invective. It has also been thought to be calculatedly antithetical to Dante's *Vita Nuova*. Readings from both (i) and (ii) are given below.

Uncleanness

1   'Your studies should have shown you (and did show you, had you wished to see it) what women are. Of these a great many call themselves and have themselves called "ladies", although very few are found among them.[56] A woman is an imperfect creature excited by a thousand foul passions,[57] abominable even to remember, let alone to speak of. If men considered this as they should, they would go to them in the same way and with the same desire and delight with which they go to any other natural and inevitable necessity; just as they hastily flee those places when their superfluous burden is released, so they would flee women, after they have done their duty to restore deficient human progeny (as do all other creatures who are far wiser in this than men!).[58] No other creature is less clean than woman: the pig, even when he is most wallowed in mud, is not as foul as they. If perhaps someone would deny this, let him consider their childbearing; let him search the secret places where they in shame hide the horrible instruments they employ to take away their superfluous humours. But let us pass over whatever has to do with this subject. Since they are very well aware of it, they secretly consider any man a fool who loves them, desires them, or follows them; and they also know how to hide it in such a way that it is neither known nor believed by many stupid men who consider only the outer shell; moreover, there are those who, while well knowing it, dare to say that they like it, and that they would do, and indeed do, thus and such. These are certainly not to be numbered among men!'

The dead husband briefly sketches the 'traps' of beautification by which women 'hook' the men they marry, then seize control.

[56] Distinguishing between *femmina* and *donna*.
[57] Cf. Ch. 9, *Quarrel* 2.
[58] A medieval commonplace, found also e.g. in Langland, *Piers Plowman*, 'B' xi. 334–43. See Ch. 8, *S. Passion* 4, for an antithetical argument.

168   LATER MEDIEVAL VERNACULAR ADAPTATIONS

Control and Quarrel

2 Thinking they have climbed to a high station, though they know they were born to be servants, they at once take hope and whet their appetite for mastery; and while pretending to be meek, humble, and obedient, they beg from their wretched husbands the crowns, girdles, cloths of gold, ermines, the wealth of clothes, and the various other ornaments in which they are seen resplendent every day;[59] the husband does not perceive that all these are weapons to combat his mastery and vanquish it. The women, no longer servants but suddenly equals, seeing their persons and rooms adorned like those of queens and their wretched husbands ensnared, contrive with all their might to seize control. . . .

3 'Like swift and starving she-wolves come to occupy the patrimo-- nies, property, and wealth of their husbands, hurrying now here, now there, they are in continual quarrels with servants, maids, factors, with their own husbands' brothers and children. Of the latter they pretend to be the tender guardians,[60] whereas they really only desire to ruin them—moreover, so that they may appear loving to those for whom they care little, no sleep is to be had in their beds: each one spends the night arguing and quarrelling, saying to her husband:[61] "I certainly see how much you love me; surely I'd be blind if I didn't notice that someone else is dearer to you than I! Do you think I'm fooled and that I don't know whom you're chasing, whom you're in love with, and whom you talk with every day? Of course I do; I've better spies than you think! Poor me! For it's been so long since I came here, yet you've never again said to me even once when I come to bed, 'Welcome, my love.' But, by the cross of God, I'll do to you what you're doing to me. Am I now so skinny? Am I not as beautiful as so-and-so? But do you understand what I'm saying? For one who kisses two mouths, one mouth must stink. Get over there! So help me God, you'll not touch me! Chase after those whom you deserve, for certainly you didn't deserve me; go show yourself for what you are. You'll get what's coming to you. Remember, you didn't drag me out of the mud![62] God knows who and what class of men they were who would have considered themselves lucky to have

---

[59] A topical subject in Italy at the time, when women's clothing was being regulated by statute; Cassell 1975. 101–3.
[60] Presumably referring to her stepchildren; cf. *Math* II. 3483–500.
[61] Cf. Ch. 1, Juv. 6; and Ch. 2, Jerome 12.
[62] On disdain, cf. Ch. 4, Andreas 18; elaborated further in *Corb.*, Cassell 1975, 38–9.

taken me without a dowry! I would've been lord and master of all they owned! And to you I gave so many gold florins! I could never even command a glass of water without a thousand reproaches from your brothers and servants; one would think I were their lackey! I was surely unlucky to ever have set eyes on you; may he who said the first word about it break a leg.''...

Promiscuity

4 'When the women see their possession settled, they turn all their attention to pimps and lovers. And let it be clear to you that she who seems most chaste and virtuous in this cursed multitude would rather have one eye than be content with just one man.[63] And if two or three men were enough, it would be something; and perhaps it would be tolerable if these two or three were better than their husbands, or were at least their equals. Women's lust is fiery and insatiable and for this reason knows no discrimination or bounds: the servant, the workman, the miller, even the black Ethiopian, each is good provided he is up to it.[64] I am certain that there would be those among them who would dare to deny this—as if one were unaware that, while their husbands were away or else left sleeping in their beds, many have already gone to the public brothels in disguise! And they were the last to leave these places, tired but unsatisfied.[65] What will they not dare to satisfy this bestial appetite of theirs? They pretend to be timid and fearful; and when their husbands ask them, they refuse to climb to any high place, however worthy the cause might be, for they say that they become dizzy; they refuse to go to sea because they say their stomach does not permit it; they refuse to go out at night because they claim they fear ghosts, spirits, and phantoms. If they hear a mouse in the house, or the wind moving a window, or a tiny stone falling from above, all of them shudder and their blood and strength flee them as if they were threatened by a mortal peril.[66] However, they lend great courage to the shameful things they want to do.'...

They are bold enough in their assignations with lovers, and in their abortions and infanticides.[67] The Spirit next rehearses Ovid's allegations about manic female anger, then switches to the subject of greed.

[63] Cf. Ch. 1, Juv. 2.
[64] 'Ethiopian', cf. Juv. Satire VI, 597–600; 'up to it', cf. Ch. 4, Andreas 23.
[65] Cf. Ch. 1, Juv. 3. On secret visits to brothels cf. Ch. 4, Ag. Marr. L4.
[66] Elaborated from Juv. Satire VI, 94–102.
[67] The charge of abortion is in Juv. Satire VI, 594–8, and repeated in Math. II. 3501 ff. A counter-allegation was that drunken men killed their wives' babies in the womb by beating them.

Gold-digging

5 'Let us consider to what degradation they subject themselves in order to increase their dowries a little. They will refuse as a husband no slobbering old man with rheumy eyes and trembling hands and head, as long as they hear that he is rich, since they are certain that they will be widows within a short time, and since he does not have to satisfy them in the nest. Nor are they ashamed to submit, offer, and allow their limbs, hair, and face (made up with so much care), their crowns, graceful garlands, velvets, cloths of gold, their many ornaments, necklaces, trifles, and such dainties to be fondled by the paralytic hands and toothless, slavering, fetid mouth—and this is far worse—of him whom they believe they can rob.[68] If his already dwindling nature grants him children, he has them in this way. If not, he cannot for this reason die without heirs! Others come, who make her belly swell; and even if nature has made it sterile, spurious pregnancies give him children so that, as a widow, she may longer live in lecherous pleasures at the expense of her ward.[69] Only fortune-tellers, flatterers, quacks, and groping fondlers in whom they take delight make them not merely courteous but prodigal; for these, women never show the least caution, thrift, or avarice.'. . .

Here are interjected miscellaneous brief charges: caprice, presumption, indulgence of their will; and that women are loud-mouthed.

'Knowledge' and 'Tuition'

6 'Wretched students suffer cold, fasting, and vigils, and after many years they find that they have learned very little. Women, even if they remain in church one morning just long enough to hear Mass, know how the firmament turns; how many stars there are in the sky and how big they are; what the course of the sun and the planets is; how thunder, lightning, hail, rainbows, and other things are created in the air; how the sea ebbs and flows; and how the land produces fruit. They know what is going on in India and Spain; how the homes of the Ethiopians are made, and where the source of the Nile is found; and whether crystal is generated in the north from ice or from something else; with whom their neighbour slept; by whom that

[68] This charge of deliberately marrying senile men (possibly true of May in Chaucer's *Merchant's Tale*: Mann 1991, 68) is likely to remind the reader of the *predicament* of women married off to the elderly.
[69] On illegitimate offspring cf. Ch. 4, *Ag. Marr.* I.6-I.7; *Math.* II. 3325-7; Juv. *Satire* VI, 76-7, 598-601 (followed by a passage on spurious pregnancies, 602-9).

other woman is pregnant and in what month she is to give birth; and
how many lovers that other has, and who sent her the ring and who
the belt; and how many eggs their neighbour's hen lays a year; and
how many spindles she uses to spin an ounce of linen; and, in brief,
they return fully informed about all that the Trojans or the Greeks or
the Romans ever did.[70] If they cannot find anyone else to lend them
an ear, they chatter incessantly with the maid, the baker's wife, the
green-grocer's wife, or the washerwoman, and become greatly put
out if they are reproved for talking to any of them.

7 'It is true that from this so sudden and divinely inspired knowledge of theirs springs an excellent doctrine for their daughters. They
teach them all how to rob their husbands, how to receive love letters
and how to answer them, how to bring their lovers into the house,
how to feign illness so that their husbands will leave the bed free for
them, and many other evils. He who believes that any mother
delights in having a daughter more honest or virtuous than herself is
a fool. It does not matter if they must go to their neighbours to ask for
a lie, a perjured oath, an evil deed, a thousand feigned sighs, or a
hundred thousand false tears, for when they are necessary, women
lend them. God knows where they keep them so ready and swift as
they do for their every whim (for, as far as I am concerned, I could
never begin to guess)!'[71]

8 'It is true, of course, that they are willing to let one of their defects
be proven, and especially those that others see with their very own
eyes,[72] and don't they have ready their "It wasn't like that! You're
lying in your teeth! You're seeing things! You've left your brain at
the menders! Try drinking less! You don't know where you are! Are
you all right in the head? Even without a fever you're raving and
rambling on nonsensically", and other such little barbed words of
theirs? If they say they have seen an ass fly, after many arguments to
the contrary you will have to give in entirely; if not, mortal enmity,
treachery, and hatred will immediately take the field. So brazen are
they that they say straight off to anyone who belittles their intellect
one jot, "And weren't the Sibyls wise?"—just as if every one of them
should be the eleventh! It is a wondrous thing that, in so many

[70] This passage is closely modelled on a caricature in Juv. Satire VI, 402–12.
[71] Cf. RR 19 above, and the common source in Juv. Satire VI, 231–41. Boccaccio
adds the charge of lying (ubiquitous but cf. esp. Ch. 4, Andreas 19) and ready tears (cf.
Ch. 1, Ovid 5; and RR 13,367–74).
[72] Cf. RR 24.

thousands of years that have passed since the world was made, amid so great a multitude as has been that of the feminine sex, only ten wise and celebrated women have been found among them; and each one thinks she is either one of them or worthy to be numbered among them. Among their other vanities, when they wish to exalt themselves far above men, they say that all good things are of the feminine gender: the stars, planets, Muses, virtues, and riches. If it weren't indecent, to this you would only want to reply, "It's quite true they're all feminine, but they don't piss!" '[73]

They also boast of the Virgin Mary and the female saints, while being totally unable to emulate them in chastity.[74] (Nature did a disservice to the saints anyway, in subjecting such 'virile', 'constant' hearts within a 'vile' sex.) The Spirit suggests that, although he has not exhausted the criticisms that could be levelled, he has said enough. But women would never acknowledge these defects: they would attribute his attitude to homosexuality.[75]

Perfection of Man

9 'Let us, however, turn to something else. Your studies at least should have shown you who you are, even if natural wisdom had not revealed it to you; and they should have reminded you and explained that you are a man made in the image and semblance of God, a perfect creature, born to govern and not to be governed. He who had created man a little beforehand showed this clearly in our first father by placing all the other creatures before him and having him name them, and subjecting them to his dominion and by doing the same thing later with the one and only woman in the world, whose gluttony, disobedience, and persuasions were the cause and origin of all our miseries. Antiquity excellently preserved this order; and the present world still preserves it in the papacies, empires, kingdoms, principalities, provinces, peoples, and generally in all magistratures and priesthoods and other high positions, divine as well as human, by preferring and entrusting the government of all men and women to men only, and not to women. Anyone with judgement can see quite easily how valid and cogent an argument this is to show how greatly the nobility of man exceeds that of

[73] Perhaps prompted by Juv. *Satire* VI, 264 mocking a gladiatorial woman on her chamber-pot.
[74] The Spirit heads off a key pro-feminist argument, whose limitations had however been noted also by Marbod: Ch. 8, 'The Good Woman' 6.
[75] A charge levelled elsewhere in medieval literature by women against indifferent males, e.g. Marie de France, *Lanval*. 277–86.

woman and of all other creatures.[76] Not only from this can one, or must one, grasp that this ample privilege of nobility is merely granted to a few excellent men. No, rather, it will be understood that it belongs also to some who are inferior in respect to women and the other creatures, for it will be quite clearly recognized that the basest or lowest man in the world, who is not deprived of the good of his intellect, is worth more than that woman who is temporally considered more excellent than any other, inasmuch as she is a woman.[77]

10 'A most noble thing, therefore, is man, who was made by his creator a little lower than the angels. And if the least man is of so great account, of what worth must he be whose virtue has raised him above the others to some excellence? Of what worth must he be whom sacred studies, philosophy, have removed from the vulgar herd? From their number you have taken yourself by your intellect and studies. . . . Why do you not know yourself? Why do you debase yourself in this way? How can you consider yourself of so little worth that you go and subject yourself to a wicked woman . . .?'[78]

The Spirit of the husband now begins to dissuade the dreamer from loving the widow by enumerating her faults from the private point of view of one who studied them at first hand. No sooner had he entered into an arranged marriage with her, he says, than she turned from dove to serpent, browbeating him with vulgar notions of her grand family connections, and imposing her will over him. She pampered herself with luxurious foods and greasy lotions. To her the terms 'generosity', 'courtesy', and 'wisdom' signified the satisfaction of her sexual appetite. Eventually he suggests that the dreamer's delusion is such that only the violence of foul-smelling remedies will bring him back to health. He must be told what the woman is 'really' like behind the façade. This is the pretext for a virulent passage so ruthlessly targeting the negative possibilities of a body past its prime that it borders—but presumably not unwittingly—on tastelessness. That there was a taste for this type of tastelessness, however, might be inferred from the hostile nuance in descriptions of old women elsewhere in medieval literature, such as that of Morgan in *Sir Gawain and the Green Knight*.[79]

Beneath the Façade

11 'When she arose from her bed of a morning, she had (and today

[76] Boccaccio is summarizing traditions inherited from the Fathers: cf. Ch. 8, Brut A3. On exclusion of women from important office, cf. Ch. 3, Gratian 8; *Math.* 10; and Christine de Pizan, *City* I. 11. 1.
[77] Perhaps recalling Ecclus. 42: 14; in Ch. 1, Scripture 10.
[78] Cf. Ch. 9, *City* 5.
[79] The obvious retort is in Le Fèvre, *Leesce* 419–518; age is natural and affects males too.

I believe has more than ever) a face green and yellow, discoloured with the hue of swamp-fumes, knotted like moulting birds, wrinkled and encrusted and all sagging, so different from the way it looked when she had time to preen herself that one could scarcely believe it had he not seen it as I did a thousand times in the past.[80] Who is not aware that smoke-grimed walls, not to speak of women's faces, become white when whitewash is applied to them, and what is more, become coloured according to whatever the painter chooses to put over the white? Who does not know that by kneading, dough, which is an insensible thing, not to speak of living flesh, swells up and rises whereas it had seemed musty?[81] She rubbed herself and painted herself so much and made her skin, which had sagged during the stillness of the night, swell up enough that to me, who had seen her beforehand, it seemed an unnatural wonder.

12 'If you had seen her, as I saw her most mornings, with her nightcap pulled down over her head, with the little veil around her throat, so swamp-faced, as I have just said, sitting on her haunches in her lined mantle, brooding over the fire, with livid rings under her eyes, coughing and spitting great gobs of phlegm, I have not the least fear that all her virtues, of which your friend spoke, would have had as much power to make you fall in love with her once as seeing that would have made you fall out of love a hundred thousand times. What she must have been like when the Pisans rode with red on their lances with her head swathed up tight and alleging a headache, whereas the pain was at the other end, you may imagine.[82] I am quite certain that, if you had seen her like that or saw her when you said that the flames rushed from her face to your heart at the sight of her as they do on oily things, you would have thought that you had met up with a load of dung or a mountain of manure, from which you would have fled, as you do from something disgusting;[83] and you would flee it still, and will flee it, if you reflect on the truth I am telling you.

13 'However, we must go on. You saw her big and sturdy; and it seems as certain to me as the beatitude which I await that, looking at her bosom, you judged it to be just as firm as you saw her face, without having seen the sagging wattles that her white wimple

---

[80] Early morning 'defects' are satirized in Ovid, *Cures for Love* 341–56.
[81] Cf. the use of dough in Ch. 1, Juv. 8.
[82] Periphrasis for lovemaking during her menstrual period.
[83] Cf. *RR* 15.

hides. But your judgement is far, far from the truth. And although as experts many could give true testimony to what I say, I hope that without further witnesses you will believe it from me who perhaps had longer experience of it, since I was unable to do anything else. Be assured that there is no tow or any other padding in that swelling which you see above her belt, but only the flesh of two puffed and blighted plums, which were once perhaps two unripe apples,[84] delightful to both the touch and sight—although I do believe that she brought them thus misshapen from her mother's body; but let us pass over this. They—whatever the cause may be, either because they were pulled too much by others, or because their own excess weight stretched them—are so beyond measure lengthened and dislocated from their natural position that perhaps (or rather, without doubt) if she let them droop, they would reach her navel, empty and wrinkled like a deflated bladder; and certainly if things such as these, like the hoods they wear in Paris, were in vogue in Florence, to be fashionable she could toss them over her shoulders *à la française!*[85] And what more? Her belly more or less corresponds to her cheeks, pulled taut by her white wimple; lined with thick, wide furrows like a young she-goat, it looks like an empty bag, sagging just like the empty skin that hangs from the chin to the chest of an ox; and perhaps no less than the other pieces of cloth, she must raise it aloft whenever she wishes to empty her bladder obeying natural necessity, or, following pleasure, when she wants to put the devil in the oven.

14 'The order of my discourse requires things strange and far different from those passed; the less you shun these things, or rather the more diligence with which you gather them into your intellect, the more health they will bring to your sick mind. Although truly I do not quite know where I should begin to speak of the Gulf of Setalia, hidden in the Valley of the Acheron beneath its dark woods, often russet in colour and foaming with foul grime and full of creatures of unusual species, but yet I will tell of it.[86] The mouth through which the port is entered is of such size that, although my little bark sailed with quite a tall mast, never was there a time, even though the waters were narrower then, that I might not have made

---

[84] A conventional analogy in the rhetoric of female beauty.
[85] Hoods with long tails ('liripipes') are visible in 14th c. visual art. *Math.* 1. 681–4 also makes jibes at the now bag-like breasts of the once attractive wife.
[86] Setalia; an actual, large, and windblown gulf, incongruously collocated in this ribald locution with Acheron, river of the underworld.

room for a companion sailing with a mast no less than mine without disturbing myself in the least. Ah, what am I saying? King Robert's armada all chained together at the time he enlarged it could have entered there with the greatest of ease without lowering its sails or raising its rudders.[87] A wondrous thing it is that never a boat entered it without perishing and without being hurled forth from there vanquished and exhausted, just as they say occurs with Scylla and Charybdis in Sicily: that the one swallows ships and the other casts them forth![88] That gulf, then, is certainly an infernal abyss which could be filled or sated as the sea with water or the fire with wood.[89]

15   'I will be silent about the sanguine and yellow rivers that descend from it in turn, streaked with white mould, sometimes no less displeasing to the nose than to the eyes, because the style I have picked draws me to something else. What shall I say further to you therefore about the village of Evilhole? Placed between two lofty mountains, from here sometimes just as from Mongibello, first with great thunderclaps and then without, there issues forth a sulphurous smoke, so fetid and repulsive that it pollutes the whole countryside around.[90] I do not know what to say to you about it except that, when I lived near it (for I remained there longer than I would have liked), I was offended many times by such blasts that I thought to die there something other than a Christian death. Nor can I otherwise tell of the goaty stench which her whole corporal bulk exudes when she groans excited sometimes by heat, and sometimes by exertion;[91] this is so appalling that, combined with the other things I have already spoken of, it makes her bed smell like a lion's den, so that any squeamish person would stay with far less loathing in the Val di Chiana in midsummer than near that.'[92]

[87] In 1338 King Robert of Naples assembled a huge fleet to regain Sicily.
[88] Cf. Ch. 4, Marbod 6.
[89] Probably adapting Prov. 30: 16; cf. Ch. 2, Jerome 8; Ch. 4, Ag. Marr. J9; Ch. 5, Gautier 17, 21.
[90] Referring to Mount Etna.
[91] Goats were associated with women in medieval portrayals of Lust: see Plate 7 (Sensuality)
[92] The Chiana was then an unhealthy, swampy river.

JEHAN LE FÈVRE

FROM *THE LAMENTATIONS OF MATHEOLUS** (*C.*1371–2)

Note: Throughout this anthology, Matheolus (*abbreviated to* Math.) *designates this text by Le Fèvre, not the Latin work by Mathieu (nicknamed 'Matheolus') of which Le Fèvre's text is a translation.*

Le Fèvre's work is a translation of a subtle poem, the *Liber lamentationum Matheoluli,* written around 1295 by Mathieu of Boulogne.[93] Mathieu asserts that his tirade against wives and women is autobiographical, for it has been prompted by the collapse of his career as cleric and advocate owing to his marriage to a widow. This was, as he states, an infringement of canon law, which prohibited clergy other than those in minor orders from marrying, and which termed a priest's marriage to a widow 'bigamy'. Evidence in the poem suggests that Mathieu, who had studied law and logic for six years at Orléans, and was associated with ecclesiastical dignitaries in Thérouanne to whom he addresses his 'Lament', attended the very Council of Lyon in 1274 at which such regulations were tightened up. Subsequently, stripped of office and humiliated (becoming, he says, a double diminutive of himself, 'Matheolulus' rather than 'Matheus'), he finds his widow not worth the sacrifice. The acerbic and witty 'Lamentations' are presented as the product of his predicament. His Latin poem did not have very wide currency, though it was being read along with Theophrastus by Deschamps and his friends late in the fourteenth century. Perhaps it interested Le Fèvre because he had already translated the pseudo-Ovidian *De vetula,* about an old bawd of a kind intermittently satirized by Mathieu. In any case, Le Fèvre's version proved an effective propagation of the satire, ensuring that 'Matheolus' continued to be a name to match Jean de Meun's for brutal antifeminism in fifteenth-century debates about women. It is probably the Le Fèvre text to which Christine de Pizan refers at the beginning of the *City of Ladies.*[94] She frowns on it as a book which treats its subject frivolously (*en manière de trufferie*) and which is allegedly not well reputed; she willingly put it aside, she says, to concentrate on something more serious. Even if we take her word for it that she did not dwell on this text, it is probable that she found much stimulus in the sequel which Le Fèvre wrote, the *Livre de Leesce,* which is a systematic refutation of Matheolus's allegations about women; some of Christine's key emphases can be traced to it.

In Book I of *Les Lamentations* Le Fèvre introduces his translation, but soon effaces himself and adopts the voice of Master (*Magister*) Mathieu, recriminating over the public disgrace caused by his marriage to 'Perrette'. Matters are made worse by the shrewishness of this widow, who according to the speaker bears out every lurid generalization about the *démonieuse* nature of

---

* New translation by Karen Pratt from *Les Lamentations de Matheolus et Le Livre de Leesce de Jehan le Fèvre,* ed. A.-G. Van Hamel, 2 vols. (Paris: Bouillon, 1892 and 1905). © Karen Pratt 1992.
   [93] The following information is based on Jehan Le Fèvre 1905, pp. cvii–cxcvi.
   [94] See Ch. 9, *City* 1.

wives (169). Consequently, he says, the poem is presided over not by Muses but by the Furies. A foretaste of irreverence to come is the seeming parody of St Paul's famous injunction, 'better to marry than burn', here modified to 'it is better for each man to have a mistress than marry and weep' (104–5). Mathieu recalls how he was bowled over by Perrette's beauty. But the sight of all that beauty, which has since turned into ugliness, clouded his knowledge of snakelike *malice femenin* (647–64). His former goddess has become a shrill contrarious opponent.

The Dominating Clock

1   (I. 732–64) This female clock is really driving me mad, for her quarrelsome din doesn't stop for a moment.[95] The tongue of a quarrelsome wife[96] never tires of chiming in. She even drowns out the sound of the church bell. A nagging wife couldn't care less whether her words are wise or foolish, provided that the sound of her own voice can be heard. She simply pursues her own ends; there's not a grain of sense in what she says; in fact she finds it impossible to have a decent thought. She doesn't want her husband to be the boss and finds fault with everything he does. Rightly or wrongly, the husband has no choice; he has to put up with the situation and keep his mouth shut if he wants to remain in one piece. No man, however self-disciplined or clear-sighted he may be, can protect himself adequately against this. A husband has to like what the wife likes, and disapprove of what she hates and criticize what she criticizes so that her opinions appear to be right.[97] So anyone who wishes to immolate himself on the altar of marriage will have a lot to put up with. Fifteen times, both day and night, he will suffer without respite and he will be sorely tormented. Indeed, 1 believe that this torture is worse than the torments of hell, with its chains, fire, and iron.

The Winning Sophistry of Wives

2   (I. 824–902) If a husband is forced to be his wife's serf, it's a terrible calamity, for he ought to be the boss. The natural order of things has been overturned by women and their madness. It's no great surprise if a husband fails to hold his own for long against a pitiless wife and the violent quarrel she often has waiting for him. Since no man can stand up to this, I don't think God would be able to

---

[95] On loquacity cf. Ch. 1, Juv. 7; Ch. 2, Chrysostom 1; Ch. 4, Andreas 21, Ag. Marr. J12; and Math. below, 11.
[96] *Femme*, ambiguous in Old (and modern) French, is translated here either as 'woman' or as 'wife' according to context, although Le Fèvre's criticisms of wives often apply, in his view, to women in general.
[97] Cf. Ch. 2, Jerome 14.

either. He would have to concede defeat, if the truth could only be told, for there's nothing worse than a woman. Their wickedness began in the days of Adam and since his fall no wife has ever obeyed her husband.[98]

3   In addition to using arguments and disputes, a woman can lead her man to false conclusions by means of five different types of sophism.[99] It's only right that I should give you some examples of their deception. Their linguistic sophistry[100] is easily demonstrated.

4   Guy found his wife in her bedroom underneath Simon, who was bonking her on the edge of the bed. Once the act was over, Guy got angry, scolded and reproached his wife, saying, 'Get out, wicked woman, may God destroy you, body and soul, for your wickedness is now only too clear.' But the woman was very quick to contradict her husband, replying, 'Are you trying to kill me? Tell me what's the matter?' And the martyr to marriage said to her, 'I want a divorce.' 'Alas,' she said, 'why do you dare to speak such evil words to me? My father was once deluded into thinking that what you are now accusing me of had happened to him, for he imagined that he had seen my mother behaving in a wifely manner underneath another man, but his eyesight was defective. I know that my mother died as a result of such an incident, and my other female ancestors in just the same way. Dear husband, tell me how you arrived at such a crazy idea. Where has this melancholy come from? Dear friend, do you wish to be the death of me? Do you want me to live or to die needlessly having done no wrong? You would be a wicked man indeed. Tell me what you want me to do.' The poor wretch wept as he embraced her and said to her, 'Sweet sister, I want you to live, for if you were ever to depart prematurely from this life as your mother did, your death would be too bitter a blow to me.' She replied, 'Then you must acknowledge publicly that I was never guilty of such a crime or, I promise you, I shall die. Now go quickly and say that it was a lie and that you dreamt it, for it was in this way that my female ancestors met their untimely ends.' Against this argument the

---

[98] Cf. Ch. 4, Map 9 and Andreas 9.

[99] Perhaps prompted by RR 15. There follows a condescending satire on women's specialization in 'sophisms' (false arguments, intended to deceive) by which they lead husbands to their 'goal' (OF methe, Latin meta: see Bloch 1987, 17). Five categories of sophism had been recognized by Aristotle (Elenchi, I. 3) and transmitted to the Middle Ages by Boethius.

[100] Sophistry of the tongue, redargutio, 'arguing by contradiction'. The following tale is also found in Marie de France, Fables, XLV.

husband could find no defence, and without further ado, retracted his accusations under oath in the presence of their female neighbours, gossips, and cousins and swore that he had lied and had wrongly accused her. Thus his wife was exculpated, while he, allowing himself to be contradicted in this way, suffered public humiliation.

Two further anecdotes show that a woman can equally refute the evidence of sight and touch. She is 'not interested in the truth.' She manipulates a husband by love and argument, by oaths and tears, to believe anything. Solomon ignored reason and abused his knowledge when he let women cajole him into idolatry. The case of Aristotle comes next, by association with the wisdom of Solomon.

Woman Over Wisdom

5 (I. 1079–166) Women can sing to more than one tune. What good were the *Perihermeneias*, the *Elenchi*, divided into several branches, the *Prior* and *Posterior Analytics*, logic, or the mathematical sciences to Aristotle?[101] For a woman surmounted all of these in mounting him and conquered the master of logic.[102] She placed a bit and headstall on his head and he was dragged into solecism, barbastoma, and barbarism.[103] The hussy used him as a horse and spurred him on like a female ass. She lifted her crotch far too high when she rode the male. The governor was governed and the roles of the sexes reversed, for she was active and he passive, willing to neigh under her. Thus the natural order of things was turned upside down. What was normally underneath was on top, and confusion reigned. For the psalterion harmonizes badly with the harp. Indeed, that ride was incongruous, improper. Thus was grammar betrayed and logic sorely dismayed. There nature had no contribution to make, since Venus forbids the old and decrepit to indulge in lechery. May the hour be cursed when he placed himself underneath her,[104] yet dared

---

[101] This ostentatious catalogue of works on logic is a reminder that many of Aristotle's writings were 'new' to the West in Mathieu's time.

[102] This is the legend of Aristotle and Phyllis, familiar in Old French through the version by Henri d'Andeli, *Le Lai d'Aristote*. The philosopher, having frowned on Alexander the Great's love for the courtesan Phyllis, is induced to fall in love with her himself; and she mocks him by promising her favours if he will let her ride him like a horse. In *Math.* the stress is on the imputed 'solecism' (the chaotic syntax, as it were) when woman rides man or when an old man imagines himself virile. See Plate 5 (*Aristotle Ridden*)

[103] Grammatical errors of various kinds.

[104] Aristotle's position beneath the female 'rider' prompts *doubles entendres* in both the Latin and the French.

to contemplate such an act: he imagined that after her ride, he would rise in her estimation as a lover. In this respect he proved to be a fool, for he was scorned by her. She deceived him also in that she had no intention of repaying him. Having dismounted from his haunches, she left, sticking her tongue out at him to express her scorn. Goodness knows what madness made him think of poking her when he couldn't even get his rod up. Nature damns the old man; way beyond his capacity, in his senile way, he longs to do far more than he is capable of. Thus he is doubly sinned against.

6   In my opinion, he had the status of a horse, and yet he was well acquainted with the power of nature, reason, and justice. Yet why did they not gallop to his aid, bringing succour to their greatest proponent and master? I don't know how this could be. What will the logicians say about the ancient art of sophistry if their celebrated teacher and master was thrown into greater confusion than any madman with a shaven head? He could not have been more confounded. Alas, what will philosophy say, given that the great master was tricked by the figure of amphiboly?[105] Never had such a thing been seen before: the woman was the mounted knight and the man, with a halter under his hoary beard, was the horse that carried the burden. Because of this unnatural act, practitioners of the liberal arts[106] are in constant and perpetual confusion. May they be eaten by evil wolves, if they have not yet taken revenge for this act. This book shows in what way, in what circumstances, and by what means I have reached this sorry pass. There is no one who can offer me a cure for it, for my wife's evil charms are too potent. She is always armed with arguments which torture me terribly. I sigh, weep, and lament, and suffer more than if I had chronic fever. How am I going to write this work? I can hardly begin to compose it without bursting into tears and lamenting.

Book I next catalogues ways in which each of a man's five senses is damaged in marriage, and concludes with a sketch of domestic squabbling.

Living With A Basilisk

7   (II. 1-114) I, who once used to compose and polish off fine poems while my studies flourished and gave me great pleasure, have now

[105] Rhetorical terminology is being turned mockingly against Aristotle, but the story does not literally hinge on 'ambiguity'—except that of 'riding'.
[106] i.e. Masters of Arts, such as Mathieu himself, who sees the disorder of his own life and writing as stemming from Aristotle's conduct.

fallen on hard times, not because of advancing age, but because of the constant nagging which upsets me. It's making me old before my time, allowing me no truce or respite. While asleep I dream of battles which end worse than they begin; I feel as if I am constantly at war, whether awake or asleep. It's not surprising if I'm fed up with suffering such a cruel life, a life worse than death; for death stops once it has killed you,[107] whereas this torture goes on and on and yet I must endure it. Since I am dying a terrible death, I should serve as a warning to all other men not to get married and to learn from my mistakes, thereby escaping woman and her wiles. If one's neighbour's house is on fire and one sees the flames leaping higher, one ought to fear for one's own house.

8 If there is anyone who is so naive that he is untutored in woman's art,[108] let him read this very work and select from it the most pleasing formulations himself. He will learn a lot from it, provided that he uses it wisely. Dear reader, make sure that you rid yourself of women. Once you are acquainted with their opinions, behaviour and character (which I shall describe if I have the chance), then I believe that justice will prevail, that you will side with me and will rightly condemn them. Woman is always quarrelsome, a nag, cruel and shrewish. Peace and quiet are foreign to her. She recites her own litany of grievances,[109] her own version of scriptures and the liturgy, just to annoy me. She often breaks her promises. My nagging wife sings her own Tenebrae;[110] 'Damn you,' she says, and haunts my lamentations. She curses all the time or nags or weeps. Every wife intones and plays the same quarrelsome tune to her husband; she sings and chimes in every hour on the hour and is a terribly perverse creature. She is in the habit of shouting out and bawling during Responses, providing her own contrafacture of the Tenebrae. She begins the antiphon with 'Damn you,' causing her husband much grief and pain. She goes on like this all the time. Whether she is weeping or nagging, her husband hears everything, whether he wants to or not. Yet he dares not complain about it, for in return for one word of complaint he would get a thousand. Instead he has to

---

[107] Cf. Ch. 4, *Ag. Marr.* J17.

[108] The narrator presents himself as instructor in an 'Art' (Latin *ars mulierum*, Old French *l'art de femmes*) no less than Guillaume de Lorris, Andreas Capellanus, and Ovid, self-styled teachers of the 'Art of Love'.

[109] Beginning a sustained metaphor whereby the wife's haranguing becomes the intonation of depressing liturgical chants.

[110] The Tenebrae were sung during Holy Week and included the Lamentations of Jeremaiah.

leave home and escape from his house. This treacherous cow treats him so badly that the man has to flee. It's true that smoke, rain, and a wife's unjustified nagging drive a man away from his home.[111] When a woman argues and disputes she is often the one to start the quarrel. The water becomes undrinkable, the smoke from the hearth clouds his sight, making his eyes weep and he is unable to stay any longer in those conditions. In order to start a fight the wife pretends that she has caught her husband in the act of adultery. She attacks or turns on him, or strikes their child so that it screams and she couldn't be bothered to calm it down, she is such a cruel viper.

9   Just as it is impossible for a fish to live out of water, so a wife can't live without abusing her husband and fighting. So I tell you truly, take in carefully what you read, for she is like a basilisk and may God protect you from this snake that kills people with its gaze.[112] Above all retain this piece of advice: the only antidote is to flee it. Man is much safer with a snake or a lion than with a woman in fighting mood.[113] I can demonstrate this with indisputable proof. You can tame all wild beasts by using chains or cages, ingenuity and cunning, and break their proud spirits, but you can't do this with your wife, for you can't get rid of an old crease in a boot.[114] Even if you could conquer a whole empire by feats of arms, you would not be able to subjugate a woman. You can see this illustrated in paintings[115] and Holy Scripture bears witness to this too. No man exists who has nothing to fear from her. If you are willing to acknowledge the truth, there is no man, however powerful, who isn't ultimately defeated by woman and her shield.

'Jangling' Woman

10 (ll. 177–250) Indeed, the birds will stop singing[116] and the crickets in summer too before woman finds the strength to hold her tongue, whatever harm comes of her words. For Calphurnia, more gossipy than a magpie, this was indeed her undoing, since she did not plead her case wisely. Her verdict was to bare her bum. Her punishment for her crime, which she fully deserved, was to reduce all

[111] See Ch. 4, *Ag. Marr.* J15 and n.
[112] See Jacquart and Thomasset 1988, 74–5 and 212 n. 82 on the connection posited in *De secretis mulierum* between the menstruating woman's glance and the 'poisonous' gaze of the mythological basilisk.
[113] Cf. Ecclus. 25: 23; in Ch. 1, Scripture 9.
[114] Idiomatic expression meaning 'old habits die hard'.
[115] Of such themes as Samson and Delilah.
[116] Adapted from lines in Ch. 1, Ovid 1.

women to the status of second-class citizens. Each is deprived of and barred from practising advocacy.[117] With her tongue and outrageous behaviour she harmed all women. They have inherited her tongue and share in her guilt, according to the laws of heredity. Condemned in this way, rightly as far as I can tell, they are forbidden for all time to question witnesses and to defend cases. We can also read about a Jewess, Mary the sister of Moses, who was a slanderer and proud. As a result of her evil tongue she became a leper, struck down by leprosy; she paid dearly for her calumny.[118]

11   Why is the raven black? Some writers lead us to believe that it was once white. She has changed her appearance as a sign of her fault, because she was a gossip, a slanderer, and a nag.[119] If only our wives were now similarly metamorphosed by divine miracle and shed their nasty traits. If I had my way, no man would have to suffer this. Indeed, the devil was told concerning woman that God, in whom all good abounds, would have made the world a peaceful place if he had removed the cursed tongues of women, so ill-trained in the art of speaking. In many a land and many a country, wars begin and are caused because of women.[120] It seems therefore that whoever gave them the gift of speech was out of his mind. If one were to dare to accuse God, He would not be able to defend Himself against the charge of giving perverse women deadly weapons when He gave them many tongues. He saw the evil that would come of it, and yet did not wish to come to our aid. It's my belief that it would be a miracle to make a mute woman speak. But truly, it would be a much greater marvel if one were able to shut up a woman once she's in full flow. The two are barely comparable. Why are women more argumentative, so full of idle gossip and more talkative than men? Because they are made of bone, while our bodies are fashioned of clay: bone makes more noise than clay.[121] Note therefore my

---

[117] Jehan Le Fèvre 1905, II. 158, quotes the *Digests* of Justinian: 'women are prohibited from pleading on behalf of others, the reason being that it would go against the modesty befitting their sex if they involved themselves in strange cases and discharged masculine functions: this goes back to a most immoral woman named Carfania, whose immodest manner of pleading disturbed the magistrate and prompted this edict.' Cf. *Corb.* 9 above; Ch. 3, Gratian 8, and Christine de Pizan, *City* I. 11. 1. Mathieu was trained in law and frequently shows it.

[118] Num. 12: 1–15.

[119] Alluding to a medieval variant of the story in Ovid, *Met.* II. 531–632.

[120] Cf. Ch. 1, Ovid 8; and Ch. 4, Marbod 1.

[121] A witticism echoed in a 15th c. sermon by San Bernadino of Siena: 'I think I am listening to a pile of bones, you rattle so much': in Brooke 1989, 28.

conclusion, which does not offer us much solace: it is their nature
which makes them all foolish and proud.

Mathieu next claims that a man's vigour is somehow depleted by marriage.
Moreover, no inspection or trial is possible, whereas in both commercial
negotiation and monastic orders there is a period during which a person can
withdraw.

Disloyalty: the Matron of Ephesus

12 (II. 451–578) There are very few women, whether married or
unmarried, ugly, rich, young wenches, middle-class, poor, low class,
or courtly, of whatever rank they consider themselves to be, who
love their husbands truly.[122] This is demonstrated in the writings of a
wise man who was familiar with the ways of women. He knew what
their love is worth. He cites the example of a handsome, charming
knight, valiant in battle and virtuous, who was captivated in the
following way. He fell so madly in love with a poor chambermaid and
was so smitten with true love that he took her as his wedded wife. He
loved her deeply in his heart. You will now hear of his ignominious
end. He was wounded during a tournament and eventually died and
passed away. His wife lamented and sighed and pretended to suffer
great grief when she saw the colour of his blood. She pulled out her
hair as she wept, claiming that she wished to die and, overcome with
grief, she longed to be buried with her husband. She did not wish to
remain alive. She was very good at pretending to weep at her
husband's grave. Thus with mournful heart did the lady behave,
saying that she did not wish on any account to return home.

13 From what I've heard, that same day a thief was hanged in the
fields which a renowned knight (Sir Gilbert was his name) was
meant to oversee in return for his fief. As he rode past, he looked at
the lady beside her husband's grave and heard her weeping and
groaning. Courteously he said to her, 'My lady, calm yourself and
pray for his soul. Nothing is gained from mourning.' She replied 'I
cannot be silent. I have lost the best man in the world and wish only
to lie dead with him in this deep pit.' Sir Gilbert comforted her, saying
that she would find another husband just as good if not better. Yet
she replied, 'You are wasting your time. I don't know what you have
in mind, go and leave me alone.' Then Gilbert galloped off. He
continued on his way to the fields, for night had already fallen. The
thief had already been removed; Gilbert started to tremble out of

[122] Cf. Ch. 4, Andreas 4.

fright, fearing that because of this oversight he had lost and forfeited his fief. Very upset and deep in thought he retraced his steps straight back to the cemetery where the lady was continuing to mourn. He then told her where he had been and all that had happened and about the conditions attached to his fief and the type of homage due and how he feared he would lose it because of the thief (may he burn in hell) whom he had failed to guard. He openly revealed his predicament to her and she immediately forgot her good husband, in the hope of retying the knot.

14 'My lord,' she said, 'do not worry. In your time of need I shall help you out of this difficult situation you are suffering, if you would like to take me as your wife.' 'My lady, indeed I would.' They pledged themselves to each other and then she said 'Cheer up,' and straight away she unearthed the coffin and pulled the corpse out of it, disinterred and dismembered. I have to tell you that he was dragged and pulled to the gibbet by his own wife. And when she arrived there she herself hung him up without delay in the correct place and on the side from which the thief had been taken down. Then she said, 'My lord, come here and keep your promise to me!' 'My lady,' he said, 'there's something missing: the thief who was taken away had two wounds on his head.' The evil creature took his sword, having no qualms about raising it, and she wounded her husband in two places, breaking three of his teeth. But then she did even worse, for she poked and gouged out his eyes and this appeared not to distress her at all. Then she said, 'Listen, my lord, do not worry any more. I have made good your loss and for that I deserve to become Gilberta. I now remind you of your promise.' He said, 'I can remember very well what I promised you. Be gone, at once. For you will never have my body. Make sure you never see me again, and give up any attempt to get me. I would prefer to be skinned alive and lose all that I value; my heart is not so susceptible that I would ever marry you. I shall never trust you. And to tell the truth, if justice were done, by my faith, you would be burnt—for you deserve to be burnt alive.' My friend, take to heart the message of this anecdote and reflect on the malice and the nature of woman's vice. You will know that I am telling the truth once you have discovered their wickedness for yourself.[123]

---

[123] This story derives from Petronius, *Satire* 111, in which, as in numerous imitations (e.g. John of Salisbury, *Policraticus* viii), the woman gives in to the 'consolations' of the soldier, who makes love to her in the sepulchre. However *Math.* adopts a variant which increases her culpability by attributing the sexual initiative to her.

The Free-wheeling Widow

15 (II. 847–946) As soon as her husband is in his coffin, a wife's only thought day and night is to catch another husband. She observes convention by weeping, but after three days can't wait to be remarried. If her children wish to claim their share of the goods and money they have inherited from their father, there's not one of them who doesn't pay dearly for it. She disagrees with everything they say, argues, and is good at reproaching them, saying 'I would already be married if it were not for your objections, for this has already happened to me three or four times. Now I'm having to dispute with you; what wretched progeny I have borne.' Then she curses the fruits of her womb[124] and tells them that, despite their objections, without delay or further procrastination, she will marry one of her suitors, who will protect her rights for her. And she is so eager to marry that she takes a husband who brings about her ruin: who spends and squanders her money, an unbridled spendthrift, who will not be restrained as long as she still has something in the loft. He leaves her with neither a penny nor halfpenny, neither land, vineyard, nor house which he hasn't sold; everything has been spent.[125] Then, when she sees how she has been used, she complains to her children and weeps for her first husband. Such tears, may God help me, with which women reproach their most recent husbands, are an indictment against the heat of their loins.[126] Their frivolity does not excuse them.

16 I don't think there is a more foolish woman than a widow all dolled up; she doesn't think of herself as past it, she often transforms and changes her appearance, adopting different hairstyles. She paints her face, rearranges her hair, wears make-up, adorns herself. One moment she is willing, the next she isn't; now she's friendly, now hostile; first she quarrels with one person then with another, praising one to the skies and piling scorn on another.[127] And if ever out of habit many men waste their time with her, she is still too dissolute, abandoning the flower for the flames. In this way she proves to be naive and foolish, resembling the dung-beetle, which leaves the perfume of the flowers to follow in the wake of carts, wallowing in horse shit. And just like the she-wolf on heat, that

[124] Cf. Ch. 5, Gautier 9; a commonplace of writings against remarriage, e.g. Jerome Letter 54.15: 'inflamed by her passions she forgets the fruit of her womb'.
[125] Cf. Ch. 5, Gautier 21.
[126] Cf. the reproaches in Ch. 5, Gautier 20.
[127] Lit., 'making one of gold, another of pewter'.

always takes the worst male as her mate, so the widow always chooses badly.[128]

17 Alas, things used to be different. A wife used to lament her husband's death and remain in mourning for a full year.[129] Now she waits no more than three days; you'd be hard pressed to find anyone waiting longer! For as soon as her first husband slips into everlasting sleep and has been disposed of in the ground, his wife begins to wage war, refusing to give up until she has found another man to stuff her tights again, for she is incapable of remaining alone. And I don't believe for a moment that she will wear black clothes to encourage mourning. Instead she will don a silk dress to indicate her joy. This is no more nor less than a disgrace. There is no bridle nor halter that could ever restrain her. She is forever coming and going; no man would ever be able to confine her to her room or to her house. She wants to be seen everywhere, so driven is she by her ardour. The burning lust of widows is an affront to decency; they creep and climb on to rooftops just like the frogs of Egypt;[130] they are not interested in beds or couches unless there is a man with them. Who would have thought they would be like this? Saint Acaire preferred to be the protector of madmen and the insane rather than to be responsible for widows. Anyone who looks into the matter knows that he was right. For these women are mad and know no bounds and so he didn't wish to be their patron. Widows are a base and immoral lot, while a madman in chains can do no harm.

Women frequent churches to find partners and to share the secrets of the cabal. They are desperate to know every last detail of their husbands' doings.

Bedroom Politics

18 (II. 1107–242) Whenever there is a secret, woman from here to the island of Crete insists on discovering it.[131] She seizes her husband, drags him off and takes him to bed, pretending that she wants to make love; then she kisses and embraces her husband and deceiving him with her words says, 'I don't know what a man has to fear, for, in the words of God, a man leaves his father and mother for his wife,

---

[128] An analogy popularized by *RR* 7749 ff.
[129] Le Fèvre has already noted (II. 579 ff.) a statement in law to the effect that widowers are not obliged to mourn wives, whereas widows by custom were supposed to mourn husbands for at least 300 days.
[130] Exod. 8: 1–14.
[131] The whole of this passage is indebted to *RR* 16,389–568.

they become one, hopefully one flesh, it really is possible. For God has
united and joined them with one indivisible bond, tying them tightly
so that they will stay together. Therefore every man should do
whatever pleases his wife.'

19   Then she strokes his head and resumes the kissing and lies
down under him and, arching her back and spine, offers to him her
carnal vessel, saying 'I'm ready to do your will and shall prove this to
you whenever you wish. I beg you to be mine, for we are one and in
any case as God says, whether you like it or not, you are mine
however reluctantly, and to my mind, rightly so.' And as they draw
together and she recognizes in his excitement that he is getting ready
to copulate, she presses her breast against his, despite the silk of the
bedclothes and blankets, saying to him; 'Here you are, I'm giving you
all I have, offering up to you my heart, body and all my limbs, but
please do not forget that you are my husband and lord. Now tell me
what I ask of you, you can tell me confidently, for indeed God will
know if I am lying. I'd prefer to suffer a terrible and sudden death
than to reveal your secrets to others. Oh wretch that I am, I would
never do it. You know how I am, you've put me to the test many a
time, fair friend, wise husband, now tell me why I am not party to
this information. Everything you know I ought to know too. No
other person will ever get to hear of it.'

20   Then she kisses and embraces him again, caressing and soothing him. With blandishments and flattery she presses herself right
up against him saying, 'How foolish and wretched I am since you
scorn and ignore my words. Alas, I am truly dishonoured by my
misguided love for you. If my neighbours[132] knew of this, I would
rightly be criticized, if the situation between us were common
knowledge. I love you more than I love myself, I am far superior to
other women, yet you deny me knowledge of your secrets—and I tell
you all I know, never omitting anything. Other women cover
themselves better, for they do not reveal their secrets, they are wise
to do this. Yet I am foolish and generous, since I behave in this way
towards you. And love alone makes me do this.' What more effective
and touching proof is there than the gift of one's heart and one's
mouth? If the man tries to draw closer, she forbids him to touch her,
pulls away, turns her back on him and weeps as if sad and upset. She
pretends to be very distressed. Then there's double trouble. She is

[132] The Old French (OF) makes it clear that these are female neighbours.

silent for a while, then sighs and in a grumbling tone says, after a few moments' silence, 'Alas, how I am deceived. I can't help but lament; whatever this man wants, I want it too. God knows his every wish would be mine, yet he would do nothing for me. I know that what he keeps hidden from me he discloses to all other women. He who says that man is deceived by woman is misguided and wrong. In this respect too I have been misled. I love you yet you don't love me at all. You aren't mine yet I am yours. And because I love you I'm telling you that you would please me greatly if you were to tell me what I ask, for I would then reveal to you all that I know, and I wouldn't lie on pain of death. Alas, I am your chambermaid. I'd rather be far away and be lying dead in a pit. The matter would have to be very important indeed for me to be able to hide it from you, yet you do not wish to reveal anything to me. I serve you as my lord, as a very important and superior person, yet you turn a deaf ear to my words. Our love is hardly mutual.'

21   The man is dismayed and ponders awhile but can find no defence against this attack; he does not notice the malice in her words and replies, 'What's the matter, my love? Please turn round. I have never been so upset as I am now over your complaint. I love you truly and there is nothing else so dear to me.' She then turns to face her husband, offering him her mouth and breast. He is completely taken in by her lecture. In response to a barrage of requests and supplications, he reveals everything to her, thus committing great folly, for from then on, she is the lady and mistress, while he lives the wretched life of a serf. Perrette wants me to tell her everything, concentrating all her efforts on making me angry. If I don't resist, believe me, I shall be treated just as you have heard.

Disobedience

Not only are women burdensome to men, impeding their attempts to serve God as the parable of the wedding feast suggests: they are also instinctively disobedient. The story given in Chapter 4, Andreas 15, is retold, followed by a strategically aberrant account of Eurydice.

22   (II. 1315–36) Orpheus knew the theory behind all musical instruments. His wife, Eurydice, was being held against her will in hell. In order to win back his wife, Orpheus went up to the gates of hell. There he demonstrated his musical skills and played wonderfully melodious music. When the king of hell heard this he returned Orpheus's wife to him, but on condition that if she looked back, she

would have to return to hell, never to leave again. Orpheus said to her, 'Sweet lady, I beseech you, do not turn round.' Eurydice paid dearly for her unwillingness to obey and, reacting against the prohibition, she broke the condition. Thus the foolish, unfortunate woman was taken back to darkest hell.[133]

After more discussion of disobedience, Matheolus alleges women's envy— her obsession with precedence—and greed, to the extent of selling her body for profit. (Le Fèvre dissociates himself from Matheolus here, insisting that he is a mere tanslator who has no personal animosity against women.)

Women and Lechery

23 (II. 1571–1702) People say that women are lecherous. On the surface, these words sound insulting. However, with due respect to all ladies, it is necessary to speak as one finds, and so that you don't think that I have made this up, I shall provide you with an example. Queen Semiramis[134] introduced a general law that every woman should take as her husband whomsoever she liked and that they would be allowed to do this without any regard to consanguinity. This precaution was to her own advantage for, as we learn from history, she married her own son. Heavens, this law was very shameful indeed, dirty, vile, and incestuous. And Pasiphaë, another queen, lay down under a bull disguised in a hollowed out wooden cow.[135] This was barefaced lechery. Just like a brutish animal, Pasiphaë placed her crotch where there was a crack in the artificial cow to receive the bull's prick. It is quite right that she has the reputation of a whore. Scylla committed an outrageous act for which she deserved to be hated and disgraced throughout the world. She burned with passion for Minos; her ardour was so insane and ill-fated that she cut off her own father's head. Her lust burned hotter than stubble. Minos won Scylla and the whole kingdom. Because Scylla was cruel, outrageous, and lecherous and had a reputation for treachery, she shares her name with one of the perils of the sea.[136]

24 No fever has a hotter flame than that of a woman on heat. Their ardour is more bitter and violent than toothache or other affliction.

[133] The usual point of this legend (Orpheus' love for his wife making him unable to keep his promise not to look back as they escape) is coolly twisted by transferring the promise to her instead.
[134] A mythical queen of Nineveh.
[135] For Pasiphaë, Scylla, Myrrha, and Biblis, see Ch. 1, Ovid 1.
[136] Following Ovid, there is confusion between Scylla, whose infatuation with Minos caused the death of her father Nisus, and the sea-monster of the same name.

Myrrha was not afraid of what people might say. She slept with her father and accepted intercourse with him, which so dishonoured him. The daughters of Lot sinned too, for they slept with their father. If Myrrha lay with her father, Biblis did so with her brother. It would be almost impossible for me to remain silent on this subject; Canace lay with Macareus, receiving her brother carnally in debauchery, which was her downfall.[137] Phaedra, the daughter of the king of Crete, was not very discreet in love. She loved with an illicit passion, besotted by Hippolytus, the son of her husband Theseus. When she had had the last remnants of that old pot she turned to her stepson for some banging. Venus turned her into a crazed stepmother. Phyllis committed a horribly devilish act. You would never find another woman so insane, so wretched, so mad, so out of control because of her passion. She abandoned herself to shameful dishonour when she hanged herself because of Demophöon. I don't know what made her hang herself; all I know is that she couldn't wait because she was overcome with despair and her beloved did not seem to be coming. Nine times she went to the seashore, then she hanged herself with her girdle. Dido, the queen of Carthage, also went too far because of Aeneas, her guest, who had dipped into her bread-basket. There's much to criticize in Dido's actions. When she saw Aeneas out at sea on his way to Lombardy, she did a terrible and reckless thing. Aware that she was heavy with child, weeping, lamenting, and insane with love, she took destiny into her own hands by killing herself, using Aeneas' sword.[138] Ill-fated was the hour when she was born. I could list many more examples, but I shan't do so for brevity's sake.

25   If there is anyone who says that women with their tits and boobs are colder than the male,[139] let him lose his purse and its contents.[140] If anyone has come to this conclusion, he hasn't looked at the evidence carefully enough. For, by Saint Acaire of Haspre, their lust is much stronger than ours and turns into greater ardour.[141] A woman underneath a man gets very excited. But let's say no more about it at present. The great authorities on the subject put forward many reasons for this and say that women burn more passionately, and more frequently spill their own blood than men,

[137] See Ovid, *Heroides*, Epistle XI.
[138] On Phyllis and Dido, cf. *RR 27–8*, and Ch. 1, Ovid 7.
[139] The belief that women were 'colder' came from Aristotle and Galen: see Ch. 1 (iii).
[140] *Double entendre* for the male genitals.
[141] Cf. Ch. 1, Isidore 2.

and are quicker to desire union with the male. Uguccione[142] himself claims that she is more eager to consummate the relationship; for the word 'woman' (*femme*) comes from the Greek 'fire' (*fos*), because she burns more than a man, or from 'thigh' (*femur*) via 'breeches' (*femourailles*). Women have heat in their loins and adore the 'thigh' game. Even supposing that you could find some who are frigid, cold humours are difficult to digest and such matter needs to be purged through bonking—for desperation gets even an old woman going, whose desire is that much keener since it stems from frigidity.[143] They are by nature very weak and frail and more fragile than glass. Ovid says that woman is only chaste when no man courts or chases her.[144] Given their lust, the pope has granted them permission to marry without delay in order to pay the tribute their flesh demands.[145] For otherwise they would hardly manage to wait and would offer or sell themselves to all comers.

The theme of lust is continued, leading into extended satire on old women and their roles as procuresses and abortionists; women's alleged love of superstition; manipulation of tears; inability to keep secrets; and lying. Now the narrator finds a new way of repeating himself, commencing a satire on their manifestation of the seven deadly sins. Suddenly he pauses, to cater for objectors.

In Defence of Antifeminism[146]

26 (II. 2589–648) Yet one might disagree with me, criticize my conclusion, and, putting forward the opposite point of view, suggest that my words are completely untrue. For, if some women are evil and perverse and abnormal, it does not necessarily follow that all of them are so cruel and wicked; nor should all of them be lumped together in this general reproach. A speech is badly composed if one's general conclusion is only partly valid. Logic hates this type of argumentation. Nevertheless, this present work, which expresses the pain in my heart, wishes me to exclude nothing, but commands me to push my argument to its logical, if extreme, conclusion, which is

---

[142] Uguccione of Pisa, author of an etymological dictionary: the same etymology is in Ch. 1, Isidore 2.
[143] Woman's 'innate' lust can thus be predicated upon either hypothesis, whether she is physiologically hotter, or colder, than man.
[144] *Amores*, I. 8. 43–4.
[145] Referring to dispensations by Popes Urban III and Innocent III, allowing widows to remarry speedily.
[146] Lines 2589–708 are not in extant MSS of the Latin text; but Van Hamel argues that Matheolus originated them nevertheless: Jehan Le Fèvre 1905, II. 184.

that no good woman exists. Solomon, in his works, makes an amazing comment, which supports my case, for he exclaims, 'Who could find a virtuous woman?'[147] The implication here is, of course, that this would be impossible. Since he says this, who am I to disagree? Why should I be shocked? What's more, he says that a base and broken man is worth more than a woman when she's doing good.[148] Thus there is no woman worth anything at all; I don't need to look for further proof. That's enough logical demonstration.

27   ... My exposition is clearly valid, for woman has—and there is ample evidence of this—deceived all the greatest men in the world; I shall be basing myself on rational argument. If the greatest are deceived, then the lesser naturally fall. In the street where I live they say that what applies to the greatest amongst us applies even more to lesser mortals. Who were the greatest lords? Who has ever heard of greater men than Solomon or Aristotle? Yet good sense, riches and reason were not worth a dung-beetle to them; all were made to look as if they had gone out of fashion; these men were both out-manoeuvred by women, deceived, vanquished, and tamed. Com-monplaces and similes, which one learns to use during one's studies and which are my weapons in the fight, decorate my speech beautifully.

The discussion of the seven sins is resumed, culminating with sloth.

Mother of Calamity

28   (II. 2759–90) It's true that women are lazy, but they are always ready to do harm. An evil woman just gets worse, becoming even more evil and wicked. It would take far too long for me to tell you everything about them, so for brevity's sake I shan't. Woman is not wise in this respect, for in her eagerness to do harm she only brings about her own ruin. According to the law, as I understand it, woman is not rational, nor does her love reside deep in her heart, but is there in her gaze for everyone to see.[149] She entrusts her honour openly to her eyes, yet they can't help but fail to protect it, since folly animates her gaze. With all her words, her chatter, and her talk, she could break a heart of glass; all her actions are stupid and foolish. Woman

[147] Prov. 31: 10
[148] Ecclus. 42: 14, in Ch. 1, Scripture 10; worried over by Christine, Ch. 9, Quarrel 4.
[149] In Aucassin et Nicolete 14.20 it is likewise claimed that woman's love is shallow (residing in her eye, nipple, and big toe) whereas man's is planted deep in his heart.

can do no good; indeed, goodness is destroyed and obliterated by her. Many a war is begun by women and many a murder committed throughout the world; castles are burned and ransacked and the poor made destitute. As every man and woman knows, there isn't one war in a thousand that isn't started by a woman and by her sowing of discord.[150] She is the mother of all calamities; all evil and all madness stem from her. Her sting is more venomous than a snake's; there isn't anyone who has anything to do with her who doesn't live to regret it.

Book II continues with a long cynical investigation of the traditional reasons for marrying, leading to the following conclusion.

Monstrous Woman

29 (II. 4095–142) Now you can see how foolhardy it is to take a wife. What will your response be? What is the point of your studying the matter? Don't get married, have mistresses. If you are weak by nature, it will be safer for you to have a hundred of them rather than devote yourself to one;[151] treat them as if they were no more important than a straw. And if you are strong, take my advice, don't plunge yourself in the mire or frequent either one woman or many— I forbid you to have anything to do with them, for in the garden lurks a snake; and no one approaches it without regretting it afterwards.[152]

30 Now I should like to rest for a while, for whoever sets out to expose the evils of the female sex, finds her poisonous acts too numerous to relate. Nature shows and teaches us that every woman is a real monster and that she is quite happy to put up with her own faults. There is no shortage of proof of this, or demonstration of how monstrous she is. It is said that woman was conceived without nature's consent. A philosopher testifies to this quite clearly in his works, saying that nature, having embarked on creation, was shocked when she contemplated her mistake and blushed as she became aware of it.[153] Woman is a monstrous hermaphrodite, proving to be a chimaera with horns and a tail bigger than a

---

[150] Cf. Ch. 1, Ovid 6; Ch. 4, Marbod 1; and Juv. *Satire* VI, 242 ff.

[151] Cf. Ch. 4, Map 24.

[152] Cf. *RR* 35.

[153] An allegation deriving from Ch. 1, Aristotle 6 or 8. See also Ch. 9, *City* 4, rebutting the notion of Nature's shame at woman's creation.

peacock's or pheasant's.[154] Thus she bears the marks of a monster, as this treatise informs you.

31   And if anyone were to say that women in general are slandered without taking account what each individual woman might do, and that some, who are specially favoured, deserve our respect and praise, I would venture to say that this would be an unnatural thing and that there has never been such a great miracle. For their sex in no way prepares them to be virtuous or to do good, indeed they are predisposed to do the very opposite.

Book III of the *Lamentations* is something of a pastiche, peculiarly poised between gravity and levity. In a vision the narrator remonstrates with God about the creation of woman and the institution of marriage. Moreover, he objects to the injustice of the punishment for the Fall, and argues that God, as good shepherd, must save people, whatever their sin.

Termination of the Female Sex

32   (III. 1399–459) 'You should gather up your sheep and wander through the fields calling them, in case you find any that have gone astray, so that they can be saved by you. You must do all you can for their safety, chasing away the wolves with your dogs and staff, and your shouting. If one dies, and you see it, you should immediately try to revive it; for if a shepherd allows a ewe to die through his own fault, ignorance, or laziness, he must, according to the law, pay compensation, if he was in a position to protect it and even if Argus himself had tried to prevent this.[155] And since the ordinary shepherd is expected to make reparation, you are expected to do so all the more, you who are all-seeing and all-powerful, and the lord of all shepherds. Thus it follows logically that, since you are capable of saving your flock and your sheep, then you must and will save them. If you are not moved by pity, you will be the cause of our deaths.

33   'Yet whatever one might say about us men, who are in a position to be saved, I do not believe that you can have or save the

---

[154] The OF *peue* is untraceable unless related to *peu-peu* which probably means 'hoopoe'. Since the latter does not have a distinctive tail, the translation 'pheasant' is suggested. The *double entendre* in 'tail' (Le Fèvre's source has *cauda*, sometimes meaning 'penis') presumably explains the designation 'hermaphrodite'. 'Chimaera' recalls Ch. 4, Marbod 5, and Map 6.

[155] The sheep which many-eyed Argus has failed to protect appears, tantalizingly, to be female.

soul of a woman. For you know and have clear proof of the fact that she was the cause of our fall and the reason for your death. Therefore you should not strive at all for her salvation. And when, on judgement day, Adam is resurrected and his body becomes whole again, then the whole female sex, which, as I have said, is full of venom, will revert to nothingness and will thus disappear.[156] For otherwise Adam could not be whole again: if his rib were not replaced in its rightful spot (from which it was taken, and with which you created woman many years ago in your earthly paradise and then forbade her entry into it), Adam would not be complete. However, once his rib has been replaced, woman will be no more.[157] Thus she will not be saved or resurrected.

34 'Alas, gentle and omnipotent God, I am aware of my error; I know that my words are erroneous, but my heart is so full of melancholy. I am oppressed by anger and suffering. If there is madness in my words, forgive me, glorious God!'

God answers, justifying marriage as a purgatorial experience enabling men to gain the eternal prize. This is confirmed when the narrator sees his own destined celestial throne among the elect, i.e. husbands, whose torments on earth give them precedence in heaven over celibates. Such is the narrator's consolation, when he awakes to the sound of his nagging wife.

[156] A facetious argument against the view that woman would be resurrected as woman at Judgement Day: Ch. 2, Augustine 7–9.

[157] A jingle in the OF on restituée ... destituée (1449–50) mocks this idea of woman's deconstitution at the moment of man's reconstitution.

7

The Wife of Bath

GEOFFREY CHAUCER (c.1343–1400)

*THE WIFE OF BATH'S PROLOGUE** (c.1390–5)

Chaucer was a subtle purveyor of the old wine of received classics, including texts given earlier in this volume, into new bottles. While he easily emulated Walter Map's urbanity in the standard mode of 'dissuasion from matrimony' (*Envoy to Bukton*), he also reinvigorated the antifeminist favourites by situating them in strange new contexts, as when Ecclesiasticus 7: 29 becomes a bone of contention for Pluto and Proserpina while they are presiding over the *fabliau* denouement of *The Merchant's Tale*. Many of his poems also challenge consideration as narratives in defence of women. However, the Wife of Bath's speech partly fulfils that function even in the process of submerging the reader in a welter of misogynistic quotations. It therefore functions in this anthology as a kind of interface between readings from antifeminism and responses to antifeminism.

Her Prologue comes 'out of the blue' in *The Canterbury Tales*, so needs little introduction save to recall that she is one of only a few women participating in the pilgrimage and in the story-telling competition which the pilgrims conduct. The Prologue can be divided into three main sections. The first (1– 9) tackles Jerome's argument with Jovinian about marriage and virginity, vigorously re-manipulating some of the ideas and scriptural texts which constituted their battleground. It has seemed to most that in the process she backs some conspicuous losers as well as trenchant winners; so she is shadowed by the stereotype of the intellectually flawed female. Ambivalence continues into the second section (14–33), ostensibly an account of her first three husbands but largely a brilliantly simple *riposte* to Theophrastan slurs. She indignantly retails these same slurs as the 'lies' her husbands have thrown at her (she pretends) in their drunkenness. Her tirade, as Mann has said, 'thus functions simultaneously as a demonstration of female bullying and a witness to masculine oppression', demonstrating how 'each feeds off the other'.[1] The last section comments on her other spouses and represents the combined forces of antifeminism as one huge book, *Of Wikked Wyves*— recited to her daily by her fifth, clerical, husband. Suffocated by a procession of hostile androcentric writings, the Wife retaliates against both book and husband. She rips out three pages, once again vindicating woman only at the cost of conforming to a (male) caricature of philistine female rancour.

---

* Tr. David Wright; Geoffrey Chaucer, *The Canterbury Tales* (Oxford: Oxford University Press, 1985), 219–39. © David Wright. Reprinted by permission of the Peters Fraser and Dunlop Group Ltd.

[1] Mann 1991, 79.

1   (1) 'Experience—and no matter what they say
In books—is good enough authority
For me to speak of trouble in marriage.[2]
For ever since I was twelve years of age,
Thanks be to God, I've had no less than five
Husbands at church door—if one may believe
I could be wed so often legally![3]
And each a man of standing, in his way.
Certainly it was told me, not long since,
That, seeing Christ had never more than once
Gone to a wedding (Cana, in Galilee)
He taught me by that very precedent
That I ought not be married more than once.

2   (14) 'What's more, I was to bear in mind also
Those bitter words that Jesus, God and Man
Spoke in reproof to the Samaritan
Beside a well—"Thou hast had", said He,
"Five husbands, and he whom now thou hast
Is not thy husband."[4] He said that, of course,
But what He meant by it I cannot say.
All I ask is, why wasn't the fifth man
The lawful spouse of the Samaritan?
How many lawful husbands could she have?
All my born days, I've never heard as yet
Of any given number or limit,
However folk surmise or interpret.
All I know for sure is, God has plainly
Bidden us to increase and multiply—
A noble text, and one I understand!
And, as I'm well aware, He said my husband
Must leave father and mother, cleave to me.
But, as to number, did He specify?
He named no figure, neither two nor eight[5]—
Why should folk talk of it as a disgrace?

---

   [2] 'Trouble' refers to *tribulatio*, from St Paul on marriage as 'tribulation of the flesh';
1 Cor. 7: 28.
   [3] She has contracted marriage at the church door (preceding nuptial mass inside)
five times since the minimum legal age for a girl.
   [4] John 4: 18; cited in *Ag. Jov.* 1. 14.
   [5] Jerome (*Ag. Jov.* 1. 15) and Juvenal (Ch. 1, 5) both name eight marriages (the
'multiplication' understood by the Wife from Gen. 1: 28) as a mind-boggling number.
On her interest in explicit biblical statement, see Blamires 1989.

3   (35) 'And what about that wise King Solomon:
       I take it that he had more wives than one!
       Now would to God that I might lawfully
       Be solaced half as many times as he!
       What a God-given gift that Solomon
       Had for his wives! For there's no living man
       Who has the like; Lord knows how many a bout
       That noble king enjoyed on the first night
       With each of them! His was a happy life!⁶
       Blessed be God that I have married five!
       Here's to the sixth, whenever he turns up.
       I won't stay chaste for ever, that's a fact.⁷
       For when my husband leaves this mortal life
       Some Christian man shall wed me soon enough.
       For then, says the Apostle Paul, I'm free
       To wed, in God's name, where it pleases me.
       He says that to be married is no sin,
       Better it is to marry than to burn.⁸
       What do I care if people execrate
       The bigamy of villainous Lamech?
       I know that Abraham was a holy man,
       And Jacob too, so far as I can tell;
       And they had more than two wives, both of them,
       And many another holy man as well.⁹

4   (59) 'Now can you tell me where, in any age,
       Almighty God explicitly forbade
       All marrying and giving in marriage?
       Answer me that! And will you please tell me
       Where was it He ordained virginity?
       No fear, you know as well as I do, that
       The Apostle, where he speaks of maidenhood,
       Says he has got no firm precept for it.¹⁰
       You may advise a woman not to wed,

⁶ 3 Kgs. 11: 1–11 mentions 700 wives and 300 mistresses, under whose influence he relapsed into paganism: cf. Ch. 2, Jerome 24; and Jerome 6 on 'what Solomon thought of marriage'.
⁷ i.e., she will not take a vow of celibate widowhood.
⁸ Cf. Ch. 2, Jerome 4.
⁹ 'Vengeance' on Lamech is mentioned in Gen. 4: 24. In citing Abraham and Jacob, the Wife is taking sides with Jovinian against Jerome: Ag. Jov. I. 19.
¹⁰ I Cor. 7: 25 (and Ag. Jov. I. 12).

But by no means is advice a command.
To our own private judgement he left it;
Had virginity been the Lord's command,
Marriage would at the same time be condemned.
And surely, if no seed were ever sown,
From what, then, could virginity be grown?
Paul did not dare command, at any rate,
A thing for which the Lord gave no edict.
There's a prize set up for virginity:
Let's see who'll make the running, win who may!

5   (77) 'This teaching's not for all men to receive,
Just those to whom it pleases God to give
The strength to follow it. All I know is,
That the Apostle was himself a virgin;
But none the less, though he wished everyone
—Or so he wrote and said—were such as he,
That's only to *advise* virginity.
I have his leave, by way of concession,
To be a wife; and so it is no shame,
My husband dying, if I wed again;
A second marriage can incur no blame
Though it were good for a man not to touch
A woman—meaning in his bed or couch,
For who'd bring fire and tow too close together?
I think you'll understand the metaphor!
Well, by and large, he thought virginity
Better than marrying out of frailty.
I call it frailty, unless he and she
Mean to live all their lives in chastity.

6   (95) 'I grant all this; I've no hard feelings if
Maidenhood be set above remarriage.
Purity in body and in heart
May please some—as for me, I make no boast.
For, as you know, no master of a household
Has all of his utensils made of gold;
Some are of wood, and yet they are of use.
The Lord calls folk to Him in many ways,
And each has his peculiar gift from God,
Some this, some that, even as He thinks good.

7 (105) 'Virginity is a great excellence,
And so is dedicated continence,
But Christ, of perfection the spring and well,
Did not bid everyone to go and sell
All that he had, and give it to the poor,
And thus to follow in His tracks; be sure
He spoke to those who would live perfectly;[11]
And, sirs, if you don't mind, that's not for me.
I mean to give the best years of my life
To the acts and satisfactions of a wife.

8 (115) 'And tell me also, what was the intention
In creating organs of generation,
When man was made in so perfect a fashion?[12]
They were not made for nothing, you can bet!
Twist it how you like and argue up and down
That they were only made for the emission
Of urine; that our little differences
Are there to distinguish between the sexes,
And for no other reason—who said no?
Experience teaches that it is not so.
But not to vex the scholars, I'll say this:
That they were fashioned for both purposes,
That's to say, for a necessary function
As much as for enjoyment in procreation
Wherein we do not displease God in heaven.
Why else is it set down in books, that men
Are bound to pay their wives what's due to them?[13]
And with whatever else would he make payment
If he didn't use his little instrument?
It follows, therefore, they must have been given
Both to pass urine, and for procreation.

9 (135) 'But I'm not saying everyone who's got
The kind of tackle I am talking of
Is bound to go and use it sexually.
For then who'd bother about chastity?

---

[11] Matt. 19: 21. Marriage, widowhood, and virginity were three ascending 'grades' of perfection.

[12] The Wife is re-asking questions which Jerome had struggled to quash: *Ag. Jov.* I. 36.

[13] The reciprocal sexual 'debt' of marriage, as in Ch. 3, Gratian 2, based on I Cor. 7: 3–4; but the Wife plays down the reciprocity.

Christ was a virgin, though formed like a man,
Like many another saint since time began,
And yet they lived in perfect chastity.
I've no objection to virginity.
Let them be loaves of purest sifted wheat,
And us wives called mere barley-bread, and yet
As St Mark tells us, when our Saviour fed
The multitude, it was with barley-bread.[14]
I'm not particular: I'll continue
In the condition God has called us to.
In married life I mean to use my gadget
As generously as my Maker gave it.
If I be grudging, the Lord punish me!
My husband's going to have it night and day,
At any time he likes to pay his dues.
I shan't be difficult! I shan't refuse!
I say again, a husband I must have,
Who shall be both my debtor and my slave,
And he shall have, so long as I'm his wife,
His "trouble in the flesh". For during life
I've "power of his body" and not he.
That's just what the Apostle Paul told me;
He told our husbands they must love us too.
Now I approve entirely of this view—'

10   (163) Up leapt the pardoner—'Now then, madam,
I swear to you by God and by St John,
You make a splendid preacher on this theme.
I was about to wed a wife—but then
Why should my body pay a price so dear?
I'll not wed this nor any other year!'

11   (169) 'You wait!' said she. 'My tale has not begun.
It is a different cask that you'll drink from
Before I've done; a bitterer brew than ale.
And when I've finished telling you my tale
Of tribulation in matrimony
—And I'm a lifelong expert; that's to say
That I myself have been both scourge and whip—
You can decide then if you want to sip

[14] Cf. Ch. 2. Jerome 1.

Out of the barrel that I mean to broach.
But you had best take care if you approach
Too near—for I've a dozen object-lessons
And more, that I intend to tell. "The man
Who won't be warned by others, he shall be
Himself a warning to all other men."
These are the very words that Ptolemy
Writes in his *Almagest*: you'll find it there.'

12   (184) 'Let me beg you, madam,' said the pardoner,
'If you don't mind, go on as you began,
And tell your tale to us and spare no man,
And teach all us young fellows your technique.'

13   (188) 'Gladly,' said she, 'if that's what you would like;
But let no one in this company, I beg,
If I should speak what comes into my head,
Take anything that I may say amiss;
All that I'm trying to do is amuse.

14   (193) 'And now, sir, now, I will begin my tale.
May I never touch a drop of wine or ale
If this be not the truth! Of those I had,
Three were good husbands, two of them were bad.
The three good ones were very rich and old;
But barely able, all the same, to hold
To the terms of our covenant and contract—[15]
Bless me! you'll all know what I mean by that!
It makes me laugh to think, so help me Christ,
How cruelly I made them sweat at night!
And I can tell you it meant nothing to me.
They'd given me their land and property;
I'd no more need to be assiduous
To win their love, or treat them with respect.
They all loved me so much that, heavens above!
I set no store whatever by their love.
A wily woman's always out to win
A lover—that is, if she hasn't one.
Since I'd got them in the hollow of my hand,
And they'd made over to me all their land,
What point was there in taking pains to please,

[15] The conjugal 'debt' of intercourse, as in *8* above.

Except for my advantage, or my ease?
Believe you me, I set them so to work
That many a night I made them sing, "Alack!"
No flitch of bacon for them, anyhow,
Like some have won in Essex at Dunmow.[16]
I governed them so well in my own way,
And kept them happy, so they'd always buy
Fairings to bring home to me from the fair.
When I was nice to them, how glad they were!
For God knows how I'd nag and give them hell!

15   (224) 'Now listen how I managed things so well,
You wives that have the wit to understand!
Here's how to talk and keep the upper hand:
For no man's half as barefaced as a woman
When it comes to chicanery and gammon.[17]
It's not for knowing wives that I say this,
But for those times when things have gone amiss.
For any astute wife, who knows what's what,
Can make her husband think that black is white,[18]
With her own maid as witness in support.
But listen to the kind of thing I'd say:

16   (235) '"So this is how things are, old Mister Dotard?[19]
Why does the woman next door look so gay?
She can go where she likes, and all respect her,
—I sit at home, I've nothing fit to wear!
Why are you always over at her house?
She's pretty, is she? So you're amorous!
What did I catch you whispering to the maid?
Mister Old Lecher, drop it, for God's sake!
And if I've an acquaintance or a friend,
You rage and carry on just like a fiend
If I pay him some harmless little visit!
And then you come back home pissed as a newt,

---

[16] The side of bacon could be won by a married couple lasting a year without quarrelling.

[17] The translation presupposes a pun (not present in Chaucer's source, *RR* 18136–7) on *lyen*, in *half so boldely kan . . . no man / Swere and lyen*. On lying, cf. Ch. 4, Andreas 19.

[18] Lit. 'that the chough is mad'.

[19] Cf. the 'complaints' in Ch. 2, Jerome 12, imitated in *Miroir* 1625–48; and in Ch. 6, *Corb. 3*.

And preach at me, confound you, from your bench!
What a great shame—just think of the expense—
To marry a poor woman, so you tell me.[20]
And if she's rich, and comes of a good family,
It's hell, you say, to put up with her pride,
And her black moods and fancies. Then, you swine,
Should she be beautiful, you change your line,
And say that every rakehell wants to have her,
That in no time she's bound to lose her honour,
Because it is assailed on every side.

17   (257) '"You say that some folk want us for our riches,
Some for our looks, and others for our figures,
Or for our sex appeal, or our good breeding;
Some want a girl who dances, or can sing,
Else it's our slender hands and arms they want.
So the devil takes the lot, by your account!
None can defend a castle wall, you say,
For long if it's attacked day after day.

18   (265) '"And if she's plain, why then you say that she's
Setting her cap at every man she sees:
She'll jump upon him, fawning like a spaniel,
Till someone buys what she has got to sell.
Never a goose upon the lake so grey
But it will find its gander, so you say.
Says you, it's hard to manage or control
A thing no man would keep of his own will.
That's how you talk, pig, when you go to bed,
Saying that no sane man need ever wed,
Nor any man who hopes to go to heaven.
Wretch, may your withered wrinkled neck be broken
In two by thunderblast and fiery lightning!

19   (278) '"And then, you say, a leaky roof, and smoke,
And nagging wives, are the three things that make
A man flee from his home.[21] Oh, for God's sake!
What ails an old man to go on like that?

[20] This introduces a passage based ultimately on Ch. 2, Jerome 15; cf. Ch. 6, RR 3–4.
[21] Cf. Ch. 4, Ag. Marr. J15.

20   (282) '"Then you go on to claim²² we women hide
        Our failings till the knot is safely tied,
        And then we show them—A villainous saying,
        A scoundrel's proverb, if I ever heard one!

21   (285) '"You say that oxen, asses, horses, hounds,
        Can be tried out and proved at different times,
        And so can basins, washbowls, stools, and spoons,
        And household goods like that, before you buy;
        Pots, clothes, and dresses too; but who can try
        A wife out till he's wed? Old dotard! Pig!
        And then, says you, we show the faults we've hid.

22   (293) '"You also claim²³ that it enrages me
        If you forget to compliment my beauty,
        If you're not always gazing on my face,
        Paying me compliments in every place,
        If on my birthday you don't throw a party,
        Buy a new dress, and make a fuss of me;
        Or if you are ungracious to my nurse,
        Or to my chambermaid, or, even worse,
        Rude to my father's kinsfolk and his cronies,—
        That's what you say, old barrelful of lies!

23   (303) '"And about Jankin you've the wrong idea,
        Our apprentice with curly golden hair²⁴
        Who makes himself my escort everywhere—
        I wouldn't have him if you died tomorrow!
        But, damn you, tell me this—God send you sorrow!—
        Why do you hide the strongbox keys from me?
        It's mine as much as yours—our property!
        What! I'm the mistress of the house, and you'll
        Make her look like an idiot and a fool?
        You'll never be, no matter how you scold,
        Master of both my body and my gold,
        No, by St James! For you'll have to forgo
        One or the other, take or leave it! Now,
        What use is all your snooping and your spying?

²² Based on Ch. 2, Jerome *13*, expanded in Ch. 6, *RR 7*, as also in *Miroir* 1538–59
and *Math.* III. 293–418.
²³ As in Ch. 2, Jerome *14*.
²⁴ Still adapting Jerome *14* ('the effeminate steward . . .').

I sometimes think you want to lock me in
That strongbox of yours, when you should be saying
'Dear wife, go where you like, go and have fun,
I shan't believe the tales they tell in malice,
I know you for a faithful wife, Dame Alice.'
We love no man who watches carefully
Our coming and our going; we want liberty.

24   (323) '"Blessed above all other men is he,
That astrologer, Mister Ptolemy,
Who set down in his book, the *Almagest*,
This proverb: 'Of all men he is the wisest
Who doesn't care who has the world in hand.'[25]
From which proverb you are to understand
That if you have enough, why should you care
A curse how well-off other people are?
Don't worry, you old dotard—it's all right,
You'll have cunt enough and plenty, every night.
What bigger miser than he who'll not let
Another light a candle at his lantern—
He won't have any the less light, I'm thinking![26]
If you've enough, what's there to grumble at?

25   (337) '"And you say if we make ourselves look smart
With dresses and expensive jewellery,
It only puts at risk our chastity;
And then, confound you, you must quote this text,
And back yourself up with the words of Paul,
As thus: 'In chaste and modest apparel
You women must adorn yourselves,' said he,
'And not with braided hair and jewellery,
Such as pearls and gold; and not in costly dress.'[27]
But of your text, and your red-letter rubric,
I'll be taking no more notice than a gnat!

26   (348) '"And you said this: that I was like a cat,
For you have only got to singe its skin,
And then the cat will never go from home;

---

[25] Probably from a collection of sayings attached to a Latin translation of Ptolemy's astronomical text.
[26] A popular *double entendre*; in RR 7399 ff. and Ovid, *Art of Love* III. 89 ff.
[27] 1 Tim. 2: 9, in Ch. 1, Scripture 14; and cf. Ch. 8, *Dives* 20.

But if its coat is looking sleek and gay,
She won't stop in the house, not half a day,
But off she goes the first thing in the morning,
To show her coat off and go caterwauling.
That's to say, if I'm all dressed up, Mister Brute,
I'll run out in my rags to show them off!²⁸

27   (357) '"Mister Old Fool, what good is it to spy?
If you begged Argus with his hundred eyes
To be my bodyguard—what better choice?—
There's little he would see unless I let him,
For if it killed me, yet I'd somehow fool him!²⁹

28   (362) '"And you have also said, there are three things,
Three things there are that trouble the whole earth,
And there's no man alive can stand the fourth—
Sweet Mister Brute, Jesus cut short your life!
You keep on preaching that an odious wife
Is to be counted one of these misfortunes.
Really, are there no other comparisons
That you can make, and without dragging in
A poor innocent wife as one of them?

29   (371) '"Then you compare a woman's love to Hell,
To barren lands where rain will never fall.
And you go on to say, it's like Greek fire,
The more it burns, the fiercer its desire
To burn up everything that can be burned.
And just as grubs and worms eat up a tree,
Just so a woman will destroy her husband;³⁰
All who are chained to wives know this, you say."

30   (379) 'Ladies and gentlemen, just as you've heard
I'd browbeat them; they really thought they'd said
All these things to me in their drunkenness.
All lies—but I'd get Jankin to stand witness

---

²⁸ The cat simile occurs in *Miroir* 3208–15, and in *Math.* ii. 3071–80. On showing off clothes, see Ch. 5, Gautier 7; Ch. 6, *RR* 30 and *Math. 17*.
²⁹ The hundred-eyed Argus tried (ineffectually) to guard Io on Juno's behalf against the advances of her husband Jupiter. Women were proverbially too wily for him: Ch. 1, Ovid 4; also in *RR* 14381–4.
³⁰ The Wife is reacting to verses from Proverbs presented in Ch. 2, Jerome 8; and cf. Ch. 4, *Ag. Marr. J9*.

And bear me out, and my young niece also.
O Lord! the pain I gave them, and the woe,
And they, heaven knows, quite innocent of course.
For I could bite and whinny like a horse.
I'd scold them even when I was at fault,
For otherwise I'd often have been dished.
Who comes first to the mill, is first to grind;
I'd get in first, till they'd be glad to find
A quick excuse for things they'd never done
In their whole lives; and so our war was won.
I'd pick on them for wenching; never mind
They were so ill that they could barely stand!

31   (395) 'And yet it tickled him to the heart, because
He thought it showed how fond of him I was.
I swore that all my walking out at night
Was to spy out the women that he tapped;
Under that cover, how much fun I had!
To us at birth such mother-wit is given;
As long as they live God has granted women
Three things by nature: lies, and tears, and spinning.[31]
There's one thing I can boast of: in the end
I'd gain, in every way, the upper hand
By force or fraud, or by some stratagem
Like everlasting natter, endless grumbling.[32]

32   (407) 'Bed in particular was their misfortune;
That's when I'd scold, and see they got no fun.[33]
I wouldn't stop a moment in the bed
If I felt my husband's arm over my side,
No, not until his ransom had been paid,
And then I'd let him do the thing he liked.
What I say is, everything has its price;
You cannot lure a hawk with empty hand.[34]
If I wanted something, I'd endure his lust.
And even feign an appetite for it;
Though I can't say I ever liked old meat—

---

[31] See Ch. 9, *City* 7 and n.
[32] Cf. Ch. 4, *Ag. Marr.* J14, and Ch. 6, *Math.* 8.
[33] A tradition seen in Ch. 1, Juv. 6 and Ch. 6, *Corb.* 3; and see *Math.* 1 and 7.
[34] Cf. Ch. 4, Andreas 5. On sex 'sold' at a 'price', also in 35 below, cf. Ch. 4, *Ag. Marr.* L3, Ch. 6, *RR* 25, etc.

And that's what made me nag them all the time.
Even though the Pope were sitting next to them
I'd not spare them at table or at board,
But paid them back, I tell you, word for word.
I swear upon my oath, so help me God,
I owe them not a word, all's been paid back.
I set my wits to work till they gave up;
They had to, for they knew it would be best,
Or else we never would have been at rest.
For even if he looked fierce as a lion,
Yet he would fail to get his satisfaction.

33   (431) 'Then would I turn and say, "Come, dearest, come!
How meek you look, like Wilkin, dear old lamb!
Come to me, sweetheart, let me kiss your cheek!
You ought to be all patient and meek,
And have ever such a scrupulous conscience—
Or so you preach of Job and his patience!
Always be patient; practise what you preach,
For if you don't, we've got a thing to teach,
Which is: it's good to have one's wife in peace!
One of us has got to knuckle under,
And since man is more rational a creature
Than woman is, it's you who must forbear.[35]
But what's the matter now? Why moan and groan?
You want my quim just for yourself alone?
Why, it's all yours—there now, go take it all!
By Peter, but I swear you love it well!
For if I wished to sell my pretty puss,
I'd go about as sweet as any rose;
But no, I'll keep it just for you to taste.
Lord knows you're in the wrong; and that's the truth!"
All arguments we had were of that kind.
Now will I speak about my fourth husband.

34   (453) 'My fourth husband was a libertine;
That is to say, he kept a concubine;
And I was young, and passionate, and gay,
Stubborn and strong, and merry as a magpie.

---

[35] She cleverly turns against the male the allegation of inferior female rationality
found, e.g., in Ch. 3, Rule 5; Ch. 4, Andreas 9; Ch. 6, Math. 28; Ch. 9, City 10.

How I would dance to the harp's tunable
Music, and sing like any nightingale,
When I had downed a draught of mellow wine!
Metellius, the dirty dog, that swine
Who with a club beat his own wife to death
Because she drank—if I had been his wife,
Even he would not have daunted me from drink![36]
And after taking wine I'm bound to think
On Venus—sure as cold induces hail,
A greedy mouth points to a greedy tail.
A woman full of wine has no defence,
All lechers know this from experience.

35   (469) 'But, Lord Christ! when it all comes back to me,[37]
And I recall my youth and gaiety,
It warms the very cockles of my heart.
And to this day it does my spirit good
To think that in my time I've had my fling.
But age, alas, that cankers everything,
Has stripped me of my beauty and spirit.
Let it go then! Goodbye, and devil take it!
The flour's all gone; there is no more to say.
Now I must sell the bran as best I may;
But all the same I mean to have my fun.
And now I'll tell about my fourth husband.

36   (481) 'I tell you that it rankled in my heart
That in another he should take delight.
But he was paid for it in full, by God!
From that same wood I made for him a rod—
Not with my body, and not like a slut,
But certainly I carried on with folk
Until I made him stew in his own juice,
With fury, and with purest jealousy.
By God! on earth I was his purgatory,
For which I hope his soul's in Paradise.[38]
God knows he often had to sit and whine

---

[36] The Metellius story is from Valerius Maximus; cf. Ch. 4, Andreas 20 on women and drink.
[37] A passage based on RR 12932–48.
[38] In Math. III. 1674 ff. marriage is a purgatorial trial by which men may attain salvation; and cf. Ch. 4, Ag. Marr. J20.

When his shoe pinched him cruellest!³⁹ And then
How bitterly, and in how many ways,
I wrung his withers, there is none can guess
Or know, save only he and God in heaven!
He died when I came from Jerusalem,
And now lies buried under the rood beam,
Although his tomb is not as gorgeous
As is the sepulchre of Darius
That Apelles sculpted so skilfully;
For to have buried him expensively
Would have been waste. So goodbye, and God rest him!
He's in his grave now, shut up in his coffin.

37   (503) 'Of my fifth husband I have this to tell
—I pray God keep and save his soul from hell!—
And yet he was to me the worst of all:
I feel it on my ribs, on each and all,
And always will until my dying day!
But in our bed he was so free and gay
And moreover knew so well how to coax
And cajole when he wanted my *belle chose*,
That, though he'd beaten me on every bone,
How quickly he could win my love again!
I think that I loved him the best, for he
Was ever chary of his love for me.
We women have, I'm telling you no lies,
In this respect the oddest of fancies;
If there's a thing we can't get easily,
That's what we're bound to clamour for all day:
Forbid a thing, and that's what we desire;⁴⁰
Press hard upon us, and we run away.
We are not forward to display our ware:
For a great crowd at market makes things dear;
Who values stuff bought at too cheap a price?
And every woman knows this, if she's wise.

38   (525) 'My fifth husband—may God bless his soul!
Whom I took on for love, and not for gold,
Was at one time a scholar at Oxford,

³⁹ Cf. Ch. 4, Map 26.
⁴⁰ Cf. Ch. 4, Andreas 14–15; and Ch. 6, RR 31.

But had left college, and come home to board
With my best friend, then living in our town:
God keep her soul! her name was Alison.
She knew me and the secrets of my heart
As I live, better than the parish priest:
She was my confidant; I told her all—
For had my husband pissed against a wall,
Or done a thing that might have cost his life—
To her, and also to my dearest niece,
And to another lady friend as well,
I'd have betrayed his secrets, one and all.
And so I did time and time again, dear God!
It often made his face go red and hot
For very shame; he'd kick himself, that he
Had placed so great a confidence in me.[41]

39   (543) 'And it so happened that one day in Lent
(For I was ever calling on my friend,
As I was always fond of having fun,
Strolling about from house to house in spring,[42]
In March, April, and May, to hear the gossip)
Jankin the scholar, and my friend Dame Alice,
And I myself, went out into the meadows.
My husband was in London all that Lent,
So I was free to follow my own bent,
To see and to be seen by the gay crowd.[43]
How could I know to whom, and in what place,
My favours were destined to be bestowed?
At feast-eves and processions, there I was;
At pilgrimages; I attended sermons,
And these miracle-plays; I went to weddings,
Dressed in my best, my long bright scarlet gowns.[44]
No grub, no moth or insect had a chance
To nibble at them, and I'll tell you why:
It was because I wore them constantly.

[41] Cf. Ch. 4, Andreas 13, 22; Ch. 5, Gautier 11; Ch. 6, RR 34–7.
[42] Cf. 1 Tim. 5: 13; in Ch. 1, Scripture 13.
[43] Cf. Ch. 2, Tert. 16; Ch. 5, Gautier 8. Note that the Wife of Bath shares the name
'Alison' (see 60) with her friend (38), here referred to as 'Alice'.
[44] Wives' alleged abuse of 'pilgrimages', etc. (Ch. 4, Ag. Marr. 14, Ch. 6, RR 29) is
answered in Ch. 9, City 6.

40   (563) 'Now I'll tell you what happened to me then.
        We strolled about the fields, as I was saying,
        And got on so well together, he and I,
        That I began to think ahead, and tell him
        That if I were a widow we could marry.
        For certainly—I speak without conceit—
        Till now I've never been without foresight
        In marriage matters; other things as well.
        I'd say a mouse's life's not worth a leek
        Who has but one hole to run to for cover,
        For if that fails the mouse, then it's all over!⁴⁵

41   (575) 'I let him think that he'd got me bewitched.
        It was my mother taught me that device.
        I also said I dreamed of him at night,
        That he'd come to kill me, lying on my back,
        And that the entire bed was drenched in blood.
        And yet I hoped that he would bring me luck—
        In dreams blood stands for gold, so I was taught.
        All lies—for I dreamed nothing of the sort.
        I was in this, as in most other things,
        As usual following my mother's teachings.⁴⁶

42   (585) 'But now, sirs, let me see—what was I saying?
        Aha! Bless me, I've found the thread again.
        When my fourth husband was laid on his bier
        I wept for him—what a sad face I wore!—
        As all wives must, because it's customary;⁴⁷
        With my kerchief I covered up my face.
        But, since I was provided with a mate,
        I wept but little, that I guarantee!

43   (593) 'To church they bore my husband in the morning
        Followed by the neighbours, all in mourning,
        And one among them was the scholar Jankin.
        So help me God, when I saw him go past,
        Oh what a fine clean pair of legs and feet

---

⁴⁵ Cf. Ch. 6, RR 26.
⁴⁶ For satire on women's tuition by mothers (already in Juv. Satire VI, 231–41), see
Ch. 6, RR 19, Corb. 7. For the dream, cf. Ch. 5, Gautier 4.
⁴⁷ Cf. routine grief in Ch. 5, Gautier 1–7; and Ch. 6, Math. 15. On fraudulent tears,
cf. Ch. 5, Jacques de Vitry 5.

Thought I—and so to him I lost my heart.[48]
He was, I think, some twenty winters old,
And I was forty, if the truth be told.
But then I always had an itch for it!
I was gap-toothed; but it became me well;
I wore St Venus' birthmark and her seal.
So help me God, but I was a gay one,
Pretty and fortunate; joyous and young;
And truly, as my husbands always told me,
I had the best what-have-you that might be.
Certainly I am wholly Venerian
In feeling; and in courage, Martian.
Venus gave to me lust, lecherousness;
And Mars gave me my sturdy hardiness.
Taurus was my birth-sign, with Mars therein.[49]
Alas, alas, that ever love was sin!
And so I always followed my own bent,
Shaped as it was by my stars' influence,
That made me so that I could not begrudge
My chamber of Venus to a likely lad.
I've still the mark of Mars upon my face,
And also in another secret place.
For, sure as God above is my salvation,
I never ever loved in moderation,
But always followed my own appetite,
Whether for short or tall, or black or white;[50]
I didn't care, so long as he pleased me,
If he were poor, or what his rank might be.

44   (627) 'There's little more to say: by the month's ending,[51]
This handsome scholar Jankin, gay and dashing,
Had married me with all due ceremony.
To him I gave all land and property,
Everything that I had inherited.
But, later, I was very sorry for it—
He wouldn't let me do a thing I wanted!

[48] Husband-hunting at a funeral is found in Miroir 1966–77, also Ovid, Art of Love III. 431.
[49] Cf. Juv. Satire VI, 553–81, and Ch. 4, Andreas 24, on women and astrology.
[50] Cf. Ch. 6, Corb. 4; Juv. Satire VI, 597–600; and for the insinuation of insatiability Ch. 4, Ag. Marr. J8–9, Andreas 23.
[51] On hasty remarriage see Ch. 6, Math. 17 and 25.

My God, he once gave my ear such a box
Because I tore a page out of his book,
That from the blow my ear became quite deaf.
I was untameable as a lioness;
My tongue unstoppable and garrulous;
And walk I would, as I had done before,
From house to house, no matter how he swore
I shouldn't; and for this he'd lecture me,
And tell old tales from Roman history;[52]
How one Simplicius Gallus left his wife,
Left her for the remainder of his life,
Only because one day he saw her looking
Out of the door with no head-covering.

45   (647) 'He said another Roman, Whatsisname
Because his wife went to a summer-game
Without his knowledge, went and left her too.
And then he'd get his Bible out to look
In Ecclesiasticus for that text
Which with absolute stringency forbids
A man to let his wife go gad about;[53]
Then, never fear, here's the next thing he'd quote:
"Whoever builds his house out of willows,
And rides a blind horse over the furrows,
And lets his wife trot after saints' altars,
Truly deserves to be hung on the gallows."
But all for nothing; I cared not a bean
For all his proverbs, nor for his old rhyme;
And neither would I be reproved by him.
I hate a man who tells me of my vices,[54]
And God knows so do more of us than I.
This made him absolutely furious;
I'd not give in to him, in any case.

46   (666) 'Now, by St Thomas, I'll tell you the truth
About why I ripped a page out of his book,
For which he hit me so that I went deaf.
He had a book he loved to read, that he
Read night and morning for his own delight;

[52] Chaucer draws two incidents from the Roman historian Valerius Maximus.
[53] Ecclus. 25: 34.
[54] Cf. Ch. 6, RR 24, Corb. 8.

Valerius and Theophrastus, he called it,
Over which book he'd chuckle heartily.
And there was a learned man who lived in Rome,
A cardinal who was called St Jerome,
Who wrote a book attacking Jovinian;
And there were also books by Tertullian,
Chrysippus, Trotula, and Heloise,
Who was an abbess not far from Paris,
Also the parables of Solomon,
Ovid's *Art of Love*, and many another one,
All bound together in the same volume.[55]

47   (682) 'And night and morning it was his custom,
Whenever he had leisure and freedom
From any other worldly occupation,
To read in it concerning wicked women:
He knew more lives and legends about them
Than there are of good women in the Bible.[56]
Make no mistake, it is impossible
That any scholar should speak good of women,
Unless they're saints in the hagiologies;
Not any other kind of woman, no!
Who drew the picture of the lion? Who?
My God, had women written histories[57]
Like cloistered scholars in oratories,
They'd have set down more of men's wickedness
Than all the sons of Adam could redress.
For women are the children of Venus,
And scholars those of Mercury; the two
Are at cross purposes in all they do;
Mercury loves wisdom, knowledge, science,

[55] Jankin's book is exaggeratedly eclectic, but Map ('Valerius'), the Theophrastus material, and portions of Jerome were often bound together in the period: Pratt 1962. 'Trotula' and 'Chrysippus' represent mere name-dropping—the latter recalled from *Ag. Jov.* I. 48. Conceivably, Chaucer knew of the Heloise–Abelard correspondence (Ch. 3 above) at first hand: Mann 1991, 54.

[56] The *Lives* (*Vitae*) of evil women are humorously compared with the *Lives* of holy women. For a list of biblical heroines, see Ch. 8, Marbod 6; and cf. Christine de Pizan's conviction that misogyny was a phenomenon of secular, not biblical, culture: *City* III. 18.1 and Ch. 9, *Letter 10*.

[57] In an Aesopic fable, a man 'proves' his superiority over lions to a lion by showing a picture of a man defeating a lion: see Blamires 1987, 52–4. Christine, too, stresses that misogyny is sustained through a male monopoly of authorship: Ch. 9 below, *Letter 8*.

And Venus, revelry and extravagance.
Because of their contrary disposition
The one sinks when the other's in ascension;
And so, you see, Mercury's powerless
When Venus is ascendant in Pisces,
And Venus sinks where Mercury is raised.
That's why no woman ever has been praised
By any scholar. When they're old, about
As much use making love as an old boot,
Then in their dotage they sit down and write:
Women can't keep the marriage vows they make![58]

48   (711) 'But to the point—why I got beaten up,
As I was telling you, just for a book:
One night Jankin—that's my lord and master—
Read in his book as he sat by the fire,
Of Eva first, who through her wickedness
Brought the whole human race to wretchedness,
For which Jesus Himself was crucified,
He Who redeemed us all with His heart's blood.
Look, here's a text wherein we plainly find
That woman was the ruin of mankind.

49   (721) 'He read to me how Samson lost his hair:
He slept; his mistress cut it with her shears,
Through which betrayal he lost both his eyes.

50   (724) 'And then he read to me, if I'm no liar,
Of Hercules and his Deianeira,
And how she made him set himself on fire.[59]

51   (727) 'He left out nothing of the grief and woe
That the twice-married Socrates went through;
How Xanthippe poured piss upon his head,
And the poor man sat stock-still as if dead;
He wiped his head, not daring to complain:
"Before the thunder stops, down comes the rain!"[60]

52   (733) 'And out of bloody-mindedness he'd relish
The tale of Pasiphaë, Queen of Crete—

[58] Christine attributes misogyny to frustration and impotence in Ch. 9, *Letter* 5.
[59] Eve, Samson, Deianeira are conventional examples, all in Ch. 4, Map 9, 10, 31.
[60] Cf. Ch. 2, Jerome 20.

Fie! say no more—it's gruesome to relate
Her abominable likings and her lust!

53   (737) 'Of the lechery of Clytemnestra,
How she betrayed her husband to his death,
These things he used to read with great relish.

54   (740) 'He also told me how it came about
That at Thebes Amphiarus lost his life:
My husband had a tale about his wife
Eriphile, who for a golden brooch
Had covertly discovered to the Greeks
Where they might find her husband's hiding-place,
Who thus, at Thebes, met a wretched fate.[61]

55   (747) 'He told of Livia and Lucilia,
Who caused their husbands, both of them, to die;
One out of love, the other out of loathing.
Hers, Livia poisoned late one evening,
Because she hated him; ruttish Lucilia,
On the contrary, loved her husband so,
That she mixed for him, so that he should think
Only of her, an aphrodisiac drink
So strong that before morning he was dead.
Their husbands always have the worst of it![62]

56   (757) 'Then he told me how one Latumius
Once lamented to his friend Arrius
That there was a tree growing in his garden
On which, he said, his three wives, out of dudgeon,
Had hanged themselves. "Dear friend," said Arrius,
"Give me a cutting from this marvellous tree,
And I shall go and plant it in my garden."[63]

57   (765) 'Concerning wives of later days, he read
How some had killed their husbands in their bed,
And let their lovers have them while the corpse
Lay all night on its back upon the floor.[64]
And others, while their husbands slept, have driven

---

[61] Pasiphaë, Clytemnestra, Eriphyle are conventional examples, in Ch. 2, Jerome
21; and Ch. 1, Ovid 1, 7.
[62] From Ch. 4, Map 30.
[63] From Ch. 4, Map 25.
[64] Partly reminiscent of *Math. 12–14*.

Nails through their brainpans, and so murdered them.
Yet others have put poison in their drink.
He spoke more evil than the heart can think.

58   (773) 'On top of that, he knew of more proverbs
Than there is grass and herbage upon earth.
"Better to live with a lion or dragon,"
Said he, "than take up with a scolding woman.
Better to live high in an attic roof
Than with a brawling woman in the house:[65]
They are so wicked and contrarious
That what their husbands love, they always hate."[66]
He also said, "A woman casts off shame
When she casts off her smock,"[67] and he'd go on:
"A pretty woman, if she isn't chaste,
Is like a gold ring stuck in a sow's nose."[68]
Now who could imagine, or could suppose,
The grief and torment in my heart, the pain?

59   (788) 'When I realized he'd never make an end
But read away in that damned book all night,
All of a sudden I got up and tore
Three pages out of it as he was reading,
And hit him with my fist upon the cheek
So that he tumbled back into our fire,
And up he jumped just like a raging lion,
And punched me with his fist upon the head
Till I fell to the floor and lay for dead.
And when he saw how motionless I lay,
He took alarm, and would have run away,
Had I not burst at last out of my swoon.
"You've murdered me, you dirty thief!" I said,
"You've gone and murdered me, just for my land!
But I'll kiss you once more, before I'm dead!"[69]

60   (803) 'He came close to me and kneeled gently down,
And said, "My dearest sweetheart Alison,
So help me God, I'll not hit you again.

[65] Ecclus. 25: 23; in Ch. 1, Scripture 9: and Prov. 21: 9; in Ch. 2, Jerome 7.
[66] Cf. Ch. 1, Juv. 5.
[67] Ch. 2, Jerome 21.
[68] Prov. 11: 22.
[69] Ch. 5, Gautier 23–4, provides an interesting precedent for this finale.

You yourself are to blame for what I've done.
Forgive it me this once, for mercy's sake."
But once again I hit him on the cheek:
"You robber, take that on account!" I said.
"I can't speak any more; I'll soon be dead."
After no end of grief and pain, at last
We made it up between the two of us:
He gave the reins to me, and to my hand
Not only management of house and land,
But of his tongue, and also of his fist—
And then and there I made him burn his book!

61   (817) 'And when I'd got myself the upper hand
And in this way obtained complete command,
And he had said, "My own true faithful wife,
Do as you please from now on, all your life:
Guard your honour and look after my estate."
—From that day on we had no more debate.
So help me God, to him I was as kind
As any wife from here to the world's end,
And true as well—and so was he to me.
I pray to God Who reigns in majesty,
For His dear mercy's sake, to bless his soul.
Now if you'll listen, I will tell my tale.'

8

Responses to Antifeminism

There are four factors which need to be borne in mind by readers of Chapters 8 and 9 of this anthology.

(i) One or two important early 'responses' have been omitted—most notably Plato's *Republic*—on the basis that they were practically unknown to the Middle Ages.[1]

(ii) If the allocation of space seems in itself to disadvantage the 'defence of woman', that is a reflection of the small proportion of medieval writing which seeks to respond in any direct way to misogynistic discourse. Some medieval specialists might be a little surprised, in fact, to discover that defence was offered on a scale as *large* as this: after all, didn't Christine de Pizan feel that the 'philosophers and poets' *en masse* spoke with one voice against women?[2]

(iii) Some passages from the Church Fathers in Chapter 2 might have warranted inclusion in the present chapter instead (e.g. Jerome 9–11, 25, and 26 on loyal wives, on the Virgin, and on men's sexual hypocrisy; Augustine 7–9 on women at doomsday; and Ambrose 1 on Deborah). Yet it is a moot point how far most of these passages were fundamentally intended to defend women, rather than to advertise virginity or chaste widowhood. Again, the antifeminism in the sermon by Jacques de Vitry (excerpted in Chapter 5) is qualified, but not formally confronted, by the criticism of complacent males incorporated with it. The sermon begins with an attack on men who, far from being content with one wife, range among women with destructive lust like a wolf strangling all the sheep in a sheepfold even though a single sheep would satisfy its hunger. It remained for later apologists to build such materials into consciously pro-female polemic.[3]

(iv) By segregating defence from attack, this anthology simplifies a situation whereby these impulses were sometimes directly juxtaposed or entwined in the same author (e.g. Abelard, Gottfried von Strassburg, Chaucer) or even in the same work. Marbod's twinned poems have here been subjected to an improper divorce, though it will be seen that in the trial of Walter Brut, 'Counsel for Prosecution' and 'Defence' are necessarily presented together. The first text given below stands, however, as the volume's main representative of the impetus towards juxtaposition.

[1] For the relevant passage, see e.g. Agonito 1977, 23–39.
[2] Cf. Ch. 9, *City* 1–2.
[3] e.g., the 'wolf' analogy appears in *Leesce* 3894–904.

THE THRUSH AND THE NIGHTINGALE*
(LATE 13TH CENTURY)

This English verse debate is introduced at this point, out of chronological sequence, as a succinct exemplar of the many texts which encompassed both positive and negative views, pitting them against each other in the dialectical mould so favoured during the Middle Ages. The poem belongs to a category of debate literature in which issues were entertainingly explored by representing the antagonists as birds. Their debate is resolved in quite a conventional way, because the vindication of woman finally comes about by invoking the Virgin Mary: a common strategy, complained about in the *Corbaccio*.[4] The poem is relatively unambitious, but sustains an interesting cultural and social distinction between the birds (on top of a gender distinction whereby the Nightingale is female, her opponent male). The Thrush refers only to 'women', while the Nightingale most often speaks of 'ladies'; she, moreover, assumes solidarity with 'ladies' both by asserting territorial rights over their garden (17) where the debate occurs and by stressing their *corteisy* (5, 13, 17) and—since nightingales were symbols of romantic love—by claiming confidential access to their emotional lives (18).

1   Summer and love have come around
With blossom and with songbird's sound—
Which springs from the hazel as dales fill with dew
While amorous nightingales prompt the birds' tune.

2   Two birds I heard that started to fight,
One took the dour view, one the bright;
The one champions women and speaks of their grace—
As you'll hear in a moment, to the other they're a disgrace.

3   The Nightingale was the one, in fact,
Who'd keep the name of woman intact.
She'd ward off threats:[5] but the Thrush snipes away,
Insists non-stop 'They're in the fiend's pay:[6]

4   'They let down the man who trusts them most
However nice the look in their face.
They're a fickle lot, for they fail under test:
Best be without them, they spread such distress.'

* New translation by Alcuin Blamires, from the edition by John W. Conlee in his *Middle English Debate Poetry* (East Lansing, Mich.: Colleagues Press, 1991), 237–48.
⁴ Cassell 1975, 32–3.
⁵ The feminine pronoun *hoe* is used for the Nightingale here in l. 15 and also in l. 49.
⁶ Lit., 'the devil's companions' (*fendes i-fere*).

5 *Night.*   'I'd rather you'd stop giving ladies the blame—   (25)
Since they're noble and gentle, it's a real shame.
You won't find disruption wrought with such force
That woman can't cure it, whatever the cause:

6   'Soothing ill tempers amongst high and low
With sparkling welcome is a thing they well know.
A poor world it would be if woman weren't born—
Created man's ally she's sweeter than all.'

7 *Thr.*   'I can't praise women at all. I'm advised   (37)
They're fickle; at heart they are liars.
Radiant and fair they may be to see
But they're cheats underneath, as found out by me.

8   'Alexander the Great had trouble with them
Despite being the world's most powerful man.[7]
I call on men of conspicuous success
To witness their ruin at the hands of that sex.'

9 *Night.*   'Bird', cried the angry Nightingale,   (49)
'To me you seem loathsome in telling these tales.
Take a line of ladies and count them with care:
Not one in a thousand is evil, I'd swear.[8]

10   'They care for their honour, being meek and mild,
Behind the closed doors of their rooms inside.
There's no lovelier thing for a man to embrace,
She's a delight to behold—why not confess?'

11 *Thr.*   'Your claim, kind bird, doesn't match what
                    transpires   (61)
In bedrooms where they have fulfilled my desires.
For a little present they'll do furtive deeds[9]
Losing their souls amidst sinful intrigues.

12   'Bird, you seem to me disingenuous
For you speak your mind though a creature of "peace".
As for me, the case of our very first man
Proves the vice of woman—witness Adam.'

---

[7] Probably alluding to an episode in which Candace deceives Alexander.
[8] Implicitly denying Eccles. 7: 28–9; in Ch. 1, Scripture 8.
[9] On desire for presents (*mede*), cf. Ch. 4, Andreas 4, etc.; but see also S. *Passion* 2, below, on men using presents to cajole women.

13 Night. 'Thrush, if you don't know better than that,   (73)
These insults to women suggest you're mad.
There isn't a sweeter source of love—
In gracious behaviour she's way above.

14   'What greater bliss for man can be rated
Than when she's brought to his arms and united?
To blame these ladies is such a disgrace
You're going to regret it: from here you'll be chased!'

15 Thr. 'You're wrong, Nightingale, yet you want to drive (85)
Me from this land for stating what's right?
I appeal to Sir Gawain the famous knight
Whom Christ gave such power and strength in fight:

16   'As far and wide as he took his way
Not one true woman he found, night or day.[10]
Your tongue is false and you ought to beware.
When this talk becomes known, be out of here!'

17 Night. 'I've leave to stay in this orchard spot,   (97)
Here in the garden I sing my note—
Yet the manners of ladies known to me are fine,
Always noble, on top of the joy that they bring.

18   'They tell me a lot of delightful things.
They live, my friend, a life of longings:
Yet you slander them from your perch on a bough
And it's these *your* words that will spread around now.'

19 Thr. 'Of course they'll spread, such talk is not new.   (109)
A person not knowing it should hear it from *you!*
But I'll show you women's ways, bird, if you listen
Since you have not bothered to learn the lesson.

20   'Take Constantine's queen, soon to regret
(For *haute couture* befitted her best)
That she shared with a cripple her bed and her table:[11]
Now, how can you claim that women are faithful!'

21 Night. 'My song still sings that you, Thrush, are wrong, (121)
And men have known that all along.

---

[10] Gawain was also associated with antifeminism at this period in *Ag. Marr*: see Ch. 4.
[11] There were stories in circulation about unfaithful queens (including Constantine's) having affairs with deformed or ugly men. (*Haute couture* translates a clichéd reference to aristocratic furs.)

A beautiful woman outdoes in her glamour
The dawn of a long warm day in the summer.

22   'If you should trespass on woman's land
She'll put you in prison, and there you'll stand
Until you renounce the lies you've uttered—
And then what humiliation you'll suffer!'

23 Thr.   'Nightingale, you speak for yourself   (133)
In saying that women will put me to death.
Damn it! Check Scripture, and there you'll find
They bring both the proud and the strong man to ground.

24   'For instance the wife of Samson the strong—
It's clear when she sold him she did him great wrong.[12]
Just survey the hoard of Eden's bliss,
The worst that Christ made there was woman, I guess!'[13]

25 Night.   'You're quick with your tales,' said the
Nightingale,   (145)
'But listen now, bird, to *my* words as well!
Woman's a flower which lasts a long time,
Most praised everywhere for her beauty's so fine.

26   'With her sensitive mind and solicitude
She's hard to match for healing men's wounds.
You'll regret your opinions,[14] they're no avail.
Bird, stop it now and abandon this evil!'

27 Thr.   'It's not wise to set value on them so high.   (157)
Your returns will surely be lean in supply
Because, Nightingale, in one hundred scarce five
Will keep themselves chaste whether young girls or wives.

28   'They'd rather make trouble all over the place
Or bring men to ruin—that's clearly the case.
But while over women we conduct our debate
Not once will you speak the truth at this rate.'

29 Night.   'Now, bird, this time you've shot your bolt![15]   (169)
Through whom was the fate of this world revoked?

---

[12] The Philistines bribe Delilah in Judg. 16: 5. Samson is representative of several examples in Scripture: cf. Ch. 2, Jerome 24, and *Dives* 14, below.

[13] With a possible pun on 'whore' in the expression *worste hord of pris.*

[14] Reading *thou rewest al thi thohut*, not (with Conlee 1991) . . . *mi thohut.*

[15] Lit., 'you have disgraced your mouth' (*thi mouth the haueth i-shend*).

            —Through a maiden meek was born that holy child,
            At Bethlehem, who can tame what's wild.
30   'She knew nothing of sin or shame:
            May Christ protect her, Mary by name.
            I prohibit you now from this woody glen—
            You've pleaded false, so get out and be gone.'[16]

31 Thr.   'Nightingale, I was a real fool   (181)
            Or too inexperienced to argue with you.
            I admit defeat because of that one
            Who bore a five-fold wounded Son.[17]

32   'I swear now by His holy name
            That henceforth women'll be safe from my blame
            Since out of this land I mean to fly
            Away somewhere—who cares where?'

MARBOD of RENNES, (c.1035–1123)

THE GOOD WOMAN (DE MATRONA), FROM THE BOOK
WITH TEN CHAPTERS (LIBER DECEM CAPITULORUM),
CHAPTER IV*

On Marbod, see Chapter 4. Given below is the encomium on woman which is
twinned with the invective preceding it in the *De meretrice*.

1   Of all the things which are seen to have been bestowed
through God's gift to the advantage of humanity, we consider
nothing to be more beautiful or better than a good woman,[18] who is
a part of our own flesh, and we part of her own flesh. Quite rightly we
are compelled by the law of nature to love her, and this is to the
benefit of society,[19] even if she troubles us. For since we are the same
our lives are governed by the same conditions and there is nothing
we do not have in common, being alike in all things save in
difference of sex. In the beginning the law of nature treated us

---

[16] The Thrush's allegation that not 5% of women are chaste is held to be 'false
pleading' because it takes no account of the Virgin Mary.
[17] The five wounds suffered by Christ on the cross.
* New translation by C. W. Marx from Marbod of Rennes, *Liber decem capitulorum*,
ed. Rosario Leotta (Rome: Herder, 1984). © C. W. Marx 1992.
[18] Reminiscent of the 'what is better . . . ?' jingle; see Albertano 8.
[19] Augustine had stressed the social good of marriage at the beginning of *On the
Good of Marriage*.

equally: we eat the same food; our need for clothing is the same; we provoke tears and laughter by similar emotions. We distinguish with equal understanding what things are good or bad, what is just or unjust, and we speak the same language. We know how to express thanks in turn as equals and how to deserve gifts from one another for our kindnesses, how to give advice by which harm may be averted.

2 (18) Man and woman are equally capable of all these things, which it is apparent are denied to dumb animals. Yet many desire animals and admit that they are lovable. Although they lack reason, they are alive and have motion, they are linked to us in nature's second tier.[20] Herbs and flowers and every living thing on earth, which the mixture of heat and moisture nourishes and fosters, giving growth and the power of producing fruit—all these, men consider beautiful; fully aware that they lack a soul, yet they move and grow. Their place in the third tier instructs us that they are the less to be esteemed. Clothes, silver, jewels and gold, all things devoid of motion even if visually attractive, are, however, very far removed from us; they belong in fact to the fourth place in nature's law.[21] Yet even those things to which these faculties [motion, etc.] are denied bring qualities to be admired.

3 (34) Therefore, since woman is more worthy than all these, more beautiful than silver, more precious than yellow gold, more radiant than jewels—since they lack the light of reason—from what has been said we consider it conclusively proved that she ought to be admired, or rather loved, more than they. By these causes, although coming from a single order (which, however, each sex shares equally), we are joined by the bond of Nature's just love, and those things are no less appropriate to man than to woman. But there are many things in which womanly concern is superior, and woman-kind has her own purpose in the world. If you remove this, the entire human race will perish; for I ask you, if there were no field, what use would your seeds be? Who could be a father, if there were no woman to be a mother? I shall not dwell on the hard and prolonged labours of pregnancy or the anxious moments of one suffering the pains of giving birth. This is the price of bearing a child which the careworn

[20] Referring to a fourfold model of creation, whereby humans and animals are in the second tier, vegetable things in the third, and inanimate things in the fourth.

[21] Cf. Boethius, *Consolation of Philosophy* II, pr. 5, arguing that, although precious stones have a residual element of creation's beauty, they lack motion and soul so are fundamentally inferior to humanity.

230 RESPONSES TO ANTIFEMINISM

mother pays in bringing us into the light, but she soon forgets such
sorrows. Who, I ask, makes up for such kindness with love to match?
Or who can say he does not have a mother?

4 (54) Woman alone contributes many things which are less
important[22]—yet which daily life in the community demands; for
who but woman may take on the responsibility of a nurse? Is any
man able to nourish life without a woman? Who will draw out wool
or thread? Who will turn the spindle? Who will return completed the
day's work of spinning or who will patiently weave? Yet these things
are done for our benefit; they are so useful that if they were to be
lacking, the quality of life would diminish.

5 (62) Moreover, woman accomplishes more efficiently with
special female care very many things which looking after a household requires, and she puts up with much that our male pride
disdains. She treats the sick more gently, is more painstakingly
attentive at the bedside, provides food and drink more devotedly. She
has a greater liking for, and is more quick to respond to, commands.
She can be shaped into the pattern of goodness like soft wax,[23] and is
proved to be more submissive to discipline, whereas the stubborn
mentality of stiff-necked man resists and scarcely endures the yoke of
discipline, all the while denying that he is inferior.

6 (72) In addition to this, in the weaker sex a zeal for virtue is more
laudable, and her faults more easily forgiven.[24] Yet, neither has
virtue often been found to be lesser in the inferior sex, nor has
wrong-doing been found to be greater: for what woman has been so
bad as to outdo the sheer evil of Judas,[25] and what man could equal
the worth of Mary? But leaving that on one side because it constitutes something unique,[26] we read that plenty of women have shown
the courage of men or have even surpassed men, and because of their
brave heart have earned a just reward and well-deserved praise. We
read that Sara, Rebecca, Rachel, Esther, Judith, Anna, and Naomi,[27]

[22] i.e., than childbearing.
[23] Cf. Ch. 4, Andreas *12*. Woman as yielding wax is found also in Ovid, *Met.* x. 85.
[24] Cf. Abelard 7. Marbod's defence does not extend to challenging prevailing views
of woman's inferiority.
[25] Picked out because instrumental in the betrayal of Christ: cf. Ch. 9, *City 15*.
[26] A 'disqualification' eagerly noted in antifeminist discourse, e.g. *Corb.*: Cassell
1975. 32–3.
[27] Sara, wife of Abraham, Gen. 17: 15 ff.; Rebecca, wife of Isaac, Gen. 24: 1 ff.;
Rachel, second wife of Jacob, Gen. 29: 16 ff.; Anna, wife of Elcana, 1 Kgs. 1: 2 ff. On
Judith, Esther, and Naomi, see nn. 28–30.

like seven stars which ancient times produced, equalled or surpassed men. Judith performed a remarkable feat which none of the men had dared attempt: returning after killing Holofernes when safety was granted to the city of Bethulia by means of a woman, she drove the beaten enemy away from the other cities.[28] Eternal fame surrounds Queen Esther, for even though married to a cruel tyrant, like lamb to wolf, she did not fear, at the risk of her life, to enter the doorway through which no one came out who had not been ordered to enter.[29] She risked her own safety for the sake of her own nation and turned against the enemy the decree of death which they had passed on her people. I pass over the full story of Ruth, who having attended alone her virtuous mother-in-law was judged worthy to bear off-spring who became part of a royal lineage when she fled her homeland and parents in the name of the faith.[30]

7 (98) But under the New Law, since the glory of female purity in the virgin birth shone out, honoured throughout the world, history has been full of countless young women who have valued their chastity more than life, and in prevailing over enemies have given lessons to men that mental courage can be unmoved by torture. Among the number of those not inferior in their worth, Agnes, Fides, Agatha, Lucy, Cecilia, and Thecla conquered ruthless tyrants by their outstanding virtue.[31]

8 (107) I could also call to mind young pagan women famous for their scorn of death and for their chaste modesty. In her dying Lucretia earned an everlasting reputation, reacting to the injuries to her chastity by speedily committing suicide, when she fled from the light as a result of her dishonour.[32] People tell how Alcestes saved the

[28] Judith's sensational liberation of the city of Bethulia, narrated in the Vulgate Bible Book of Judith 12–15, fascinated the Middle Ages. She murdered her people's enemy, the tyrant Holofernes, by beheading him with his own sword in the tent to which she allowed him to have her brought. See Plate 10.
[29] Book of Esther, 4: 11: 'whosoever cometh into the king's inner court, who is not called for, is immediately to be put to death....' Esther took this risk by presenting herself, uncalled, to plead with her husband King Ahasuerus on behalf of the Jews when persecution was threatened by Aman. She got the decree of persecution reversed in 8: 3 ff.
[30] After the death of her husband and two sons, Naomi decided to return to Bethlehem (Ruth 1: 1 ff.). Her daughter-in-law Ruth—though not an Israelite—loyally followed her there, subsequently marrying Boaz, by whom her son Obed was to be the grandfather of David (4: 13 ff.).
[31] Saints Agnes, Fides, Agatha, Lucy, Cecilia, and Thecla were all celebrated as virgin martyrs.
[32] Cf. Ch. 6, RR (5).

life of her husband the king by her own death, under the terms of a harsh agreement whereby the cruel fates were seeking the death of one or other of them.[33] Chaste Arria pierced her breast with a sword, wishing to anticipate the destiny of her condemned husband. As she was handing the sword to her beloved, she said: 'Take this; the wound I have inflicted on myself does not cause me pain, but your wounds, Pethus, which you will inflict will cause pain to me even after death.'[34]

9 (120) It is clear from these examples and from the arguments which we have presented in the very beginning of this poem that woman ought not to be censured simply because she is female,[35] nor ought any man be heaped with praise simply because he is a man, but rather that vice should be censured in both sexes and virtue deserves praise equally in both.

ABELARD (1079–1142)

FROM LETTER 6, 'ON THE ORIGIN OF NUNS'* ('DE AUCTORITATE VEL DIGNITATE ORDINIS SANCTIMONIALIUM)

On Heloise and Abelard, see Chapter 3 above. Heloise took responsibility for a community of nuns some time after the traumatic end of her intimacy with Abelard. In that capacity she wrote asking him to expound the origin of female orders, and this brought out all Abelard's most positive thoughts on women. Underlying his response were (i) the conviction that woman's 'weakness' made God cherish her devotion all the more (women having, as it were, a greater handicap); (ii) a belief that on the whole women were nevertheless not to be distinguished from men so far as the spiritual life was concerned; and (iii) a constructive reappraisal of the importance of women in the earliest development of Christianity. All this added up to something rather more far-reaching than traditional panegyric on women, for by critical scrutiny of his biblical and other sources he was able to underpin the conventional examples (such as Judith, Esther, the Virgin) with evidence supporting a more active role for women in the Church than the Church allowed them. In this letter he meditates first on the significance of Christ's

---

[33] Alcestis was celebrated in classical culture for agreeing to die so that her husband Admetus should live: Hercules later retrieved her from the underworld.

[34] This story of Arria preceding her husband in suicide when he was condemned to death under Emperor Claudius derives almost verbatim from Martial, *Epigrams* I. 13.

[35] The 'woman–female' distinction here acknowledges a likely conceptual distinction in l. 122 between *mulier* and *femina*.

* New translation by Alcuin Blamires from J. T. Muckle, 'The Letter of Heloise on Religious Life and Abelard's First Reply', *Mediaeval Studies*, 17 (1955), 255–8, 264, 268–9, 270–1. For the whole letter see Scott Moncrieff 1974, 129–75.

being *anointed* by Mary Magdalene,[36] as He never was by a man, with great fervour and with sacramental implication.

Sacramental Office

1   Weigh carefully the dignity of woman,[37] by whom Christ was twice anointed during His life,[38] both on the feet and on the head, receiving from them the sacraments of kingship and priesthood.[39] . . . The disciples were indignant at a woman being so presumptuous, for Mark mentions that they muttered against her.[40] However, after softening their anger with gentle answers, He extolled her kindness to such an extent that He insisted it should be inserted in the Gospel, so that it could be preached wherever that was preached, both in reminder and praise of the woman who had done this thing (which *they* alleged involved no small presumption). We do not read that any other services, rendered by any person whatever, were commended or ratified in such a way on the authority of the Lord.

Men did various things for Christ, Peter even boasting how he and his fellows had left all to follow Him. But Christ commended women more, and they demonstrated their loyal devotion at His death, while the disciples fled and even denied knowledge of Him.[41]

Women at the Passion

2   The rams, or rather the very shepherds of the Lord's flock, flee: the ewes remain undaunted. The Lord reproved the former as weak flesh because they 'could not watch one hour' with Him at the time of His Passion.[42] It was the women, spending a sleepless night at His sepulchre, who deserved to be first to see the glory of the risen Christ.[43] More in their actions than in their words, they showed Him, by their loyalty at His death, how much they had loved Him during His life. . . .

3   When the Sabbath was over, Mary Magdalene and Mary the mother of James, and Salome, came to the sepulchre very early on

[36] Matt. 26: 6 ff., Mark 14: 3 ff., Luke 7: 36 ff., John 12: 1 ff.
[37] McLaughlin 1975, 291, suggests that Abelard deliberately emulates contemporary discussion of the 'dignity of man', *dignitas hominis*.
[38] Men, too, anointed Him at death: John 19: 38–40.
[39] Sacraments only administered afterwards, as Abelard earlier pointedly remarks, by men.
[40] Mark 14: 4.
[41] Cf. Ch. 1, Scripture *11–12*.
[42] Matt. 26: 40, where the disciples have fallen asleep at Gethsemane.
[43] Cf. Albertano 3 and S. *Passion 1* below.

the morning of the day of the Resurrection itself. As we have demonstrated their devotion, let us now see what honour they merited. . . . Mark does not hide the fact that they were first sent by the angel to tell the news to the disciples. He writes of the angel's words to the women: 'He is risen, He is not here; but go, tell His disciples and Peter that He goeth before you into Galilee.'[44] Also the Lord Himself, appearing first to Mary Magdalene, says to her 'Go to my brethren, and say to them: I ascend to my Father', etc.[45] We infer from all this that these holy women were appointed, so to speak, as Apostles over the Apostles because, sent to the Apostles either by the Lord or by angels, they proclaimed the supreme joy of the Resurrection for which everyone was waiting—so that the Apostles might first learn from these women what afterwards they would preach to the whole world.[46]

Women accompanied the Apostles subsequently, too. Abelard reviews evidence about women's inclusion in early communities of prayer; then he comments on Miriam as epitome of woman's active role in ancient divine liturgy; suggests that in the case of the priestly Levites 'it appears that the religion of women was not divided from the clerical order';[47] and interprets the instructions in 1 Timothy 5: 9–11 as rules for the selection of widows as deaconesses.[48]

Deaconesses

4   It must certainly be the case that one of these deaconesses was that Phebe whom the Apostle earnestly commends to the Romans. Appealing to them on her behalf, he says 'I commend to you Phebe our sister, who is in the ministry of the church, that is in Cenchre: that you receive her in the Lord as becometh saints: and that you assist her in whatsoever business she shall have need of you. For she also hath assisted many, and myself also.'[49] In commenting on this passage, both Cassiodorus and Claudius declare that she was a deaconess of that Church. Cassiodorus says: 'It means that she was a deaconess of the mother Church, a function still carried out in Greek areas today, in the interests of training. To them [deaconesses] the practice of baptizing in the Church is not denied.' Claudius says: 'This

---

[44] Mark 16: 6, 7.
[45] John 20: 17.
[46] For more grudging views, see Ch. 2, Ambrose 3–7, and Ch. 9, City 7.
[47] Muckle 1955, 262.
[48] See Ch. 1, Scripture 13 and n.
[49] Rom. 16: 1–2.

passage teaches on apostolic authority that women too may be
appointed in the Church's ministry. . . .'[50]

Abelard testifies to the notable sanctity of the consecrated virgin, then
develops a favourite theme—the special divine grace reserved for the virtue
of the 'weaker' sex.

More Perfect in Weakness

5 Just because the sex of women is weaker, their virtue is more
pleasing to God and more perfect, according to the testimony of the
Lord Himself.[51] When encouraging the Apostle to struggle despite his
weakness for the crown of victory, He says 'My grace is sufficient for
thee: for power is made perfect in infirmity.'[52] Also, speaking through
the same Apostle about the 'limbs' of His 'body' (that is, the
Church)—but as if He would particularly commend the worth of
such weak 'limbs'—He added in the First Epistle to the Corinthians:
'Much more those that seem to be the more feeble members of the
body, are more necessary. And such as we think to be the less
honourable members of the body, about these we put more abundant
honour. . . .'[53] But where can we say that this was ever so thoroughly
realized, through the dispensation of divine grace, as in that weakness of women's sex, which both sin and nature had made contemptible?[54] Analyse the various strata of this sex, not just virgins and
widows or married women[55] but even unspeakable whores, and you
will see that Christ's grace is more capacious among them, in
accordance with the saying of the Lord, 'The last shall be first, and
the first last', and 'Where sin abounded, grace did more abound.'[56]

6 If we seek out afresh from the very beginning of the world the
favours or honour shown by divine grace to women, we shall
immediately discover a certain dignity enhancing woman's creation,

---

[50] Abelard quotes a now lost Cassiodorus commentary, and a commentary by
Claudius of Turin: see McLaughlin 1975, 299.
[51] Cf. Marbod 6 above.
[52] 2 Cor. 12: 9.
[53] 2 Cor. 12: 22–3.
[54] This paradoxical doctrine establishing woman's superior gift of grace on her
inferiority in 'nature' (Allen 1985, 278) is voiced elsewhere by Abelard in Radice
1974, 97, and supported by Heloise in Radice 1974, 164–5.
[55] Alluding to the traditional three 'strata' or *gradus* of women, as in Chapter 2,
Jerome 4.
[56] Matt. 20: 16 and Rom. 5: 20, respectively.

since she was made in paradise, but man outside it.[57] Consequently women are warned to take special note that paradise is their native country and that they are more amply suited to follow the celibate life of paradise. . . .[58] Also the Lord restored Eve, the origin of all evil, in Mary before He renewed Adam in Christ. And just as sin began from woman, so grace began from woman, and the privilege of virginity has blossomed again.[59] . . .

Conventional eulogies are offered on Deborah (see Chapter 2, Ambrose 1) and Judith and Esther (see above, Marbod 6) along with less conventional ones on a mother tortured by Antiochus and on the self-sacrifice of Jephtha's daughter.[60]

Privilege of Bearing Christ

7   Setting aside everything else, what has been so essential to our redemption and to the salvation of the whole world as the female sex, which produced for us the Saviour Himself? . . . Can any glory match what the sex attained in the person of the Lord's mother? If He had wished, our Redeemer could have assumed His body from a man, just as it was His will to form the first woman from the body of a man. However, He transferred this unique grace of His humility as an honour to the weaker sex. Also, He could have been born of another, worthier, part of the woman's body than other men, who are born out of precisely the same base portion of the body where they are conceived. But, to the incomparable honour of the weaker body, He consecrated its genitals far more, in His birth, than He had consecrated those of man through circumcision.[61]

Abelard now continues his gallery of exemplary women, dwelling on the Sibyl, and the Samaritan woman at the well whom Christ favoured with conversation as well as His request for drink.[62] Moreover, His love for women was such that He raised the dead for them. Abelard rounds off the Letter with reflections on virginity drawn mainly from Jerome.

---

[57] One of the conventionally recognized 'privileges' of women: cf. Ch. 9, *Letter 10, City 4.*
[58] Here Abelard cites Ambrose (Ch. 2, 2), a somewhat double-edged witness.
[59] Cf. Ch. 2, Jerome 25.
[60] 2 Macc. 7, and Judg. 12: 30 ff.
[61] There is precedent for some of these ideas in Augustine.
[62] Cf. Christine de Pizan, *City* I. 10.6.

ALBERTANO of BRESCIA (c. 1193–?1260)

FROM *THE BOOK OF CONSOLATION AND ADVICE** (*LIBER CONSOLATIONIS ET CONSILII:* 1246)

Albertano was an Italian judge quite prominent in the troubled regional politics of his period, who regaled each of his sons with an edifying treatise as they came of age. The present treatise gained an enormous circulation during the thirteenth and fourteenth centuries, being translated into several European languages. A French abridgement by Renaud de Louens (after 1336) is known in at least twenty-six manuscripts, and was translated in turn by Chaucer as the *Tale of Melibee*. The work is cast as a debate between Melibeus, a nobleman keen to revenge himself on enemies who have violently raided his home, and his sage wife Prudentia, who begs him not to hasten into such retaliation. The text's nineteenth-century editor, with a now embarrassing condescension, not to say missing the entire point, thought that Albertano's regrettable taste for scholastic distinctions was here 'the more obvious' a fault 'because it appears particularly in the replies of the female interlocutor' who 'quotes all sorts of authors' and 'reasons ... like an accomplished lawyer'.[63] In the extract given below, Melibeus's initial scorn at his wife's intervention prompts her to a calm critical appraisal of his antifeminist clichés.

Chapter 3: Criticism of Women

1 Melibeus said, 'For many reasons I have decided to make very little use of your advice. First, because everyone would think me foolish if I changed on account of your advice or understanding what is an opinion firmly held by such a large number of people. Second, because women are wicked and no good one may be found, as Solomon declares who said: "I have found one good man among a thousand, but I have not found one good woman among them all."[64] Third, because if I were to act according to your understanding and advice, I would seem to give you supremacy over me, and so through this I would make you dangerous to me, and give you power over me when you ought to have very little. For Jesus the son of Sirach said, "If a woman has supremacy, she is dangerous to her husband,"[65] and Solomon said, "Hear, you people and all nations and rulers of the Church, do not give power over yourself in your life-time to your

---

* New translation by C. W. Marx from Albertano of Brescia, *Liber consolationis et consilii*, ed. Thor Sundby, Chaucer Society, 2nd ser. 8 (1873; reprinted 1973), 12–19. © C. W. Marx 1992.

   [63] Albertano 1873, pp. xv, xvii.
   [64] Eccles. 7: 28; in Ch. 1, Scripture 8.
   [65] Ecclus. 25: 30; in Ch. 1, Scripture 9. The book was attributed to 'Jesus the son of Sirach'.

son and wife and brother and friend, for it is better that your sons be dependent on you than you be dependent on the hands of your sons."[66] The fourth reason is that if I were to follow your advice, whenever it might be necessary to keep a secret, then it would inevitably be revealed because you could not keep it; for it is written, "The babbling of women knows how to conceal only what it does not know."[67] Finally, the fifth reason is because of the word of the philosopher who said "Women conquer men through their evil advice."'[68]

Chapter 4: The Justification of Women

2 Then the lady Prudence, when she had patiently and kindly heard and understood these things which her husband said, begged for permission to reply and said: 'I can answer the first argument which you put forward because "it is not foolish advice to change one's opinion on a question,"[69] for although you promised to do what you said before, you might not be accused of lying if you were to change your mind for a just reason. For it is written, "the wise man does not lie when he changes his opinion for the better". Nor is what you say an obstacle, namely that your advice would be firmly held by many people, for it is always better that the truth and benefit of issues be ascertained by a few wise men than determined by a noisy crowd, "for the tiresome crowd has no virtue".[70]

3 'To your second argument, that all women are evil because no good one can be found, I reply (with due respect to you) that you ought not to despise women in such general terms and condemn their ignorance,[71] for he who despises all offends everyone; as Seneca said in the *Guide for the Honourable Life*, "You may despise the ignorance of no one; you may be a remarkable speaker, but should be tolerant in listening to others speak: serious, not harsh; cheerful, not scorning; eager for wisdom and easily taught; you should without arrogance communicate what you know to one who asks, and ask kindly to be told what you do not know, without suggesting

---

[66] Ecclus. 33: 19–20, 22.
[67] Seneca, *Controversiae*, II. 13, 12; cf. Ch. 6, RR 33–7, and *Math. 18–21*.
[68] From the maxims (*Sententiae*) of Publilius Syrus (1st c. BC), 324.
[69] Seneca, *De beneficiis* IV. 38, 1.
[70] A legal maxim.
[71] Cf. objections to generalization, countered in Ch. 6, *Math. 26*; and upheld in Ch. 1, Ovid 7; *S. Passion* 6 below; and Ch. 9, *Letter* 2.

your ignorance."[72] For there are a great many good women and this can be shown through divine reason, for if no good woman could have been found Jesus Christ would have refused to take life within a woman and would not have taken on human flesh from a virgin.[73] No one may ignore the fact that there are many holy and good women. And even our Lord Jesus Christ, because of the goodness of women, regarded it as fitting after His Resurrection to show Himself to women before men, because He showed Himself to Mary Magdalene before the Apostles.[74] What Solomon said, namely, "I have not found a good woman among them all", is no obstacle, because although he did not find one many others have found good women, and perhaps Solomon was thinking of women who were of the highest order of excellence, and none is to be found. For no one is perfect in all respects nor perfectly good except God alone, as He Himself said in the Gospel.[75]

4 'Your third reason was that if you were to act according to my advice and understanding, you would seem to give me supremacy and power over you. I think this is silly and indeed of no account. For if we were to grant supremacy and lordship over ourselves to everyone from whom we took advice, no one would want to take advice from anyone else. For we have free choice to disregard or pay attention to the advice given us.

5 'In the same way, I hold of no account your fourth reason where you said, "The babbling of women knows how to conceal only what it does not know", nor do I think this applies here, for this refers to the worst type of babbling and prating women about whom it is commonly said, "there are three things which drive a man from the house; smoke, the steady dripping of water, and a bad wife".[76] It was about these that Solomon said, "It is better to live in a desert place than with a quarrelsome and irritable woman."[77] However, you have not found me to be such a one; indeed, you have frequently experienced my most solitary silence and my reluctance to speak.

6 'What you said in the fifth argument, namely, "Women over-

[72] Albertano 1873, 14, identifies the source as Martinus Dumiensis, *Formula honestae vitae*, ch. III.
[73] Cf. *Thrush* 29–31 and Abelard 7, above.
[74] Cf. Abelard 2–3 above, and S. *Passion* 1, below.
[75] Luke 18: 19.
[76] See Ch. 4, *Ag. Marr.* J15 and n.
[77] Prov. 21: 19

come men through evil advice", cannot apply here because you do not wish to follow bad advice. For even if you wished to follow bad advice and women, in advising you to do good, overcame you in this bad counsel, they ought not to be blamed but rather praised. For the blessed Paul said in the Epistle to the Romans, "Do not be conquered by evil but conquer evil with good."[78] If, however, you were to say that women badly advise men who wish to take good counsel and overcome them by this, then this must be charged to men who are in control of advice in that they can reject evil counsel and choose good. For the same Paul said in the first Epistle to the Thessalonians, towards the end, "Put everything to the test; hold to what is good."[79] Or, you may say that this argument is relevant when vicious and most wicked women advise foolish men. But this does not apply here.'

Chapter 5: Praise of Women

7 'When you have heard these arguments for the justification of women, you may hear and understand five other reasons why it can be shown that women are good and especially kind partners in marriage, and that their counsel should be listened to and, if it is good, followed. First, because it is commonly said, "counsel from women is either excessively valuable or quite worthless". I understand "excessively valuable" as "most highly valued", because there is nothing superfluous about it, just as is said about the friends of God, "Your friends, O God, are esteemed beyond measure."[80] And certainly, although there are villainous women whose counsel is worthless, nevertheless, the best counsel is found in many. For Jacob through the good counsel of his mother Rebecca obtained the blessing of his father Isaac and dominion over his brothers.[81] In the same way Judith, through her good counsel, freed the city in which she dwelt from the hands of Holofernes, who wanted to destroy it in a siege.[82] Also, Abigail through her own good counsel freed her husband Nabal from the anger of King David who wanted to kill him.[83] In a similar way, Esther raised up the Jews through her good

[78] Rom. 12: 21
[79] 1 Thess. 5: 21.
[80] Ps. 138: 17.
[81] Gen. 27: 1 ff. Rebecca's ingenuity enables Jacob to masquerade as his brother Esau and pre-empt him in obtaining the blessing of his ailing father.
[82] Cf. Marbod 6 above.
[83] 1 Kgs. 25. Nabal ungenerously refuses David's request for provisions, but Abigail mollifies David by quickly remedying this and apologizing.

counsel along with Mordecai during the reign of King Ahasuerus.[84] And so, many examples can be found of the innumerable good women and their counsel.

8 'The second reason why counsel of good women must be heard and, if it is good, followed, is demonstrated because of the first name assigned by God to women; for when God made man He said, "Let us make a helper for him,"[85] and He created Eve using a rib from his body and called her a helper, since women ought to help men and look after them. And rightly women can be called "helper" and so consequently "adviser", for without the help and counsel of women the world would not be able to endure. And certainly it would have been a very poor help-mate which God had given to man if man was obliged to seek counsel from women only as a last resort, since one can hardly exist without the other.

9 'The third reason brought to bear in addition to these is that woman is better than gold and precious stone and even understanding itself, and her understanding is sharper and surpasses others, as we are accustomed to say in verse: "What is better than gold? Jasper. What is better than Jasper? Understanding. What is better than understanding? Woman. What is better than woman? Nothing."[86] Seneca brings a fourth reason to bear, in addition to these, commending kind wives above all things; for he said, "Just as nothing is better than a kind wife, so nothing is more cruel than a troublesome wife. Just as a wise woman risks her own life for the safety of her husband, so a mean woman puts her own life before the death of her husband."[87]

10 'Cato introduced then the fifth argument in support of women, saying, "Remember to endure the tongue of your wife if it is honest."[88] "Therefore you may know that in a good wife is good fellowship," and, as is customarily said, "A good woman is a faithful protector and her home is good."[89] For a good woman by doing well and by obeying her husband attracts him alone, so that not only is she able to consult him but also may seem to exercise authority over

[84] Cf. Marbod, *Good Woman* 6 above.
[85] Gen. 2: 18.
[86] A popular jingle, but susceptible to subversion ('What is more capricious than flame? water? wind? woman?—Nothing'): see Chaucer, 1987, n. to 1107–8; also Mann 1991, 122.
[87] Albertano 1873, 18, gives as the source Fulgentius, *Mythologiarum* I. 27.
[88] Dionysius Cato, *De moribus* III, Dist. 24.
[89] Both quotations from Petrus Alfonsi, *Disciplina clericalis*, 15.11, 15.12.

him; as is customarily said by wise men, "A chaste married woman rules by obeying her husband," and "he who serves wisely has a share of power".[90] Therefore, if you wish to act wisely and with good counsel, if the Lord will grant it, I will bring your daughter back to full health, and I will see to it that you come out of this with honour.'

11   When Melibeus heard this his face brightened slightly and he said, 'Eloquence is a honeycomb of sweetness; it is pleasant to the soul and gives health to the body.[91] For through your good and sweet words and through my previous experience, I have recognized that you are wise and faithful to me and discerning, and so, having changed my opinion, I wish to act according to your advice.'

THE *RESPONSE** TO RICHARD DE FOURNIVAL'S *BESTIARY OF LOVE* (*LI BESTIAIRE D'AMOUR*: c. 1250)

Richard de Fournival (b. 1201) was a surgeon and church dignitary in Amiens. Among other fruits of his erudition was an unusual hybrid prose work adapting ideas from medieval animal lore to the purposes of a suitor's address to an unreciprocating beloved. The suitor's posture is a mixture of humility, cajolery, sentiment, and aggression. The text soon acquired a clever riposte, possibly written by a woman, systematically reusing the same animal lore to substantiate the necessity for a woman to be on guard against the dangerous power of a sweet-talking man. Richard had given the *Bestiary* a portentous Aristotelian opening—no one person can know everything, but what one person does not know, another will. The *Response* begins by taking up this cue and presenting a heterodox account, one he 'won't know', of creation: Adam appears as murderer of his first partner, and inferior to his second. This theory of dual creation was familiar to the twelfth-century biblical scholar Peter Comestor. The Jews, he wrote, noticed the word 'now' in Adam's comment on the creation of Eve ('This now is bone of my bones, and flesh of my flesh'[92]), and deduced that before Eve there had been another woman, created, like Adam, from earth.[93]

1   Fair master, I beg you in accordance with what you have told me, not to interpret it as villainy if I aid myself with your intelligence, according as I have retained some of it. For although I cannot know all that you know, yet I know something that you do not. Wherefore

---

[90] Publilius Syrus, *Sententiae*, 93 and 544.
[91] Prov. 16: 24.
* Tr. Jeanette Beer, *Master Richard's Bestiary of Love and Response* (Berkeley, Los Angeles, and London: University of California Press, 1986), 41–3. © 1986 by the Regents of the University of California. Reprinted by permission of the publisher.
[92] Gen. 2: 23: in Ch. 1, Scripture 2.
[93] *Historia Scholastica*, quoted in Beer 1986, p. xxxi.

it is very useful for me to aid myself with that since my need is great, I who am a woman in conformity with Our Lord's good pleasure, who did not want to make me of less good substance than He made you. And it pleases me to tell you how, although you have not made mention of this in your work.

2   God who by His dignity and power created the whole world and first made heaven and earth and all that is established in the one and in the other, afterward made man to be the noblest creature He could devise. And it pleased God to make man out of a substance that is not among the most suitable of substances. And from this substance, according to certain authorities, He formed such a woman as did not please the man whom He had previously made. Then it came to pass that when God had given life to the one and to the other, Adam killed his wife, and God asked him why he had done this. He replied, 'She was nothing to me and therefore I could not love her.' So Our Lord came then to Adam where he slept, and took one of his ribs, and from it fashioned Eve, whence we are all descended. Wherefore some maintain that if that first woman had remained, Adam would never have yielded to the sin for which we are all in pain. But for the very great love Adam had for the woman who was made from him, he loved her in the way that became apparent. For that love for her took precedence over the commandment of Our Lord,[94] as you have heard on other occasion how they ate the fruit that had been forbidden them.

3   But I must abridge this matter and attend to what I began. So, since it is the case that Our Lord gave man mastery over every creature, even over the woman whom He had made of more suitable substance than man, Scripture puts forward a reasonable argument for why He did this. None the less, He who was Lord of all formed man of whatever material was at hand. Then He took from man himself, as was said earlier, and made and fashioned from it Woman.

4   This is why I say that, inasmuch as man had been fashioned by such a noble artisan, the substance was much improved after this process. So for this reason woman was made of equal if not better material than man. And in this regard let no one come forward to challenge the following truth: that if Our Lord's grace had not been so abundant as to cause Him to intend man to have dominion over

---

[94] Cf. Ch. 2, Augustine 6.

every human creature we are created of nobler stuff than you were,[95] fair master, but must nevertheless obey you by the command of our Sovereign. But God never did anything without reason, for it is fitting that this thing which derives from the other should be obeisant to it. Thus woman must obey man, and man the earth, and the earth God, for God was the Creator and Sovereign of its every creature. Wherefore everyone must know that he must obey that wherefrom he came, and principally Him Who made all, as has been said above.

5   For which reason, lord and master, I who am a woman must obey you who are a man, which is to say that I intend to put to use what seems good to me, and if there be anything else remaining, let it wait until it can be useful either to me or to another.

THE SOUTHERN PASSION* (LATE THIRTEENTH CENTURY; BEFORE 1290)

This detailed narrative of the Passion of Christ in medieval English verse expands that found in a slightly earlier text known as The Ministry and Passion, partly by incorporating more observations with a personal flavour. Of these, the most remarkable occurs when the reviser develops an extended argument on behalf of women from the source text's remark that the resurrected Christ honoured all women by appearing first to a woman. Since women's conspicuous loyalty to Christ during the Passion was a point often noted in their favour,[96] this part of the crucifixion story is apt for a protest against conventional misogyny. What seems more surprising is the indignation of this particular protest and its uncompromising stance against society's double standard in sexual matters. The poem's editor was wrong, however, to think this the product of independent authorial observation:[97] for analogous arguments appeared in the Church Fathers (see Chapter 2, Jerome 26) and must always have been available, as they were to the author of Dives and Pauper (below) and to Christine de Pizan (Chapter 9).

1   (1899) This, then, was the first time that the sweet king Jesus appeared to any mortal person after His Resurrection. On Easter Day He chose rather to show himself to a woman, Mary Magdalene, than to any other person, and in this He did a great honour to woman— indeed to all sinful people, in that she was such a sinner. (We sinners

[95] One of the 'privileges' of woman: cf. Ch. 9, Letter 10 and City 4.
* New translation by Alcuin Blamires from The Southern Passion, ed. Beatrice Brown, EETS, os 169 (London, 1927), but with revisions generously made available by O. S. Pickering from a new edition (Pickering 1992) of this part of the poem.
[96] Cf. Abelard 2–3 above, and Ch. 9, Letter 9.
[97] Brown 1927, 99. The conventionality of the topic is implied in Ch. 4, Andreas 1–2.

need not lose hope, seeing that Jesus wants to come to us in such a way.) Here in this example any person of understanding can perceive that women are loyal enough when they commit themselves to virtue;[98] for, although the disciples whom our Lord loved and his closest kin, Saints James and John, were full of grief, they left Him abandoned in His sepulchre without a friend, whereas Mary sought Him out. Yet even after Peter and St John had gone to the sepulchre, they went off again and let things be. But she stayed there weeping, in much distress, unwilling to leave. . . . (1921) She alone showed more love for Him than any person alive, even disciples and kin as we have said.

2   (1923) So I conclude that ultimately there is no love as loyal as that of a morally committed woman. How is it then that women are so criticized in verses and sayings and books, which claim that they are false, untrustworthy, fickle, and wicked, to many a man's cost? Tell me truthfully, where is any woman who goes asking *men* to lie with her[99]—whereas all the time men ask *women* to do this, using their wealth[100] to give silver or other presents in order to satisfy their lust? What foolishness! Where would you find a man so steadfast, if a nice, attractive, charming woman were to come and keep on begging him for sex, that he would not change his tune and do it in the end? If he didn't, he'd be reckoned a saint fit to lie in a shrine! So, how should we rate a *woman* (and this includes most women) who does not give in to any amount of importuning, as can be seen every day? *She* won't be thought a saint—it will pass without notice. What logic is there in this attitude? Who on earth can see sense in it?[101] But if a woman is discovered to have gone astray just once, she will be blamed at least a thousand times more than a man; moreover, if a woman is given a bad reputation—however contrary to the facts— any man will be loath to marry her, as one sees all the time. Yet take a man who has slept with a hundred women and may be the vilest lecher on earth, and there is still no delay in a wife being found for him, whether he is knight, baron, or whatever, so long as he's rich. The girl can be absolutely virginal and innocent, her spouse as corrupt as you like. What logic can anyone see in this? It should

___

[98] The disconcerting qualifier *whare they turneth to good* here and at 1924 may be a concession to Mary Magdalene's previous life of sin.

[99] On pursuit as a male prerogative, cf. Gower 2 and *Dives* 19 below, and Ch. 9, *Letter 6*.

[100] Based on Pickering's reading, *of here auere*

[101] Based on Pickering's reading, *Day that hit conne ise.*

properly be described as debauchery and wickedness and rampant promiscuity.

3   (1953) If it is as evil to do lechery as the Bible and the Lord Himself tell us,[102] then who is the more blameworthy: the one who instigates it, or the one who doesn't so much do it as suffer what men do to her? You know very well that it is the male who *does* it,[103] and whoever says otherwise is wrong and is lying through his teeth, unless[104] he has no teeth—and would to God he hadn't.

4   The nature of all other animals will teach us the real truth, that women's goodness and chastity exceed men's, so that it is unfair for them to be criticized. You can see clearly that among sheep, oxen, dogs, hens and geese, horses, all sorts of animals, the female keeps herself quietly to herself, unexcited, as if sex didn't exist, except when her season duly comes round. Indeed, some of them are sexually inactive for a whole year or even two unless put to lush pasture. What do you think of the males? Do they behave similarly?—No, not many of them, if they get the chance, because they are always ready for it, summer or winter, when they can find a mate; very few hang back. And if they pick up a mating scent from the far end of town, they'll soon be there, doing the act so sinfully that it doesn't bear thinking about.[105]

5   Let louts learn a lesson from this, and stifle their malicious talk! (1959) When they are enjoying themselves on the pub bench, with a jug and a glass and a barman there to serve up, then their chatter and their fun is to pass judgement on some innocent girl—would to God they'd drown in a beer barrel for it! Why won't they reflect on other animals, as I have just said, and see that woman's nature is more chaste than their own? These loudmouths and liars sitting with their friends commit slander against women; I'll explain how. If a cleric or priest has stupidly committed theft or lechery, up jumps each lout with a bit of coarse slander: 'Just look what these clerics get up to! So-and-so stole an ox and did such-and-such wrong, and so-and-so went to bed with that man's wife. These lousy clerics, they're

---

[102] Based on Pickering's reading, *and oure lord sulf therto*.
[103] Cf. the 'active–passive' gender categorization in Ch. 3, Aquinas 1, and Aristotle, *Generation of Animals* 729[b].
[104] Here begins one of several passages found only in one MS of the poem, relegated to the Notes of Brown's edition but convincingly reinstated by Pickering.
[105] Writers more usually invoked the animal world when castigating men for continuing to have sex with wives who were pregnant: cf. Ch. 6, *Corb. 1*.

all the same—they ought to be butchered down to the last one.' So, if men come across one cleric who has done wrong, every lout will say it is characteristic of *all* clerics. How rational is this? Tell the truth: stop yourself lying about it! It is simply malicious intent and foul gossip to generalize about all men on the basis of the culpability of one man seen doing wrong.

6 (1973) Women fare just the same among malicious tongues. When the men hear (which is seldom) that one woman is going astray—no doubt at the importuning of some lecher, since few would do so otherwise—then plenty of louts will voice their smut: 'Do you see that woman who seduced that reeve,[106] who puts on such goody-goody airs and graces (so much for believing any woman) and acts as pious as a nun?[107] D'you see what she's done, how she has behaved? It's clear what they are—not one's to be trusted—for they are all wicked and false, shame on the lot of them.' So, for one lapse that a good-for-nothing brings a woman to, though it happens rarely or is even a lie, they'll criticize every woman including good ones and claim they all behave like that. But what reasoning is this, to criticize an innocent majority who seldom make a slip, for a single act?[108] This is not right. (1979) Why can't blame be borne individually for individual guilt? Instead, one person's wrongdoing gets blamed on all. But for the love of Christ, those of you with some sense, do not blame the innocent without cause. For if, every time you see one man doing wrong, you're going to accuse all men likewise, it won't take long in any one day before you'll be saying that all men ought to be hung. If one man is a rogue, are all men too? No, there's no logic in that; you know what's true. Were a man hung or dismembered for theft, and they proposed to dish up the same treatment to you, you wouldn't consider it legal. You would look quite unamused, and take the liberty of bidding goodbye to all who pronounced that sort of judgement. Think of others as you would have them think of you. Should a woman importuned by a lecher do wrong, don't thrust forward your half-baked logic claiming falsely that all women behave so, and all deserve disgrace. Don't blame any woman unfairly for another's guilt. Let each bear guilt individually as is only right— and as you'd wish to be upheld in your own case if you were innocent.

[106] Based on Pickering's reading, *that ilke reue.*
[107] Based on Pickering's reading, *ockir nonne.*
[108] Cf. objections to generalization in Albertano 3 above; also Ch. 1, Ovid 7, and Ch. 9, Letter 2.

7 (1983) When all is said, may God bring shame on all who blame
a good woman without reason, for there is no greater mildness and
goodness in any earthly creature, no greater kindness and loyalty
than in a good woman. You see how Mary Magdalene alone sought
our Lord, when the Apostles who were with Him all abandoned Him.
Whose love was clearer in this case, hers or theirs? Don't tell a lie!
Was there anyone more steadfast[109] than holy Mary Magdalene?

JOHN GOWER (1325?–1408)

FROM *A LOVER'S CONFESSION* (*CONFESSIO AMANTIS*: 1386–90)

Gower's English poem in eight books is a major attempt to construct a
framework sympathetic both to traditional courtly expression of unrequited
love and to rational and moral discipline. Its narrator, the Lover (Amans) is
convinced that he is the powerless victim of his own love for a lady, whose
bland indifference renders his obsessive attentions risible. Eventually the
Lover's Confessor puts it to him that everyone is a miniature kingdom: it is
up to the individual not to 'misrule' that kingdom (VIII. 2111–25). The
infatuated lover is therefore a victim only of his own assent to the
infatuation. This stress on personal responsibility has already prompted an
exculpation of women from the allegations of 'bringing men down' so readily
heaped on them in misogynistic writings. (Disconcertingly, the argument
depends also upon a conviction that infatuation 'reduces' men to womanli-
ness.) The passage occurs during the Confessor's analysis of Five 'Points of
Policie' which Aristotle was supposed to have taught the young Alexander.

1 (VII. 4239) The fifth element of statecraft is chastity, which very
seldom makes its appearance anywhere these days. Even so, there is
no one who can be wholly chaste without an exceptional dispensation of grace. But in view of a king's elevated position, anointed and
consecrated as head of the secular order, for the sake of the dignity of
his crown he should be more looked up to than anybody of humble
rank who is not of such noble consequence. Therefore a prince ought
to stop and think before lapsing into debauchery, and beware

---

[109] 'More steadfast' here renders *stablour* ('more stable', 1990). The writer deliberately echoes the earlier question, 'Where would you find a man so steadfast?', *so stable*
(1932), in order to crush a common allegation that woman (unlike man) is
inconstans—'unsteady' or 'inconstant'; cf. Brut *A4* and *Dives 21* below, and Ch. 2,
Ambrose 4.

* New translation by Alcuin Blamires from *The English Works of John Gower*, ed. G.
C. Macaulay, 2 vols., EETS, ES 81 (London, 1900), ii. 354–5.

especially of such infatuation as would transform the quality of his manhood into effeminacy.[110]

2   (4257) I have read how Aristotle told Alexander that it would lift his spirits if he looked at the faces of beautiful women. Yet he also gave him a guideline that he should so control his body, that he did not exceed the bounds of behaviour so as to commit self-deception.[111] There is no deception on the part of the woman, where a man bewilders himself: if he deludes his own wits, I can certainly acquit the women. Whatever man allows his mind to dwell upon the imprint his imagination has foolishly taken of women, is fanning the flames within himself—and, since the woman knows nothing about it, she is not to blame. For if a man incites himself to drown, and will not restrain himself, it is not the water's fault.[112] What can gold do about it, albeit people covet it? If a man wants to tie himself up in love, the woman has not constrained him. If he wounds his own heart, she cannot prevent his foolishness. And even if it should happen that he gains friendliness from her, still it is a man who chases first.[113] The woman retreats and he pursues, so that it stands to reason that whatever happens it is the man's responsibility that he so often falls, where it is difficult to get up again.

3   (4292) Nevertheless, many wise men have made fools of themselves before now. As it still is with men nowadays and always was, the strong is weakest in this situation. Nature's way makes it appropriate for a man to love, but it isn't natural that a man should lose his wits for love. (If the month of July freezes and December is hot, I know the year's cycle has gone haywire.) To see a man lose his status because of his effeminate infatuation,[114] abandoning what a man should do, is like seeing stockings outside shoes: an aberration for any man.

---

[110] *To change for the wommanhede / The worthinesse of his manhede*: cf. Ch. 1 above, Isidore 2; and the opinion that lechery 'gendryth wommanys condicionys' in Manzalaoui 1977, 135.

[111] Cf. *Dives* 19, below.

[112] Cf. Ch. 9, *City* 3.

[113] Cf. *S. Passion* 2–3 above; *Dives* 17 below, and Ch. 9, *Letter* 6.

[114] *Thurgh his sotie effeminat*. The ensuing story of Sardanapalus shows that 'effeminacy' is antithetical to military leadership and *chivalerie*.

THE TRIAL OF WALTER BRUT (1391)

Women and the Priesthood

In the Middle Ages heterodox sects sometimes made a point of dissociating themselves from the disparagement of women implicit in orthodoxy. The religious movement known as Lollardy, which derived from the teachings of Wycliffe and began to alarm the authorities in England during the 1380s and 1390s, was one example. Instruction of the laity—men and women alike—through preaching was high on the Lollards' agenda. They fiercely resented the Church's control of the right to preach; indeed, they wanted to dismantle the ecclesiastical hierarchy which they felt Rome ('Antichrist') had imposed on the Christian laity. They soon became targets for accusations of heresy. Walter Brut was an educated lay Lollard whose trial in 1391 seems to have been a showpiece. A whole team of academic theologians was assembled to refute his propositions, of which the first to be cited by prosecution witnesses was that 'any Christian without sin, even a woman' could consecrate the body of Christ.[115] Documents associated with the trial reveal that he also championed women's power and authority to preach and to give absolution.[116] There are scraps of surviving evidence suggesting that some Lollard groups put similar views into practice,[117] which doubtless served to reinforce age-old suppositions about women's susceptibility to heresy in the traditionalist mind.[118] But since it has been argued that the religious 'emancipation' of women in some heretical sects of the Middle Ages was only skin-deep,[119] it is rather refreshing to discover that a concerted attempt to justify their inclusion in the ministry *could* be mounted at this date. The justification is not easy to exemplify, though, because successive layers of Brut's argument have to be untangled from two overlapping documents: the episcopal record or *Registrum*, and a treatise composed by theologians as a formal refutation of Brut's opinions on this and other matters. To represent the relevant opinions as fully as possible, we give in *A* the arguments it is thought he advanced in defence of women preaching, which are catalogued then attacked in the treatise; in *B* what seem to be his initial arguments asserting women's power to consecrate the eucharist, again catalogued by his opponents; and in *C* his development of further views on the latter in a 'response' transcribed into Bishop Trefnant's *Register* (though this too is summarized in the treatise).

---

[115] Capes 1914, 279.
[116] Capes 1914, 364, no. 30, summarizes Brut's condemned opinions on women exercising priestly functions.
[117] Aston 1984, 55, 62 ff.
[118] The Waldenses, flourishing in parts of Europe from the 12th c., are another example of a sect which gave women a sacerdotal role.
[119] E. McLaughlin 1976.

A FROM THE TREATISE IN REFUTATION OF BRUT: 'ON WHETHER WOMEN ARE PERMITTED TO INSTRUCT MEN ASSEMBLED IN PUBLIC'.*

In this discussion the heretical arguments are first listed, then, where appropriate, 'confirmed' or (most often) refuted.

A1   (i) It says in Proverbs 4: 3–4, 'I was an only son in the presence of my mother, and she taught me.'

(ii) Whoever is fit to prophesy is fit to instruct, since to prophesy is to make public; as Cassiodorus says, 'prophecy is declaring the course of events with unshakeable truth through divine inspiration.' But women are allowed to prophesy, as is made clear about Deborah in Judges 4, and about the prophetess Huldah, wife of Shallum in 2 Kings 22: 14, and about the four daughters of Philip in Acts 21: 9. And in the first epistle to the Corinthians, 11: 5, the Apostle intimated the same when he said, 'Every woman that prays and prophesies, [etc.]'. Therefore, women are permitted to instruct.

(iii) Everyone who has the grace of wisdom and knowledge is obliged to share it with those who are ignorant, as we read in the first epistle of Peter 4: 10: 'Each one who has received grace should share it among others.' But certain women will receive the grace of wisdom and knowledge, and therefore they too are obliged to share it with the ignorant. And therefore she is obliged to instruct because it is only through instruction that she can share grace with others.

(iv) To teach is one of the spiritual works of mercy, as is shown by this verse, 'counsel, chastise, forgive, comfort, teach, give, pray'. No one is forbidden to perform the works of mercy; indeed, they are required of all since all will be examined about them on the day of judgement. Therefore, women are permitted to perform them, and therefore to teach.

A2   *Confirmation*. It is agreed that it is a mortal sin to withdraw from the poor those alms which will sustain the body. How much more is it a sin to withdraw alms from those who are in spiritual need! A woman is not permitted to sin. Therefore, she is not allowed to refuse to teach the needy.

Another Confirmation. It is confirmed, for we read that the blessed Mary Magdalene preached publicly in Marcilia and in the area round

---

* Transcribed and translated by C. W. Marx from 'Utrum liceat mulieribus docere viros publice congregatos', a section from one of two sets of discussions on points raised by Brut, BL MS Harley 31, fos. 194^v–223^r (the present section comprising 194^v–196^v). © C. W. Marx 1992. Aston identifies Cambridge scholars John Necton and William Colville, among those present at the trial, as possible authors (1984, 54).

about, which through her preaching she converted to Christ. Because of this she is called the 'Apostle of Apostles'.[120]

A3   *In Contradiction.* In contradiction, we read in the first epistle to Timothy 2: 12, 'I do not permit a woman to teach.'

The First Conclusion. Women are not permitted to teach men publicly in church. No one is allowed to teach in public unless they are one of those who are allowed to investigate the fine details of scripture. Women are not allowed to investigate the fine details of scripture; therefore, they are not allowed to teach in public. . . .

The hierarchy of the Church was ordained and arranged on the pattern of the hierarchy of Heaven. . . . In the heavenly hierarchy the lesser angels purify; the greater ones are the source of light and carry out their work through intermediaries, and not vice versa. So ought it to be in the hierarchy of the Church that the greater ones, that is, bishops and archbishops, ought by the light and grace of their teaching to purify through intermediaries, that is priests and preachers, to enlighten and help the lesser lay people, namely women, and not vice versa. St Thomas argued the same in the *Summa theologiae*, and put forward three reasons:[121]

(i) First, because to teach and strive to convince publicly in church is the work not of subjects but of prelates. A woman, because of her female sex, is by nature subject to man, or if not by nature, at least by command of the Lord. Therefore, it is not her place to teach in public.

(ii) Second, although the beauty of her appearance and every movement of woman may lead men to sexual desire, it is chiefly the sweetness of her voice and the pleasure of hearing her words that does this. The lips of the wicked woman dripping scandal and the conversation of woman ignite men like fire. You may say that this does not apply to a holy and devout woman, but to a wicked or foolish one. You are wrong because, all things being equal, a man ought to be *more* attracted by the beauty and soft voice of a good woman than of a bad because he knows that the first will keep faith with him but the second will not. Thus we read in Ecclesiasticus 42: 12–14, 'Do not linger in the company of women; from clothes there comes a moth and from a woman wickedness. The wickedness of a man is better for a man than a well-meaning woman.' . . . So that men will not be led into sexual desire by the public teaching of a

[120] Cf. Abelard 3, above. That Mary Magdalene had travelled to France and preached there was a legend current in the Middle Ages.

[121] IIa IIae, Quaestio 177, though with expansion of Aquinas's three points. See also *S. Th.* Supp., Quaestio 39, art. 1.

woman, it is forbidden to them to teach in public because in so doing they would harm men rather than benefit them.

(iii) The third reason is that women in general have weak and unstable natures and thus they are incomplete in wisdom; therefore, they are not allowed to teach in public.

(iv) In addition, Henry of Ghent supplies a fourth reason; in his *Summa*, article 11, question 2, he says that four things are required to teach in public and officially.[122] These are: consistency of teaching, effectiveness of performance, authority of teaching, and energy of speech. (*a*) Consistency of teaching means that one's thoughts are not easily diverted from the truth. For this reason teachers are likened to a light because they do not grow dim, as is mentioned in Matthew 4: 16. (*b*) Effectiveness of performance means that one does not cease from one's work because of weakness. For this reason, teachers are compared to eternity which never fails because the stars are for ever and ever, as in Daniel 12: 3. (*c*) Authority of teaching means that the listeners pay attention to him who believes in himself. For this reason they are compared to a lamp which is placed upon a lampholder because of its brightness, as in Matthew 5: 15. And (*d*) energy of speech means that, by correcting vices, teachers encourage their listeners to virtue. For this reason, they are compared to salt which preserves meat from rotting, as in Matthew 5: 13.

A4   But (*a*) a woman does not have consistency of teaching because she is changeable and easily led astray.[123] Thus, the Apostle said in the first epistle to Timothy 2: 12 and 14, 'I do not permit a woman to teach'; she is subject because of what happened to Adam: 'he was not seduced but the woman was seduced.' (*b*) She is not effective in performing this office on account of the weakness of her sex, which is not sufficient to speak at length in public and work strenuously. Consequently, the Apostle wishes woman to be silent, and in 1 Corinthians 14: 35 he says: 'if a woman wishes to learn, she is to ask her husband at home'. (*c*) She is not able to have the authority of teaching because her sex does not permit her to be free to go out, 'because you will be under the power of the man and he will rule over you': Genesis 3: 16. Therefore the Apostle makes woman

---

[122] Henry of Ghent (d. 1293), *Summa in tres partes precipuas digesta*, 3 vols., i, 193 ff.
[123] The whole of *A4* is borrowed from Henry of Ghent. On woman's alleged lack of 'consistency' of teaching (*constancia predicandi*) cf. *C1* below, and n. Humbert of Romans also listed four reasons: women's inadequate intelligence; their inferior role in life; the risk of their provoking immoral response; the disastrous consequences of Eve's 'teaching': Owst 1926, 5.

subject and 'will not allow her power over man', as when he says 'I do not permit . . .' 'Adam was formed first' as a sign of his lordship, 'then Eve' (1 Timothy 2:12–13). Hence it would be improper and embarrassing if she were to assume the authority of someone taking precedence. And so the Apostle says: 'it is a disgrace for a woman to speak in church'.[124] (d) She does not have the energy of speech to destroy sins, but rather to promote them. On this the gloss on 1 Timothy 2: 12, 'I do not permit a woman to teach', says it is much more the case that a man is encouraged to lechery by her, and her speech kindles fire in the heart of the one who listens to her.

A5   It is clear from these teachers what is in the mind of the Apostle, that for these four reasons a woman is not permitted publicly to teach men. Therefore, we read in 1 Timothy 2: 12, 'I do not permit women to teach', that is, in church. And this same idea is confirmed in 1 Corinthians 14: 35, 'If a woman wishes to learn, she is to ask her husband at home.' If therefore a woman is not allowed to learn in public, how much more is she not allowed to teach in public? Thus, 1 Timothy 2: 11 says, 'let a woman learn in silence'. Therefore, I think that it is heretical to say that a woman should be allowed to teach men in public. It is true that the Apostle said, in 1 Corinthians 14: 31, 'you can all prophesy that all may learn'. But in case anyone should believe that women as well as men should be allowed to prophesy, he added, 'women are to be silent in church, for they are not permitted to speak there', that is, in churches, 'but are subjects, as the law says, and if a woman wishes to learn she is to ask her husband at home'.

The second Conclusion further insists that the prohibition against women teaching in public should avert any notions of their taking precedence over men—while conceding that women may teach women and children in private, and that abbesses may teach nuns in the cloisters.

A6   *Third Conclusion.* Although women may not be allowed to teach in public, there are certain cases however where they are allowed to do so. This is approved in three situations. First, if it is granted to them as a special favour, as it was to women in the Old as well as the New Testament, as is made clear in the second Confirmation above. The second situation is when it is granted to women as a reproach to men who have become effeminate. It was for this reason that government of the people was granted to women, as appears in Judges 4 concerning Deborah. The third situation is when there is a

---

[124] 1 Cor. 14: 35.

great abundance of harvest but only a few to reap it. It was for this reason that it was granted to the women, Mary and Martha, to preach in public and to the Four daughters of Philip to prophesy in public. [125]

The quotation from Proverbs in (A1) (i) is next neutralized, but the writer then wriggles desperately over the point in (A1) (iv) that teaching is enjoined on all as a 'work of mercy'. Women should fulfil the injunction by teaching ignorant women, and girls and boys, 'but not men'.

A7 To this confirmation I admit that to deny bodily and spiritual alms to one in need is a sin when they cannot be assisted in any other way than this. But when it is required of another by virtue of office, as it is required of prelates and teachers, to teach the laity, woman is nevertheless excluded from teaching in public ... however few teachers there may be, however big a harvest, and however great the lack of preachers. Situations like these should allow women to teach and preach as it was said of the Magdalene and Martha,[126] but they do not.

A8 In general terms I suggest that this whole subject can be reduced to one question: Is it permitted to anyone to teach or preach when it is likely that this will harm those who hear more than it will benefit them? ... It is likely that a beautiful woman will inflame her hearers to lechery by the power of her words more than she will stamp it out. On the other hand, people share the grace which they have received from Heaven in various ways according to the diversity of their conditions. Therefore, if women have the grace of wisdom and learning, they can share it by teaching in private but not in public.

B FROM THE TREATISE IN REFUTATION OF BRUT: 'ON WHETHER WOMEN ARE SUITABLE MINISTERS TO CONSECRATE THE SACRAMENT OF THE EUCHARIST'*

Brut's propositions are surveyed. They turn chiefly on the Lollard claim that priestly office should be grounded essentially on merit.

[125] Acts 21: 9; quoted from Henry of Ghent. Fathers such as Chrysostom knew of the active role of women in the early Church, but could not imagine that role being continued in their own times: Clark 1979, 20. The subject is reviewed in Abelard 4, above.
[126] See *A2* above.
* Transcribed and translated by C. W. Marx from 'Utrum mulieres sunt ministri ydonei ad conficiendum eukaristie sacramentum', BL MS Harley 31, fos. 196ᵛ–205ʳ. © C. W. Marx 1992.

B1 (i) Every holy person is a priest, according to Chrysostom, because that is said about all the faithful in 1 Peter 2: 9: 'You are a chosen people, a royal priesthood, a holy nation.' Every chosen good woman is holy; therefore, every such one is a priest; therefore, every such one can consecrate.

(ii) Although the power to baptize belongs to priests alone by virtue of their office as is clear from the *Sentences*, book IV, distinction vi, nevertheless a layman and a woman can baptize in the case of necessity.[127] Therefore by the same token they can consecrate in case of necessity. . . .

(iv) A good layman and a good woman are more worthy than a bad priest, and therefore more suitable to carry out a worthy task. Now, to consecrate the body of the Lord is the most worthy task; therefore, a good layman and a good woman are more worthy for it.

(v) The Holy Spirit operates more through those in whom it is than through those and for those in whom it is not; therefore, it wishes more to work through a good layman and for him, and through a good woman, than through a bad priest. . . .

(vii) It is proposed that a bishop may ordain a woman to the priesthood by saying with an intercessory prayer the words of the sacrament, 'do this in memory of me; take, eat, [etc.]', and she may receive the character of a priest.'. . .

(viii) If a woman may have goodness of life and may be ordained, why cannot she consecrate? We find frequently in the Holy Scripture that there were women elders and priests in the early church. Also, a woman can bear the body of Christ; therefore, she can consecrate. The basis for this argument is obvious in the case of the Blessed Virgin, as we find in Anselm. . . .

B2 Second Conclusion[128]

Here Brut firmly declares the spiritual equality of men and women.

Gender is not a qualification for the priesthood: the female sex is not proved to be necessary for the priesthood seeing that a man can be a priest; nor is the male sex, because a woman can be a priest in the case of absolute necessity. There is no contradiction here: it is proved that a woman is capable of priestly power because her soul itself shares in that essence of priestly power, and this is because the soul

---

[127] The clause in Peter Lombard's *Sentences* reads: 'A woman, however devout, may not presume to baptize, except when necessity compels it.' See further *C1* below.

[128] Fos. 198ʳ–198ᵛ.

of man and the soul of woman are of the same particular species. Therefore, since the soul of man may be capable of priestly power, it follows equally that the soul of woman may be capable of the same power. The bodies of men and women are of the same particular species, and so are their souls and the matter of which they are composed. Therefore, woman is able to exercise whatever spiritual power a man can, and it is clear that anyone may bestow the priestly power on a woman by their own absolute authority. Nothing more is required for someone to become a priest except that he be admitted by God. He is admitted for this purpose, that God may wish to change bread into the body of Christ whenever the priest might say the words of the sacrament with the intention of consecrating; or, that the words of the sacrament uttered by him may have the power of changing the bread, and he has received the sign of his admission which is called the 'character'. All these things can be done as much for women as for men. An angel by the absolute power of God can accomplish such things as consecrating churches, baptizing, confirming and administering last rites; therefore, gender is not a qualification for the priesthood.

Brut now suddenly turns Pythagorean, postulating that transmigration of souls must give rise to occupation of male (priest's) bodies by female souls and vice versa, hence further undermining the concept of a gender-exclusive ministry.

*C FROM THE REGISTER OF BISHOP TREFNANT**

Women, Baptism, the Eucharist

Brut places his discussion of women in the context of a summary history of priesthood, suggesting that Christ never envisaged the sharp distinction between the apostolate and the laity which has come to exist in the Roman Church. Then he turns to the issue of the Eucharist.

C1 Having made these comments, let us see whether women are able—as is here questioned—to effect this sacrament and administer it to the people. Women *are* able to baptize;[129] and according to the traditions of the Roman church the sacrament of baptism is the most

---

* New translation by Alcuin Blamires from *The Register of John Trefnant, Bishop of Hereford*, ed. William W. Capes (Hereford, 1914), 345–7.

[129] The Church had long (though not universally) conceded that in emergencies laypersons, including women, might baptize if no cleric was available. Brut builds heavily on this: his opponents retort that in such a case the woman is merely God's instrument.

necessary of all since, as is said, 'little children dying unbaptized are to be tortured in eternal fire'[130] but if they have had that sacrament even without receiving any other they are saved, which is clear from scrutiny of the sacraments individually. So if women are able to perform this principal sacrament, I dare not state that they cannot administer the others. But certainly I do not wish to state that the administering of any sacrament is appropriate for them or for laymen, however good they are, except in the absence of others constituted for this purpose in the Church. Teaching and preaching God's word is appropriate to priests, and they have been ordained to this end in the Church as much by Christ as by the Apostles. Paul teaches that women should learn in silence with all subjection, and does not permit a woman to teach or to exercise authority over men.[131] However Paul does *not* state that women are *not able* to teach or to exercise authority over men—nor do I presume to affirm it, since women, devout virgins, have steadfastly[132] preached the word of God and have converted many men while priests dared not speak a word.

Brut includes at this point an argument that preaching takes precedence over the Eucharist.

C2   Since in baptism there is complete remission of sins, women absolve from sin those they baptize; hence women have the power of releasing from sin. But the powers of 'binding and releasing'[133] are interconnected, so women have the power to 'bind and release' which is said to have been granted to priests. Therefore women do not seem to be excluded from Christian priesthood even though their power is restrained so long as others are ordained to perform the functions of the priesthood. In baptism women also confer the Holy Spirit on those who are baptized in the name of the Father, Son, and Holy Spirit, and they fulfil the sacrament of marriage, since that sacrament is effected in the words of a man and a woman who become betrothed, not in the words of the priest when he blesses them, since *his* words are not of the essence of the sacrament even if they may be instituted for its embellishment and solemnization.[134]

[110] In Capes 1914, 331, Brut traces this quotation via canon law to Augustine.
[131] 1 Tim. 2: 11-12.
[132] This word (*constanter*) pointedly refers to allegations of women's *inconstantia*; cf. Brut A4(a) above; also S. *Passion 7* above, *Dives 21* below, and Ch. 2, Ambrose 4
[133] The power to 'bind and loose' conferred on St Peter by Christ (Matt. 16: 19), central to papal and priestly office in Catholicism.
[111] The Church acknowledged that marriage was above all constituted by a couple's

C3 So, women administer many of the sacraments which priests are said to be ordained to administer. As to whether women can confer holy orders, let us look at Joan—a Roman pope, yet female in sex; governing the Church of Rome for more than two years; conferring diverse orders on diverse people during that time; and performing other things appropriate to the office of pope.[135] If all her acts of this kind are void and groundless, we must doubt whether popes and priests now alive are validly ordained and whether they may administer sacraments, for we do not know whether those now ordained are in succession to those *she* ordained. If her acts were valid, why should good women not now be able to minister sacraments since she, a prostitute, administered such things?

Brut adds here that he supposes women can effect the relatively minor sacrament of extreme unction; and why not the Eucharist too?

C4 Canon law states that in the consecration of the body of Christ a good priest is no more efficacious than a bad one and a bad one no less than a good one, because (as they say) it is not through the priest's virtue but through the virtue of the words of Christ—He himself being the active force—that the bread is consecrated as the body at the priest's invocation.[136] If God effects the consecration of bread into His body at the invocation of an evil priest, I do not see why He could not do the same at the invocation of a devout woman making invocation with reverent love; unless someone is to claim the power of Christ to be limited because His body can only be consecrated in conformity with the regulation of the Roman pope. But that cannot really be said, considering the omnipotence of Christ, which is not to be limited by any finite power. And, if Christ were to effect this at the invocation of a devout woman uttering those sacramental words, in what respect (I ask) would the sacrament accomplished by her differ from that which is consecrated by priests?

exchange of vows, their mutual consent (known as *verba de praesenti*): see Brooke 1989, 128 ff. The priest's blessing was secondary.

[135] From the 13th c. a story circulated that a woman in male disguise had held papal office for over two years before dying suddenly after giving birth to a child during a liturgical procession. The Harley treatise (fo. 204ʳ) condemns the story while also offering reassurance that pseudo-ordinations over that brief span could not have been so numerous as to invalidate the priesthood *en masse*.

[136] Brut is pursuing some implications of the orthodox retort (fos. 197ʳ–198ʳ) to his earlier position (*B1* (iv)) on evil priests and devout laity.

C5 Think how many miracles Christ enacted for women and at their request.[137] Didn't He turn water to wine at Cana in Galilee at His mother's request?[138] Didn't He bring Lazarus back to life when he had been dead in a tomb for four days, at the request of Mary and Martha?[139] Isn't it said that He imprinted the image of His face indelibly on a linen cloth for Veronica, to remember Him by?[140] How then can we say that Christ could not, or would not, consecrate bread into His body at the request of a devout woman asking with reverent intention (not presumptuously) and uttering the sacramental words? Taking all these things into account, I dare not claim, unless I am otherwise taught, that women are unable to consecrate the body of Christ; though I do agree that it does not befit them, or laymen, to do this where there are those present who are constituted in the Church to administer sacraments. Thus, there seems to me no reason why women should not be able to be priests, so far as the ministration of sacraments is concerned.

*DIVES and PAUPER** (1405–10)

This exposition of the Ten Commandments is conducted in the form of a dialogue between a rich person ('Dives') who seems to represent a conventionally minded, worldly layperson, and a poor man ('Pauper'). Pauper is a clerical voice whose affiliations are hard to pin down, for he propounds orthodox doctrine with a tinge of radicalism which makes the book quite bracing and caused the authorities in the post-Wycliffe era to be somewhat wary of it. In the case of the discussion of the Sixth Commandment ('Thou shalt not commit adultery') this 'radicalism' actually derives from the unimpeachable authority of Augustine. His sermon *The Ten Strings*, on the Commandments, vigorously criticized husbands who refused to apply to themselves the standards of sexual restraint they demanded of their wives.[141] The association between this line of thought and outright defence of women is already apparent in some earlier texts such as *The Southern Passion*; but Pauper develops it comprehensively and with a degree of commitment (albeit still prepared to uphold the concept of 'natural' and divinely ordained male primacy) that takes Dives by surprise. The extract

[137] Cf. Abelard: Scott Moncrieff 1974, 164–5.
[138] John 2: 1.
[139] John 11: 1–44.
[140] According to 14th c. legend, Veronica offered a scarf to Jesus to wipe His face on the path to Calvary; He gave it back with His features imprinted on it.
  * New translation by Alcuin Blamires from *Dives and Pauper*, ed. Priscilla Barnum, i. p. 2. EETS, 280 (Oxford, 1980), 66–72, 80–93.
[141] Sermon IX, *PL* 38, cols. 75 ff., esp. 77–8, 83–4; also in *CSEL*, 41 (1961), 105–51. There is a résumé of the sermon's arguments in Augustine's treatise, *Adulterous Marriages* ii. 8: Huegelmeyer 1955, 108–9.

below begins at a point where Pauper has mentioned the creation of Adam
and Eve as a paradigm of marriage.

Creation of Adam and Eve

1   (Commandment VI, Chapter 4) *Dives.* 'Why did God make
woman out of Adam's rib rather than out of another bone?' *Pauper.*
'—Because the rib is closest to the heart, signifying that He made her
to be man's companion in love, and helper. Just as the rib is the
closest bone to the heart, so a wife should be closer in love to her
husband than all other women and men. God did not make woman
out of the foot, as if to be man's slave, nor out of the head, as if to be
his superior, but out of his side and his rib, so as to be his companion
in love and his helper in difficulty.[142] But when Eve sinned, woman
was made subject to man, so that the wife should be ruled by her
husband and be in awe of him and serve him—as companion in love,
helper in difficulty, and closest comfort in distress: not as slave and
serf in base subjection, for the husband ought to respect and esteem
his wife in that they are both one flesh and one blood.'

2   *Dives.* 'Why didn't God make woman separately out of the earth,
like Adam?' *Pauper.* 'The reason was to increase their love together,
and also to give woman grounds for humility. It increased their love
together because, woman being part of man's body, he must love her
as his own flesh and blood, and she must also love man as her origin
and as her flesh and blood. Moreover she ought to see considerable
grounds for humility, thinking how man is her perfection and her
origin: she should respect man as her perfection, her principal, and
her origin who preceded her in the order of creation.[143] God made all
humankind out of one person, since He wanted all humankind to be
united in charity, just as they all come from one.'

Adultery in Men and Women

3   (Ch. 5) *Dives.* 'Is adultery a greater sin in man than in woman?'
Pauper. 'Generally it is more sinful in man than in woman because
the higher one's position, the worse the fall and the more serious the
sin. By nature, man has greater strength and greater intelligence and

---

[142] This explanation was very widely disseminated and is found e.g. in Chaucer's
Parson's Tale and in Jacques de Vitry, *Sermones vulgares* no. 66. It goes back at least to
Hugh of St Victor (*De sacramentis*) and would have been familiar from its use in Peter
Lombard's *Sentences* (Dist. XVIII, Ch. 2).
[143] Cf. Ch. 3, Aquinas 3.

reason with which to withstand and be on guard against the devil's guile. And because he is made woman's master and guardian, to direct her in virtue and protect her from vices, if *he* lapses into vices and adultery, he is much more to blame than woman and deserves to be ignominiously rebuked. Hence St Augustine in his work *The Ten Strings* reproves husbands who lapse into adultery, addressing each of them thus: "God bids you not to commit lechery, that is, not to have sex with any woman except your wife. You ask of *her* that she should not have sex with anyone except you—yet you are not willing to observe the same restraint in return. Where you ought to be ahead of your wife in virtue, you collapse under the onset of lechery. You want your wife to conquer lechery and overpower the devil, yet you are willing to be conquered like a coward and prostrate yourself in lechery. Notwithstanding that you are 'the head of your wife',[144] she goes to God in front of you while you, 'the head', go backward to hell. . . . Complaints are always being made about men's lechery, yet wives do not dare to find fault with their husbands for it. Male lechery is so brazen and so habitual that it is now sanctioned, to the extent that men tell their wives that lechery and adultery are legitimate for men but not for women." This is what Augustine says.'

4   *Dives*. 'Sometimes one hears of wives being caught in the act with their servants, and being brought to court before the judge in great disgrace. But as for any husband being similarly brought to court for sleeping with any of his servants, that is seldom seen.' *Pauper*. 'Yet, as St Augustine says in the same book, it is as great a sin in the husband as in the wife, in fact more so; but, he says, it is not God's truth but male wickedness that holds men less guilty of the same sin. Men are less often caught or punished for adultery than women, not because they are less guilty but because they are more guilty—and bolder and more cunning in passing off their sin, while they practically all support each other in it. It is men who are witnesses, judges, and enforcers of punishment against adultery in women. And because they are deeply guilty of it themselves, they are more or less unanimous in their efforts to back up their promiscuity. Since adultery is seldom seen in women, it attracts more notoriety and severe punishment when it occurs: but it is so commonplace among men that hardly any disgrace attaches to it.'

Augustine points out that husbands would be appalled if wives imitated

[144] Eph. 5: 23.

them in claiming that adultery with a servant were a trifling matter. Fortunately, wives do not copy, but rather endure, their husbands' infidelities.

5 '"It is better for her to suffer distress for your sin than for her to emulate your wicked example. Your wife is chaste, a devout true Christian woman. She is distressed over your lechery more out of charity than for physical reasons: she wishes you were not doing wrong, not because *she* is not doing wrong but because it is not beneficial to you.". . .'

Christ encourages such a wife to be patient. Let her follow not the 'head' who is her earthly husband, but her spiritual husband Christ, the 'head' of the Church.

6 '"Change your ways, lecherous men," says Augustine there, "and from now on be chaste. Don't say that you cannot keep yourselves chaste; it is a disgrace to say that a man cannot do what a woman does or be as chaste as a woman. Woman quite properly has flesh as weak as man's, and she was first deceived by the serpent. Your chaste wives show you that you too can be chaste if you will."'

In Chapter 6, Pauper argues that women's greater chastity derives not just from the closeness with which they are watched, as Dives supposes, but from their God-fearing nature and their concern for decent behaviour and for not shaming their husbands. Men are given greater freedom and thereby greater responsibility by God, but betray that trust in their promiscuity.

7 'As St Augustine says, "you are not ashamed of your sin because so many men commit it. Man's wickedness is now such that men are more ashamed of chastity than of lechery. Murderers, thieves, perjurers, false witnesses, plunderers and fraudsters are detested and hated by people generally, but whoever will sleep with his servant girl in brazen lechery is liked and admired for it, and people make light of the damage to his soul. And if any man has the nerve to say that he is chaste and faithful to his wife and this gets known, he is ashamed to mix with other men, whose behaviour is not like his, for they will mock him and despise him and say he's not a real man; for man's wickedness is now of such proportions that no one is considered a man unless he is overcome by lechery, while one who overcomes lechery and stays chaste is considered unmanly." These are St Augustine's words in the same work.'

8   Dives. 'I am very surprised that St Augustine, and you too, accuse men of lechery so much, and attribute greater fault to man than to woman.' *Pauper.* 'Christ did just the same. . . .'

The gospel story of the woman taken in adultery implies that Christ found her male accusers more guilty of sexual sin than she. This leads into discussion of various legal questions raised by adultery, then of fornication between unmarried people.

Woman as 'Snare'?

9   (Ch. 10) Dives. 'I am driven by reason and Holy Scripture to agree that both adultery, and fornication between unmarried people, are serious sins (though adultery is the more serious), and I would like to guard against both sins. But women are the devil's snares, and tempt men so much towards lechery that it is very hard to keep one's guard. "Women deceived Adam and Samson, Peter, David, and Solomon: who can be safe from woman's guile?" '[145]

10   Pauper. 'Many men have been deceived by wicked women— more through their own folly than through woman's deceit—but many more women have been maliciously deceived by men than ever men were maliciously deceived by women.[146] Certainly the lecherous woman is called the snare of devils, who hunt man's soul; for Solomon says in Ecclesiastes 7: 27, "I have found woman more bitter than death. She is the hunter's snare, her heart is a net and her hands are cords binding tight. He who pleases God shall escape her, but the sinful man will be caught by her." However, men are not just called the "devil's snare" but also "his net spread wide on the hill of Thabor to trap many at once" (Hosea 5: 1). Man's malice is called a "net spread wide on a high hill" because it is blatant and brazenly committed, not by a few but by many; and hence when Holy Scripture reproves men's malice it speaks in the plural as if addressing many, but when it reproves woman's malice it speaks in the singular as if addressing few, indicating that there are more wicked men than women and generally more malice among men than among women even though some women are quite malicious. Fighting, robbery, manslaughter, unconcealed lechery, gluttony, guile, falsehood, perjury, treachery, fraud, and other loathsome sins dominate man more than woman.'[147]

[145] Dives quotes a simple Latin verse, of the kind Christine de Pizan perhaps has in mind when she suggests that elementary education is antifeminist: Ch. 9, *Letter 3.*
[146] Cf. Ch. 9, *Letter 6* and 9.   [147] Cf. Ch. 9, *Letter 11, City 15.*

11 'This fraudulent excuse whereby men blame their sin on the "malice" of woman began with Adam, and made him and all mankind forfeit, because when God rebuked him he sinfully blamed his sin on woman and attributed the fault to her. Also he attributed fault to God for having made woman when he answered arrogantly (just as men still do): "The woman whom you gave to me to be my companion gave me of the tree and I ate,"[148] as if as to say: "If you had not given her to me to be my companion, I should not have sinned." So even though his fault was greater than the woman's, he would not acknowledge any fault but attributed it to woman, and principally to God who made woman.' *Dives.* 'How was Adam's fault the greater?' *Pauper.* 'Because it was to him chiefly that God gave the command that he should not eat of that tree: Eve only knew it from Adam. Woman was remarkably tempted by the devil in the shape of the serpent, which moved upright at that point and had a face like a woman according to Bede and Peter Comestor; and she was deceived by his nice promises and his cunning speech, for he promised her they would not die but be like gods, with knowledge of both good and evil. Adam had no external temptation, only the artless words of his wife who offered him the apple.[149] We do not find that she spoke any deceitful words to him.'

12 'Thus, since man was forbidden by God's own mouth, she only by man; and since man had less temptation than woman, and moreover would not accuse himself or admit guilt but attributed the fault to woman and to God, therefore he sinned more than woman, for woman admitted her guilt yet asked no mercy. Offering no such excuse, she largely admitted her guilt by saying "The serpent has deceived me."[150] In that she acknowledged that she was deceived, she acknowledged that she had done wrong and unwisely and contrary to what she ought to have done. And because woman abased herself and acknowledged her lack of wisdom and folly, God at that juncture placed hope for our salvation in woman, when He said to the serpent: "I shall put enmity between you and woman and between your seed and her seed, and she shall crush your head."'[151]

Woman's 'seeds' were her good deeds, and Christ. Adam was wiser than Eve and would not have believed the devil's tales.[152] But the wiser he was, the

---

[148] Gen. 3: 12.
[149] Cf. Ch. 9, *Letter 10*.
[150] Gen. 3: 13. Eve's 'admission of guilt' had been noted even by Ambrose: *Paradise* XIV. 71: Ambrose 1961, 349.
[151] Gen. 3: 15. [152] Cf. Ch. 2, Augustine 4–6.

more he sinned, and deceived himself with a pride no less than Eve's. That his sin exceeded hers overall is attested by St Paul's statement that all men died through the sin of Adam.

13   'Christ became man, not woman, to save humankind so that, just as humankind was lost through man, humankind should be saved through man: hence it was in manhood that He wished to die for humankind, because manhood had lost humankind. Moreover, He became man, not woman, to preserve the order of nature; and because woman's sin was less serious than Adam's and harmed humankind less; and because woman was less corrupted in the first transgression than was man. Therefore God took His manhood solely from woman, without the participation of a man. So, in that He became man, He did man great honour—but in that He took manhood solely from woman, without the participation of man, He did great honour to woman,[153] for it was only out of woman's progeny that He made medicine for the sin of Adam, to heal humankind from the grievous illness of Adam's sin.'

14   Dives. (Ch. 11) 'Your words are remarkable, but I cannot disagree with you, for fear of our Lady, mother and virgin, who brought forth grace for humankind and can help us in every need. But I still say, as I said before, woman deceived Samson, who was so strong.'[154]

15   Pauper. 'Woman did not deceive him until he had deceived himself through lechery and failure to govern himself properly.[155] First, he married a heathen woman out of lust and sinful love, against God's law and against the will of his parents.[156] Next, he slept with a heathen prostitute.[157] Then he took another heathen woman, called Delilah, as his mistress, and she deceived him and brought him to his death. He was disloyal to God, and women were disloyal to him. Women saw that he was foolishly infatuated with them, so they treated him as a fool. He deceived himself and behaved unwisely when he allowed a woman to tie him up among his enemies, and told a heathen woman his secret—in what way his enemies could most harm him. And although God turned his foolish actions to the honour of Himself and His law, nevertheless Samson was not excused by that, for he did much wrong and was very stupid.[158]

---

[153] Cf. Abelard 7, above.
[154] Cf. Thrush 24, above.
[155] The theme of 'misgovernance' is continued in 19 below; cf. Gower 2, above.
[156] Judg. 14–15.   [157] Judg. 16: 1   [158] Judg. 16: 4–31.

16 'David, too, was deceived by his own sinful lust and lechery and not by the woman Bathsheba, as you claimed in your quotation.[159] We read in Holy Scripture in 2 Kings 11: 2–17 that one day when King David got up from his sleep after midday, and was strolling on the upper floor of his palace, he saw a beautiful woman washing herself in her upper storey. He didn't know the woman; nor did she think about him or know anything of his wicked will, as the Bible makes clear. Soon afterwards he sent messengers for this woman, and when she came to him he slept with her and got her pregnant. As soon as she knew that she was pregnant, in order to conceal his sin he sent for her husband Urias so that he would come home and have intercourse with his wife, and the child would be identified as his and not David's. But Urias was a good knight who would not approach his wife or indulge in sexual pleasure while God's army was in the field, besieging a city called Rabat. So David sent him away again with letters about his death to Joab the commander of the army, and treacherously arranged for him to be killed. Here you can see how David was overcome by lechery and deceived by the devil *before* the woman came to him—for, as Christ says in the Gospel, whoever looks at a woman and is willing to sin with her, immediately commits lechery and transgresses the commandment, "Thou shalt not commit adultery."[160] David looked at that woman and was willing to commit lechery, while the woman had no evil thoughts. He sent for her as if for his liege woman, and she did not know why. And when she came to him, as her king, he slept with her sinfully: it was very hard for her to prevent him.'

Pauper argues that women were not to blame for Peter's denial of Christ. As for Solomon, the initiative for taking heathen concubines was his, and while they were 'stable' in their faith he was 'unstable' in his. His lechery preceded their compliance.

17 'Lecherous men walk and ride from town to town to get women to do their pleasure. They seek out the women, not the women them.[161] They plan all sorts of tricks to procure women's consent to sin. Men generally take the initiative in instigating lechery, and then whether the woman consents or not it is the man who is guilty. Frequently it happens that, when a man thinks he is sure of the

---

[159] Behind Dives's quotation lay discussions such as Ch. 3, *Rule 4*, and Ch. 4, *Map 10*.
[160] Matt. 5: 28.
[161] Cf. *S. Passion* 2–3 and Gower 2 above; and Ch. 9, *Letter 6*.

RESPONSES TO ANTIFEMINISM

woman's consent, she will not do so for fear of God; or, if she has already consented and promised to do the man's pleasure, she may repent of it and withdraw from his wicked company. Then, that lecherous man will defame all women and say that they are false and deceitful, for it is precisely because such lechers cannot satisfy their filthy appetites with women at will, that they make the vilest allegations about them.[162] Since they cannot defile them with their bodies, they defile them with their tongues, making evil insinuations, slandering them, and doing them as much harm as they can.'

The point is confirmed in the story of Susanna, whom two elderly governors tried to 'frame' when she resisted their advances.[163]

18   (Ch. 12) *Dives*. 'Nevertheless, many women will consent quite readily to sexual advances when they are made.' *Pauper*. 'That is true, but women are not so ready to consent as men are to make advances, and the one who makes advances and initiates is the one who first consents and is more in the wrong.' *Dives*. 'You keep on acquitting women and accusing men.' *Pauper*. 'I accuse no good man, only wicked lechers. Nor do I acquit any wicked woman, only good women slanderously accused of lechery, and not only individually but in their sex generally—for man in his arrogant malice irrationally defames the female sex and (as Adam did) assigns his sin to woman and will not lay the blame on his own malice in order to obtain mercy.' *Dives*. 'Solomon said much about the evil of women.' *Pauper*. 'And Solomon said much about the good of women. . . .'

A short battle of quotations ensues, culminating when Dives paraphrases Ecclesiasticus 19: 2.

19   *Dives*. '"Wine and women make wise men dote and forsake God's law and do wrong."' *Pauper*. 'However, the fault is not in the wine, and often not in the woman. The fault is in the one who misuses the wine or the woman or other of God's creations. Even if you get drunk on the wine and through this greed you lapse into lechery, the wine is not to blame but you are, in being unable or unwilling to discipline yourself.[164] And even if you look at a woman and become caught up in her beauty and assent to sin, the woman is

---

[162] Cf. Ch. 7, *WoB* 47; and Ch. 9, *Letter* 5, on the psychological motivation of misogyny.
[163] Dan. 13: 1–64.
[164] Cf. Gower 2 above.

not to blame nor is the beauty given her by God to be disparaged: rather, you are to blame for not keeping your heart more clear of wicked thoughts. Where you ought to praise God, you have evil intentions and you offend against God by misusing His fair creation. If you feel yourself tempted by the sight of a woman, control your gaze better. If she flirts and stirs up lust in you, escape from her flirtation. If you know that she is eager for sex, escape from her company; for flight is the best means of combating lechery.[165] You are free to leave her. Nothing constrains you to commit lechery but your own lecherous heart.'

Women's Dress Sinful?

Dives criticizes women for dressing provocatively. Pauper agrees that this can be reprehensible, in either sex, but modifies the effect of the traditional biblical authorities by re-contextualizing them.

20   (Ch. 13) *Pauper*. '... In 1 Timothy 2: 9–10 St Paul bids women dress in respectable clothing, modestly and soberly, not braiding their hair elaborately or using gold or silver or pearls or extravagantly expensive material. St Peter says the same in his first Epistle, 3: 3–5, where he bids men to respect their wives and keep them in honour.' *Dives*. 'Women dress up these days very contrary to the teaching of Peter and Paul, so I fear they sin most seriously.' *Pauper*. 'Peter and Paul did not comprehensively forbid dressing up: they forbade women to dress up in that way out of pride, or so as to incite people to lechery, or in a style exceeding their status.[166] We find that St Cecilia and many other devout women went dressed in cloth of gold and in fine pearls, yet wore hair-shirts under that grand attire. Moreover, Peter and Paul said those words chiefly in relation to times of prayer, such as Lent, Ember days, Rogation days, Fridays, vigils, and in times of crisis when public processions are conducted. At such times men and women should abandon all ostentation and showiness in dress; for, as the biblical gloss says, showy clothing procures no good from God and makes people form the wrong impression, especially if it goes beyond the bounds of respectability. The chief intention of St Paul where he says those words is to inform men and women about prayer—for whom they should pray, why and how and where (as the gloss says), and he instructs them to pray humbly, without dressing up elaborately in ostentatious clothing. ...'

---

[165] An Ovidian idea: cf. Ch. 4, Marbod 7.
[166] Dress was regulated by statute according to one's class in the Middle Ages.

The Question of Reliability

21   *Dives.* 'Since it is the case that man takes precedence over woman in the natural order, and is more steadfast[167] and stronger and of greater discretion than woman in the natural course of things, and ought (as you have well said) to be more virtuous and steadfast in goodness than woman, how does it come about that women often sustain their chastity more than man, and are more steadfast in goodness than man?' . . . *Pauper.* 'By nature man *is* more steadfast than woman and has greater discretion than she, but through grace, women are often more steadfast in goodness than men, and have better discretion in goodness than many a man.' *Dives.* 'Why is that?' *Pauper.* '—Because men are too self-reliant and do not put as much trust in God as they should. Women, knowing their weakness, do not put faith in themselves but only in God, commending themselves to God more than do men. They are more afraid of offending God than men are.'

MERELAUS THE EMPEROR, FROM STORIES OF THE ROMANS (GESTA ROMANORUM)*

The *Gesta* was an anthology of tales, each with an accompanying allegorical interpretation, compiled in Latin at or just before the beginning of the fourteenth century, possibly in England. It attained wide circulation and was subject to numerous regional variations in content. Sometime in the early fifteenth century an English prose translation was made, from which the sixty-ninth story is presented below in modern English. This story's contemporary appeal is attested by the fact that Christine de Pizan and Hoccleve made adaptations.[168] It can serve as a paradigm of eulogistic narrative in which woman is both suffering victim of, and ultimately moral victor over, predatory men.

1   Merelaus was a wise emperor who had married the daughter of the King of Hungary, a beautiful and very charitable woman.[169] There came a time when the emperor formed a resolution in bed one night to visit the Holy Land. So in the morning he called the empress

[167] The word is *stable*; cf. its use in *S. Passion* 7 above, and n.

* New translation by Alcuin Blamires from *The Early English Versions of the Gesta Romanorum*, ed. Sidney J. H. Herrtage, EETS, ES 33 (London, 1879), 311–19.

[168] *City of Ladies* ('Florence of Rome') II. 51.1, where Christine states that she has taken it from Gautier de Coinci; and Hoccleve ('The Emperor Jereslaus's Wife'): Hoccleve 1970, 140–78.

[169] *Full of werkis of mercy*, perhaps with reference to specific Christian 'Works of Mercy' (including the comfort of prisoners and of the sick) such as she subsequently enacts.

and his brother to him and said: 'Madam, I shall not conceal or keep it from you that I intend to go to the Holy Land. I am fully resolved to do so, and therefore I formally appoint you to govern the empire in my place, upholding my honour, and to the benefit of my people.' Then she said, 'Since this must be so, may it be done as you wish. In your absence I shall be a turtle-dove deprived of its mate, but I trust that you will return home in good health.' The emperor comforted her with kind and gentle words, kissed her, took his leave, and went on his way.

2 When he had gone, his brother grew arrogant. He oppressed both rich and poor and also tempted the empress towards a sinful liaison with him; but, as a good woman ought, she refused to consent so long as her husband was living. He would not leave it at that, but kept on tempting her whenever he could find her alone. At last, when the empress saw that his misconduct[170] was incorrigible, she summoned three or four worthy lords and said to them: 'Sirs, as you well know, my lord put me in control of the empire. His brother was to serve under me as steward and not act independently of me— yet, as will be clear to you, he is oppressing poor, ordinary folk and plundering the wealthy and powerful, and would do even more harm if he could. I require you, therefore, to have him tied up and to put him in prison.' They said: 'Certainly he has done great wrong since the emperor went, and we shall be glad to carry out your will.' Immediately they laid hands on the steward, and shackled him with iron fetters in prison, where he remained for a long time.

3 Eventually word came that the emperor was on the way home. The steward thought to himself: 'If my lord finds me here when he returns, he will inquire into the reason for my imprisonment, and his wife will tell him how I tempted her to sin. Then I shall never get his favour, and maybe I shall lose my life.' So he quickly sent a message begging the empress to come and let him speak to her in the prison. When the empress heard the message she came, and asked him what he wanted. 'Noble lady,' he said, 'show mercy to me, for if my lord finds me here I am as good as dead.' 'If I knew', she said, 'that you would stop your misconduct and prove to be a good decent man, you could still obtain my goodwill.'[171] And he said, 'Yes,' pledging his trustworthiness.

---

[170] Translating the word *foly*, a euphemism for sexual advances.
[171] Her word *grace* carries unwitting irony: it could mean 'sexual favour'.

4   Then she brought him out of prison and had him bathed, his hair cut, and his beard shaved. After giving him fine clothing to wear she said: 'Brother, take your horse now, and come and ride with me to meet our lord.' With this steward and a great crowd of other lords and officials, she rode out to meet the emperor. But as they were riding a hind came running swiftly, and seeing it, everybody went in pursuit with the hounds as fast as they could, so that no one was left with the lady except the steward. As soon as he realized this he said, 'Madam, beside us here is an unfrequented forest: let's go into it—I have loved you for a long time—and let me make love with you.' She responded: 'What on earth do you mean! Didn't I release you from prison only yesterday on condition that you would stop your misconduct—and now are you at it again straight away? I tell you now as before, that no one shall do it with me except my husband, who can claim it by law.'[172] 'Unless you give in to me,' he said, 'I shall hang you up by the hair on a tree in this forest where nobody will come across you, and you'll have a nasty end.' But she replied, 'You can behead me or use whatever torture you like against me, but you will never force me into sin.' Then he stripped her right down to her smock, strung her up by the hair on an oak tree, and tethered her palfrey close by. After doing this he rejoined the others and stated that a great throng of people had abducted the lady from him. Consequently there was great sorrow throughout the empire.

5   Three days later an earl went hunting in the forest, and as his hounds tracked some wolves, they caught a different scent and stopped their chase, directing their course towards the tree. The earl was very surprised by this and spurred his horse in pursuit until he came to the tree where the lady hung. When he saw her strung up there by the hair, he had great compassion for her, she was so beautiful, and said 'Woman, who are you, and why are you hanging like this?' By divine miracle she was still alive, and said: 'I am a woman from foreign parts, and God knows, I have no idea how I come to be hanging here!' 'Whose horse is this next to the tree?' said the earl. 'It is mine, sir,' she replied. Suspecting that she was some great noblewoman, the earl's pity for her grew all the more. 'Dear friend,' he said, 'you seem a noble lady. At home I have a little child, a young daughter: if you will undertake to bring her up and teach her you shall be delivered from this torment, and be well rewarded

---

[172] The 'carnal debt' of marriage sanctioned in canon law: see Ch. 3, Gratian 2.

for it too.' She replied 'Sir, I shall do as you wish to the best of my ability.'

6 The earl took her down, brought her to his castle, and committed his daughter to her care. The empress slept in the same bedroom as the earl's wife, with the girl between them and a lamp burning there every night. Such was the empress's behaviour that she was loved by everyone. But in the earl's household was a steward much attracted to her, who often propositioned her sinfully. She kept on answering that she had vowed to God that she would never love any man in that way except the one whom God's law allowed her to. Then in great indignation the steward said, 'So, in no way will you grant me your love?' 'No,' she replied: 'What more do you want me to say? I mean to keep the vow I have made to God.' The steward went off, thinking 'I'll be avenged on you, if I can.'

7 One night it happened that the door of the earl's bedroom was left open and the steward spotted it and went in, to find everyone asleep. He looked around by the lamplight and saw the empress's bed. Seeing the empress lying beside the earl's daughter, he drew out a knife and slit the child's throat. Then furtively he placed the knife in the empress's hand, so that when the lord woke up he would see the bloodstained knife, suspect her of murdering the child with her own knife, and consign her to a vile death.

8 Soon after the steward had done this the earl's wife chanced to wake, and as she looked up from her bed she saw how the empress had a bloody knife in her hand. Nearly out of her wits at the sight, she shouted to her husband, 'Sir! Sir! Wake up, and look at the lady's bed and look what she's holding in her hand!' The earl woke up and looked. Much disturbed on seeing the bloody knife he called out to the empress: 'Wake up, woman! What's that in your hand?' The shouts awoke the empress; the knife dropped from her hand; she looked and saw the child dead; and felt the bed full of blood. Then she shouted loudly: 'Help! My lord's daughter has been killed!' Hearing her daughter was dead, the earl's wife cried out with a distraught voice to her husband: 'Kill this devil, or woman, whichever she is, who has murdered our daughter!' Then she said to the empress: 'It is absolutely plain that you have killed my child with your knife, with your own hands; and you'll be die a hideous death for it.' Then the earl said to her with heavy heart: 'Woman, if it were not for fear of God, I would sever your head from your body with my sword, seeing

that I saved you from death, yet now you have slain my daughter. As it is, I shall not harm you: but I order you to leave my country quickly, because if I ever find you in it after this day, you'll never eat bread again!'

9   Full of distress, the empress put on her clothes, mounted her palfrey, and went eastwards. As she rode she saw a gibbet on her left, and officers taking a man to his death. Stirred by pity she spurred her horse up to the gibbet and spoke to the officers. 'I am ready to purchase this man's life if you are willing to accept money to save him.' They said 'Yes,' so she came to an agreement with them and thus rescued the man. She said to him, 'Dear friend, since I have saved your life, be an honest man from now on.' 'Yes, lady,' he replied, 'I promise you that.' He accompanied her as her servant, and when they reached a city she asked him to go ahead and choose some respectable lodgings for her. He did this, and she stayed many days in the city. Men there who were very struck by her beauty often propositioned her, without success.[173]

10   Soon afterwards a ship arrived loaded with all sorts of merchandise; and when the lady heard about it she asked her servant, 'Go to the ship and see if there is any good cloth for me.' Going on board, and finding numerous fine materials, the servant requested the captain to come and speak with his lady. He agreed, so the servant reported back to her that the captain was coming, and when the latter arrived he greeted her respectfully. Assenting to the lady's request for dress materials, he returned to the ship accompanied by the servant, to whom he said: 'Friend, I'll let you into my confidence if I can trust you; and if you'll keep my plan secret I will reward you well.' The other said, 'I'll swear on the Bible to keep your plan secret, and help you as much as I can with it.' So the captain said: 'I love her more than you would believe; she has such beauty, and I'd give all my goods to have my will of her. If you can help me to get her I'll pay you whatever you ask.' The servant responded: 'Tell me what you want me to do to, to bring her to you.' 'Go to her,' he said, 'and tell her I won't allow my cloth off the ship for anybody, and so make her come on board—but not until a strong wind blows up. Then I shall take her away with me, there'll be no escape for her.'

11   'It's a good plan,' said the treacherous servant. 'Give me my

---

[173] In Hoccleve this provokes a digression against allegations that women are *variant*. When propositioned they show the *constance* of *wommanhode*, since it is their nature to be *stidefast*: see *Jereslaus's Wife*, lines 484–97.

money and I'll give you what you want.' After receiving the money this traitor went back to his lady and told her how the captain would not send his cloth out of his ship, 'but asks you to come down to the dock, where you can view and choose materials as you wish.' Since she believed him, she went to the ship and boarded it. But while her treacherous servant stayed ashore, the captain, seeing a strong wind begin, hoisted sail and gave orders to row fast. And when the lady perceived this treachery she was deeply disturbed and said: 'What kind of treason is this you're doing to me?' 'No treason,' he said, 'except that I mean to have sex with you, and wed you as my wife.'

12 'Sir,' she said then, 'I have made a vow to God that I shall never commit that deed except with him to whom I am lawfully bound.' 'Don't say that,' he replied. 'You are now in the middle of the ocean, and if you don't consent I shall throw you right into the water.' Then she said, 'Since there's no option, find me a suitable place in the ship, and I shall do your will rather than die.' The captain believed what she said. But once in the place she drew a curtain across between herself and him, and kneeled down to pray.[174] 'My Lord God, who have protected me since my youth, preserve me from defilement in this hour, that I may give you my soul with a pure heart.' When her prayer was done such a great storm blew up on the sea that the ship broke in two, and everyone drowned except the lady and the captain, she by getting to a plank which carried her to land, and he by holding on to another, though neither knew that the other had reached safety.

13 The lady found her way to an abbey occupied by nuns, where she was respectfully received. For a long time she lived a devout life there such that God lent her the grace to cure many who were sick, with the result that sick people all around the abbey went there in hopes of a cure—successfully so, to their delight.

14 Now her husband's brother, who had strung her up by the hair, had become a vile leper. The knight responsible for killing the earl's daughter and placing the bloodstained knife in her hand, was deaf and blind. The servant who had betrayed her was crippled. And the ship's captain had half lost his mind. When the emperor heard tell that such a devout and virtuous woman was in that place, he said to his brother, 'Dear friend, let us go to this abbey so that the holy

---

[174] Clearer in Hoccleve, *Jereslaus's Wife*: lines 645–58, where the captain curtains off a corner in response to her request for a discreet place to satisfy his desire, away from the crew's gaze; she prays within while he speaks to some crewmen.

woman can cure your leprosy.' 'Yes, my lord, if that were possible,' he replied; and without any delay the emperor took him in person to see the nuns, who made a procession to meet him when they heard that he was coming. The emperor enquired of the prioress whether there were any such holy woman among them, and when she said yes, he asked for her to come forward. They made the empress come forward and speak with the emperor. Hiding her face behind a wimple so as not to be recognized, she approached and respectfully greeted him.

15 'Fair lady,' he said, 'can you cure my brother's leprosy? If you can, you may have whatever you ask.' The empress looked carefully. She saw the emperor's brother standing there, an ugly leper with worms coming out of both sides of his face, and she saw that because the emperor had come there with his sick brother, every sick person in that area had come to be healed. She said to the emperor, 'Sir, if you gave me your whole empire, I couldn't cure your brother unless he made a public confession.' The emperor turned to his brother and told him to confess openly so that he could be cleansed.[175] He made a confession covering his whole life—except about the way he hanged the empress by the hair, which he was unwilling to mention. The empress said to the emperor, 'Sir, it would be a waste of time for me to apply my medicine to him because he has not yet made a full confession.' The emperor turned to his brother and said: 'You peasant! What miserable wretchedness has got into you? Can't you see, you're a disgusting leper? Will you not disclose everything, so as to be cleansed and made whole? Confess quickly, or you'll be excluded from my company for good!'

16 'My lord!' he said: 'I cannot confess until I have a guarantee of your favour and mercy.' 'What?' said the emperor, 'Have you done some offence against me?' 'Yes, sir,' said the other, 'I have committed a grave offence against you, and for that reason I am asking your mercy before saying what it is.' There was no thought of the empress in the emperor's mind, since he believed her to be dead long ago. He said, 'State confidently what offence you have done me, for there is no doubt I shall forgive you.' Then his brother explained how he had tried to get the empress to sin, and consequently hanged her by the hair. Hearing this the emperor was furious: 'False debauchee! Divine vengeance has overtaken you for it! If I had known this before, I

---

[175] The word clansid discloses the connection assumed in that period between outer deformity (especially leprosy) and inner sin.

would have made you die the most hideous death any man could suffer.'

17   The steward who killed the earl's daughter then spoke up. 'I don't know what lady you speak of, but it was in such a forest that a lady hung by the hair, and my lord the earl took her down and brought her to his castle to be a nurse; and I did my best to make her sin with me. Because I could not have my will of her I killed my lord's daughter sleeping beside her, and put the knife in the lady's hand so that she would get the blame for it; consequently the earl threw her out of his country, though I don't know where she went afterwards.'

18   Then the rescued thief (the treacherous servant) spoke. 'I don't know what lady you speak of, but there was a beautiful lady who saved me from death by hanging, on the gibbet, by paying a large sum of money; but after that, I betrayed her to a ship's captain so he could take her as his mistress. When I lured her to his ship by trickery, he set sail and took her away, though what happened afterwards I don't know, nor where she went.'

19   Then the captain said: 'Yes, it was such a lady that I received on board through her servant's deceit. And when we were in the middle of the ocean I intended to sin with her, and she started praying; and when her prayers were finished a storm arose and shattered the ship so that everyone drowned; I reached land with the help of a plank. But what became of the lady, whether she was drowned or saved, I don't know.'

20   Then the empress cried out with a loud voice, saying 'You have all made a thorough confession, and I am therefore willing to apply my medicines to you.' So she healed them all; then revealed her face among them all. When the emperor realized it was she, in his joy he ran to her, embraced her, kissed her, and wept like a child. 'Blessed be God,' he said, 'for I have found what I have supremely desired!' In great happiness he brought her home to the palace, and lived out his life well, in peace and charity.

9

A Woman Defends Women

CHRISTINE DE PIZAN (1365–c. 1430)

Christine de Pizan was born in Italy but brought up in cultured circles at the court of Charles V of France, where her father was appointed as astrologer. He was a well-read man, and according to Christine he took an unusually positive view (for its time) of her own wish to develop her intellectual gifts; her mother on the other hand sought in vain to mould her more convention-ally—'with spinning and silly girlishness'.[1] Married at fifteen, Christine was fortunate that her husband further encouraged her literary talents, for these were to stand her in good stead when she lost both him and her father and had to support her three children after 1389. Her literary output covered some forty years. It was immense and wide-ranging, and it was rather remarkable for the extent to which some of it took issue with the disparage-ment of women. People have argued that she cannot properly be regarded as a forbear of modern feminism, because she was too committed to conserva-tive, quiescent ideals of womanly decorum.[2] Moreover, the present antho-logy shows how she availed herself of certain defence-of-women arguments which were not new, for they had long been in circulation—among men. In particular, she owed a substantial debt, without acknowledging it, to Jehan Le Fèvre's *Livre de Leesce*. Notwithstanding these reservations, Christine's attempt to redefine the cultural profile of woman was potent. She saw with great clarity how women had accepted and internalized an unjustifiable devaluation of their sex, including a presupposition of their limited intellect, for centuries.[3] She pinpointed the hypocrisy with which men unjustly put women down while claiming a God-given right to do so.[4] She understood (taking up a cue from Le Fèvre) how a successful challenge to misogyny entailed undermining the authority of prestigious literary authorities such as Ovid. She protested that the reality of women's behaviour did not vindicate the allegations misogynists flung at them. She suspected that misogyny was a kind of conspiracy wrought by senile male lechers and buttressed by jealous fear of female potential.[5] What is striking, even in the light of the capacious precedent of the *Leesce*, is the comprehensiveness of her approach to the subject. She demonstrated intellectual courage and good sense as she systematically confronted the whole gamut of misogynistic notions, covert

[1] *City* II. 36.4
[2] *Letter* 12; *City* III. 19.2; and see Gottlieb 1985, Delany 1990, 88–103.
[3] *City* I. 28.1.
[4] *City* I. 3.3.
[5] *City* I. 8.8 speaks of men attacking women out of jealousy at their superior intellect and behaviour; possibly prompted by *Leesce* 1155–61.

as well as explicit, in order to expose their speciousness. It has been argued that her view of woman was 'not antithetically constructed' in reaction to misogyny— that she did not rely on refutation by 'counter-cliché'.[6] Perhaps the latter is more true than the former. *Of course* her view was antithetically constructed. In that epoch this was inevitable, and the time was long overdue for people to start coming forward to dismantle the accumulated dogma of antifeminism. But to do so rationally and constructively, rather than by descending to the kind of 'Women-are-evil / No-they-aren't' squabbling which the dogma promoted, this was the great task, and Christine rose to it.

FROM *THE LETTER OF THE GOD OF LOVE** (*L'EPISTRE AU DIEU D'AMOURS*: 1399)

This poem assumes the form of an Official Statement by the God of Love, publishing the complaints lodged at his court by multitudes of women concerning their mistreatment by false lovers and protesting especially against the defamation arising from men's casual talk of sexual conquest. What is the point of such defamation, it is asked, among those who ought rather to be the protectors of women's honour?

1 (168) Every man should feel affection in his heart for woman, who is mother to each and every one of them, and who, rather than being horrible or cruel to him, is gentle, sweet, and loving, offering compassion and help when he needs them. She has done so much for him and continues to do so, for her actions are very effectively designed to nurture a man's body gently. From his birth, through life to death, women help and succour him, providing compassion, sweetness, and support.[7] And if a man refuses to acknowledge this and, lacking in gratitude, harshly slanders them, my response is to repeat my view that a man who utters defamatory remarks, insults, or reproaches against women by criticizing them (whether it be one, two of them or women in general) offends against nature.[8]

2 (185) Let us suppose that there do exist stupid women, or those tainted with every conceivable vice, faithless and incapable of love or loyalty, proud, vicious, full of cruelty, inconstant, fickle, flighty, false, deceitful, and given to trickery: should we because of this lock them

---

[6] Christine de Pizan 1982, p. xxxiii.

* New translation by Karen Pratt from the Old French text in *Œuvres Poétiques de Christine de Pisan*, ed. Maurice Roy, ii (Paris: SATF, 1891); see also Fenster and Erler 1991. © Karen Pratt 1992.

[7] The natural debt to woman as mother is argued in e.g. Ch. 8, Marbod 3–5; also Leesce 1026–36; and *Bien des Fames* 19 ff.: in Fiero *et al.* 1989, 107–9.

[8] The charge of 'ingratitude' recurs in *City* I. 8.9, I. 38.4. Andreas also refers to the 'offence to nature' in antifeminism: *On Love* III. 52–3.

all up and claim that there is not a single one of any worth? When God on high made and created the angels, cherubim, seraphim, and archangels, were there not some whose deeds were evil? Should one therefore call all angels evil? But let any man who knows an evil woman be wary of her, without casting aspersions on a third or quarter of all women and without criticizing women in general and condemning their female ways.[9] For there have been many, still are and will be, who are virtuous and fair and hence deserve our praise, women in whom we find virtue and good qualities, and whose kindness amply demonstrates their good sense and worth.

Attacking vices is one thing; condemning individuals by name is another— indeed, it is disallowed by God. The slanderers should ponder the better example set by exponents of chivalry such as Othon de Grandson. But Christine now turns our attention to the inheritance of literary 'defamation'.

3 (259) The aforementioned ladies complain about many clerks who attribute all sorts of faults to them and who compose works about them in rhyme, prose, and verse, criticizing their conduct in a variety of different ways. They then give these works as elementary textbooks to their young pupils at the beginning of their schooling, to provide them with exempla and received wisdom, so that they will remember this teaching when they come of age.[10] In their verse treatises these clerks say that Adam, David, Samson, Solomon, and countless other men were brought down by women morning, noon, and night. Is there therefore a man alive who would be able to protect himself from them? Another says that women are very deceitful, scheming, false, and of little worth. Others say that they are great liars, fickle, inconstant, and flighty. They accuse them of many another serious vice and are very critical of them, finding no excuse for them whatsoever.

4 (277) This is the way clerks behave day and night, composing their verse now in French, now in Latin. And they base their opinions on goodness only knows which books, which are more mendacious than a drunk. Ovid, in a book he wrote called *Cures for Love*, says many evil things about women, and I think he was wrong

---

[9] On unjust generalization, cf. Ch. 8, *S. Passion* 6, and Albertano 3; and Ch. 1, Ovid 7. Generalization is supported in Ch. 6, *Math.* 26, 31.

[10] Christine specifies Ovid's *Remedia amoris* as one of these 'elementary textbooks' in 4 below. Ovid seems to have been studied in schools from at least the 11th c. Cf. Ch. 6, *RR* 3 commenting that Theophrastus' book is 'a good one to study in school'; and on Adam, Samson, etc., cf. Ch. 8, *Dives* 9.

to do this. He accuses them of gross immorality, of filthy, vile, and wicked behaviour. (I disagree with him that they have such vices and promise to champion them in the fight against anyone who would like to throw down the gauntlet. I mean, of course, honourable women, for I do not include worthless ones in what I have to say.) Thus, clerks have studied this book since their early childhood as their grammar primer and then teach it to others so that no man will undertake to love a woman. . . .

5 (309) And if anyone says that we ought to believe books written by reputable men of sound judgement, who never debased themselves by lying, yet demonstrated the wickedness of women, my response is that those men who wrote such things in their books, I have discovered, never sought to do anything but deceive women in their private lives; nor could they get enough of them: they wanted a different woman every day and couldn't be faithful even to the most beautiful. How many did David have, or King Solomon? This angered God and he punished them for their excess. There were many others like them, notably Ovid, who lusted after so many women, then had the nerve to slander them. And all those clerks, who had so much to say about them, were—more than other men—maddened with lust not for just one, but for thousands of them![11] Now if such men had ladies or wives who refused to pander to their every whim or who concentrated their efforts on cheating them, what is so surprising about that? For there can be no doubt that, when a man plunges into such filth, he certainly does not seek out worthy ladies or virtuous, modest women of good character: these women he neither knows nor has anything to do with. He wants only those who suit his purpose, and has a constant supply of tarts and whores on his arm. Does a rake deserve to possess anything of worth, since he chases everything in skirts and then imagines he can successfully hide his shame by slandering them with complex arguments once he has grown old and is past it?[12] But if they were to criticize only fallen and loose women, and were to advise against pursuing them (for pursue them is what these men actually did), then some good could come of it. For this would be a very reasonable thing to do, worthy, fair, and commendable advice, and would not be defamatory to women in general.

---

[11] This psychological explanation is echoed in Ch. 8, *Dives 17*, and expanded with reference to Ovid in *City* I. 9.2, where a story that Ovid was embittered by castration is borrowed from *Leesce* 2709–22.
[12] Cf. Ch. 7, *WoB 47*.

6 (348) And if we turn now to the question of deceit, I simply cannot conceive of or comprehend just how a woman might deceive a man. She isn't the one who pursues him or tracks him down, seeking his love or begging for his favours at his house.[13] She does not constantly think about him or have him on her mind, whereas man comes round to deceive and seduce her. How does he seduce her? In such a way that no trouble is too great for him, and there is no burden he will not bear in order to have her. He has no other diversion, devoting himself exclusively to seducing women, dedicating his heart, body, and wealth to the task. It often happens that this period of privation and trial lasts a long time, yet they frequently fail in their aims, even though they try very hard. These are the men Ovid speaks about in his poem on the *Art of Love*; for out of the deep sympathy he felt for them he composed a book in which he describes and teaches them openly how to seduce women through trickery and to win their love. He called this work the *Art of Love*, but, far from teaching the rules and conventions of noble love, it teaches the very opposite. For any man who decides to put into practice the precepts of this book will never love properly, however much he may be loved. For this reason, this book is inappropriately named: it is in fact a book on the art of sheer deceit and dissimulation—that is what I call it.

7 (379) Yet if women are so flighty, fickle, changeable, susceptible, and inconstant (as some clerks would have us believe), why is it that their suitors have to resort to such trickery to have their way with them? And why don't women quickly succumb to them, without the need for all this skill and ingenuity in conquering them? For there is no need to go to war for a castle that is already captured. And the same applies to a poet as skilful as Ovid, who was later sent into exile, or Jean de Meun in his *Romance of the Rose*—what a long-winded business that is! What a complicated task! What well-known and recondite knowledge he brings to bear on this, and what great adventures are involved. And the help of so many people sought and requested and so much effort, and so many tricks devised in order to seduce a mere slip of a girl (for this is the ultimate aim) with deceit and guile. Is a violent attack necessary then against a weak and defenceless site? How can one perform a great leap from such close quarters? I simply cannot see or understand why it requires such an

---

[13] The argument that men, not women, are sexual predators is in *Leesce*, 2970 ff., 3846 ff., and Ch. 8 above, *S. Passion 2*, Gower 2. *Dives 17*.

enormous effort, skill, ingenuity, and great cunning to capture a weak place.[14]

8 (402) Therefore, since it *is* necessary to call on such skill, ingenuity, and effort in order to seduce a woman, whether of high or humble birth, the logical conclusion to draw is that women are by no means as fickle as some men claim, or as easily influenced in their behaviour. And if anyone tells me that books are full of women like these, it is this very reply, frequently given, which causes me to complain. My response is that women did not write these books nor include the material which attacks them and their morals. Those who plead their cause in the absence of an opponent can invent to their heart's content, can pontificate without taking into account the opposite point of view and keep the best arguments for themselves, for aggressors are always quick to attack those who have no means of defence.[15] But if women had written these books, I know full well the subject would have been handled differently.[16] They know that they stand wrongfully accused, and that the cake has not been divided up equally, for the strongest take the lion's share, and the one who does the sharing out keeps the biggest portion for himself.

The loyalty of Medea, Dido, and Penelope disproves allegations of women's fickleness.[17] In fact it is because women are so often victims of male deceit that they have to be wary. The God of Love will punish men who turn against him and against women; worse still are those who besiege women till they give in, then generalize that women are easy prey.

9 (559) But, whoever may have slandered or denigrated them in their writings, I can find no ill spoken of women in any book or work on the subject of Jesus, His life and death (the latter brought about by envy), nor in the acts of the Apostles, who endured great suffering for the faith, nor in any gospel,[18] but instead women are attributed with many a virtue, many an important act, great wisdom, good sense and unwavering constancy, perfect love, unshakeable faith, great charity, a determined will, a strong and steadfast heart eager to serve

[14] The 'siege' metaphor is prominent in *RR*; and cf. Ch. 1, Ovid 6.
[15] This is the germ of Christine's idea for the well-defended 'City' of Ladies: cf. *City* I. 3.3.
[16] Cf. Ch. 7, *WoB* 47.
[17] On Medea, see Ch. 6, *RR* 27; on all three, see Ch. 1, Ovid 7.
[18] Christine again emphasizes a favourable attitude to women in the New Testament and in Christian legend (as against the misogyny of pagan literature) in *City* III. 18.1.

God; and they gave ample proof of these qualities, for they did not abandon Him in life or death. Sweet Jesus, injured, wounded, or dead, was forsaken by everyone except for the women.[19] The whole of our faith rests on that of a woman. Thus, a man who denigrates women is a fool indeed, if only because of the respect owed to the Queen of Heaven, in acknowledgement of her goodness, for she was so noble and worthy that she deserved to bear the son of God! God the Father honoured women greatly when He decided that she should be His wife and mother, the temple of God united with the Trinity. A woman should rightly be joyful and glad, since she shares the same form as the Virgin; for God never created anything as worthy or as perfect, apart from Jesus incarnate. Thus, anyone who criticizes women in any way at all is a real fool, since a woman sits on such a lofty throne next to her son and at our Father's right hand; a great honour indeed for woman as mother.[20] Nor do we ever find sweet Jesus denigrating them: instead He loved and held them in high esteem.

10   (595) God created woman in His noble image[21] and bestowed upon her the wisdom and insight necessary to achieve salvation, and the gift of understanding. He also gave her a most noble shape and she was created out of very noble material; for she was not fashioned out of the clay of the earth, but exclusively out of the rib of man, whose body was at that stage, to tell the truth, the most noble part of earthly creation.[22] And the authentic Old Testament stories in the Bible, which cannot be untrue, tell us that woman, not man, was created first in earthly paradise;[23] but as far as the deception is concerned, for which our mother Eve is blamed and which resulted in God's harsh sentence, I can assure you that she never did deceive Adam, but innocently swallowed and believed the words of the devil, which she thought were sincere and true, and with this conviction she went on to tell her husband. There was therefore neither trickery nor deceit in this, for innocence devoid of all hidden malice should

[19] Cf. Ch. 8, Abelard 2–3, S. Passion 1.
[20] Cf. Ch. 8, Abelard 7, Albertano 3.
[21] Christine's insistence that woman was created 'in God's image' has to be seen against a history of theological controversy: cf. Ch. 2, Augustine 5; Ch. 3, Gratian 4, 10; and d'Alverny 1977. The points in this paragraph are further developed in City 4 below.
[22] Cf. Ch. 8, Response to Richard 1–4; also in Leesce 1210–25.
[23] Cf. Ch. 2, Ambrose 2; Ch. 8, Abelard 6; Leesce 1226–8.

not be called deception.[24] No one deceives without intending to deceive, otherwise it is not real deception. . . .

11   (643) If one judges the matter correctly, one will discover that the so-called 'greatest evil' is capable of doing little harm. Women do not kill anyone, wound or torture them; they do not plot or carry out treacherous acts, they are not arsonists, nor do they disinherit anyone, administer poison, steal gold or silver, trick people out of their possessions or lawful inheritance, through fraudulent contracts, nor harm kingdoms, duchies, or empires.[25] They are hardly a source of evil, not even the worst of them. Usually one exception does not make a general rule. And if anyone wishes to insult me by citing historical or biblical examples of one, two, or several women who were wicked and reprehensible, they are still exceptional, for I am speaking about women in general and there are very few who indulge in such tricks.

12   (661) If someone says to me that women's nature and character are not conducive to their waging war, killing people, or kindling tinder to start fires, or committing similar acts, and that therefore no credit, praise, or advantage can or should be attached to them for avoiding or resisting such actions, my response, with due respect for the speaker, is to agree that their hearts are not predisposed to such behaviour nor to committing acts of cruelty. For woman's nature is noble, very compassionate, timid, and timorous. She is humble, gentle, self-effacing, and full of charity, loveable, devout, and quietly modest. She fears war, is innocent and pious; when annoyed, her anger is quick to subside; she cannot bear to witness cruelty or suffering, and in a word, this is the female character, which clearly stems from her nature.

13   (681) And any woman who is, by chance, not like this, is quite wrongly acting against her nature. For cruelty is reprehensible in a woman, who should be the source of pure gentleness. And because they are not accustomed or predisposed to shed blood or to kill, or to commit other heinous, ugly, and terrible crimes, and are therefore innocent of and indeed exempt from the greatest and most serious sins (for everyone is stained with some vice), they will therefore not

---

[24] Cf. Ch. 8, *Dives* 11. Christine's *simplement* ('innocently', 612) and *simplece* ('innocence', 617) attribute to Eve a quality much prized in women at this period.

[25] One of Christine's favourite themes: cf. *City* 15 below; also in Ch. 8, Marbod 6, *Dives* 10; and in *Leesce* 1177 ff., 3927 ff.

be found guilty of or be caught in the act of committing great misdeeds; thus, they will not be punished for them with either torments or suffering, because they are not guilty. Hence I can say, without being heretical, that God on high favoured them greatly in creating them without those qualities which make one likely to be damned;[26] for inclinations lead to actions, the results of which for many people weigh heavily on their souls. Thus it is much better not to have the inclination in the first place, which, if satisfied, would result in eternal death.

All this proves that men should not attack but cherish women; slanderers gain only a bad reputation anyway. Every man comes from a woman, and it is natural for woman—mother, sister, girlfriend—to bring him joy. Man is not disparaged by woman's worth, which passes from mother to son. But these things are said not to flatter women's vanity but to stir them to become yet more worthy. As for men who defame or trick women, the heaviest penalties of the God of Love are pronounced against them.

FROM *THE QUARREL OF THE ROSE*[*] (*LA QUERELLE DE LA ROSE*: C.1400–C.1403)

Christine was a key protagonist in a literary debate about the moral value of the *Romance of the Rose* which seems to have flared up at the time she was writing the *Letter of the God of Love*. Dignitaries of court and church took sides, Gontier and Pierre Col defending the *Rose* with Jean de Montreuil, and the Chancellor of the University of Paris formidably reinforcing Christine's own distaste for the poem. She thought Jean de Meun's part of the *Rose* rather dissolute; she censured among other things the use of indecent language, the condoning of deceitful behaviour, and the denigration of women. But since the exchange of letters is quite complex, brief excerpts only are given here to exemplify the debate about antifeminism and also to show what condescension Christine had to tolerate on the part of her male opponents.

Christine's Letter to Jean de Montreuil (1401): On the Speech of Genius, and Jean de Meun's Antifeminism

1   (16/163) What good can possibly come from it, and what point is there in [Jean de Meun's] excessive, violent, and totally unfounded criticism, denigration, and defamation of women, insofar as he claims that they are guilty of many a terrible vice and that their

---

[26] Repeated in *City* I. 14.2.
[*] New translation by Karen Pratt, with page and line references to the Old French edition by Eric Hicks, *Le Débat sur le Roman de la Rose* (Paris: Champion, 1977). For translation of the whole *Quarrel* see Baird and Kane, 1978. © Karen Pratt 1992.

behaviour is perverse in every conceivable way; yet, despite all the talking and the like each of his characters indulges in, he can never get his fill of the subject. For if you wish to tell me that the Jealous Man does this because he is governed by passion, I fail to see how it fits in with the role of Genius to encourage and urge men to go to bed with women without omitting to perform the act which he praises so highly. And Genius is the one who, more than any of the other characters, fulminates so vehemently against women, saying, in fact, 'Flee, flee, flee the venomous serpent.' Then he tells men to pursue them relentlessly.[27] There is a terrible contradiction here in ordering men to flee what he wishes them to pursue, and to pursue what he wishes them to flee. But since women are so perverse, he should not have commanded men to approach them at all; for he who fears harm ought to keep well out of its way. Thus he strongly forbids a man to reveal his secrets to a woman, who is so keen to discover them (so he claims, although I really do not know where the devil he found so much nonsense and irrelevant arguments, which he sets out in great detail). But I ask all those who really believe that his teaching is true and place so much faith in it, to tell me if they can how many men they have seen accused, killed, hanged, or publicly defamed by the accusations of their women?

Christine's Letter to Gontier Col (1401): 'Excessive Emotion'

2 (25/19) After you had read and thoroughly scrutinized my letter and since your erroneous position had been undermined and deflated by the truth, you wrote in a fit of impatience your second, more insulting, letter, criticizing me as a member of the female sex (which you claim to be excessively emotional by nature[28]) and accusing me of folly and presumption in daring to correct and contradict a teacher as renowned, well qualified and learned as you declare the author [Jean de Meun] of that work to be. Therefore you urge me insistently to recant and repent, after which mercy and compassion will still be extended to me, but if I do not, I shall be treated just like the publican.[29]

---

[27] Genius bids men flee from women (*RR* 35) yet afterwards summons all men to procreate (19505 ff.); so (Christine argues) his antifeminism does not project credible 'characterization' even if the Jealous Husband's does.
[28] Gontier's *impacience* is ironically juxtaposed with his allegation that Christine's *femmenin sexe* is *passioné*: cf. Ch. 6, *Corb. 1*, describing woman as a creature *passionato da mille passioni*.
[29] Matt. 9: 10 ff.

3   (25/29) Oh superior and ingenious intellect! Do not deliberately allow your keen mind to be clouded and narrow in its views. Consider the matter clearly and fairly, guided by the methods of the queen of learning—theology—and, far from condemning what I have written, you will ask yourself whether those particular passages I have criticized really do deserve to be praised. And moreover, you should carefully note throughout the work those things I take issue with and those I do not. And if you despise my arguments so much because of the inadequacy of my intellect, which you denigrate with the words 'like a woman [emotional by nature]' etc., rest assured that I do not consider this insulting or in any way defamatory, since I derive comfort from the knowledge that there are, have been, and continue to be huge numbers of excellent women who were and are highly praiseworthy and thoroughly versed in all the virtues, whom I would prefer to resemble than to be enriched with all of fortune's gifts. Furthermore, if for this reason you still insist on belittling my forceful arguments with your antifeminist attacks, please remember that a small dagger or knife point can pierce a great sack bulging and bursting with material possessions; and surely you know that a little weasel can attack a great lion and sometimes put it to flight. So, even if you threaten me with your insults and subtle reasoning, methods which generally create fear in the faint-hearted, do not for one moment think that I am fickle in my opinions or that my mind might easily be changed.[10]

Christine's Reply to Pierre Col (1402): Ambrose and Ecclesiasticus

Gontier Col's brother, Pierre, has joined in the fray on Jean de Meun's side. In responding to his letter, Christine notes his claim that St Ambrose somewhere criticizes women more harshly than Jean, on grounds of their habitual deceit.

4   (135/652) You say that St Ambrose was more critical of the female sex than [Jean] was, for he says that it is a sex practised in deception. My reply to this is that surely you are well aware that the pronouncements of the Church Fathers, and even the sermons of Jesus Christ himself, were meant to be understood on two levels. Thus it is necessary to realize that St Ambrose did not make such a statement against women themselves, for I am convinced that the good man would have wished to condemn only vice. For he knew full

---

[10]   Christine pointedly eschews the 'fickleness' (*légièreté*) attributed to women, as she notes in *Letter 7* above.

well that there were many holy women, but he wanted to say that it is because of the female sex that man frequently betrays his own soul.[31] Similarly, when Solomon said that the misdeed of a man is better than the good deed of a woman,[32] we know that it is wrong to take this literally. Yet Solomon himself can serve as an example of this; for the misdeed of a man would have been far better for him, whatever the circumstances, than any goodness he could see in the woman with whom he was so infatuated that he took to worshipping idols.[33] Solomon's statement could also be read as a prophecy, for the misdeed of Judas has been of far greater worth to us than the good deed of Judith, who killed Holofernes, or of any other woman.

FROM *THE CITY OF LADIES** (*LE LIVRE DE LA CITÉ DES DAMES* (1405–)

Augustine had written of the 'City of God' in contradistinction to the 'city of this world'. In writing of the establishment of a 'City of Ladies', therefore, Christine signals her ambition and her seriousness of purpose. But, more than Augustine's, her 'city' is a *defensive* structure: it is built on the reputation of women conspicuous in every field of endeavour or morality, but it is thereby above all a stronghold designed to offer new protection to the sex which has previously been totally undefended against the serried ranks of antifeminism. (Doubtless Christine is also advertising her opposition to the cynical Ovidian view, perpetuated in *Romance of the Rose* 7669 ff., that the 'fort' of womanhood defends itself from male importunity with a strategic laziness that aims at defeat.) The process of building is of course active as well as defensive; a reconstitution of what woman is and can be, as demonstrated by historical and legendary example. Christine draws extensively on Boccaccio's *De mulieribus claris* (*Concerning Famous Women*) in narrating these examples, which make up the bulk of her book. Few of them can be accommodated in the present volume, for it has seemed a greater priority to represent as fully as possible the framework they illustrate, namely Christine's point-by-point investigation of antifeminist shibboleths. Her questions are bold and penetrating; they reach frequently to the wellsprings of misogyny. Why, she asks, should husbands—and wives under their influence—be less happy at the birth of daughters than sons (II. 7.1)? The reasons suggested are anxieties about the cost of a daughter's dowry, and about safeguarding a young daughter from sexual corruption. Then comes the retort: sons cost a great deal more in education and in consum-

[31] Christine appeals to the argument for male responsibility, as in Ch. 8, Gower 2, *Dives* 19.
[32] Ecclus. 42: 14; in Ch. 1, Scripture 10.
[33] 3 Kgs. 11: 1–10; cf. Ch. 2, Jerome 24.
* Christine de Pizan, *The Book of the City of Ladies*, tr. Earl Jeffrey Richards (New York: Persea Books, 1982), 3–5, 17, 23–4, 26, 28–9, 71–2, 77, 80, 118–19, 127–8, 130–1, 165, 169–70, 185–6, 219–22. © Persea Books 1982. Reprinted by permission of the publisher. Old French text in Curnow edition (Christine de Pizan 1975).

ables, they easily slide into a dissolute life, and they are more interested in quick access to their inheritance than in caring for elderly parents—a task left to daughters while sons roam as they please. Although (but also because) all this might seem to understate the patriarchal mentality which in the Middle Ages privileged the male line *per se*, such an analysis is thoroughly absorbing, not least for the extent to which it might be conditioned by, for instance, conventional literary arguments on the inconveniences of off-spring, a sub-category of misogyny.[14] Then again, she crushes all the fuss about women's dress in one calm statement: one's conscience is not to be judged by what one wears.[15]

The *City* is a response to a wide range of misogynistic texts. Some of the worst offenders are paraded in 1. 9 and 1. 10 (see 8 below). But Christine chooses the compendious *Lamentations* of Matheolus (probably in Jehan Le Fèvre's translation) as the chief bogey. The opening of the *City* tells of her starting to read this for relaxation, but finding herself distinctly unamused.

Reaction to Matheolus

1 (1. 1.1) Just the sight of this book, even though it was of no authority, made me wonder how it happened that so many different men—and learned men among them—have been and are so inclined to express, both in speaking and in their treatises and writings, so many wicked insults about women and their behaviour. Not only one or two, and not even just this Matheolus (for this book had a bad name anyway and was intended as a satire), but, more generally, judging from the treatises of all philosophers and poets and from all the orators—it would take too long to mention their names—it seems that they all speak from one and the same mouth. They all concur in one conclusion: that the behaviour of women is inclined to and full of every vice.

2 Thinking deeply about these matters, I began to examine my character and conduct as a natural woman and, similarly, I con-sidered other women whose company I frequently kept—princesses, great ladies, women of the middle and lower classes—who had graciously told me of their most private and intimate thoughts, hoping that I could judge impartially and in good conscience whether the testimony of so many notable men could be true. To the best of my knowledge, no matter how long I confronted or dissected the problem, I could not see or realize how their claims could be true when compared to the natural behaviour and character of women. Yet I still argued vehemently against women, saying that it would be impossible that so many famous men—such solemn scholars, pos-

sessed of such deep and great understanding, so clear-sighted in all
things, as it seemed—could have spoken falsely on so many occasions that I could hardly find a book on morals where, even before I
had read it in its entirety, I did not find several chapters or certain
sections attacking women, no matter who the author was. . . . Like a
gushing fountain, a series of authorities, whom I recalled one after
another, came to mind, along with their opinions on this topic. And I
finally decided that God formed a vile creature[36] when He made
woman. . . .

Sunk in grief, Christine experiences a visitation by three crowned and light-
giving women later identified as Reason, Rectitude, and Justice. Reason
assures her that the word of the authorities—even Aristotle—is not infall-
ible, while daily experience disproves the poets' satires on wives. The trio
have come to supply the defence that women have lacked in centuries spent
suffering, and believing, criticism of their sex. It is destined that Christine
shall build a citadel for worthy women. Foundations can be prepared by
digging out the 'dirt'—getting at the roots—of misogyny, an unnatural and
irrational phenomenon for which there are various motives.

What Motivates Antifeminism?

3   (I. 8.3) [Reason] 'Some have attacked women with good intentions, that is, in order to draw men who have gone astray away from
the company of vicious and dissolute women, with whom they might
be infatuated, or in order to keep these men from going mad on
account of such women, and also so that every man might avoid an
obscene and lustful life. They have attacked all women in general
because they believe that women are made up of every abomination.'
    'My lady,' I said then, 'excuse me for interrupting you here, but
have such authors acted well, since they were prompted by a
laudable intention? For intention, the saying goes, judges the man.'
    'That is a misleading position, my good daughter,' she said.
. . . 'Causing any damage or harm to one party in order to help
another party is not justice,[37] and likewise, attacking all feminine
conduct is contrary to the truth, just as I will show you with a
hypothetical case. Let us suppose they did this intending to draw
fools away from foolishness. It would be as if I attacked fire—a very
good and necessary element nevertheless—because some people

---

[36] Referring to the myth of female 'deformity': see 4 below.
[37] Rectitude later (II. 54.1) insists that the 'benefit' is partisan, if male trickery is
deleted from the record.

burnt themselves, or water because someone drowned.[38] The same can be said of all good things which can be used well or used badly. But one must not attack them if fools abuse them. . . .'

The city's foundations need to be cleared of debris, i.e. antifeminist detritus such as Ovid's *Art of Love* and *Cures for Love* (described as the embittered products of a warped ex-lecher) and the pseudo-scientific *Secrets of Women*[39] whose author perpetrates palpable 'lies' about the 'defects' of women's bodies.

Imperfection and Impiety

4   (I. 9.2) [*Christine*] 'I recall that, among other things, after he has discussed the impotence and weakness which cause the formation of a feminine body in the womb of the mother, he says that Nature is completely ashamed when she sees that she has formed such a body, as though it were something imperfect.[40]

'But, sweet friend, don't you see the overweening madness, the irrational blindness which prompt such observations? Is Nature, the chambermaid of God, a greater mistress than her master, almighty God, from whom comes such authority, who, when He willed, took the form of man and women from His thought when it came to His holy will to form Adam from the mud of the ground in the field of Damascus and, once created, brought him into the terrestrial Paradise which was and is the most worthy place in this world here below?[41] There Adam slept, and God formed the body of woman from one of his ribs, signifying that she should stand at his side as a companion and never lie at his feet like a slave, and also that he should love her as his own flesh.[42] If the supreme craftsman was not ashamed to create and form the feminine body, would Nature then have been ashamed? It is the height of folly to say this! Indeed, how was she formed? I don't know if you have already noted this: she was created in the image of God. How can any mouth dare to slander the vessel which bears such a noble imprint? But some men are foolish enough to think, when they hear that God made man in His image,

[38] An argument echoed in Ch. 8, Gower 2, and still current in Webster's *White Devil* III. ii. 203–6.
[39] This 13th-c. gynaecological treatise, which exaggerated the negative associations of menstruation, was commonly ascribed to Albertus Magnus, not Aristotle, and was circulating widely at this time: Lemay 1978.
[40] Cf. 2 above. Nature's 'shame' is also quoted in *Math.* 30: on the theory of 'imperfection', see Ch. 1, Aristotle and Galen extracts.
[41] See *Letter 10* above and notes for some of the conventions in this paragraph.
[42] This is the 'rib topos' (D'Avray and Tausche 1980, 106): cf. Ch. 8, *Dives 1*.

that this refers to the material body. This was not the case, for God had not yet taken a human body. The soul is meant, the intellectual spirit which lasts eternally just like the deity. God created the soul and placed wholly similar souls, equally good and noble, in the feminine and in the masculine bodies. Now, to turn to the question of the creation of the body, woman was made by the supreme crafts- man. In what place was she created? In the terrestrial Paradise. From what substance? Was it vile matter? No, it was the noblest substance which had ever been created: it was from the body of man from which God made woman.'

5 'My lady, according to what I understand from you, woman is a most noble creature. But even so, Cicero says that a man should never serve any woman and that he who does so debases himself, for no man should ever serve anyone lower than him.' She replied, 'The man or the woman in whom resides greater virtue is the higher; neither the loftiness nor the lowliness of a person lies in the body according to the sex, but in the perfection of conduct and vir- tues. . . .'[43]

After opposing a couple of antifeminist apophthegms ascribed to Cato, Reason argues that, since so few women are found in brothels or taverns, sobriety rather than lechery or gluttony is their natural characteristic; they frequent churches instead.

6 (I. 10.1) [Reason] 'You can see them quite well in big crowds and groups near churches during sermons and at confessions, reciting the Our Father and the Offices.' 'This is obvious, my lady,' I said, 'but these men say that women go there all dressed up to show off their beauty and to attract men to their love.'[44] She responded, 'This would be believable if you saw only young and pretty women there. But if you watch carefully, for every young woman whom you see, you will see twenty or thirty old women dressed simply and honestly as they pray in these holy places. And if women possess such piety, they also possess charity, for who is it who visits and comforts the sick, helps the poor, takes care of the hospitals, and buries the dead? It seems to me that these are all women's works and that these same works are the supreme footprints which God commands us to follow.'[45] . . .

[43] Cf. Ch. 6, *Corb.* 10.
[44] Alleged in *Math.* II. 947 ff.; and see Ch. 6, *RR* 19, and Ch. 4, *Ag. Marr.* L4, on religion as pretext.
[45] i.e., women perform the 'works of mercy' commended by medieval preachers: cf. Ch. 8, *Gesta* 1. (This response, that women frequent churches because devout Catholics, is precedented in *Leesce* 1777–804.)

The Old Proverb: Women, Talk, and Tears

Christine mentions the proverb used by men to disparage women: 'God made women to speak, weep, and sew.'[46] Reason protests that Mary Magdalene earned God's special grace through her tears, while the great luminary of the Church, St Augustine, was converted by his mother's tears. Then she confronts the criticism of woman's speech.

7   (I. 10.5) [Reason] 'If women's language had been so blame-worthy and of such small authority, as some men argue, our Lord Jesus Christ would never have deigned to wish that so worthy a mystery as His most gracious Resurrection be first announced by a woman, just as He commanded the blessed Magdalene, to whom He first appeared on Easter Day, to report and announce it to His Apostles and to Peter.' [Christine] '. . . Some foolish preachers teach that God first appeared to a woman because He knew well that she did not know how to keep quiet so that this way the news of His Resurrection would be spread more rapidly.'[47]

8   She answered, 'My daughter, you have spoken well when you call them fools who have said this. It is not enough for them to attack women. They impute even to Jesus Christ such blasphemy, as if to say that He wished to reveal this great perfection and dignity through a vice. I do not know how a man could dare to say this, even in jest, as God should not be brought in on such joking matters. But as for the first question, regarding talking—in fact, it was fortunate for the woman from Canaan who was so great a talker and who would not stop yelling and howling after Jesus Christ as she followed Him through the streets of Jerusalem, crying, "Have mercy on me, Lord, for my daughter is sick."[48] And what did the good Lord do? He in whom all mercy abounded and abounds and from whom a single word from the heart sufficed for Him to show mercy! He seemed to take pleasure in the many words pouring from the mouth of this woman ever perseverant in her prayer. But why did He act like this? In order to test her constancy; for when He compared her to the dogs—which seemed a little harsh because she followed a foreign cult and not that of God—she was not ashamed to speak both well

---

[46] For the adage *fallere, flere, nere, statuit deus in mulier* ('God made woman to lie, cry, and spin') cf. Ch. 7, *WoB* 31. Christine touches only lightly on women's 'spinning', which is commended in Ch. 8, Marbod 5, and in *Bien des Fames* 83 ff.: Fiero et al. 1989, 110–13.

[47] As asserted in *Math.* II. 2309 ff. and elsewhere (e.g. Langland, *Piers Plowman* 'B' XIX. 161–2). But see Ch. 8, Abelard 3, Albertano 3.

[48] Matt. 15: 22–8.

and wisely when she replied, "Sire, that is most true, but the little dogs live from the crumbs from their master's table." "O most wise woman, who taught you to speak this way? You have won your cause through your prudent language which stems from your good will." And one could clearly see this, for our Lord, turning to His Apostles, testified from His mouth that He had never found such faith in all of Israel and granted her request. Who could sufficiently sum up this honour paid to the feminine sex which the jealous despise?'

Reason adds that Christ did not disdain to talk to the Samaritan woman at the well, and that the Gospels record the fortunate words of the woman who couldn't stop herself crying, 'Blessed is the womb which bore you!'[49]

Not an Inferior Intellect

The book is particularly concerned to repudiate insinuations about the inadequacy of women's minds. Reason attributes woman's exclusion from legal office, not to the 'Caphurnia' fantasy (*Matheolus* 10: Chapter 6 above), but to a sensible distribution of functions between the sexes.[50] But women are perfectly fit for executive roles; indeed, what they might lack in physical power they make up for in sharpness of mind. Although their knowledge is frequently limited through their restriction to a domestic realm, examples prove not only their ability to learn but also their innovative capacity— especially the case of Nicostrata, or 'Carmentis', who gave Italy laws and a new language.

9   (I. 33.1) [*Reason*] 'This lady knew through divine inspiration and the spirit of prophecy (in which she was remarkably distinguished, in addition to the other graces she possessed) how in time to come this land would be ennobled by excellence and famous over all the countries of the world. Therefore it seemed to her that, once the grandeur of the Roman Empire, which would rule the entire world, had been established, it would not be right for the Romans to use the strange and inferior letters and characters of another country. Moreover, in order to show forth her wisdom and the excellence of her mind to the centuries to come, she worked and studied so hard that she invented her own letters, which were completely different from those of other nations; that is, she established the Latin

[49] John 4: 3–26 and Luke 11: 27–8. Both instances were noted in woman's favour by Abelard (Scott Moncrieff 1974, 162–4), and the second is quoted by Margery Kempe in defence of women 'speaking of God': Meech and Allen 1940, 126.
[50] Reason conservatively accepts the assumption in canon law (Raming 1976, 28) that for women to practise law would be an impairment of the *verecundia* or modesty (*City* 'onnesteté') befitting their sex.

alphabet and syntax, spelling, the difference between vowels and consonants, as well as a complete introduction to the science of grammar. She gave and taught these letters to the people and wished that they be widely known. This was hardly a minor or unprofitable contribution to learning which this woman invented, nor one for which she merits slight gratitude; for, thanks to the subtlety of this teaching and to the great utility and profit which have since accrued to the world, one can say that nothing more worthy in the world was ever invented.'[51]

10   (I. 37.1) [Christine] 'My lady, I greatly admire what I have heard you say, that so much good has come into the world by virtue of the understanding of women. These men usually say that women's knowledge is worthless. In fact, when someone says something foolish, the widely voiced insult is that this is women's knowledge. In brief, the typical opinions and comments of men claim that women have been and are useful in the world only for bearing children and sewing. . . . (1. 38.4) Henceforth, let all writers be silent who speak badly of women, let all of them be silent—those who have attacked women and who still attack them in their books and poems, and all their accomplices and supporters too—let them lower their eyes, ashamed for having dared to speak so badly, in view of the truth which runs counter to their poems; this noble lady, Carmentis, through the profundity of her understanding, taught them like a schoolmistress—nor can they deny it—the lesson thanks to which they consider themselves so lofty and honoured; that is, she taught them the Latin alphabet!'

The Propaganda against Wives

In Book II, Rectitude takes over Reason's role. Christine asks her whether 'Valerius' (Walter Map) and Theophrastus were right when they claimed that the shortcomings of wives destroy men's peace in marriage, and that servants provide more loyal care.[52]

11   (II. 13.1) [Rectitude] 'I assure you that women have never done what these books say. Indeed, I have not the slightest doubt that whoever cared to investigate the debate on marriage in order to write a new book in accordance with the truth would uncover other data. How many women are there actually, dear friend—and you yourself know—who because of their husbands' harshness spend their weary

---

[51] This achievement is also presented in *Leesce* 3618–31.
[52] Cf. Ch. 2, Jerome 16.

lives in the bond of marriage in greater suffering than if they were slaves among the Saracens? My God! How many harsh beatings—without cause and without reason—how many injuries, how many cruelties, insults, humiliations, and outrages have so many upright women suffered, none of whom cried out for help? And consider all the women who die of hunger and grief with a home full of children, while their husbands carouse dissolutely or go on binges in every tavern all over town, and still the poor women are beaten by their husbands when they return, and *that* is their supper![53] . . . For men are masters over their wives, and not the wives mistresses over their husbands, who would never allow their wives to have such authority. . . .'

12 (II. 19.1) [*Christine*] 'I still recall that the philosopher Theophrastus, whom I spoke of above, said that women hate their husbands when they are old and also that women do not love men of learning or scholars, for he claims the duties entailed in the upkeep of women are totally incompatible with the study of books.'[54] She replied, 'Oh dear friend, keep still! I can immediately provide you with examples contradicting and disproving such statements.'

13 (II. 21.1) 'The noble lady Xanthippe possessed great learning and goodness, and because of these qualities she married Socrates, the greatest philosopher. Although he was already quite old and cared more about searching for knowledge and researching in books than obtaining soft and new things for his wife, the valiant lady nevertheless did not stop loving him but rather thought of the excellence of his learning, his outstanding virtue, and his constancy, which, in her sovereign love and reverence, she considered to be a sign of his excellence. Upon learning that her husband had been condemned to death by the Athenians because he had attacked them for worshipping idols and had said that there was but one God, whom one must worship and serve, this brave lady could not bear it, but, completely dishevelled, overcome with grief and weeping, she quickly rushed to the palace where her husband was being held, and she found him among the deceitful judges who were administering to him the poison to end his life. Arriving at the moment when Socrates was about to drink, to put the cup to his mouth to drink the poison, she rushed towards him and angrily tore the cup from his hands and

---

[53] Christine characteristically appeals to experience—though the paradigm envisaged here is conventional (*Leesce* 3763–70; *Piers Plowman* 'B' v. 358–9).
[54] Cf. Ch. 2, Jerome 20.

poured it all out on the ground.[55] Socrates reproved her for this and urged her to be patient and comforted her. As she could not prevent his death, she was very grieved and said, "What a great wrong and what an enormous loss to put such a just man to death wrongfully and sinfully." Socrates continued to console her, saying that it was better that he died wrongfully than justifiably, and so he died. But the grief in the heart of the woman who loved him did not abate for the rest of her life.'

The Question of Constancy

Biblical and other examples are presented to disprove women's alleged unchastity, and Lucretia's story is told to refute the misogynistic insinuation (which angers Christine) that women offer only token resistance to sexual violence. Then she turns to the allegation of inconstancy.

14   (II. 47.1) [Rectitude] 'Let me point out to you the contradiction in what these men say concerning the variability and inconstancy of women: since they all generally accuse women of being delicate and frail by nature, you would assume that they think that they are constant, or, at the very least, that women are less constant than they are. Yet they demand more constancy from women than they themselves can muster, for these men, who claim to be so strong and of such noble condition, are unable to prevent themselves from falling into many, even graver, faults and sins, not all of them out of ignorance, but rather out of pure malice, knowing well that they are in the wrong. All the same, they excuse themselves for this by claiming it is human nature to sin. When a few women lapse (and when these men themselves, through their own strivings and their own power, are the cause), then as far as these men are concerned it is completely a matter of fragility and inconstancy. It seems to me right, nevertheless, to conclude—since they claim women are so fragile—that these men should be somewhat more tolerant of women's weaknesses and not hold something to be a crime for women which they consider only a peccadillo for themselves. For the law does not maintain, nor can any such written opinion be found, that permits them and not women to sin, that their vice is more excusable. In fact, these men allow themselves liberties which they are unwilling to tolerate in women, and thus they—and they are many—perpetrate many insults and outrages in word and deed. Nor

[55] This episode is probably presented in conscious antithesis to Xanthippe's more notorious action, pouring slops over her husband: cf. Ch. 2, Jerome 20; and Ch. 7, WoB 51.

do they deign to repute women strong and constant for having endured such men's harsh outrages. In this way men try in every question to have the right on their side—they want to have it both ways!'[56]

Men have little to boast about in the domain of constancy, to judge from certain Roman Emperors and some subsequent dignitaries of Church and State.

15   (II. 49.5) [Rectitude] 'Regardless of what philosophers and other authors may say about the changeableness of women, you will never find such perversion in women as you encounter in a great number of men. The most evil women whom you will find written about were Athalia and Jezebel her mother, queens of Jerusalem, who persecuted the people of Israel; Brunhilde, queen of France; and several others.[57] But consider, for my sake, the perversity of Judas Iscariot who cruelly betrayed his good master whose apostle he was and who had done so many good things for him, or the harshness and cruelty of the Jews and of the people of Israel who killed not only Jesus Christ out of envy but also several holy prophets who lived before Him as well: they murdered some, and slaughtered the others with other methods. Take the example of Julian the Apostate, whom some consider to have been one of the Antichrists because of his perversity, or of Denis, the treacherous tyrant of Sicily,[58] who was so detestable that just reading about his life is a dishonest act, and along with these consider all the evil kings in various countries, disloyal emperors, heretical popes, and other unbelieving prelates filled with greed—the Antichrists who must come—and you will find that men should really keep quiet and that women should bless and praise God who placed their precious souls in feminine vessels.'

Christine applauds the evidence of female constancy (such as the instances of Griselda, and Florence of Rome), but knows her critics will maintain that not all—in fact very few—women are good.

16   (II. 53.2) [Rectitude] 'What a surprise that all women are not good! In the entire city of Nineveh, which was so large, not a single

---

[56] This discussion of the 'double standard' should be compared with Ch. 8, *S. Passion* 2, *Dives* 3–7, and Ch. 2, Jerome 26.

[57] Athalia and Jezebel exemplify wickedness in Ch. 4, Marbod 4, and in *Math.* II. 2547–66. On Judas, cf. Ch. 8, Marbod 6.

[58] Emperor Julian campaigned to revert to paganism during his brief rule from AD 361. Denis of Sicily is in a catalogue of male reprobates in *Leesce* 3812–19.

good man could be found when Jonah the prophet went there on behalf of our Lord to destroy it unless it turned away from its evil.[59] It was even worse in the city of Sodom, as was obvious when fire from heaven destroyed it after Lot's departure. Moreover, note that in the company of Jesus Christ, where there were only twelve men, there was still one very bad man among them. And men dare to say that all women must be good and that one should stone those who are not! I would simply ask them to look at themselves and then let him who is without sin cast the first stone.'[60]

The Steadfast Female Martyr

In Book III, Justice identifies for Christine the most noble occupants of the completed City of Ladies, after establishing the Virgin Mary as 'Empress'. First come Mary Magdalene and the other women who remained so devoted and steadfast during Christ's Passion. Next come the women martyrs, whom God favoured with no less constancy and courage than He did men.

17   (III. 3.2) 'First let me tell of the blessed Catherine, the daughter of King Costus of Alexandria.[61] This holy maiden found herself at the age of eighteen the heiress of her father and governed herself and her inheritance nobly. She was a Christian woman, totally dedicated to God, and refused to marry. It happened that the emperor Maxentius came to Alexandria on a solemn feast day when the city was busy with splendid preparations for the imposing sacrifices to the gods. Catherine was in the palace and so heard the bellowing of the sacrificial animals and the din of the musical instruments. After enquiring about what was going on, she learned that the emperor had already gone to the temple to sacrifice, and she hurried there and began to reprimand the emperor with learned arguments. As a well-lettered woman, versed in the various branches of knowledge, she proceeded to prove on the basis of philosophical arguments that there is but one God, Creator of all things, and that He alone should be worshipped and no other. When the emperor heard this beautiful, noble, and authoritative maiden speak, he was completely amazed and utterly speechless; nevertheless, he stared at her intently. He summoned from everywhere the wisest philosophers known in the land of Egypt, then quite famous for philosophy, and some fifty philosophers were assembled who were quite unhappy to learn why

[59] An oblique retort to the oft-cited Eccles. 7: 28 (one good woman not found among a thousand).
[60] Alluding to the Woman Taken in Adultery: cf. Ch. 8, *Dives* 8.
[61] Medieval tradition held that St Catherine was persecuted in AD 307.

they had been sent for, and said that a trifle had moved the emperor to assemble them from such distant lands in order to debate with a maiden.[62] In short, when the day of the debate arrived, the blessed Catherine so successfully overwhelmed them with her arguments that they were confounded and unable to answer her questions. On this account the emperor was beside himself with anger, which had no effect at all, for they all converted, thanks to the divine grace in the holy words of the virgin, and confessed the name of Jesus Christ. The emperor had them burnt alive for this disrespect, and the holy virgin comforted them in their martyrdom. . . .'

18 'The tyrant Maxentius, in his great lust for the blessed Catherine, tried through flattery to bend her to his will. Seeing that this was of no use to him, he turned to threats and then to tortures. After having her roughly beaten and then imprisoned for twelve days without visitors, he tried to weaken her with hunger. The angels of the Lord, however, were with her and comforted her. And when she was brought before the emperor after the twelve days, he saw that she was healthier and fresher than before and, convinced she had received visitors, ordered the prison guards tortured. But Catherine, taking pity on them, claimed that she had received no comfort except from heaven. The emperor did not know what harsher tortures he could use to compel her, and so, following his prefect's advice, he had wheels built and fitted out with razors which turned against one another so that whatever was between them would be sliced in two. Then he had Catherine placed naked between these wheels. During the entire time, with her hands clasped in prayer, she worshipped God, whereupon the angels descended and with great force broke the wheels apart so that the torturers themselves were killed. Upon seeing the miracles which God had performed for Catherine, the emperor's wife was converted and attacked the emperor for what he was doing. She went to visit the holy virgin in prison and asked her to pray to God on her behalf, and because of this the emperor had his wife tortured and her breasts torn off. And the virgin told her, "Do not be afraid of the tortures, most noble queen, for today you will be received into endless joy." The emperor had his wife beheaded, along with a large number of other converts. The emperor then asked Catherine to be his wife, but, after he realized that she was rejecting all of his requests, he finally issued the sentence that she be

[62] Right from the earliest known account written in 866 by Emperor Basil I, St Catherine was celebrated as a Christian intellectual, so it is no surprise that Christine (champion of woman's talent for learning) gives her pride of place here.

beheaded. And she prayed, asking intercession for all who remembered her passion and for all who invoked her name in their suffering, and a voice came from heaven declaring that her prayer had been granted. So she finished her martyrdom, and milk poured from her body rather than blood. And the angels took her holy body and carried it to Mount Sinai. . . .'

Bibliography

Abelard and Heloise, correspondence: *see* McLaughlin, Muckle, Radice, and Scott Moncrieff entries.

AERS, D., *Community, Gender, and Individual Identity: English Writing 1360–1430* (London: Routledge, 1988).

AGONITO, R. (ed.), *History of Ideas on Woman* (New York: G. P. Putnam's Sons, 1977).

ALBERTANO OF BRESCIA, *Albertani Brixiensis Liber consolationis et consilii*, ed. T. Sundby, Chaucer Soc., 2nd ser., viii (London, 1873).

ALLEN, Sr PRUDENCE, RSM, *The Concept of Woman: The Aristotelian Revolution 750 BC–AD 1250* (Montreal: Eden Press, 1985).

—— 'Plato, Aristotle, and the Concept of Woman in Early Jewish Philosophy', *Florilegium*, 9 (1987), 89–111.

AMBROSE, St, *Expositio evangelii secundum Lucam*, ed. M. Adriaen, CCSL, xiv (Turnhout: Brepols, 1957).

—— *Hexameron, Paradise, and Cain and Abel*, tr. J. J. Savage, FOC, xlii (New York: Fathers of the Church, Inc., 1961).

—— *The Principal Works of St Ambrose*, tr. H. de Romestin, Select Library of Nicene and Post-Nicene Fathers, 2nd ser., x (Oxford: James Parker; and New York: Christian Literature Co., 1896).

ANDREAS CAPELLANUS, *Andreas Capellanus On Love*, ed. and tr. P. G. Walsh (London: Duckworth, 1982).

AQUINAS, St THOMAS, *Summa Theologiae*, gen. ed. Thomas Gilby, OP, 60 vols. (London: Blackfriars, in conjunction with Eyre and Spottiswoode; and New York: McGraw-Hill, 1963–).

ARISTOTLE, *Generation of Animals*, tr. A. L. Peck (Cambridge, Mass.: Harvard University Press, 1963).

ASTON, M., 'Lollard Women Priests?' in her *Lollards and Reformers* (London: Hambledon Press, 1984), 49–70.

ATKINSON, C. W., ' "Precious Balsam in a Fragile Glass": The Ideology of Virginity in the Later Middle Ages', *Journal of Family History*, 8 (1983), 131–43.

AUGUSTINE, St, *Adulterous Marriages*, tr. C. T. Huegelmeyer, in *Saint Augustine: Treatises on Marriage*, tr. C. T. Wilcox, M. M. Charles, C. T. Huegelmeyer and others, FOC, xxvii (Washington, DC: Catholic University of America Press, 1955), 61–132.

—— *City of God*, tr. H. Bettenson (Harmondsworth: Penguin, 1984).

—— *Confessions*, tr. R. S. Pine-Coffin (Harmondsworth: Penguin, 1961).

—— *The Literal Meaning of Genesis*, tr. J. H. Taylor, Ancient Christian Writers, nos. 41–2 (New York: Newman Press, 1982).

—— *Earlier Writings*, tr. J. H. S. Burleigh, Library of Christian Classics, vi (London: SCM Press, 1953).

—— *The Trinity*, tr. Stephen McKenna, FOC, xlv (Washington, DC: Catholic University of America Press, 1963).

304   BIBLIOGRAPHY

BADEL, PIERRE-YVES, *Le Roman de la Rose au XIV* *siècle: étude de réception de l'œuvre* (Geneva: Droz, 1980).
BAILEY, D. S., *The Man–Woman Relation in Christian Thought* (London: Longmans, 1959).
BAIRD, J. L., and KANE, J. R., *La Querelle de la Rose: Letters and Documents* (Chapel Hill: University of North Carolina Press, 1978).
BEER, J. (tr.), *Master Richard's Bestiary of Love and Response* (Berkeley: University of California Press, 1986).
BELL, LINDA A. (ed.), *Visions of Women* (Clifton, NJ: Humanities Press, 1983).
BELL, SUSAN G., 'Christine de Pizan (1364–1430): Humanism and the Problem of a Studious Woman', *Feminist Studies*, 3 (1976), 173–84.
BENNETT, J. A. W., and SMITHERS, G. V., *Early Middle English Verse and Prose* (Oxford: Clarendon Press, 1966).
BENSON, L. D. (ed.), *The Riverside Chaucer* (Boston, Mass.: Houghton Mifflin, 1987; and Oxford: Oxford University Press, 1989).
BENTON, JOHN F., 'Trotula, Women's Problems, and the Professionalism of Medicine in the Middle Ages', *Bulletin of the History of Medicine*, 59 (1985), 30–53.
BERNARDUS SILVESTRIS, *Commentary on the First Six Books of Virgil's 'Aeneid'*, tr. E. G. Schreiber and T. E. Maresca (Lincoln: University of Nebraska Press, 1979).
BLAMIRES, ALCUIN, *The Canterbury Tales* (London: Macmillan, 1987).
—— 'The Wife of Bath and Lollardy', *Medium Ævum*, 58 (1989), 224–42.
BLOCH, R. HOWARD, 'Medieval Misogyny', *Representations*, 20 (1987), 1–24.
BOCCACCIO, GIOVANNI, *Concerning Famous Women*, tr. G. A. Guarino (London: Allen & Unwin, 1964).
—— *Il Corbaccio*, ed. T. Nurmela, Suomalaisen Tiedakatemian Toimituksia: Annales Academiae Scientiarum Fennicae, ser. B, no. 146 (Helsinki, 1968).
—— *The Corbaccio*, tr. A. K. Cassell (Urbana: University of Illinois Press, 1975).
—— *The Decameron*, tr. G. H. McWilliam (Harmondsworth: Penguin, 1972).
The Book of Margery Kempe, ed. S. B. Meech and H. E. Allen, EETS 212 (London: Oxford University Press, 1940).
BOREN, J. L, 'Alysoun of Bath and the Vulgate "Perfect Wife"', *Neuphilologische Mitteilungen*, 76 (1975), 247–56.
BORNSTEIN, D. (ed.), *Ideals for Women in the Works of Christine de Pizan* (Detroit: Michigan Consortium for Medieval and Early Modern Studies, 1981).
BØRRESEN, K., *Subordination and Equivalence: The Nature and Role of Women in Augustine and Thomas Aquinas*, tr. C. H. Talbot (Washington, DC: University Press of America, 1981).
BROOKE, CHRISTOPHER N. L., *The Medieval Idea of Marriage* (Oxford: Oxford University Press, 1989).
BROWN, BEATRICE (ed.), *The Southern Passion*, EETS, os 169 (London: Oxford University Press, 1927).
BROWN, CARLETON, 'Mulier est Hominis Confusio', *Modern Language Notes*, 35 (1920), 479–82.

BROWN, D. CATHERINE, *Pastor and Laity in the Theology of Jean Gerson* (Cambridge: Cambridge University Press, 1987).

BROWN, PETER, *The Body and Society: Men, Women, and Sexual Renunciation in Early Christianity* (New York: Columbia University Press, 1988).

BÜCHER, K., *Die Frauenfrage im Mittelalter* (Tübingen, 1922).

BULLOUGH, V. L., 'Medieval Medical and Scientific Views of Women', *Viator*, 4 (1973), 485–501.

—— and BULLOUGH, BONNIE, *The Subordinate Sex: A History of Attitudes toward Women* (Urbana, Ill.: University of Illinois Press, 1973).

CAIRD, G. B., 'Paul and Women's Liberty', *Bulletin of the John Rylands Library*, 54 (1971), 268–81.

CAPES, W. W., (ed.), *Registrum Johannis Trefnant* (Hereford, 1914).

CARRUTHERS, M., 'The Wife of Bath and the Painting of Lions', *Publications of the Modern Language Association*, 94 (1979), 209–22.

CASSELL, A. K., 'The Crow of the Fable and the *Corbaccio*: A Suggestion for the Title', *Modern Language Notes*, 85 (1970), 83–91.

—— '*Il Corbaccio* and the Secundus Tradition', *Comparative Literature*, 25 (1973), 352–60.

—— (tr.), *The Corbaccio* by Giovanni Boccaccio (Urbana: University of Illinois Press, 1975).

CHAUCER, GEOFFREY, *The Riverside Chaucer*, ed. L. D. Benson (Boston, Mass.: Houghton Mifflin, 1987; and Oxford: Oxford University Press, 1989).

CHRISTINE de PIZAN, *Œuvres Poétiques*, ed. M. Roy, SATF (Paris: 1886–91).

—— *The Book of the City of Ladies*, tr. E. J. Richards (New York: Persea Books, 1982).

CLARK, ELIZABETH, *Jerome, Chrysostom, and Friends* (New York: Edwin Mellen, 1979).

—— *Women in the Early Church*, Message of the Fathers of the Church ser., xiii (Wilmington, Del.: Michael Glazier, 1983).

CONLEE, J. W. (ed.), *Middle English Debate Poetry: A Critical Anthology* (East Lansing, Mich.: Colleagues Press, 1991).

CONROY, C., *1–2 Samuel, 1–2 Kings* (Wilmington, Del.: Michael Glazier, 1983).

COURTNEY, E., *A Commentary on the Satires of Juvenal* (London: Athlone, 1980).

CRANE, T. F., *The Exempla or Illustrative Stories from the Sermones Vulgares of Jacques de Vitry* (London: Folk-Lore Society, 1890).

CROW, J. (ed.), *Les Quinze Joyes de mariage* (Oxford: Blackwell, 1969).

CURNOW, M. 'The *Livre de la Cité des Dames* of Christine de Pisan: A Critical Edition', Ph.D. dissertation, Vanderbilt University, 1975.

D'ALVERNY, M.-T., 'Comment les théologiens et les philosophes voient la femme', *Cahiers de civilisation médiévale*, 20 (1977), 105–29.

D'AVRAY, D. L., and TAUSCHE, M., 'Marriage Sermons in *ad status* Collections of the Central Middle Ages,' *Archives d'histoire doctrinale et littéraire du moyen âge*, 47 (1980), 71–119.

DELANY, S., *Medieval Literary Politics: Shapes of Ideology* (Manchester: Manchester University Press, 1990).

DELHAYE, P., 'Le Dossier anti-matrimonial de l'*Adversus Jovinianum* et son influence sur quelques écrits latins du xiie siècle', *Mediaeval Studies*, 13 (1951), 65–86.

DESCHAMPS, EUSTACHE, *Le Miroir de mariage*, in *Œuvres complètes*, ix, ed. G. Raynaud, SATF (Paris: Firmin-Didot, 1894).

DINSHAW, C., *Chaucer's Sexual Poetics* (Madison: University of Wisconsin Press, 1989).

Dives and Pauper, i., pts. 1 and 2, ed. P. Barnum, EETS 275, 280 (London: Oxford University Press, 1976 and 1980).

DOW, B. H., *The Varying Attitude towards Women in French Literature of the Fifteenth Century: The Opening Years* (New York: Institute of French Studies, 1936).

DRONKE, P., *Abelard and Heloise in Medieval Testimonies* (Glasgow: University of Glasgow Press, 1976).

—— *Women Writers of the Middle Ages: A Critical Study of Texts from Perpetua to Marguerite Porete* (Cambridge: Cambridge University Press, 1984).

EICHMANN, RAYMOND, 'The Anti-feminism of the Fabliaux', *French Literature Series*, 6 (1979), 26–34.

FARMER, S., 'Persuasive Voices: Clerical Images of Medieval Wives', *Speculum*, 61 (1986), 517–43.

FENSTER, T. S., and ERLER, M. C. (eds. and trs.), *Poems of Cupid, God of Love* (Leiden: Brill, 1991).

FERRANTE, J., *Woman as Image in Medieval Literature from the Twelfth Century to Dante* (New York: Columbia University Press, 1975).

FIERO, G. K., PFEFFER, W., and ALLAIN, M. (eds. and trs.), *Three Medieval Views of Women: 'La Contenance des Fames', 'Le Bien des Fames', 'Le Blasme des Fames'* (New Haven: Yale University Press, 1989).

FREMANTLE, W. H. (tr.), *The Principal Works of St. Jerome*, Select Library of Nicene and Post-Nicene Fathers, 2nd ser., vi (Oxford: James Parker; and New York: Christian Literature Co., 1893).

FRIEDBERG, AEMILIUS, *Corpus Iuris Canonici*, pt. 1, *Decretum Magistri Gratiani* (Leipzig, 1879; reprinted Graz, 1955).

FRUGONI, C., 'L'Iconographie de la femme au cours des Xe–XIIe siècles', *Cahiers de civilisation médiévale*, 20 (1977), 177–88.

FYLER, JOHN, 'St Augustine, Genesis, and the Origin of Language', in *Saint Augustine and His Influence in the Middle Ages*, ed. Edward B. King and J. T. Schaefer (Sewanee: The Press of the University of the South, 1988), 69–78.

GALEN, *On the Usefulness of the Parts of the Body*, tr. M. T. May (Ithaca, NY: Cornell University Press, 1968).

GARBATY, T. J., '*Pamphilus, De Amore*: An Introduction and Translation', *Chaucer Review*, 2 (1967), 108–34.

Gesta Romanorum: The Early English Versions of the Gesta Romanorum, ed. S. J. Herrtage, EETS, ES 33 (London: Oxford University Press, 1879).
GOTTFRIED VON STRASSBURG, *Tristan*, ed. P. Ganz (Wiesbaden: Brockhaus, 1978).
GOTTLIEB, BEATRICE, 'Feminism in the Fifteenth Century', in J. Kirshner and S. F. Wemple (eds.), *Women of the Medieval World: Essays in Honor of John H. Mundy* (Oxford: Blackwell, 1985), 337–64.
GOWER, JOHN, *The English Works of John Gower*, ed. G. C. Macaulay, EETS, ES 81 and 82 (London: Oxford University Press, 1900–1).
GREEN, RICHARD F., 'Chaucer's Victimized Women', *Studies in the Age of Chaucer*, 10 (1988), 3–21.
GUILLAUME DE LORRIS and JEAN DE MEUN, *Le Roman de la Rose*, ed. E. Langlois, 5 vols., SATF (Paris: Didot/Champion, 1914–24).
—— *The Romance of the Rose*, tr. C. Dahlberg (Princeton, NJ: Princeton University Press, 1971).
GULDAN, E., *Eva und Maria: Eine Antithese als Bildmotiv* (Graz/Cologne, 1966).

HASENOHR, G., 'La Locution verbale figurée dans l'œuvre de Jean Le Fèvre', *Le Moyen Français*, 14–15 (1984), 229–81.
HAYS, H. R., *The Dangerous Sex: The Myth of Feminine Evil* (London: Methuen, 1966).
HELLMAN, R., and O'GORMAN, R. (trs.), *Ribald Tales from the Old French* (New York: Thomas Y. Crowell, 1965).
Heloise, correspondence with Abelard: *see* McLaughlin, Muckle, Radice, and Scott Moncrieff entries.
HENRY OF GHENT, *Summa in tres partes precipuas digesta*, 3 vols. (Ferrara, 1642–6).
HEXTER, R. J., *Ovid and Medieval Schooling: Studies in Medieval School Commentaries on Ovid's 'Ars Amatoria', 'Epistulae ex Ponto', and 'Epistulae Heroidum'* (Munich: Arbeo, 1986).
HICKS, E. (ed.), *Le Débat sur 'Le Roman de la Rose'* (Paris: Champion, 1977).
HOCCLEVE, THOMAS, *Hoccleve's Works: The Minor Poems*, ed. F. J. Furnivall and I. Gollancz; rev. J. Mitchell and A. I. Doyle, EETS, ES 61, 73, reprinted in one vol. (London: Oxford University Press, 1970).
HODGART, M., *Satire* (London: Weidenfeld & Nicolson, 1969).
HOROWITZ, M. C., 'Aristotle and Woman', *Journal of the History of Biology*, 9 (1976), 183–213.
HUEGELMEYER, C. T. (tr.), *Adulterous Marriages*, in *Saint Augustine: Treatises on Marriage*, tr. C. T. Wilcox and others, FOC xxvii (Washington, DC: Catholic University of America Press, 1955), 61–132.
HUGH OF FOUILLOY, *De nuptiis*: PL 176.
HUMPHRIES, R. (tr.), *The Satires of Juvenal* (Bloomington: Indiana University Press, 1958).

INNOCENT III, POPE, Lotario dei Segni, *De miseria condicionis humane*, ed. and tr. R. E. Lewis (Athens, Ga.: University of Georgia Press, 1978).
ISIDORE OF SEVILLE, *Isidori Hispalensis Episcopi, Etymologiarum sive Originum*, ed. W. M. Lindsay (Oxford: Clarendon Press, 1962).

JACQUART, D., and THOMASSET, C., *Sexuality and Medicine in the Middle Ages*, tr. M. Adamson (Cambridge: Polity Press, 1988).

JEHAN LE FÈVRE, *La Vieille*, ed. H. Cocheris (Paris, 1861).

—— *Les Lamentations de Matheolus et le Livre de Leesce*, ed. A.-G. Van Hamel, 2 vols. (Paris: Bouillon, 1892, 1905).

JEROME, St, *Adversus Jovinianum*, PL 23. 211–338.

—— *The Principal Works of St Jerome*, tr. W. H. Fremantle, Select Library of Nicene and Post-Nicene Fathers, 2nd ser., vi (Oxford: James Parker; and New York: Christian Literature Co., 1893).

—— *Select Letters*, tr. F. A. Wright (London: Heinemann; and Cambridge, Mass.: Harvard University Press, 1933).

JOHN CHRYSOSTOM, St, *The Homilies of St John Chrysostom on the Epistles of St Paul to Timothy, Titus and Philemon*, Library of Fathers of the Catholic Church (Oxford: John Henry Parker, 1843).

JOHN OF SALISBURY, *The Frivolities of Courtiers and the Footprints of Philosophers*, tr. J. B. Pike (Minneapolis: University of Minnesota Press; and London: Oxford University Press, 1938).

—— *Policratici sive De nugis curialium et vestigiis philosophorum*, ed. C. C. Webb, 2 vols. (Oxford: Clarendon Press, 1909).

JOHNSON, LESLEY, 'Women on Top: Antifeminism in the Fabliaux?' *Modern Language Review*, 78 (1983), 298–307.

JUVENAL, *Juvenal and Persius*, ed. and tr. G. G. Ramsay; rev. ed. (Cambridge, Mass.: Harvard University Press, 1940).

—— *The Satires of Juvenal*, tr. R. Humphries (Bloomington: Indiana University Press, 1958).

KAHR, M., 'Delilah', *Art Bulletin*, 54 (1972), 282–99.

KELLER, J. E. (tr.), *The Book of the Wiles of Women* (Chapel Hill: University of North Carolina Press, 1956).

—— (ed.), *Libro de los engaños*, 2nd edn. (Chapel Hill: University of North Carolina Press, 1959).

KELLY, F. DOUGLAS, 'Reflections on the Role of Christine de Pisan as a Feminist Writer', *sub-stance*, 2 (1972), 63–71.

KELLY, J. N. D., *Jerome: His Life, Writings, and Controversies* (London: Duckworth, 1975).

KELLY, JOAN, 'Early Feminist Theory and the *Querelle des Femmes*, 1400–1789', *Signs*, 8 (1982), 4–28.

KRAUS, HENRY, 'Eve and Mary: Conflicting Images of Medieval Woman', in his *The Living Theatre of Medieval Art* (Bloomington: Indiana University Press, 1967), 41–62.

LANGLAND, WILLIAM, *The Vision of Piers Plowman*, ed. A. V. C. Schmidt (London: Dent; and New York: Dutton, 1978).

LECLERCQ, J., 'Un témoin de l'antiféminisme au Moyen Âge', *Revue bénédictine*, 80 (1970), 304–9.

LEICESTER, H. MARSHALL, 'Of a Fire in the Dark: Public and Private Feminism in *The Wife of Bath's Tale*', *Women's Studies*, 11 (1984), 157–78.

LEMAY, HELEN, 'Some Thirteenth- and Fourteenth-Century Lectures on Female Sexuality', *International Journal of Women's Studies*, 1 (1978), 391–400.
LIVINGSTON, C. H., *Le Jongleur Gautier le Leu: étude sur les fabliaux* (Cambridge, Mass.: Harvard University Press, 1951).
LUCAS, ANGELA M., *Women in the Middle Ages: Religion, Marriage and Letters* (New York: St Martin's Press; and Brighton: Harvester, 1983).
LUSCOMBE, D. E., 'The Letters of Heloise and Abelard since "Cluny 1972"', in *Petrus Abaelardus (1079–1142): Person, Werk und Wirkung*, ed. P. Thomas, with J. Jolivet, D. E. Luscombe, and M. de Rijk, Trierer Theologische Studien, 38 (Trier, 1980), 19–39.
LYDGATE, JOHN, *Minor Poems*, ed. H. N. MacCracken, 2 vols., EETS, ES 107, OS 192 (London: Oxford University Press, 1911 and 1934).

McLAUGHLIN, ELEANOR, 'Equality of Souls, Inequality of Sexes: Women in Medieval Theology', in *Religion and Sexism: Images of Women in the Jewish and Christian Tradition*, ed. Rosemary Ruether (New York: Simon & Schuster, 1974), 213–66.
—— 'Les Femmes et l'hérésie médiévale: un problème dans l'histoire de la spiritualité', *Concilium*, 111 (1976), 73–90.
McLAUGHLIN, M. M., 'Peter Abelard and the Dignity of Women: Twelfth Century "Feminism" in Theory and Practice', in *Pierre Abelard—Pierre le Vénérable: les courants philosophiques, littéraires et artistiques en occident au milieu du xiiᵉ siècle, Actes*, Colloque International, Cluny 1972 (Paris: CNRS, 1975), 287–334.
McLaughlin, T. P. (ed.), 'Abelard's Rule for Religious Women', *Mediaeval Studies*, 18 (1964), 241–92.
McNAMARA, JO ANN, 'Sexual Equality and the Cult of Virginity in Early Christian Thought', *Feminist Studies*, 3 (1976), 145–58.
MAKOWSKI, ELIZABETH M., 'The Conjugal Debt and Medieval Canon Law', *Journal of Medieval History*, 3 (1977), 99–114.
MANN, JILL, *Geoffrey Chaucer* (Hemel Hempstead: Harvester Wheatsheaf, 1991).
MANZALAOUI, M. A. (ed.), *Secretum Secretorum*, i, EETS, OS 276 (Oxford: Oxford University Press, 1977).
MAP, WALTER, *De nugis curialium*, ed. and tr. M. R. James, rev. C. N. L. Brooke and R. B. Mynors (Oxford: Clarendon Press, 1983).
MARBOD OF RENNES, *Liber decem capitulorum*, ed. Rosario Leotta (Rome: Herder, 1984).
MATTHEWS, WILLIAM, 'The Wife of Bath and All Her Sect', *Viator*, 5 (1974), 413–43.
MEECH, S. B., and ALLEN, H. E. (eds.), *The Book of Margery Kempe*, EETS OS 212 (London: Oxford University Press, 1940).
MENOUD, P.-H., 'Saint Paul et la femme', *Revue de théologie et de philosophie*, 19 (1969), 318–30.
METZ, R., 'Recherches sur la condition de la femme selon Gratian', *Studia Gratiana*, 12 (1967), 377–96.

MIGNE, J.-P. (ed.), *Patrologiae cursus completus, series latina* (Paris, 1844–64).
MOORE, ARTHUR K., 'Studies in a Medieval Prejudice: Antifeminism', Ph.D. dissertation, Vanderbilt University, 1943.
MORAWSKI, J., *Proverbes français antérieurs au xv⁵ siècle*, Classiques français du moyen âge, 47 (Paris: Champion, 1925).
MORGAN, FIDELIS, *A Misogynist's Source Book* (London: Jonathan Cape, 1989).
MUCKLE, J. T., 'Abelard's Letter of Consolation to a Friend', *Mediaeval Studies*, 12 (1950), 175–211.
—— 'The Personal Letters of Abelard and Heloise', *Mediaeval Studies*, 15 (1953), 47–94.
—— 'The Letter of Heloise on Religious Life and Abelard's First Reply', *Mediaeval Studies*, 17 (1955), 240–81.
MURTAUGH, D. M., 'Women and Geoffrey Chaucer', *English Literary History*, 38 (1971), 473–92.
MUSCATINE, C., 'The Wife of Bath and Gautier's *La Veuve*', in U. T. Holmes (ed.), *Romance Studies in Memory of Edward Billings Ham* (Hayward, Cal.: Valencia Press, 1967), 109–14.
—— *The Old French Fabliaux* (New Haven: Yale University Press, 1986).

NOLAN, J. G., *Jerome and Jovinian*, Studies in Sacred Theology, 2nd ser., no. 97 (Washington, DC: Catholic University of America Press, 1956).
NOOMEN, W., and VAN DEN BOOGAARD (eds.), *Nouveau recueil complet des fabliaux* (Assen, Pays-Bas: Van Gorcum, 1983–).

O'FAOLAIN, J., and MARTINES, L. (eds.), *Not in God's Image* (New York: Harper & Row, 1973).
OWST, G. R., *Literature and Pulpit in Medieval England* (Cambridge: Cambridge University Press, 1933).
—— *Preaching in Medieval England* (Cambridge: Cambridge University Press, 1926).
OVID, *Ars Amatoria, Book 1*, ed. A. Hollis (Oxford: Clarendon Press, 1977).
—— *The Art of Love and Other Poems*, ed. and tr. J. H. Mozley (Cambridge, Mass.: Harvard University Press, 1957).
—— *The Erotic Poems*, tr. Peter Green (Harmondsworth: Penguin, 1982).
—— *Heroides and Amores*, ed. and tr. G. Showerman, rev. G. P. Goold (Cambridge, Mass.: Harvard University Press, 1977).

PAGELS, E., *Adam, Eve, and the Serpent* (Harmondsworth: Penguin, 1990).
PATTERSON, LEE, ' "For the Wyves love of Bathe": Feminine Rhetoric and Poetic Resolution in the *Roman de la Rose* and the *Canterbury Tales*', *Speculum*, 58 (1983), 656–94.
PEDRO ALFONSO, *Disciplina clericalis*, ed. A. G. Palencia (Madrid and Granada: Consejo Superior de Investigaciones Científicas, 1948).
PERRY, BEN E. (ed.), *Secundus the Silent Philosopher*, American Philological Association, Monograph 22 (Ithaca, NY: Cornell University Press, 1964).
PETER OF BLOIS, *Epistola LXXIX, PL* 207. 243–7.

PICKERING, O. S., 'The *Southern Passion* and the *Ministry and Passion*: The Work of a Middle English Reviser', *Leeds Studies in English*, 15 (1984), 24–56.

—— 'The "Defence of Women" from the *Southern Passion*: A New Edition', in Klaus P. Jankovsky (ed.), *The South English Legendary: A Critical Assessment* (Tübingen: Stauffenburg, 1992).

PITTS, B. A. (tr.), *The Fifteen Joys of Marriage* (New York: Peter Lang, 1985).

PRATT, R. A., 'The Development of the Wife of Bath', in MacEdward Leach (ed.), *Studies in Medieval Literature in Honor of Professor Albert Croll Baugh* (Philadelphia: University of Pennsylvania Press, 1961), 45–77.

—— 'Jankyn's Book of Wikked Wyves: Medieval Antimatrimonial Propaganda in the Universities', *Annuale medievale*, 3 (1962), 5–27.

PRUSAK, B. P., 'Woman: Seductive Siren and Source of Sin? Pseudepigraphical Myth and Christian Origins', in R. R. Ruether (ed.), *Religion and Sexism: Images of Women in the Jewish and Christian Tradition* (New York: Simon and Schuster, 1974), 89–116.

RABY, F. J. E., *A History of Christian–Latin Poetry from the Beginnings to the Close of the Middle Ages* (Oxford: Clarendon Press, 1927).

—— *A History of Secular Latin Poetry in the Middle Ages*, 2 vols., 2nd edn. (Oxford: Clarendon Press, 1957).

RADICE, B. (tr.), *The Letters of Abelard and Heloise* (Harmondsworth: Penguin, 1974).

RAMING, I., *The Exclusion of Women from the Priesthood . . . : A Historical Investigation of the Juridical and Doctrinal Foundations*, tr. Norman R. Adams (Metuchen, NJ.: Scarecrow Press, 1976).

REYNOLDS, L. D., and WILSON, N. G., *Scribes and Scholars: A Guide to the Transmission of Greek and Latin Literature*, 2nd edn. (Oxford: Clarendon Press, 1974).

RICHARD DE BURY, *Philobiblon*, ed. Michael MacLagan, tr. E. C. Thomas (Oxford: Blackwell, 1960).

RICHARD DE FOURNIVAL, *Master Richard's Bestiary of Love and Response*, tr. J. Beer (Berkeley and Los Angeles: University of California Press, 1986).

—— *Li Bestiaires d'Amours di Maistre Richart de Fornival e li Response du Bestiaire*, ed. C. Segre (Milan: 1957).

RICKARD, P., DEYERMOND, A., and others (trs.), *Medieval Comic Tales* (Cambridge: D. S. Brewer, 1972).

RIGG, A. G. (ed. and tr.), *Gawain on Marriage: The Textual Tradition of the 'De Coniuge Non Ducenda'* (Toronto: Pontifical Institute of Mediaeval Studies, 1986).

ROBATHAN, D. M. (ed.), *De vetula* (Amsterdam, 1968).

ROBBINS, R. H., *Secular Lyrics of the XIVth and XVth Centuries* (Oxford: Clarendon Press, 1952).

ROBERTSON, ELIZABETH, 'The Rule of the Body: The Feminine Spirituality of the *Ancrene Wisse*', in Sheila Fisher and Janet E. Halley (eds.), *Seeking the Woman in Late Medieval and Renaissance Writings* (Knoxville: University of Tennessee Press, 1989), 109–34.

ROGERS, KATHARINE M., *The Troublesome Helpmate: A History of Misogyny in Literature* (Seattle: University of Washington Press, 1966).

ROUSSELLE, A., *Porneia: On Desire and the Body in Antiquity*, tr. F. Pheasant, (Oxford: Blackwell, 1988).

ROY, BRUNO, 'La Belle e(s)t la bête: aspects du bestiaire féminin au moyen âge', *Etudes françaises*, 10 (1974), 319–34.

RUETHER, ROSEMARY R., 'Misogynism and Virginal Feminism in the Fathers of the Church', in her *Religion and Sexism: Images of Women in the Jewish and Christian Traditions* (New York: Simon & Schuster, 1974), 150–83.

——— (ed.), *Religion and Sexism: Images of Women in the Jewish and Christian Traditions* (New York: Simon and Schuster, 1974).

RUIZ, JUAN, *The Book of Good Love*, tr. R. Mignani and M. A. Di Cesare (Albany, NY: State University of New York Press, 1970).

RUSCH, W. G., *The Later Latin Fathers* (London: Duckworth, 1977).

SALU, M. B. (tr.), *The Ancrene Riwle* (London: Burns & Oates, 1955).

SCHLEISSNER, M. (ed.), 'Pseudo-Albertus Magnus: *Secreta Mulierum cum commento*, Critical Text and Commentary', Ph.D. dissertation, Princeton University 1987.

SCHMITT, CHARLES B., 'Theophrastus in the Middle Ages', *Viator*, 2 (1971), 259–63.

SCOTT MONCRIEFF, C. K. (tr.), *The Letters of Abelard and Heloise* (1942: reprinted New York: Cooper Square Publishers, 1974).

SILVA, D. S., and BRENNAN, J. P., 'Medieval Manuscripts of Jerome, *Against Jovinian*', *Manuscripta*, 13 (1969), 161–6.

The Southern Passion, ed. B. D. Brown, EETS, os 169 (London: Oxford University Press, 1927).

SPENCER, RICHARD, 'The Treatment of Women in the *Roman de la Rose*, the "Fabliaux" and the *Quinze Joies de Mariage*', *Marche romane*, 28 (1978), 207–14.

STRAUS, B. R., 'The Subversive Discourse of the Wife of Bath: Phallocentric Discourse and the Imprisonment of Criticism', *English Literary History*, 55 (1988), 527–54.

TERTULLIAN, *Ad uxorem, De exhortatione castitatis, De monogamia*, in *Tertullian: Treatises on Marriage and Remarriage*, tr. W. P. le Saint, Ancient Christian Writers, xiii (London, 1951).

——— 'The Apparel of Women', (*De cultu feminarum*), tr. E. Quain, in *Tertullian: Disciplinary, Moral and Ascetical Works*, tr. R. Arbesmann and others, FOC, xl (New York, 1959).

——— *Opera*, ed. A. Kroymann, CCSL i–ii (Turnhout: Brepols, 1954).

THUNDY, Z. P., 'Matheolus, Chaucer, and the Wife of Bath', in *Chaucerian Problems and Perspectives*, ed. E. Vasta and Z. P. Thundy (Notre Dame, Ind.: University of Notre Dame Press, 1979), 24–58.

TOLKIEN, J. R. R. (ed.), *The English Text of the Ancrene Riwle: Ancrene Wisse, Corpus Christi College Cambridge MS 402*, EETS, os 249 (London: Oxford University Press, 1962).

TROTULA OF SALERNO (attrib.), *The Diseases of Women*, tr. E. Mason-Hohl (Los Angeles, 1940).

TRUAX, J., 'Augustine of Hippo: Defender of Women's Equality?' *Journal of Medieval History*, 16 (1990), 279–99.

UTLEY, F. L., *The Crooked Rib: An Analytical Index to the Argument About Women in English and Scots Literature to the End of the Year 1568* (Columbus: Ohio State University Press, 1944).

WALTHER, H., *Proverbia sententiaeque Latinitatis Medii Aevi*, 9 vols. (Göttingen: Vandenhoeck and Ruprecht, 1963–9).

WARNER, MARINA, *Alone of All her Sex: The Myth and Cult of the Virgin Mary* (New York: Knopf, 1976).

WEISSMAN, H. P., 'Antifeminism and Chaucer's Characterization of Women', in *Geoffrey Chaucer: A Collection of Original Articles*, ed. G. D. Economou (New York: McGraw-Hill, 1975), 93–110.

WIESEN, D. S., *Saint Jerome as a Satirist* (Ithaca, NY: Cornell University Press, 1964).

WILLARD, CHARITY C., *Christine de Pizan: Her Life and Works* (New York: Persea Books, 1984).

WRIGHT, T., *The Anglo-Latin Satirical Poets and Epigrammatists of the Twelfth Century*, 2 vols., Rolls ser. (London: Longman, 1872).

WULFF, AUGUST, *Die frauenfeindlichen Dichtungen in den romanischen Literaturen des Mittelalters bis zum Ende des XIIIen Jahrhunderts* (Halle a.S.: Max Niemeyer, 1914).

WURTELE, DOUGLAS, 'The Predicament of Chaucer's Wife of Bath: St Jerome on Virginity', *Florilegium*, 5 (1983), 208–36.

ZADDY, Z. P., 'Chrétien misogyne', *Marche romane*, 30 (1980), 301–7

Index

Italicized numbers refer to texts printed in this volume

Aristotle (cont.)
179n., 180–1, 192n., 194, 242,
248, 249, 291, Plate 5
Generation of Animals 39–41, 91–3,
246n.
Arria 232
Arrius 110, 220
Artemisia 69
Aston, M. 250n., 251n.
Athalia 101, 299
Atreus 19n., 24
Aucassin and Nicolete 194n.
audacity, women's 28, 35, 111, 169
Augustine, St 3, 14n., 64, 77–8, 84–5,
91, 223, 228n., 236n., 258n.,
294
Adulterous Marriages 77n., 260n.
City of God 81–2, 151n., 289
Confessions 78
Good of Marriage 64, 228n.
Literal Meaning of Genesis 79–81
Soliloquies 77
The Ten Strings 77n., 260, 262–4
The Trinity 78n.
avarice, see greed

backbiting:
men 246–7, 268
women 118–19
baptism, by women 234, 256–8
baths 8, 21, 58, 138n., 143, 163
Bathsheba 8, 15, 32–3, 75, 95–6, 101,
105–6, 116, 267, Plate 3
Benton, John 38n.
Bernard, St 95
Bernardus Silvestris 102n.
Bible, the 1, 6, 7, 8, 31–7, 63, 164,
183, 218, 227
Acts 62, 93, 96, 251
Corinthians 31, 52, 54, 58, 59, 62,
63, 64–6, 76, 80, 85, 88, 91,
199, 200, 202, 235, 251, 253–4
Daniel 253, 268
Deuteronomy 85, 107
Ecclesiastes 6, 34, 68, 90, 124, 127,
129, 158, 225, 237, 300
Ecclesiasticus 1, 6, 31, 34–5, 125,
127, 129, 145, 147, 163, 165,
183, 194, 198, 217, 221, 237,
238, 252, 268, 289
Enoch 50, 56
Ephesians, 7, 62, 81, 262
Esther 231
Exodus 129, 188
Galatians 3, 79, 80

Genesis 6, 31–2, 51, 57, 59, 61, 65,
79, 81, 90, 92, 95, 145, 200,
230, 242, 253, 265
Hebrews 68
Isaiah 76
Job 75, 90
John 35–6, 62, 199, 233, 234, 260,
295
Judges 75, 121, 227, 236, 251,
266
Judith 10, 231
Kings 8, 32–3, 75, 81, 90, 95, 97,
105, 200, 230, 251, 267, 289
Leviticus 38n.
Luke 35, 233, 295
Macc. 236
Mark 35, 203, 233, 234, 239
Matthew 4, 35, 52, 54, 63, 66, 76,
82, 105, 202, 233, 235, 253,
267, 287, 294
Micheas 166
Numbers 84, 184
Peter 61, 145, 251, 256, 269
Philippians 57, 72
Proverbs 2, 6, 7, 22, 33–4, 65,
67–8, 89–90, 104, 125, 127, 128,
158, 176, 194, 209, 221, 239,
242, 251
Psalms 75
Revelations 57
Romans 80, 81, 234, 235
Ruth 231
Song of Songs 68
Timothy 37, 57, 58–9, 61, 63, 67,
80, 136, 145, 164, 208, 214,
234, 252–4, 258, 269
biology, see physiology
Blamires, Alcuin 199n., 218n.
Bloch, R. Howard 3n., 4n., 5n., 9
Boccaccio, Giovanni 148, 166–7
Corbaccio 11, 25, 124n., 166–76,
224, 230n.
Concerning Famous Women 166, 289
Decameron 137n.
Boethius, Consolation of Philosophy
154n., 155, 156n., 229n.
Bonaventure, St 48n.
Book of Margery Kempe 58n., 295n.
Book of the Wiles of Women 130–5
Børresen, K. 3n., 47n., 78n.
Bromyard 4
Brooke, Christopher N. L. 87n., 184n.
brothels 77, 293
women's secret visits to 26, 126,
169

Printed in the United States
990700001B